"A unique take on leadership from an unusually gifted scholar. *Leadership Across Boundaries: A Passage to Aporia* should be on all leadership scholars' bookshelves. It is unlike anything else I have read."

—**Keith Grint**, *The University of Warwick, UK*

# LEADERSHIP ACROSS BOUNDARIES

*Leadership Across Boundaries: A Passage to Aporia* theorizes on leadership in an unprecedented manner by stepping outside of conventional leadership theory and importing into leadership studies the implications of certain innovations in the social sciences, such as pluralism, complexity theory, and the dialogical turn, to change the way scholars discuss and study leadership.

*Leadership Across Boundaries* anchors theoretical passages that generate a new way of imagining what it means to lead and follow with concrete examples about Martin Luther, the Common Law, dialogue as a practice, a painting by Diego Velázquez, synchronized fireflies, and the strange career of Francis of Assisi. This book acknowledges the limitations of existing leadership research as being too leader-centric, simplistic, static, and in many cases oblivious to the power of images to shape our understanding. To rectify these limitations, *Leadership Across Boundaries* examines alternative images of leadership grounded in concrete examples that present leadership in an unprecedented light. The book includes a discussion of invigorating ideas of homeward leadership (looking backward), extra-ordinary leadership (going forward), and what will be defined as the perennial need for aikido politics.

An interdisciplinary text, *Leadership Across Boundaries: A Passage to Aporia* will appeal not only to scholars, instructors, and students of leadership, but also to those in the many fields in which leadership theory applies, such as history, economics, sociology, archetypal psychology, the law, political philosophy, applied mathematics, and the martial arts.

**Nathan Harter** is Professor of Leadership Studies at Christopher Newport University in Newport News, Virginia. Previously, he practiced law in Indiana and became a full professor at Purdue University in the Department of Organizational Leadership.

# Leadership: Research and Practice Series

**Series Editors:**

**Georgia Sorenson,** Møller Leadership Scholar and Møller By-Fellow, Churchill College, University of Cambridge, Founder of the James MacGregor Academy of Leadership at the University of Maryland, and co-founder of the International Leadership Association.

**Ronald E. Riggio,** Henry R. Kravis Professor of Leadership and Organizational Psychology and former director of the Kravis Leadership Institute at Claremont McKenna College.

For more information about this series, please visit: www.routledge.com/
Leadership-Research-and-Practice/book-series/leadership

# LEADERSHIP ACROSS BOUNDARIES

## A Passage to Aporia

*Nathan Harter*

Routledge
Taylor & Francis Group

NEW YORK AND LONDON

First published 2021
by Routledge
52 Vanderbilt Avenue, New York, NY 10017

and by Routledge
2 Park Square, Milton Park, Abingdon, Oxon, OX14 4RN

*Routledge is an imprint of the Taylor & Francis Group, an informa business*

*Library of Congress Cataloging-in-Publication Data*
Names: Harter, Nathan, author.
Title: Leadership across boundaries : a passage to aporia / Nathan
    Harter.
Description: 1 Edition. | New York : Routledge, 2020. | Includes
    bibliographical references and index.
Identifiers: LCCN 2020028121 (print) | LCCN 2020028122 (ebook) |
    ISBN 9780367863265 (hardback) | ISBN 9780367863241 (paperback) |
    ISBN 9781003018407 (ebook)
Subjects: LCSH: Leadership. | Leadership—Case studies. |
    Leadership—Study and teaching.
Classification: LCC HM1261 .H3727 2020 (print) | LCC HM1261
    (ebook) | DDC 303.3/4—dc23
LC record available at https://lccn.loc.gov/2020028121
LC ebook record available at https://lccn.loc.gov/2020028122

ISBN: 978-0-367-86326-5 (hbk)
ISBN: 978-0-367-86324-1 (pbk)
ISBN: 978-1-003-01840-7 (ebk)

Typeset in Bembo
by Apex CoVantage, LLC

To three academic mentors: two from Butler University, professors **John Beversluis** and the late **George Hoffmann**; and one from the National Endowment for the Humanities summer seminar at the University of Chicago in 1995, the late professor **Donald N. Levine**.

# BRIEF CONTENTS

# CONTENTS

*Aikido Politics 246*
*Living Within Tensions 249*
*Looking Back, Yet Moving Forward (i.e. Sankofa) 252*

# SERIES FOREWORD

In most instances, scholars approach a subject and think that they know exactly what they are studying. They often do this because they rely on some default, or generally agreed-upon definition. Such is the case with leadership. Scholars and practicing leaders simply accept that they know what leadership is. Nathan Harter, in this important book, asks us to think more broadly about the definition of leadership and how we study or practice it. Harter shows us the complexity of leadership, which involves the dynamic interaction of the leader, followers, and context (both inside and outside of the collective). He does this through a number of disciplinary lenses—sociological, psychological, political, historical, the arts, and humanities. It is an impressive work.

For leadership scholars: Many of us try to wrap our arms around this complex phenomenon we call leadership. Harter makes it clear that we need much longer arms.

For students of leadership: Most theses begin with a definition of terms, and students strive for that precise definition of leadership. Harter's work will lead to a broadening of that definition, and your thinking.

For practitioners/leaders: This book can shed light on why, in most circumstances, it is so very hard to lead. You will be challenged to lead better.

To all: If you are serious in your quest for a better and deeper understanding of leadership, you need to read this book.

*Ronald E. Riggio and Georgia Sorenson*

# ACKNOWLEDGMENTS

I launched this project asking for help. Something in my thoughts did not make sense, so I started going to other people from the beginning. They helped me immensely. I would like to use this opportunity to mention many of them by name, even if the ultimate responsibility for what appears in these pages belongs to me.

In addition to specific recognition for particular chapters, I want to say thank you publicly to Sarah Chace, Justin Farmer, Ryan Fisher, Jess Hench, Matt Homan, James Kelly, Peter Monaghan, Moriah Poliakoff, Michael Lewis, Paul Robinson, Sarah Scott, Lynn Shollen, Brennan Smith, Tammara Sutton, Qingyan Tian, R. Elizabeth (Coltharp) Tollis, Rachel Wagner, Carly Wever, Henry Wilson, and Austin Wood. To the many contractors working for months during my sabbatical, to renovate, repair, and replace the roof after a tree fell on the house, thankfully we figured out a way to accommodate one another. Retaining Amanda Rooker of SplitSeed to develop the manuscript was prudent, instructive, and rewarding. Her editing made this whole book better. I am equally indebted to Christina Chronister, Danielle Dyal, and the anonymous reviewer at Routledge. I am further indebted to Gilbert Rajkumar Gnanarathinam and his team at Apex CoVantage, LLC.

In addition, I routinely submitted the topics herein to my private study group at Christopher Newport University in Newport News, Virginia, which is a gathering of select undergraduates whose practice of dialogue serves as the professional highlight of my week. Finally, I must acknowledge for special commendation a faithful friend and colleague, my fellow co-traveler: Willy Donaldson.

This work was supported by a sabbatical leave from Christopher Newport University, Newport News, Virginia, and by a generous grant from the Hayek

Fund, through the Institute for Humane Studies. I hereby acknowledge the kind permission of the following three journals to reprint versions of material I had previously published with them: *Journal of Leadership Studies*, *Theology of Leadership Journal*, and *VoegelinView*. Figure 3.1 and Table 9.1, plus Table 0.1 were created on the 2019 professional version of Microsoft Office, used with permission from Microsoft.

To God be all the glory. And to Karin, always, my heart.

# A PREFACE IN FOUR PARTS

## Part One: An Autobiographical Statement

When I first became a professor back in 1989, one colleague asked whether my research was quantitative or qualitative. I was frankly stumped. Are those my only choices? Little did I realize at the time that the question comes from a paradigm of scholarship that I did not share. It turns out that he was presenting me with a false dilemma.[1] Quantitative and qualitative are not the only two possibilities. In the choosing between X and Y, I was neither. But then I had to ask myself: how *would* I characterize my research? Again, I was stumped.

I did not possess the words, largely because I really was not aware what I was doing at the time. That is the honest truth. Today, I can say that looking back there was a pattern. Maybe it was unconscious. Nevertheless, thirty years later, I have the rudiments of an answer.

The "arc" of my research can be described best by my books, of which there have now been four. Imagine if you will three concentric circles labeled (from the inside out) micro, meso, and macro. Standing outside of these three and looking on with curiosity is the meta. These are familiar labels for magnitudes that are embedded within one another, ranging from the smallest or most detailed to the largest. We might think of micro as more fine-grained, whereas the macro is coarse. These labels help to categorize my books. (The macro/micro distinction will also be examined more thoroughly in a subsequent chapter.)

The first book I wrote applied Georg Simmel's notion of the sociological form to leadership, so that one could regard it as a relationship, like marriage

---

1. On the quarrels between quantitative and qualitative methods, see generally Klenke (2008, pp. 44–48, 155, and 369ff).

or friendship (Harter, 2007a). Let us call that the **macro** level of investigation. I argued at the time that there is a way to study sociological forms properly, which I had been learning from what I could find about Simmel, and although I may not have done it expertly, I was learning. I now realize that each of these magnitudes has its own integrity, with the result that from within a magnitude, there is a way to investigate something that could easily be inappropriate at other magnitudes. In my opinion, it is best to be conscious of the magnitude at which one is working and not confuse it with others. Book one, therefore, was macro.

The next book investigated what happens inside the mind of a leader, from a phenomenological approach (Harter, 2015). I wanted to know: What is judgment? And how does a person arrive at that judgment? In other words, I wanted to look within, at the moving parts of the individual human mind when a leader proposes a course of action. Despite the fact that so much more could be said, at least for that project I settled on a **micro** magnitude.

Book number three worked explicitly at the **meso** level, as I summarized the last lectures of Michel Foucault, who was trying to understand how, during the Hellenistic period, prospective leaders were trained to become subjects in their own right, i.e. relatively autonomous beings or social agents who had taken responsibility for constituting their selves (Harter, 2016). It was the level directly between the inner-personal (book two) and the interpersonal (book one). I wanted to know: How does a prospective leader become a person to begin with?

With hindsight, I could see a kind of spread or differentiation among my books. Once I had done so, I formally decided that this book should be conducted at the **meta** level, the furthest one because it is standing outside of the model altogether. After I saw that possibility, I could guide my work more consciously and choose where to go with it. I thought to myself, "Onward (and outward) therefore to the meta. . . ."

Before we get to that, let me say that the false dilemma originally presented to me about whether my research is quantitative or qualitative (X or Y) omitted a legitimate type of scholarship that has attracted me personally, which is the investigation of theory itself (Z). Needless to say, quantitative and qualitative scientists rely on theory. Theory is part of the toolkit a scientist uses.[2] Jan Patočka wrote, "Social sciences normally appeal to mere empirical data. However, they need also a philosophical foundation in order to locate their fundamental problem" (1998, p. 97; see also Klenke, 2008, p. 14). So, I wondered from the outset of my career, who pays any attention to the theories themselves? The exemplary sociologist Donald Levine—one of the mentors to

---

2. Don Levine (2018) identifies three common attitudes regarding the split between theory and practice: theory is foundational for practice, theory is disjunctive, or theory is inseparable from practice (p. 102).

whom this book is dedicated—devoted his career to doing just that (e.g. 1995; 2015, prologue). With his guidance at a National Endowment for the Humanities summer seminar in 1995 at the University of Chicago, I discovered that I wanted to do something like this. It turns out that when X and Y constitute a *false* dilemma, this means that those are not my only options. My interests lay not with X or Y; instead, I was interested in Z.

Actually, this book originated in another example of a false dilemma. But more on that later.

## Part Two: "My, What a Big Bibliography You Have!"

As most readers will already know, scholars cite their sources for a variety of reasons. One reason is to give credit where credit is due, so that it remains clear which thoughts and ideas are original and which have been borrowed from somebody else. This practice is a professional courtesy we pay to one another. If I learned a particular lesson from a given source, I should probably make that apparent. Another reason to cite a source is to give the reader a chance to go back and check—to verify that this is indeed what the original author was saying. After all, scholars have to keep one another honest! Citing my sources makes the research more transparent. In the same vein, citations give the reader a place to go if they are interested in learning more about the subject matter, for their own edification. In addition, on occasion I will cite sources that merely serve as an example. I will not go into detail on every assertion, but if you like, you can probably go find what you are looking for if you check.

Social scientists have an annoying habit of citing more than one source for single assertions, almost as though the cumulative weight is meant to impress you as authority. It might be the case that citing only one source is pretty lame if nobody else concurs. At the other extreme, writers go too far the other direction by interlarding their prose with strings of citations (Tom, 2018; Dick, 2017; Harry, 2010). Joanne Ciulla complains that "stacking up citations is not a substitute for a good argument" (2019, p. 110). Let's be honest, the most innocuous claims can be challenged by anybody, so it might be advisable to throw a citation or two in there to deter quibbles. Still, the practice can distract from good prose.

What should I cite? Some writers prefer the most recent sources, to show that they are up-to-date and know the latest stuff. I have known reviewers who take writers to task because their sources are, in their words, "outdated." Other writers prefer to go back to the seminal works, where it all branched off in a new direction to begin with. (Count me in with the latter.) There are those who insist on resorting exclusively to the great books and major theorists, such as Max Weber and Friedrich Nietzsche, scorning what they call the secondary literature; but then there are those who contend that without paying attention to the secondary literature you are missing important modifications, critiques, and qualifications to the great books. You have not done your due diligence.

Academe abounds with people who watch the citations closely—often for very good reasons. (If you are like me, one of the first things you do with a new book is flip it back to the list of references.) Even if you in particular find my citations all somewhat distracting (if not pretentious), there is a reason for them being there—mostly, to be candid, in anticipation of criticism. I find that as a reader, after a while you can ignore them, in the same way that railroad passengers quit noticing the telephone poles that run alongside the tracks. You will look past them to say, "What a gorgeous sunset!" Nevertheless, they are there if you need them.

With regard to the scholarly apparatus of this book, let me share another concern. An interdisciplinary project runs the risk of being incomplete in any one of the disciplines it chooses to include. The experts in discipline X might expect to see more from their literature, whereas the experts in discipline Y expect to see more from theirs. The interdisciplinary scholar walks a fine line between showing enough to prove credible but not so much as to disrupt the flow of the argument and veer off into the proverbial weeds. And every academic discipline has them. Weeds, that is.[3]

You will probably notice something as we go along. Certain cited works feature prominently in my thinking. I will cite them frequently or explore them at some length. A few are largely responsible for the entire structure of my argument. Other cited works are more incidental. A few fly by so quickly you may not even notice. Occasionally, I could not resist a uniquely apt phrase or clever remark that I picked up somewhere. Further complicating matters, I have developed a relationship of trust with certain authors whom I have come to cite without emphasizing their credentials. If Eric Voegelin said it, for instance, that's good enough for me. The list of these trusted authors has grown through the years, such that it would not be unusual to mention them almost in passing, as though waving my hand and saying, "Don't worry. This writer is okay." I do not see the point of going back to justify my reliance on every single person I cite. The names of those I have come to trust include James Hillman, José Ortega y Gasset, Georg Simmel, Jan Patočka, and Hannah Arendt. There are others.

You will notice that a few of the authors I cite are controversial. This pertains to men such as Carl Schmitt, Martin Heidegger, Friedrich Hayek, Georges Sorel, Ervin Laszlo, and Jordan Peterson. Sometimes, I am not citing them for that which makes them controversial. In a few spots, yes, I know perfectly well what makes the person controversial, and I do not hide from it, but I have discovered through trial and error that, not infrequently, that which

---

3. I confess that sometimes veering off into the weeds can be edifying in its own right, interesting, or even fun.

makes them controversial is incidental to their merit. You can cite Karl Marx without supporting revolution. You can cite Sigmund Freud without endorsing the Oedipus complex. Also, sometimes that which makes them controversial is what makes them especially valuable. I try to flag when that happens. But let it be said from the outset: I certainly cannot testify one way or the other about their failings otherwise.

A final remark about the citation regimen, if I may. The study of law showed me just how rich and volatile footnotes can be. They should not distract from the flow of the argument. Sometimes, they give to the curious critic a more detailed discussion of a matter that I suspect most other readers will not need. Now and then, I use that space to elaborate, giving examples or indicating another direction that things could go. Some notes exist as housekeeping, keeping the scholarship tidy. Others inject a little humor. When I do post a note, I do not intend any one exclusive purpose. You will never know why it is there until you give it a peek.

Before we begin, I must address a potential concern. I am a product of a particular culture—a culture labeled as Judeo-Christian or Western (and within that culture, American). Most of my examples and points of reference come from that culture. This tradition is what I know best. Like it or not, many of those who continue to shape leadership studies still live within that context. Nevertheless, despite my identity I have not insisted here on any particular culture or creed. I have for instance invoked Aikido (Japanese), Sankofa (Ghanaian), pagan mythology (Greco-Roman), Taoism, secular scientism, and whatever it is that Plato might have been. More transparently, in the interest of full disclosure, always looming in the background as silent witnesses to what I aspire to accomplish have been Socrates, Christ, and the Buddha. Frankly, I welcome readers from other faith traditions because I am hoping that they recognize evidence of their own wisdom in these pages. Their traditions are likely to enrich and refine what is being said here, for that is part of what a dialogical approach requires. The lessons in these pages are themselves open to challenge, befitting the fallibilism that echoes throughout the book. Nevertheless, I should not be expected to apologize for the influence of my own tradition upon my thinking. And I won't. I am simply making that influence explicit.

## Part Three: An Encomium on Pluralism

### *Or as I Like to Call It: Sitting in a Circle All Looking at the Same Thing*

If we were to accept that (a) reality is one, but that (b) we can know it in many ways, then the question becomes (c) how a person integrates this multitude of perspectives into a coherent whole, if indeed that is even possible.

Suppose that reality is one, but that it presents a variety of facets (Ortega, 1914/1961; James, 1909/1996). We should be able to subdivide our investigation into several approaches, depending on the facet with which we choose to begin. Camic and Joas (2004) have argued that because the world is so complex and our powers to grasp it intellectually so limited, never mind the finitude of language, we will find ourselves with a fragmented understanding. One might say that a compact reality has undergone differentiation, so the question is whether to integrate these "fragments" and if so, how. Certainly in sociology, this fragmentation has been a problem (or opportunity) from its inception, as Don Levine once taught me: fragmented for example into national traditions and into subdisciplines. Given this pluralistic situation, some sociologists seek a synthesis (assuming they do not ignore the fragmentation altogether), but there has been a range of voices calling to resist the necessity or even the desirability of a synthesis (e.g. Sorokin, Merton, Buber, Bakhtin, Dewey, Mead, Gadamer, Habermas, Rorty, McKeon). Don Levine is among these luminaries calling instead for dialogue (see generally Camic & Joas, 2004). A dialogue does not require synthesis.

Picture in your mind an object in the center of the room, with a circle of chairs around it facing inward. For our purposes, that object in the center of the room is leadership. Each chair represents a facet or approach to understanding leadership. We can say without much strain that these perspectives are complementary. But notice, rather than describing only the object, we are now describing the configuration in the room that includes the object, yes, but also the chairs. We have taken a giant step back, gaining a meta vision of the room. Therefore, we can adopt a multiperspectival approach in which we simply list what can be seen from each chair and then by simple addition say that the result is a composite that more accurately represents the truth of the matter. This is one way to understand a pluralistic mindset (Bernstein, 1997; James, 1909/1996). But is it enough for leadership studies? In 2003, Riggio, Ciulla, and Sorenson said in effect, "No, it's not enough." We should convert a multidisciplinary approach into an **interdisciplinary** approach (James, 1909/1996, p. 313). What is the difference?

Don Levine (2018) suggested that once you catalogue the views from all of the different chairs, there is also a way for the people in these various chairs to talk with one another and help one another (ch. 7). One way to do this is chronologically, of course, establishing a pattern of cycling through them, one at a time, building as you go. "You see this, but I see that." Such a process fits more the multiperspectival approach, which is desirable, when folks are taking turns and talking to one another (e.g. Wilson, 2016). A way to integrate these various perspectives is to use one perspective from one chair to critique all of the other perspectives, saying in effect to each in turn: "From where I sit, here's what you are missing. And here's what you are missing." Yet another is to use many perspectives to critique any one perspective, ganging up on that lone point of view, as everybody takes turns identifying what is limiting about it. These activities convert a multiperspectival activity into an *inter*perspectival activity. Consequently, we get at least these three possibilities.

What is still missing is how to choose among the chairs. Which one is correct? With so many competing choices, where should you sit in order to investigate the object in the center of the room? The answer is obvious: there is not only one. You have to get up and move, seeing it from every angle. That is not to say that a scholar could not pick a chair and just stay there, continuing to investigate the object thoroughly, without ever leaving his post. It is more than possible. And in many cases, it is perfectly reasonable, because there might be a lot to do just sitting in that one chair. One thinks for example of Tom Wren looking at leadership through the lenses of history (Wren & Swatez, 1995; Wren, 2012) or Mary Uhl-Bien looking through the lenses of complex adaptive systems (Uhl-Bien, Marion, & McKelvey, 2007; Uhl-Bien & Marion, 2008).

In leadership studies, then, we sit in a variety of chairs that we call academic disciplines. We look at leadership by means of psychology, sociology, anthropology, political science, history, and so forth (e.g. Harvey & Riggio, 2012). We can array them side-by-side and call our overall field of study multidisciplinary, as many do. We can do that chronologically, for example, reporting which came first, second, third, and so forth. Or we can try to bring these disciplines into dialogue, one with another. We can critique the other disciplines from within our own, as Joanne Ciulla does so skillfully, for instance, from her perch in philosophy (e.g. 2019). By the same token, we can all direct our attention to one discipline in particular, pointing out its many shortcomings. Each of these discursive modes would be an improvement on conflictual modes of discourse among the disciplines in which they battle for preeminence or try to define one another out of existence (Levine, 2018, p. 13).

The novelist Alexander Solzhenitsyn (1984–1991) shared the Russian folktale of the seven brothers who rode out to look at Mother Truth.

> [They] viewed her from seven sides and seven angles, and when they returned each of them had a different tale to tell: one said that she was a mountain, one that she was a forest, one that she was a populous town. . . . And, for telling untruths, they slashed each other with swords of tempered steel, and with their dying breaths bade their sons slash away at each other, to the death. They had all seen one and the same Truth, but had not looked carefully.
>
> *(p. 56)*

Here's the thing: an array based on academic disciplines is not the only array of chairs. In leadership studies, we also find ourselves using a variety of scholarly methods. We can think of each method as a different chair. That is, we can come to investigate leadership using quantitative methods or qualitative methods,

methods based on phenomenology, pragmatism, critical studies, and so forth (e.g. Riggio, 2019; Schyns, Hall, & Neves, 2017; see Levine, 2018, p. 202). Simply listing these methods and describing them is a contribution, but then what I am saying is that we should bring *the methods* into conversation, whether we use one method to critique all of the others or use all of the methods to critique one. It amounts to the same thing. Methodology is another array of chairs.

We could set up the same basic framework of object-and-chairs after differentiating leadership into other categories. Theory and practice—those are two chairs. Before and after, leader and follower, good and bad, short-term and long-term, large-scale and small-scale, and so forth. In principle, the possibilities are endless. How do people in Africa experience leadership (Gutman, 1935)? How do children experience leadership (e.g. Parten, 1933)? How do women experience leadership (Maslow, 1939)? We can generate a multitude of arrays of chairs encircling the exact same object in the center of the room. No matter how you split it, you can treat the differentia as complementary using the multiperspectival lens, or you can treat them using the interperspectival lens, whether you critique all of the other elements from only one or you critique any one element from all of the others.

What pluralism does is recognize the plurality of possibilities, but it does not tell you what to do with them. It requires dialogue to make sense of a pluralistic universe. And there are many ways to go about such a dialogue. We have mentioned only three: chronological, seeing one from all, or seeing all from one. I expect there are others.[4]

So now we have a variety of chairs in a variety of circles, which displaces the question by one level. Not only are there multiple chairs, there are multiple *arrays* of chairs. At this higher level of abstraction, we can ask: Which configuration of chairs should we adopt—the multiple disciplines, the multiple methods, or what? If a person can split our investigation into leadership in so many different ways, then which is best? You and I can do at this level what we did at the lower level: sorting chronologically, seeing all from one, or one from all. Furthermore, I am not saying that these are the only ways to conduct interdisciplinarity. Which throws us into an even higher level of abstraction: Which form or type of *interdisciplinarity* should we adopt? And once again, the answer is the same: all of them mutually engaged, in dialogue.

By now, you might be wondering how to manage so many choices. Are they all equally useful? Do they really require all of the others in dialogue to constitute anything resembling the truth about leadership?

---

4. A typical example of this kind of dialogue occurs when scholars address intersectionality and leadership (e.g. Sanchez-Hucles & Davis, 2010). To the extent that the object in the center of the room changes, of course, the means of investigation must be renewed to reflect that changing reality. For present purposes, let us assume *per impossibile* that we are dealing with an unchanging object, i.e. leadership.

Levine (2018) offered a way forward from this type of question.[5] He rejected several likely candidates—candidates frequently adopted by other scholars (see Levine, 2018, p. 196f):

- **Monism** suggests that there is only one right answer, one way to the truth. And this is it (whatever "this" is).
- **Polemicism** urges people to argue over which one is the best. Then see monism, above.
- **Semanticism** says it is just a matter of clearing up our language. What we will find is that there really is not any conflict.
- **Skepticism** doubts that any of these alternatives will work. Maybe nothing will.
- **Eclecticism** uses bits and pieces of different possibilities and mashes them together heedlessly.

Instead of these choices, Levine created a hybrid from the work of the psychologist Sigmund Freud and the sociologist Talcott Parsons. It is a version of pluralism. The correct answer, he wrote, is "it depends." The significant thing to study is **what it depends on**. Levine identified four and only four purposes that should guide a scholar in his or her choices. First (associated with the ego) is adaptation to meet one's goal, problem solving, usually by means of science and technology. Second (id) is exploring that goal itself, expressing what it means and why, usually by means of art. Third (superego) is integrating everything normatively, how things ought to be, usually by means of ethics, politics, and law. Fourth (ego-ideal) is pattern maintenance, continuity toward living up to that goal, which includes continuity through-out one's academic career and even after one is dead, usually understood by means of religion.

A couple of typical examples of the ego/adaptation in leadership studies would be the work of John Antonakis (e.g. Antonakis & Day, 2017) or Ron Riggio. A typical example of the id/expression in leadership studies would be the work of Whitney McIntyre Miller (peace) or Ben Redekop (sustainability). A typical example of superego/integration in leadership studies would be the work of Joanne Ciulla or Barbara Kellerman (e.g. 2004). And an example of ego-ideal/continuity in leadership studies is this book.

## Part Four: Where All of This Is Coming From

Given the pluralism inherent in leadership studies, one book cannot answer every conceivable question. All it can do is participate in an ongoing dialogue and contribute toward a greater understanding. This project has emerged from

5. See generally, Levine (2018, ch. 7).

existing streams of scholarship that it would repay to identify here in the preface. You should know where I am coming from, even if I do not continuously cite these sources throughout the book.

Collinson, Grint, and Jackson correctly noted in 2011 that the volume and breadth of research into leadership "has grown exponentially in the past sixty years and shows no signs of abating" (p. xli). They identify a number of competing streams, with new ones popping up every year. Accordingly, my own work does not exist in isolation; it flows with a degree of turbulence where a number of these streams have converged. It is no coincidence that just about every one of the following sources appears in their four-volume set titled *Major Works in Leadership Studies* (Sage).

Scholars in leadership studies have gradually been converging on leadership as a process among many other processes in time, requiring multiple levels of analysis, taking seriously the importance of the context (McCusker, Foti, & Abraham, 2019, pp. 10–18). I agree with the position set forth over a hundred years ago that you cannot understand leadership outside of its context (see Osborn, Hunt, & Jaunch, 2002; Bryman, Stephens, & Campo, 1996; Fiedler, 1972, citing Terman, 1904). Sometimes, because of the context, leadership as it is conventionally understood is unnecessary. The reason is that sometimes an entire structure or culture itself seems to be doing an adequate job of doing what we like to credit leaders with doing (Kerr & Jermier, 1978).[6] In fact, on occasion, leadership turns out to be not only unnecessary but also destructive, requiring resistance (Collinson, 2019; de Vries & Miller, 1985). This means that what we refer to as leadership might also be conducted from the organizational level (Hosking, 2011). Frequently, within these organizations, individuals might participate in leadership as a process in ways that are a bit harder to recognize, measure, and control, such as fostering democratic leadership (Gastil, 1994) or distributed leadership (Gronn, 2002), or working on inter-group relations (Pittinsky & Simon, 2007). Leadership often means managing within a web of contending forces. Also, I see no reason to draw too bright of a line between leaders and followers, inasmuch as followership is also a role in which people are engaged so that together leadership and followership form a unit (see Alvesson, Blom, & Sveningsson, 2017, pp. 80–86; Baker, 2007).

By moving away from isolating the **person** or **role** of leader, we open out onto more expansive images in which participants in leadership are co-creating their future and co-creating one another. Often, I find myself in this book acknowledging when two or more elements in any dichotomy are mutually constituting (Collinson, 2019; 2005; Fairhurst, 2001): leaders and followers, social agents and their structures, images and practice—the list will become

---

6. I think we mislabel this as "substitutes for leadership," rather than as leadership at a collective level (see Raelin, 2003).

quite long.[7] This way of talking about two things "co-constituting one another" fits the reality that is out there, that we presume to study: it is all one fabric—a compact reality that we in our minds differentiate in multiple ways, often without going back to explain how the differentia might be related. Because they are.

My own depiction of an ideal follows from the work of those who write about "the extra-ordinarisation of the mundane' (Spoelstra, 2018; Alvesson & Sveningsson, 2003)—that is, a stepping out from convention and from the usual ways of doing things, to cross boundaries. Without this motion, I have a hard time seeing leadership at all. The divergent practice of transgressing existing norms not only serves to detect and disarm potential sources of conflict, it also promises to infuse the mundane with new possibilities. But watch out, it also makes dissent more likely. At the core of this extra-ordinariness is attending to life's contradictions, tensions, polarities, antinomies—call them what you will (Storey & Salaman, 2009; Fairhurst, 2001). We already expect leaders to adapt and shift from one type of leadership to another based on the situation (Grint, 2005; Kaplan & Kaiser, 2003). We call this trait agility or versatility. I am urging a deeper willingness to entertain and live with things that are contrary—things such as thoughts, images, values, and paradigms. Alvesson, Blom, and Sveningsson (2017) acknowledge that leaders often view themselves as boundary-crossers. I tend to think that leadership is fundamentally contradictory, so why not say so?

Most fundamentally, perhaps, I am speaking on behalf of a Taoist model of being, in which the leader participates in a flow of energy (Prince, 2005). By moving toward a more dynamic image, in which things constantly change and different methods work best, I settle on the idea that at its root (or "pin-point") **leadership is a mode**—a mode exemplified best in the practice of dialogue.

Perhaps the following paragraph represents my intentions best. Viewing social reality as constituted by means of conflict and relentless change is nothing new. We could go all the way back to Heraclitus for these insights. More recently, a mentor to Václav Havel and a martyr to the Velvet Revolution named Jan Patočka put these two principles front and center in his analysis of social reality in the twentieth century (see generally Tava & Meacham, 2016). Everybody is moving toward something, he said—so much so because moving is intrinsic to our purpose. Movement is how people realize themselves. We are moving creatures made up of moving biological systems, and we participate in social forms that move. Our highest purpose therefore is to face up to the freedom to move, just as the highest social purpose is freedom itself and not the end toward which we seem to be striving. In our restlessness, we contend or

---

7. David Collinson (2019) writes that "even the most influential ideas in leadership studies can be prone to over-dichotomization. [Yet] studies of leadership . . . are often much less effective in exploring interconnections and tensions" (p. 260; see also p. 264).

struggle. We are in fact constituted by our struggles. All that movement sends us into collisions of one kind or another. In sports, in traffic, in business competition, in science, art, philosophy, and supremely at war, we all serve the primeval god Polemos. Life is fundamentally agonistic, whether we find ourselves striving against nature, other people, God, or even ourselves. It stands to reason, therefore, that leadership exemplifies this state or condition of struggle and at the same time contends against it. My question is why it should be so hard to imagine the struggle occurring in the leader's mind. If this is how we constitute ourselves as individuals and as a community, then it becomes paramount to accept the fact and learn to do it well. Doing it well for the individual human being is done by means of interrogation. Doing it well for the community is done by means of dialogue. And the proper desideratum in all this struggle, the proper objective toward which we should be striving—for individuals and for the community both—is gaining for oneself the freedom to engage in these practices forever, to slip the surly bonds of earth (so to speak), over and over again. As such, we all are life personified.

Among the scholars in leadership already working on these themes and upon whom I have become dependent are Mats Alvesson, David Collinson, William Donaldson, Gail Fairhurst, Keith Grint, Dian-Marie Hosking, Donna Ladkin, Sverre Spoelstra, Mary Uhl-Bien, and Suze Wilson. Consider this book part of an extended dialogue with them. More precisely, I am learning the emergent vocabulary they will have been using to talk about leadership—a vocabulary that still sounds alien at times. However, if I had to name two sources in the literature on leadership that most closely resemble what I am doing—not in style, certainly, but in substance—it would be these: the seminal article by Ronald Heifetz and Donald Laurie "The Work of Leadership" from the *Harvard Business Review* in 1997 and Karl Weick's "The Collapse of Sensemaking in Organizations: The Mann Gulch Disaster" in the *Administrative Science Quarterly* in 1995. As you will notice, I do not incessantly or fawningly cite them, but for anyone familiar with these works, you will find their fingerprints everywhere.

# INTRODUCTION

## Consider the Use of Maps

"You are here."

We orient ourselves on maps. We do this repeatedly with different kinds of maps, certainly with maps that differ as to scale (campus, commonwealth, or continent) and with maps that differ as to time (colonial Virginia, confederate Virginia, contemporary Virginia). We can even orient ourselves with imaginary maps. The Spaniard José Ortega y Gasset once wrote, "All of us carry in our imaginations a diagram of the world to whose quadrants and regions we refer all things" (1957, p. 81). Brian Eno (2011) once pointed out that a three-year-old can move from one world to another seamlessly. After watching a cartoon, a child can go chat with mom before walking upstairs to play with dolls—each world requiring its own map.

Today more than ever, we need leaders with an equivalent power to move seamlessly from one map to another, because reality is one, interconnected, without boundaries or borders. It is as vast as the galaxy and as intimate as a chair. Yet each of us occupies a distinct point on the map, giving us a distinctive perspective.

Let me be clear: all maps are, to one degree or another, imaginary. They are schemas, simplifications. They reside in the mind. Leaders have to adopt multiple points of view, from multiple magnitudes, with a variety of frameworks. Furthermore, leaders have a special obligation not only to map the reality, but also to imagine worlds that do not yet exist.

Leaders can be said to help others to orient themselves. "We are apparently here," they will say. "But we could go there." Right about now, as I pen these words, we in the Western world need this kind of leadership. Despite the good news about what is going right with the world (see e.g. Pinker, 2019; Ridley, 2011), the prevailing mood seems to be that things are going from bad to worse. We sense the need for a leadership mindful of the maps. People are asking themselves: Where are we presently? Where are we going? How do we get there?

## Maps for Leadership Studies

Leadership scholar Howard Gardner (1995) described a process by which human beings learn. We begin with what he called a five-year-old mind, relatively open and relatively empty, with simple maps to guide us. This would be true for anybody of any age who begins to learn anything new. You have to start somewhere. Through regular exertions, the student improves those maps incrementally, adding content and complexity along the way. We can call these maps models or schemas or images auditioning to become theories and concepts. Not only does this process of map-making describe the learning process that a literal five-year-old might undergo (ontogenesis), it also describes the process that our field of study has undergone, as we continue to add content and complexity (phylogenesis). In this fashion, leadership studies continually matures.

Learning therefore is a recursive process, accomplished in stages, as these maps become bigger and more detailed—or, as one might say, more extensive and more intensive (e.g. Kegan, 1982; Piaget, 1950/2005). Learning entails periodically letting go of familiar maps that no longer fit the reality we are trying to understand and exchanging them for better ones. Part of the process includes comparing these maps to the reality in order to establish just how accurate they are, so that with time we appreciate the extent to which the map is not the territory. Because of these experiences, we come to expect that this process can go on and on indefinitely. As we keep getting nearer to a complete map, the process is supposedly asymptotic. Accordingly, we start to include in our maps sections of the territory that remain unexplored. At one time, cartographers would label this *terra incognita* with a warning: "Here, there be monsters."

The map can become so big and so intricate as to become unwieldy (Borges, 1937/1993). We must keep the map sufficiently simple so as to be useful. Toward that end, we make maps of only part of the territory, for example, or we leave some details in reality off of the map, to avoid clutter. Eventually, as the five-year-old mind gives way to greater maturity, not only do the maps improve, but we realize that we can use different maps for different purposes—the same territory can be represented by different types of maps: a topographical map, a political map, a road map, and so forth. Each of them can be accurate for its unique purpose without including all of the content from the other maps. This is another way to simplify our maps without ignoring the complexity of the real world. A prominent mathematician noticed that this tendency to generate lots of maps is especially prevalent in the social sciences (Poincaré, 1914/1996, p. 19f).

The map in leadership studies was already simplified for us by the division of labor known as the academic disciplines. Scholars have been apportioning the task of map-making to different people, so that one group concentrates on sociology, while another group concentrates on anthropology, and so forth. That is to say that the academy has divided reality into parts, as a way of managing the process. The boundaries among the disciplines have been a topic of considerable debate now for centuries. Martin Heidegger and Isaiah Berlin, for example, each asserted that philosophy is separable from the sciences generally; Wilhelm Dilthey and Max Weber asserted that the social sciences are separable from the natural sciences; David Hume asserted that ethics regarding the "ought" is a separate undertaking from the study of what "is"; Rudolph Carnap replied that these differences exist only to the extent that anything other than physics engages in nonsense.

Needless to say, something similar occurs not only *between* the disciplines but also *within* each discipline, as specialization becomes increasingly fine-grained. For some time now, scholars engaged in leadership studies have wondered where they fit in all of this. Is leadership studies a distinct discipline (or sub-discipline), or does it somehow cross the boundaries in an interdisciplinary fashion? Lurking in the background is the suspicion that leadership studies does not even deserve to exist; it has no discernible boundaries, no "discipline." In the spirit of Carnap, then, is it all just nonsense? To paraphrase the philosopher Alasdair MacIntyre, "Whether [leadership] is to be classed with the electron as a notion of great explanatory power or with the ether as a bogus and empty theoretical concept is therefore the crucial question" (1997, p. 48). I am not convinced that my colleagues and I have adequately answered that threshold question.

Given its multidisciplinary origins (Harvey & Riggio, 2012), leadership studies began with a collection of very different maps (Goethals & Sorenson, 2007), donated from the various disciplines—e.g. history, political science, management, social psychology, sociology, and economics. It seems that more and more of them arrive every year. And the territory to be explored continues to widen, as scholars include more and more variables.[1] After a point, the five-year-old mind would find the situation confusing. The experts themselves don't manage much better. The situation would be especially confusing for two types of people (or for the same person in two different roles): namely, the **student** of leadership and the **practitioner**, each of whom is seeking some sort of guiding image.

---

1. I acknowledge the anonymous reviewer's observation that, although relying on a variety of academic disciplines, this book omits many humanities-based approaches such as normative ethics, religious studies, classics, linguistics, and literary criticism that would also contribute to understanding.

As Henri Poincaré explained (1914/1996), scholars exist in part to think more intently on specific questions so that non-experts do not have to (p. 33). They focus on the details and examine the terrain. Like the better cartographers, they walk the territory for themselves, taking measurements. They have to specialize. That is the job. So, if the scholars cannot agree on what it is they are doing, as they quarrel over their various maps, then everybody else who cares will experience understandable frustration and not a little impatience.

Theories of adult psychological development tell us that after the process of trying to improve the map and then trying to learn how to use multiple maps, in due time the expert learns the art of map-making for herself. Using maps well can be difficult, but *making* them is far more complicated. Rather than pick up the map that somebody else drew, the expert steps out into the wilderness herself. The expert becomes less of a consumer of maps and more of a producer.

Needless to say, one of the greatest contributions a map-maker can make is to map that section called *terra incognita* where nobody has mapped before— monsters and all. A number of scholars in leadership studies are trying to do this. I admire them greatly. But maybe the greater contribution would be to challenge the maps that everybody has already been using, to help people see the same reality in a completely different way. (And if that makes some maps obsolete, well, good riddance.) Thomas Kuhn (2012) was to refer to such a moment as a paradigm shift. One thinks for example of the geocentric model of the solar system giving way to the heliocentric model. Or Newtonian physics giving way to Einstein's. Leadership studies did this, to cite one example, when it turned away from the Great Man Theory that had persisted in our field for centuries.

This task of re-mapping is especially necessary when the territory on which those earlier maps were based is itself changing. Reality is one, but it is not static. We know that new islands emerge in the ocean, cliffs shear off, rivers alter their course, sea levels rise, climate shifts, cities expand, engineers dam up rivers, lumberjacks cut down trees—the territory is not going to stand still. Neither should the maps. A very good map may no longer be useful once the reality changes.[2]

It will be my contention that leaders do much the same five things. That is, they improve the maps that people are using. They use different maps for the same reality, as the need arises. They map uncharted territory. And ultimately, at their best, they look at the territory with fresh eyes and see what nobody else could see. Sometimes too they have to throw a few maps into the dustbin.

But now here is the curious thing. Maps are intended to depict the territory. Yet these maps also influence behavior. Not only do they describe reality, they

2. In 2018, Hurricane Walaka completely eroded East Island of the French Frigate Shoals in the Pacific Ocean. Existing maps of East Island have no further purpose now that it has been literally swept from the face of the earth.

tend to shape our choices. We rely on maps to select destinations and the routes we might take to get there. Once somebody maps *terra incognita*, we now have choices. After Christopher Columbus returned, Europeans of every stripe—monarchs and entrepreneurs and missionaries and adventurers—entertained dreams of a new world. And so they followed. In the same manner, this is leadership of a special kind, to open up what had previously been closed, to return with good report. Others will then pore over these first crude maps, which are initially pretty sketchy. And as a result, together they will change the world.

None of which is to ignore or discredit prior maps. They can be instructive. The goal is to build upon them and not to displace them entirely—not without good reason. Something of the sort is captured in the African teaching of Sankofa.

The Akan culture of West African Ghana generated a number of symbols brought by slaves to American shores (see generally Temple, 2010). These symbols succinctly represent some tenets of traditional wisdom, like an ideogram. These symbols survive in unlikely places such as tombstones, to remind the diaspora of its roots. One such image, known as Sankofa, depicts a bird walking one direction while its head is turned the other way. Sankofa has been translated as looking backward while moving forward, but it conveys more of an adage to remember the past in order to face the future, to return to one's origins and retrieve its treasure today. Another way of saying this is as follows: Do not forget where you come from. When necessary, learn your history.

Postcolonial rulers used the idea of Sankofa to reclaim their heritage. Psychotherapists also use it to help clients excavate very old thoughts and feelings. Since 1968, black studies adopted it as a theme of recovery. The important lesson is that the bird does not actually turn around and walk backwards. It continues to move ahead. But it does so grounded in what came before. In terms of the map metaphor, Sankofa accepts the need to keep the old maps while drawing new ones. Leadership moves forward, but it takes its bearings from behind.[3]

Maps influence subsequent behavior. I would take this one step further. All of this imagery of maps and map-making tells us about the process of understanding—of looking at and making decisions. Being a curator of these maps is the work of leadership studies. Even the five-year-old mind knows, however, that leaders in particular are the ones altering the reality that the rest of us are mapping. They are out there building up and tearing down, conquering and preserving, altogether engaged in the dynamics that shape our maps for years to come.

Some writers admire the so-called man of action, who actually does something in the world while the rest of us sit here and cogitate. A wholesome example might be Theodore Roosevelt (1910) singing the praises of the

---

3. A lovely example of this was written by the Ghanaian-American philosopher Kwame Anthony Appiah titled *Lines of Descent* (2014, Harvard University Press).

so-called man in the arena daring greatly, but then one can readily find troubling accounts of writers who seem to endorse even the most craven despot, so long as he leaps before he looks (e.g. Georges Sorel). Others of course will lament the rise of the man of action as the harbinger of a period barbarization (Ortega, 1958, p. 96). Yet these adventurers who make things happen, for better or worse, do so largely based on maps in their head. Leaders both (a) rely on and (b) alter their maps of reality. It is a process by which the two constitute one another. For even if the territory looks one way to the casual observer, it might look completely different in the leader's imagination. The leader is, in effect, trying to bring into existence a reality that conforms to a map that exists only in the imagination. We might say that human beings make maps, but maps also make us.

All of which sounds terribly heroic on the leader's part, or at least Faustian. Here we uncover one of the most persistent "maps" in leadership studies: namely, that the leader is a lone social actor animated by a vision of the future which, by means of other people, he or she brings to fruition. This is the image of leadership as work (to borrow a term from Hannah Arendt, 1958), not unlike a craftsman assembling raw materials in his shop, where he keeps all of his tools, so that he can construct the chair that originates in his mind. In this version, leaders make the world conform to their wishes. I will use these pages to suggest an alternative image—another image I am borrowing from Arendt. This alternative image of leadership she describes as social action, and it changes how we think about the process of leadership. But this image is in fact a composite of many things that have to be said in order to make it plausible. If I am going to ask leadership scholars to question their familiar maps and even perhaps throw some of them away, I should explain my own process of map-making, for I have spent time in *terra incognita*. I have tried to map it for you. If I am successful, leadership studies will have a different relationship with its various maps. And those experts who come after me and venture forth to draw their own maps might view their project in a new way. For this is the other job of an expert, according to Poincaré: not only to think so others don't have to; but also to show others how to think, so they can do it themselves (1914/1996, p. 33).

To that extent, of course, I am being audacious. How dare I? But then my motif has been to go out with boldness and return with care. That motif will resonate throughout the book. It also suggests something of the type of leadership the world needs: go out with boldness and return with care. We have suffered too long from leaders doing the opposite: they are trapped in outdated schemas, unwilling to think for themselves, lacking the boldness to confront the contradictions that hold us back, yet incautious in their practice. I am describing a perennial temptation we all face. Even so, I have to believe that we have the capacity at any age to outgrow a five-year-old mind.

Boldly, then, let me talk about map-making.

## Map-Making Using Subsidiary-Focal Integration (SFI)

How does one create a map? What follows in this section of the chapter is a technique that I find useful. It comes from the philosophical sub-field known as epistemology. Philosophy professor Esther Lightcap Meek (2014) has introduced a process of coming to know which she calls subsidiary-focal integration (or SFI). Based on the work of Michael Polanyi (see e.g. Harter, 2015, pp. 57–63), the process is not linear, but instead it swings from point to point, like sweeping a flashlight around a darkened room. That which appears in the beam of light is the **focus**, where you pay attention. Think of it as the image one takes from experience, the surface that presents itself to you. Meek wrote:

> To notice and wonder at something is itself a highly sophisticated act that must occur for you to come to know. You actively attend to something significant. You assign value to it as something to notice, picking it out from a background. And you must *consent* to the wonder, give yourself to it, responding hospitably to its overture.
>
> *(2014, p. 20)*

This is a critical part of the process familiar to students of leadership who watch somebody give a speech or preside at a meeting. The leader draws your attention. Leaders often attract attention. You care about what she or he is doing. In leadership studies, we often urge students to do this better, with greater sensitivity (Ladkin, 2015, ch. 4). We want them to notice with great care what is happening. But that is only a part of the SFI, only a piece of the puzzle. The philosopher Patočka told us, "Reality is never revealed to us as a whole. . . . All our explanations lead us to see the whole from the perspective of the particular" (1998, p. 168).

As Barbara Kellerman (2016) complained recently, we have tended to shine the flashlight on leaders and completely neglect the rest, as though nothing else matters. We call this error being too leader-centric. Kellerman has been urging leadership scholars to cast a wider search and not get so caught up in one part of the larger whole. To borrow the metaphor from Meek, we ought to swing the flashlight around a bit before making up our minds about what's going on.

Let us go back to the image of an unlit room. What you already know about the room and cannot presently see comprises your **subsidiary** knowledge. Were you told by somebody, for instance, that you are standing in a kitchen? That seems relevant. Is there furniture you saw previously off to the right, even though right now it is too dark to see it? Can you feel the doorframe? Do you hear the refrigerator off to the left? Your subsidiary knowledge is an accumulation of information, presumably in an integrated pattern held for the time being in your imagination, like a map. Other than what is to be seen in your flashlight (focus) and what is subsidiary, the rest is unknown.[4]

If we were to bring forward the metaphor of map-making, think of subsidiary knowledge as the map by which you operate. Focus is what you see when you actually walk the territory. You compare what you experience with what you know in your head. Each place where your attention is drawn informs you about what might be there. As you examine what you can see, you also integrate it in your imagination with everything else you know. Going back to the dark room, you can see the chair. It faces to the right. You were already aware that there is a table to the right. You infer that they go together. You file away what you learned from what you could see, and then you cast the flashlight onto something else, adding to your overall knowledge of the room. Sometimes as you walk through the room, mentally putting the pieces together into a coherent whole, you have to swing the light back onto something you thought you knew. As you go forward, maybe you would like confirmation, or you would like to see it from a fresh point of view. It is not unusual now and then to focus on things you probably already know.

That which was focal can become subsidiary, and that which was subsidiary can become focal. It is a matter of choice. This book is a lot like that. It temporarily makes subsidiary knowledge the focal point. If you were to study the presidential leadership of Ronald Reagan as your focus, let us say, the context for that leadership is not some blob or cloud; it is comprised of other things, including other leaders such as Margaret Thatcher, Pope John Paul II, and Mikhail Gorbachev (Cabrera & Cabrera, 2015, p. 56), each of whom could as easily become the focus of investigation and each of whom can serve as a point of view from which to examine the times when they lived. We should not assume that nobody else is leading just because we focus on one leader. A scholar's attention has to be selective.

Gradually, you can become familiar with a room you can hardly see, such that you could walk through it blind and not collide with anything. For Professor Meek, this explains how each of us actually comes to know the world. It is a process (in her words) of indwelling (2014, ch. 4). She writes that "most of our knowing . . . operates unseen below the surface" (2014, p. 49). Anything you encounter that is new you struggle to fit within your subsidiary knowledge. The mind integrates knowledge. Sometimes, of course, you are mistaken. But you still possess the flashlight, so in cases of uncertainty, you can

---

4. Some of it remains to be known, though not all of it. José Ortega y Gasset (1957) named that which is real but cannot be known the *compresent*. In one of his lectures, Patočka examined this problem as it pertains to phenomenology (1998, pp. 63ff). No matter how assiduously you wave the flashlight around, you will not see the radio waves floating through the air. Radio waves exist. You just cannot see them, with or without a flashlight. You have to infer their presence. For purposes of illustration, leadership scholars treat charisma as though it is compresent. But I will go further and say that leadership itself is compresent to the disinterested observer.

reorient yourself by having another look around. Meek writes, "Relatedness and particularity should not be adversarial opposites" (2014, p. 84).[5] They work together.

Do not let the metaphor obscure the lesson. Meek is not talking literally about a beam of light. She is talking about consciousness, that of which you are presently aware. This is your mind's focus. It is possible to be conscious of that which you are not presently aware—you remember things, for instance. It is also possible that your subsidiary knowledge is so much a part of you that you are not even conscious of it. You take it for granted.[6] If in that darkened room somebody moved the chair into the walkway earlier, without your knowledge, well, you could be making your way with confidence in the shadows toward the kitchen sink and suddenly stumble over it, cursing. That happens.[7]

What the SFI means is that you encounter something and immediately ask yourself how it fits with everything else you know, including that which you take for granted. You also wonder what it suggests about things you do not yet know. You are in the process of *working toward* a pattern of reality, a composite or pattern you can trust—in short, a map (Meek, 2014, p. 53). We might say that there is a knower (you), the knowable (the room), the known (what you have seen), and knowledge (the map of the room in your head).

It doesn't help, of course, that your initial knowledge is pretty limited, which is to say that, starting out with Gardner's five-year-old mind, your subsidiary knowledge is puny. You have to expand it by means of experience or reading about the experiences of other people. Plus, you acquire information, some of which just ain't so, even in textbooks! Making matters worse is the fact that reality is capable of change. What you once knew might no longer be the case.

Perhaps most disturbing is the realization that SFI might change you, might fundamentally transform you (Meek, 2014, ch. 6). As the author of this book, not only am I hoping to replace your subsidiary knowledge of patterns of reality with a better one, I am actually hoping to undermine the expectation that there is only one. I am not saying that what you thought was a kitchen is in actuality an office. I am not urging a replacement of one pattern with another. I am saying instead that one and the same room can be both. It is also a passageway to the garage, a pantry, a gathering place for breakfast, maybe even where the dog sleeps! It depends how you look at it. What I am saying is not to go in to studying leadership assuming

---

5. Matthias Freise (2018) will refer to these as alternate paradigms. You cannot do both at the same time, but you can switch back and forth.
6. Charles Sanders Peirce (1877/1955) and José Ortega y Gasset (1940/2002, appendix) referred to these as beliefs.
7. What Meek is describing is a more elaborate version of the hermeneutic circle, by which you come to know something by switching between consideration alternately of the whole and of its parts (Harter, 2007a, p. 70). Her method also resembles what Immanuel Kant meant by the basis for judgment, like seeing the same object from different points of view—from above and below, from left and right, front and back, inside and out, near and far (Harter, 2015, pp. 77–85).

there is only one right answer. Leadership can be a lot of things. It can be done in a lot of different ways. That is because the reality you want to understand contains multiple objects in multiple relationships comprising multiple, interlocking systems. You will most definitely need more than one map.

Leadership studies is less about acquiring data and other information, like harvesting vegetables; it is a communion, living with, an encounter with a particular aspect of reality. One does not know leadership until one can be said to abide with it, just as you do not really know a woman until you live with her. I would humbly suggest that the subsidiary knowledge presently being used in leadership studies needs to be reexamined periodically. That is largely what my life's work has been. We need to shine the flashlight on that which we ordinarily take for granted or leave for other people to figure out. Maybe we were wrong. That is one possibility. Maybe things have changed. Maybe the map we have been using in our imagination to navigate through the kitchen is not the only one. Are there other patterns? And are those in some situations more useful? That is what I am asking here. The novelist Marcel Proust (2003) once wrote, "The real voyage of discovery consists, not in seeking new landscapes, but in having new eyes" ("La Prisonnière," in volume 5 of *In Search of Lost Time*).

The advice that I offer to leadership scholars applies at least as much to those who would lead. I urge the same process, the same methods. Both scholars and practitioners might begin by using SFI.

## What This Book Is About: My Elevator Speech

When you disclose that you are writing a book, folks naturally want to know what it is about. I believe that leadership studies as it is currently being conducted is limited in its scope because it operates from impoverished images of its mission and of leadership itself as a phenomenon. Frankly, I will argue that literally every image we use in our teaching and our writing is potentially both enabling and limiting, simultaneously.

One of my life's mottos is attributable to Alfred Lord North Whitehead: "Seek simplicity, then distrust it." We have no choice but to operate by means of images—and by images, provisionally I mean in addition myths, symbols, narratives, schemas, models, and a whole host of similar terms. A leader must traffic in them. So also must scholars in leadership studies. But the goal should always be to transcend them, to be the master, to know the limits of each image, and to bring multiple images to bear where you can on the same reality.

When it comes right down to it, in the moment of trial, better to trust the reality, no matter how grim, than the images we use to think about that reality. Reality should always serve as a check on the imagination. William James (1909/1996) once said, "Our intelligence . . . must at any cost keep on speaking terms with the universe that engendered it" (p. 207). Nevertheless, we must become facile with our use of images, though not glib. The reality we are living and the reality we hope to bring about are the primary consideration. I am a fan of using one's imagination in both leadership and the study of leadership. We tend to neglect that element of both, to our detriment. But that imagination, no matter how rich and inspiring, must be grounded in something. And it must yield altogether when paramount reality resists. In fact, that encounter between our imagination and paramount reality constitutes the most fundamental challenge to any leadership. I will be arguing that the moment when, because of one's imagination—because of the map one is using to make sense of the world—reality proves to be intractable, a leader must still find a way forward. That moment is crucial. That experience of cognitive dissonance, when the map and the territory don't jibe, that is what I will be referring to as an *aporia*, which is a term from ancient Greek philosophy. This entire book is designed as a voyage to find passage to *aporia*—not to evade it, but to seek it out.

During the course of the journey, I will pick up and set back down a variety of images to help us understand leadership, perhaps in new ways; and not just leadership itself but the whole, messy context within which leadership takes place. Ultimately, we will discover a singular composite image that emerges from a variety of perspectives—an image of leadership and the study of leadership that, in my opinion, we have too often overlooked, or even rejected for spurious reasons. There has been a perennial wisdom or Sankofa out there that we would be right to reclaim. It is already there. Maybe we just have to see it with fresh eyes.

Yes, we need leaders who can find the right maps. But more so we need leaders who can draw new maps, who can look at things in an unfamiliar way or—more to the point—who can venture onto the parts of the map that say only: "Here, there be monsters." History tells us that merchants in the Middle Ages competed to access India quickly by familiar routes. Christopher Columbus hoped that a quicker route lay westward. He was wrong. And his error enriched Europe immeasurably (see Johnson, 2001, pp. 171–174).

## Not a Chain, But a Collage; Not a Collage, But a Chord

The story is told that a philosopher once declined to review a manuscript because it was not an argument. "Whatever it is," he said, "this is not philosophy." He understood an argument to proceed step-by-step like a Euclidean proof toward an irrefutable conclusion. QED, drop the mic, go home. I personally have great respect for this type of procedure, especially as it contributed to the titanic philosophical systems of Aristotle and Kant. Most of us understand, however, that there are other ways of knowing, which is why we should quickly grasp a distinction between chains and a collage. The structure of the chain is clear in its serial links made of sturdy iron. Break one link in the chain, and it fails in its intended purpose. My book isn't built that way. The collage is an assembly of many images, the totality of which constitutes a composite image, known as a **gestalt**.

This book is more of a collage, with multiple images, drawn from multiple academic disciplines, full of examples and metaphor, the cumulative effect of which, I hope, is plausibility. This is as much as I could aspire to. Richard McKeon (2016) once explained that problem-solving and proofs are only two methods used in the social sciences—and I am relying on neither. Mine is something else, a method that McKeon called assimilation. Admittedly, practitioners might prefer problem solving, on the one hand, and scholars might prefer proofs, on the other. But in these pages I am not doing either one. To set those as my only options constitutes a false dilemma. So, what is this thing called assimilation?

Through **assimilation**, one takes two or more perspectives and sees if, instead of treating them as separate or even opposed, we can transcend them and arrive at knowledge that encompasses them all. It is not about setting alternatives against each other in competition, winner-take-all. Assimilation is about approximating by addition, getting closer and closer to something we can say is good or true or just. That is, with assimilation we are putting the pieces together so that they fit and so that eventually we get to glimpse the image on the lid of the jigsaw puzzle box. Doing so cannot be done in a completely stepwise fashion. Starting out, we do not always know if we have all the pieces, let alone what the completed image will look like. We have to proceed in more of an "as-if" process, looking at two pieces side-by-side and wondering if they belong together.[8] Gradually, as the image becomes apparent, then our job becomes easier and we can say that we are making progress.[9]

As Nassim Nicholas Taleb wrote, "The test of originality for an idea is not the absence of one single predecessor but the presence of multiple but incompatible ones" (2010, p. 5). I like this aphorism. This should be our goal.

If the imagery of a collage does not work, let us try another. Veit Erlmann (2010) explained that the images we use to depict reason, such as "reflection," presuppose a kind of disembodied distance from that which you are trying to understand, i.e. one occupies a space apart from the phenomenon, where objectivity is key. Erlmann attributes this imagery to the visual sense. Do you "see" what I'm saying? Even my choices of the collage and jigsaw puzzle as metaphors depend on the visual sense. We often use a metaphor to tell us what reasoning is, but what if we adopt the imagery of a different sense, Erlmann asked, of listening? Here, the imagery suggests that resonance, rather than disembodied reason, could be the standard by which we judge. I think this idea has merit. My book is an attempt at resonance on behalf of resonance. I am hoping to strike a chord.[10]

---

8. For a technical analysis of philosophy "as if," see generally Appiah (2017), Vaihinger (2014).
9. For those familiar with various ways of conducting research in the social sciences, Karin Klenke (2008) once labeled this approach to studying leadership **pragmatism**, as opposed to constructivism, interpretivism, and symbolic interactionism that resemble it (p. 21f).
10. Klenke (2008) asked for research on leadership that is distinctive, rich, and resonant: "Findings are valid to the extent that they resonate with the experience of others who have experienced the phenomenon in question" (p. 231).

Like a chain, a book is a linear medium (see de Saussure, 1959, pp. 65–70). One scans across the page from left to right, from top to bottom, from page to page. The reader progresses through thoughts and ideas in sequence. That structure for an academic book appears to be inescapable. By way of contrast, neither a collage nor a musical chord is linear. The collage is a composite, an image comprised of images. A chord is multiple notes sounded simultaneously. Somehow, I must deploy a linear medium to depict or portray a non-linear image.

Poincaré once made an interesting plea to fellow mathematicians. He wrote that students are not usually equipped to grasp the subject matter when it is constructed for them logically, in a linear fashion. Pupils require images (1914/1996, p. 131). Even if they follow discrete steps in a proof, at some point they seem to lose track of the argument even when they are trying to follow—and he had to admit that losing track in this way means they are less likely to want to follow. Very few will persist to the bitter end. Instead, he wrote, give them a picture of what you are trying to do. Use their intuition to create an image before setting out on the proof. It does not qualify as "understanding" to examine steps in a proof and satisfy yourself that each one is correct (1914/1996, pp. 118, 126). Few students succeed using that method. That is the "chain" method of argumentation, and for Poincaré not only does it not work for most beginners, it is less likely to be retained later because it was not connected to anything that gave it any meaning: "In order to prove [something] we shall certainly have to appeal to experience or make an effort of intuition [without which] our theorems will be perfectly exact but perfectly useless" (1914/1996, p. 125). Logic alone does not offer that intuition of the whole. Not only this, but just because something is logically valid does not mean that it shows anything true (1914/1996, p. 127). As Poincaré said, "It is by logic that we prove, but by intuition that we discover" (1914/1996, p. 129).[11]

The distinguished mathematician then offered a humble example. You can define the operation in arithmetic known as division as the inverse of multiplication, he wrote, and that would be both simple and true, but what does that even mean to the five-year-old mind? Instead, he wrote, involve children in an exercise about sharing (1914/1996, p. 134). They will come to discover the meaning of the arithmetic operation for themselves, with only a little guidance. And it is far likelier to stick.

So now, let me give you a hint: that image toward which I am heading is not a sharply defined image either. It is more of a blur, a turbulence to be experienced, the cumulative effect of which will open out onto a more realistic and more useful understanding of the turbulent phenomenon of interest to us all. What this imagery requires of leadership will be the topic in this book's final chapter, as we examine aikido politics and mediation—similar methods for

---

11. In his lectures on pluralism, William James (1909/1996) said, "Reality, life, experience, concreteness, immediacy, use what word you will, exceeds our logic, overflows and surrounds it" (p. 212).

taking preexisting social energies dedicated to conflict and converting them to processes of reconciliation. Just as the Aikido master embraces an assault and treats it as an invitation to dance, and just as the mediator brings opposing parties into direct conversation for the sake of their mutual understanding, leadership works with turbulence as a generative force, an opportunity and not a threat. One bends toward the paradox, transforming it.

## Aporias

In the hurly-burly of social life, we ascribe leadership to certain participants (see generally Meindl, 1995; Pfeffer, 1977). In these pages, I will claim that, to a great extent, leadership may be an optical illusion. Either it exists and we can observe and measure it, or it is an inference from that which we can observe and measure. Sometimes, all we get is a palimpsest of leadership. Or it is an illusion. Those seem to be our only choices (MacIntyre, 1997, p. 71). Except that maybe it is our understanding of leadership that has been impoverished.

The term *aporia* means "without portal" or "without a way through."[12] It refers to cognitive perplexity when one is confronted by two or more propositions that are logically inconsistent (Rescher, 1995, p. 41; cf. Beversluis, 2000, p. 1, n. 2). They cannot both be true. A person is said to be stuck between them, with no way out. Socrates was famous for drawing his interlocutors step-by-step toward a moment of *aporia*, when the poor fellow realizes that he must contradict himself—or backtrack from one of his avowed positions. This process was known as the *elenchus* (see generally Beversluis, 2000; Vlastos, 1982). Cohen wrote that it was Plato (more so than Socrates) who "loves to construct fallacies based on confusing types of opposition" (1962, p. 170). He speculated that Plato built them into his best dialogues on purpose (1962, p. 174). A scholar named Vasilis Politis (2009) explained that Plato had two uses for *aporias*: one was to induce perplexity, to show somebody that he didn't know what he was talking about, but the other was to help the guy start to think afresh by recognizing how untenable his position might be. In doing so, Politis differentiated the **subjective** experience of *aporia* as bewilderment from the **objective** condition of a genuine puzzle or problem to be solved—a usage that Aristotle would later adopt (2009, p. 88ff).

This book repeatedly runs up against *aporias* as boundaries, thresholds, lines that it would be difficult, if not impossible, to cross. There are boundaries among academic disciplines, among participants in a dialogue, between the two sides in a lawsuit, between leaders and institutions, etc. The very process of differentiation creates the potential for *aporias*. Jacques Derrida dedicated an entire book to the topic of *aporias* as "the limits of truth" (1993).

---

12. The original Greek plural was *aporiai*. As an adjective, one would use the term "aporetic." The experience of profound uncertainty, to feel at a loss how to proceed, is known as *aporein*.

It is my contention that leaders in particular are charged with navigating *aporias*—not only logical *aporias* but also practical, psychological, and social *aporias*. And they do this by (a) being made aware of them first, (b) appreciating to the full their compelling force, and (c) figuring out a way to sail on through. Afterwards, leaders return to their people with the solution, the good news, perhaps even bearing the head of a giant they had to slay.[13] It is an old story.

George Orwell (1940, p. 30) once wrote about the story of Jonah and the whale. He noticed the extent to which people fantasize finding themselves in that situation. He wrote:

> Being inside a whale is a very comfortable, cosy, homelike thought. The historical Jonah, if he can be so called, was glad enough to escape, but in imagination, in day-dream, countless people have envied him. It is, of course, quite obvious why. The whale's belly is simply a womb big enough for an adult. There you are, in the dark, cushioned space that exactly fits you, with yards of blubber between yourself and reality, able to keep up an attitude of the completest indifference, no matter *what* happens.

Perhaps, Orwell wondered, people prefer being contained within an *aporia*, because it means you have no decisions to make, no way out. You yield yourself to the predicament. "A problem with no solution is only a fact." It is what it is. As Orwell expressed it, "Short of being dead, it is the final, unsurpassable stage of irresponsibility." A person who reaches this conclusion "has performed the essential Jonah act of allowing himself to be swallowed, remaining passive, *accepting*." Whereas Charles Sanders Peirce (1877/1955) had considered the experience of an *aporia* unsettling and a spur to action, Orwell suspected that for many people it was supremely comforting. Well, not so for leaders.

One of the most perceptive definitions of leadership appears in Wilfred Drath's 2001 excellent book *The Deep Blue Sea*, where he posits that leadership fulfills three basic tasks: setting direction, creating and maintaining commitment in others to the purpose, and facing adaptive challenges (p. xvii). Here, as elsewhere, leadership adopts the metaphor of travel, moving from point A to point B, traversing that deep, blue sea. From within this metaphor, then, *aporias* constitute obstacles, blockades, cul-de-sacs, without passage to anything on the other side. Thus, one of the tasks of a leader is to locate and do something about these *aporias*. Are they genuine? Is there a way around them? Or should we just accept them and stick to familiar trade routes? Maybe it is comforting to have been swallowed by a whale, but is that really the task? Or are we, like the original Jonah, fleeing from our mission?

---

13. A classmate of mine in law school once stated that according to Aristotle, the law of non-contradiction means that contradictions are not philosophically interesting. My ears perked up. I said, "But that's when philosophy becomes most interesting!"

## Is the Goal to Solve Life's *Aporias*?

David Bohm (1996a) has described a kind of progression in problem solving that can be applied to any *aporia*. To begin, you can simply ignore the problem and hope that it goes away or that somebody else deals with it. Russell Ackoff (2010) called this **absolving** yourself from the problem. Frequently, that attitude will suffice. President Calvin Coolidge is reputed to have said, "Don't you know that four-fifths of all our troubles in this life would disappear if we would just sit down and keep still?" Sometimes you should probably just go with the flow.

But let us say that you do decide to address the problem. At the lowest level, you stick to familiar methods, replicating past successes. Bohm called this **reacting** to a problem in a mechanical fashion. And in most instances, that will suffice. You take a routine approach to finding a way forward. When that works, Ackoff (2010) calls this **resolving** the problem. At the next highest level, you can consider possible responses, selecting from among familiar methods. He called this **reflecting**. It is still a relatively mechanical process. The only room for discretion is making a selection. Which tool in the toolbox was designed for this job? Bohm gave the example of accidentally losing a dime you dropped in the design of the carpet, making it hard to see, until you change the angle where you are looking in order to use a nearby lamp and scan for the glint of metal (1996a, p. 18). When this works, Ackoff (2010) called this **solving** the problem. The next higher level after this is somewhat creative, as you fashion a new method based on familiar methods, like a composite or adaptation. You engage in what is called *bricolage*—a term I have had reason to use before. There is nothing cheap or simple-minded about using one's ingenuity here. Still, it is based on the same paradigm that would have been used at lower levels. If absolving, resolving, or solving works successfully, then you can relax. End of story.

Unfortunately, these three do not always work (Bohm, 1996a, p. 69). You would then appear to have bumped up against a genuine *aporia*. Is there a way past? The highest level—and the one of greatest relevance—is based completely on creativity, seeing the predicament in a new way that requires nothing already familiar. It escapes the old paradigm, without a viable alternative ready at hand. You have to map this *terra incognita*. In such a spirit, Bohm wrote what others have been saying, namely that before you try to change society, maybe you need to change your thinking first (1996a, p. 23). Is it possible that by altering one's mindset, the problem evaporates? Or transforms into an opportunity? Ackoff (2010) called this possibility **dissolving** the problem (see Table 0.1).

The three lowest levels (absolving, resolving, or solving) are variations of what Heifetz called technical problems (1994, pp. 73ff). A true *aporia* resists these; in such instances, nothing works. At which point, you face what Heifetz referred to as an adaptive problem (1994, pp. 73ff). Bohm gave the example of Einstein

**TABLE 0.1** Terms for Problem-Solving.

| **Bohm** | Ignore | React | Reflect | Create |
|---|---|---|---|---|
| **Ackoff** | Absolve | Resolve | Solve | Dissolve |

initially stumped by the model of the speed of light as though it is not unlike the speed of sound, only much, much faster. The evidence told him that this was not possible. He had to choose between the evidence and the theory—and he rose up above them both with insights regarding relativity (1996a, pp. 58–61). Not unlike what Newton had done previously, mind you, with regard to gravity. The leader says, "We've been looking at this all wrong." How that breakthrough happens can be mysterious. Bohm wrote that this imaginative insight is

> something that everybody experiences when he is thinking about a problem containing a number of contradictory or confused factors. Suddenly, in a flash of understanding involving in essence no time at all, a new totality appears in the mind, in which this contradiction and confusion have vanished.
>
> *(1996a, p. 54)*

Poincaré weighed in on the topic as it pertains to "mathematical discovery" (1914/1996, ch. 3). He said much the same thing about the suddenness with which insight bursts into the mind, usually after a long period of intense investigation that seemed to be going nowhere. Somehow, maybe in the subconscious, a way is found. Because the *aporia* is only apparent at first—and may not actually exist—let us call it a tension, a possible contradiction where you find yourself torn, indecisive. As Aristotle wrote, "Those who search without first engaging with *aporiai* are like those people who don't know where they need to be going; moreover, they do not even know whether or not they have found what they are searching for" (quoted in Politis, 2009, p. 89).

The first chapter will address the importance of thinking about these tensions in terms of images.

# 1

# SURROUNDED BY ICONS

## Seeing Through Images

## Introduction to the Chapter

Nobody understands leadership completely. Nobody ever will. I begin with a premise that nobody can understand any phenomenon completely. Whatever we study is in principle inexhaustible (Patočka, 1998, p. 92; see Simon, 2000; Simon, 1982).

This chapter explains the importance of being mindful of the images one uses when studying any complex phenomenon, but especially when studying leadership. Joanne Ciulla recently insisted that leadership is a creation of the imagination (2019, p. 118). Images are literally intermediate; they convey meaning. (But beware: they can also mislead.) For simplicity, the chapter begins with the image of splitting that which is **compact** into two, by an act of **differentiating**. Accordingly, it explains what I mean by **dichotomies** as products of the process of differentiation that students undergo in order to select what it is that they intend to study. That is, one needs to have some idea about that which is X and that which is Y. Frankly, my book (like most of leadership studies) is full of dichotomies.[1] Dichotomies help to orient us in an inchoate world, like separating the map into north and south and east and west. Having said that, one will have to guard against becoming trapped in dichotomies, as victims of **either/or thinking**.[2] Dichotomies are useful, but they are not the reality itself.

One of the simplest dichotomies familiar to students of leadership is the leader as protagonist, the one person (figure) who made a difference in the

---

1. The term "dichotomies" at this point includes distinctions, polarities, dualities, antinomies, tensions, and the like. More precision will be supplied as it is needed.
2. Either/or thinking is also known as **disjunctive thinking**.

world (ground), i.e. who changed things for the better. This image, by which we single out the leader as the focus of our attention, belongs to the troubadour tradition of leadership, where leaders are celebrated in story and song (Hogan & Kaiser, 2005).[3] Mats Alvesson calls this the Hollywoodization of leadership (2019, p. 29f). In casual conversation, we say that Abraham Lincoln freed the slaves and Rosa Parks launched the bus boycott, Columbus discovered the new world and Julius Caesar subdued Gaul. (He even said so himself.) Those heroic accounts can be useful images. They are often entertaining and instructive. They are also simplistic. They certainly will not suffice for the study of leadership. Such imagery might suffice for what Howard Gardner (1995) called the five-year-old mind; yet expertise requires that we see past this limited image (pp. 24–30). Alvesson issues equivalent warnings against idealization and idolization (2019, p. 34). The next chapter, which is about one of the most consequential characters in European history—namely the Protestant reformer Martin Luther of Saxon Germany—attempts to do just that. One should want to get past the crude models of social action that unduly valorize a lone champion. As experts, though, we have to acknowledge that leadership studies as a field of academic interest originated with this image of the Great Man and has not completely outgrown it (Harter & Heuvel, 2018).

Once one differentiates into X and Y, of course, you have to investigate the relationship between X and Y. What are they to each other? Are they polar opposites? Are they locked in rivalry or in symbiosis? Beware the possibility of a false dilemma! Often, good thinking proceeds from an apparent duality (X and Y) to a point transcending them both (Z). If we succeed, though, one moves along from (a) a **compact reality** to (b) **differentiation** and then to some kind of (c) **integration**. In this way, one passes through either/or thinking toward both/and thinking (see e.g. Cabrera & Cabrera, 2015, ch. 7). In the history of leadership studies, accordingly, we took up considerations of the leader *in relationship* with the follower and *in relationship* with the organization and *in relationship* with the culture and so on. As William James put it, "The full truth about anything involves more than that thing. In the end nothing less than the whole of everything can be the truth of anything at all" (1909/1996, p. 90). We in leadership studies have properly tried to grow beyond what is known as a leader-centric approach to show how it all fits together.

This chapter considers the extent to which images disclose something about the reality we wish to understand. Images also shape how we construct that reality, so it pays to become mindful of the images by which we operate in leadership studies. One of the most basic images is dividing or splitting something into two (or more) parts, then figuring out how those parts might be related. To what extent, however, do such images limit our understanding?

---

3. Don't get me wrong: studies of prominent leaders will continue to be legitimate contributions to the field of study (see e.g. Rustow, 1970).

## Images as Intermediate Symbols

> Signs are small measurable things, but interpretations are illimitable. . . .
> —*George Eliot,* Middlemarch *(1871–1872)*

Kenneth E. Boulding wrote *The Image: Knowledge in Life and Society* in 1956. There, he made the case for a new integrative study of what he called eiconics, which is the character and life of images. He illustrated its utility for such fields as organizational studies, biology, anthropology, sociology, economics, politics, history, and culture—tying it together in the last chapter with a review of its philosophical implications. Throughout, he found opportunities to mention mythology and religion, as well.[4] He treated images almost in the same fashion as subsequent attempts to characterize genes (Dawkins, 1976/2006) and memes (Distin, 2005). In one sense, I hope to contribute to Boulding's project.

Forty years after *The Image*, Gareth Morgan was to write *Images of Organization* (2nd edition, 1997/2006). There, Morgan wrote about organizations as machines, organisms, brains, cultures, political systems, psychic prisons, domination, and flux—in the process making each metaphor at least plausible. What you and I conceive as a single, unitary entity (the organization) can be viewed profitably in any one of several guises. So much of what one thinks about it depends on the imagery you choose.[5] In a similar vein, George Lakoff and Mark Johnson came out with *Metaphors We Live By* (1980). Then, in 2011, Mats Alvesson and André Spicer decided to edit a volume of *Metaphors We Lead By*, in which leadership itself is viewed by means of multiple, alternative images, such as saint, gardener, buddy, commander, cyborg, and bully.

The following work also relies on a series of images. These images are meant to capture or represent something about reality. They are not representations of reality as one sees it with your eyes, like a portrait intended to look like the Duchess of Alba; instead, they are conceptual in nature and might not look at all like the reality one sees. As Boulding explained, you are not meant to focus on the image itself (**idol**), except as it conveys meaning of some sort (**icon**).[6]

---

4. See generally Eliade (1991). Ironically, Boulding did not emphasize the value of his new idea to psychology, although he later complained when psychology had not paid due attention to his work (1989, p. 378).
5. Impairing the capacity to do this would be an uncritical commitment to literalism. For a sustained critique of literalism, see e.g. Hillman (1975).
6. Religion gave us the distinction between the icon, which is transparent to a deeper reality, and the idol, which is opaque (see Spoelstra, 2018, p. 95). Klenke (2008) credits Pandofsky (1970) with formalizing iconography as a method in the social sciences, in which the researcher asks (a) what is seen (focal awareness), (b) what it symbolizes, and (c) what that all says to the observer (p. 272f). Semiologist Ferdinand de Saussure (1959) would concur that the image (or signifier) is associated in the mind with a concept (or signified). Each "recalls" the other. However, he denied that the sign comprised of signifier and signified has any necessary association with the real world. Instead, he argued, these associations are completely a matter of convention, as part of a comprehending language system (see generally, pp. 65–70).

There is something *behind* the image, something far more elaborate and surprising than you could ever hope to include in any single image. Nevertheless, some meaning can be said to pass through the image. The classic organizational chart, for example, is supposed to convey the order and flow of authority. To be clear, such a chart is only one way to depict this. There can be others.[7]

The image is like an impression one has of the surface of reality. The Spaniard José Ortega y Gasset, in his first book *Meditations on Quixote* (1914/1961), wrote about the dichotomy between surface and depth, which is what we are talking about. He wrote that "depth is fatally condemned to become a surface if it wants to be visible" (p. 59). Yet it cannot exhibit or display itself entirely. We all know this. Which is why in every encounter, we sense something that is not apparent, he wrote, something fugitive. "Everything has within it an indication of its possible plenitude" (1914/1961, p. 32). Later, he wrote, "Impressions form a superficial tapestry from which ideal paths seem to lead us toward a deeper reality" (1914/1961, p. 74). Part of the problem is that the same thing can present itself in different ways (1914/1961, p. 63), so that it will appear in one form to person A and in another form to person B. Or in different forms to the same person who looks again. This is largely why interpretation is necessary. Accordingly, critics interpret works of art, jurists interpret passages in a constitution, and lovers interpret furtive glances. With our conceptual powers, we penetrate past "the barbarous, brutal, mute, meaningless reality of things" (1914/1961, p. 145). An image is what one gets with your focal awareness using SFI. Whatever your flashlight reveals, it belongs to a reality that you cannot presently see (i.e. the subsidiary knowledge). Surface and depth is a basic dichotomy.

Sometimes, of course, one gets things wrong as to what an image means, or you go too far, seeing things that are not even there.[8] Sometimes, what you discover hidden in the dark heart of reality will retaliate, like a boar in the underbrush. But, no matter how far you take your interpretations, you never exhaust reality.

In light of these thoughts, we might depict leadership as an invitation, with (a) the leader serving as the surface and (b) some shared adventure as the depth.

---

7. The image is only an image and not the reality itself. The map is not the territory. A failure to make this distinction leads to the Fallacy of Misplaced Concreteness (see Harter, 2007a, crediting Alfred Lord North Whitehead).

8. By adulthood, we engage in **perpetual hermeneutics**, reading into things, seeing shapes in the clouds and constellations in the stars. Critics of revelation often complain about this tendency to take phenomena for which there is a natural explanation and insist that God meant something by it (see Guthrie, 1993). The phenomenon of finding meaning where there is none is known as *pareidolia* (see Liu, Li, Feng, Tian, & Feng, 2014)—a term that actually has the word "idol" as its root. Leonardo da Vinci famously recommended to painters that they gaze upon stains, because shortly their minds will "see" any number of interesting images (Zwijnenberg, 1999, p. 60). Our minds are meaning-making machines, even when—to be honest—there is no meaning.

The leader presents himself or herself to prospective followers in such a way as to intimate, if not explicitly regale them about what awaits them beyond (Ortega, 1914/1961, ch. 17). If the leader is successful, together, they set themselves upon the living flux.

Sadly, as Ortega admitted, we all tend to resist the call to adventure, for we become too familiar with our habitation. We know the circle that bounds our daily activity. We lack genuine curiosity. We come to accept the world as we experience it. Subsidiary knowledge will suffice. Mostly, looking inward we penetrate our selves only so far, accepting what we see in the mirror (1914/1961, p. 157). We do not believe in ourselves, that we were ever made for anything more. Yet Ortega also wrote that in our depth, in the plenitude of each person's being, we bear what he called "the rudiments of the hero" (1914/1961, p. 156). In my opinion, the leader is the one who summons that potential from out of the depths of followers, literally evoking it, so that it might break through the encrustations of habit, appetite, convention, and sloth. And then, calling to the archetype in each of us, the leader says, "Let us away."

Archetypal psychologists will contend that certain images are already freighted with meanings—meanings of which one may not be aware, even as you use them (see generally Sells, 2000; Peterson, 1999; contra de Saussure, 1959, pp. 65–70). Our brains are so organized that these archetypes say something about the enduring structures of human experience. For instance, pools of water suggest the unconscious; mountaintops and the sky, heaven. It does not seem to matter when or where you live. Claude Lévi-Strauss (1963) marveled at "the astounding similarity between myths collected in widely different regions . . . [H]ow are we going to explain the fact that myths throughout the world are so similar?" (p. 208; see Vico, 1744/2001, pp. 41, 80). He took it as his mission "to derive constants which are found at various times and in various places from an empirical richness and diversity that will always transcend our efforts at observation and description" (1963, p. 82f). Mythology, madness, dreams, and the arts traffic in these archetypes. Interestingly, systems thinking also finds them significant in conveying the reality we encounter (e.g. Kim, 1993).[9] Once again, these images or icons are like transfer functions, where meaning is converted into understanding. A well-chosen image can be said to "transport" a thought or idea into one's mental enclosures; images are **literally inter-mediate**, the in-between. One must "unpack" them. This is what Poincaré was calling for a hundred years ago in math education: more images.

Another related field of study pertinent to the usage of images—and especially of what one might call universal images—is semiotics and more specifically structuralism and its handmaiden in the natural sciences neuro-anthropology. There, for example, Lévi-Strauss (1978) detected a recurring

---

9. It is probably no coincidence that Boulding was one of the founders of general systems thinking.

pattern of differentiation into opposition and then some kind of resolution.[10] Again: compact → differentiation → integration. This three-stage imagery will be a recurring theme in my book. The signs or symbols that can vary widely across time and around the world correspond, in his judgment, to deep structures that all human beings are thought to share (1978, p. 19). It was his purpose to work backwards from the signs and symbols to the underlying structures. Perhaps the most popular demonstration of this project—and one that is especially pertinent to leadership studies—was conducted by Joseph Campbell regarding the hero's quest (2008). Lately, Antonio Damasio (2006) has invoked findings from neuroscience to make the strong claim that there can be no such thing as imageless thought (see also Klenke, 2008, p. 13; cf. N. Thomas, 2018).

It is not my purpose here to defend archetypal psychology or structural anthropology as distinct intellectual pursuits. These are alternate ways of capitalizing on a primitive and less controversial insight about the importance of images as a way by which meaning can be shared. From this, scholars could move toward studying language and hermeneutics and what Karl Weick called sense-making (1995). The possibilities are abundant.

Jürgen Habermas, who expressed his misgivings about structuralism generally, saw in the use of symbols a uniquely powerful opportunity for human beings to gain some critical distance from paramount reality and instead represent that reality by means of pictures, words, gestures, architecture, and the whole of culture. Images allow us to break from the immediacy of existence, permitting us to be thoughtful and reflective, as well as capable of communicating more expeditiously with others of our kind (Habermas, 2001, ch. 1). We are not simply passive recipients of messages from beyond, waylaid by angels; we also *create* the portals through which reality must pass. In that way, we win a measure of freedom from the press of circumstances. We can stop and ponder our situation, generating alternate responses and imagining how they might work, before we reengage the world. This capability gives us, as a species, tremendous advantages. We get to interpose images between ourselves and our reality.

For the sake of thoroughness, of course, we must acknowledge that sometimes images also help to obscure, as for example in the use of masks and facades (see Klenke, 2008, p. 275, citing Loizos, 2000 and Moeller, 1989). The

---

10. Lévi-Strauss (1978) recounts the curious example of the hare-lip in American lore. The split face of the hare represents a dividedness that does not exist in the purely good divinity (no division at all) or in sets of twins (complete separation of good and evil into two different beings). The one who is hare-lipped is unitary in one sense, yet split in another sense. It is a creature that is divided within itself between good and evil. As such, it can bless or curse, save or endanger, lead or mislead. At the social level, therefore, this represents the dual prospects of the leader as good and evil, although at the psychological level this represents the dual prospects we all encounter, inasmuch as the line between good and evil goes down, straight down, into every human heart (ch. 3). The apparent division or split creates a both/and.

purpose is not always for anything to "pass through" but instead to prevent what is there to pass through and so to occlude or block, to mislead. We complain about leaders who are fake and put us on, living a charade, using smoke and mirrors. Often, the purpose is for something else to pass through, something perhaps deeper; but in any case, the image serves as a substitute for that which is otherwise apparent. This is not a trivial use of imagery. One thinks for example of clothing to hide our nakedness or staging a house we are trying to sell in hopes that prospective buyers don't notice evidence of structural damage. In leadership, we call this impression management.

As mythology reminds us, and as the first philosophers explicitly told us, the messages from the gods are often hermetic and enigmatic. Even when they wish to communicate, they do so indirectly. As Heraclitus wrote, "Nature loves to hide"; and again, "Men are deceived in the recognition of what is obvious"; and yet again, "The lord whose oracle is in Delphi [namely, Apollo] neither declares nor conceals, but gives a sign" (see Kahn, 1979). So it is that in such instances messages do not pass through completely. Or if they do, they are the wrong message. At best, they are nearly inscrutable. That can be frustrating. The theologian Paul Tillich once wrote that because of human limitations, revelation "is received always in a distorted form" (1966, p. 81).

Interestingly, the brain sometimes uses this capacity to use images in order to give us distance from any trauma that we undergo (Krell, 2019, p. 288; Benjamin, 1968, pp. 108–111). In that sense, it serves as a palliative. Rather than helping one understand reality, images can offer an escape from a painful reality, a tactic for self-care in troubled times. On the flip side, there are schools of psychoanalysis claiming that we do this to ourselves in a self-destructive manner: interposing images in order not to deal with reality, i.e. to protect ourselves. Therefore, we can be said to mislead ourselves by the use of images, often unintentionally (see e.g. Levine, 2014).[11]

Whether the portal opens from beyond in order to deliver a message to us from another reality or we create it ourselves as an evolutionary strategy in order to ponder our choices in a given situation, the image of a portal (whether open or closed) remains the same. What is more, many of the same dynamics surround it. The image of the portal itself therefore is quite versatile.[12]

The images in this book are not the message. They are tools. Sometimes, they may seem misleading or worse. Nevertheless, if you accept from the outset what they promise to deliver and look through them, as icons of meaning, then you should be able to avoid some of the problems of regarding images as idols, as so often happens in leadership studies as well as in life.

---

11. Images serve other functions, of course, such as entertainment and adornment.
12. When one image has multiple uses, this might suggest an underlying affinity between two things, yet it can also sow confusion. We cannot declare that the walnut is medicine for the brain just because the two things look alike (Jelliffe, 1967).

## The Role of Metaphor and Analogy in the Sciences

> Metaphors are the means by which the oneness of the world is poetically brought about.
>
> —*Hannah Arendt (1968)*

Metaphor and analogy use images to show things figuratively and not literally. Martin Kemp (2004) has written that analogy "is still much used today as a way of enhancing understanding, by referring to something difficult and unfamiliar in terms of the known" (p. 134f). Metaphor and analogy are suggestive, we might say, although not a substitute for investigation. Metaphor and analogy are thought to be more of a poetic device, adjunct to understanding. They give to the five-year-old mind something familiar and then say that something else is like that. If you understand A, then you can also understand B. But, is that all that metaphor and analogy can provide?

Leonardo da Vinci (1452–1519) relied heavily on analogy, in many cases as evidence of the interconnectedness of all things. He could imagine the same basic principles at work in the cascade of falling waters and in the curls in a woman's hair. In the same manner, he noticed similarities between the network of rivers across a landscape and the distribution of veins in human flesh. Analogy is not only suggestive; it betokens a unity in the created world (e.g. Jaspers, 1953/1964, p. 93). With patience and close observation, rendered in complex drawings, he could derive general principles from what he saw of how things work. His studies of fluid dynamics were unsurpassed for centuries. Metaphor and analogy can be more than aids in instruction.

In the spirit of Leonardo, then, something called systems theory coalesced around the time of the Second World War (1939–1946), when scholars from different areas of study came together to devise general systems theory (or GST). The GST, widely credited to Ludwig von Bertalanffy (1968), was intended to describe every conceivable system, from molecules to the Milky Way. Using GST, we find some version of systems thinking in such diverse academic disciplines as sociology, psychology, business, biology, and mathematics. Like the metaphor of turbulence, which I will return to later, systems thinking has manifold uses. It is a handy image.

A comparable example described in some detail by Steven Johnson (2001) is "emergence," which coalesced from out of a myriad of sources, such as Adam Smith, Friedrich Engels, Charles Darwin, and Alan Turing, and from investigations into ciphers, ant colonies, migrating slime mold, artificial intelligence, urban planning, and online gaming. Johnson quipped that looking back one can witness the emergence of emergence, as many unrelated local problems in physics, biology, mathematics, and sociology converged on the same basic, underlying precept.

Poincaré made much of the fact that mathematics itself originated in this capacity to detect patterns across unlike phenomena. Adding two apples to two apples is, in the abstract, the same operation as adding two oranges to two oranges. Like Ortega and Leonardo before him, Poincaré wrote,

> Facts would be barren if there were not minds capable of . . . distinguishing those which have something hidden behind them and recognizing what is hidden—minds which, behind the bare fact, can detect the soul of the fact.
>
> *(1914/1996, p. 28)*

The true discoverer, he wrote, "has brought out the relation" between seemingly unrelated facts. Science proceeds by unearthing and then examining up close the "unexpected concurrences" in nature (1914/1996, p. 39; see also p. 51). He even said that "the great progress of the past has been made when two of these sciences have been brought into conjunction, when men have become aware of the similarity of their form in spite of the dissimilarity of their matter" (1914/1996, p. 39f).

As recently as 2003, a professor of applied mathematics named Steven Strogatz celebrated the role of metaphor and analogy in contemporary science because they do often suggest some undetected principle that two or more phenomena share (e.g. p. 156). He quoted Albert Einstein: "It is a wonderful feeling to recognize the unity of a complex of phenomena that to direct observation appear to be quite separate things" (2003, p. 154). Strogatz explained how the rhythm of fireflies illuminating the woods at twilight obeys the same basic laws that regulate the beating of the heart and the orbit of the moon. Sometimes, in other words, Leonardo was correct: there is a unifying precept at work in disparate events. Metaphor and analogy are sometimes more than an explanatory tool. Yet Strogatz also relied on metaphor and analogy for the educational purpose as well (2003, p. 5). So, which is it? If it can be both suggestive and metaphorical, then perhaps the scholar ought to make it abundantly clear which is the case when he or she uses these metaphors and analogies. What is the image supposed to be saying?

There is a third possibility about the relationship of metaphor and analogy with the practice of science. Brian Eno (2011) has made the remarkable claim that we have it backwards. We do not use analogies to serve our understanding of phenomena in the real world, like handmaidens or poor country cousins to the real work of science; rather, we use scientific understanding to enrich our participation in multiple worlds, to feed the imagination with more possibilities. Science tells us about many of these worlds, such as the atom, the galaxy, and the mitochondrion.[13] It also informs science fiction, architecture,

---

13. E.g. Frederick Turner (1997) celebrated the burgeoning "anthology of forms" created by mathematicians studying chaos. On the nature of myths in science generally, see Back (1997).

and fashion. If anything, he wrote, science is the handmaiden. (Now that's a bold position to take.)[14]

Along these lines, one can see Leonardo the artist immersing himself in the study of the world in part to enable him to create worlds in his paintings that are sufficiently plausible, but not literally true to reality (see Kemp, 2004, p. 149; Goethe, 1817/1994, p. 43). He knew how to depict reality with extraordinary fidelity to what he saw. His powers to do this were unsurpassed. Then he took that knowledge and adapted it to his art, where he alone is sovereign (Boorstin, 1992, p. 407; Jaspers, 1953/1964, p. 41). For him, there was no such thing as art for art's sake, on the one hand, and science for science's sake, on the other (contra Clark, 1939, p. 191). They were meant to serve one another.[15] Another both/and.

"The one thing that bridges art and science is the use of visualization to describe your observations," claims Rebecca Kamen.

> There is so much we share in common and I think it is not such a great leap. I think chemists imagine things the way artists do too. We go through steps, exploring what that is, and then use the power of observation.
> *(Brouwer & Schaefer, 2011, p. 5; see e.g. Kamen, 2018; Kamen, 2012; Beveridge, 1950)*

So, imagery can be an effective teaching tool for scientific knowledge. It can also suggest affinities and similarities that express an underlying unity. It can also mislead, of course. But then, as Eno insists, it can be the entire purpose of the science to generate the imagery. Can we say, I wonder, that imagery and the practice of science constitute or give form to one another (see Bohm, 1996a, ch. 2)? I accept that position.

## The Role of Metaphor and Analogy in Describing and Also *Creating* Reality

I commend Lois Farfel-Stark (2018) for her study of the history of images that shape civilization—a tasteful exemplar of Boulding's eiconics. The shape of our artifacts, she writes, corresponds with the shape in our thinking. They do seem

---

14. But then Richard Rorty (1989) takes this to a completely new level, citing Mary Hesse (1980) to the effect that scientific revolutions as associated with Nicolaus Copernicus and Galileo are more accurately understood to be "metaphoric redescriptions," so that science is mostly a series of progressively useful metaphors (p. 16f). But then for Rorty, all of language is metaphorical. What we call "literal" means a familiar metaphor.

15. See Jaspers (1953/1964, p. 3). Ortega even explained once how science has what he called an "imaginative character" (1958, p. 15). Freud (1924/1961) wrote of Leonardo's "vacillation between art and science" (p. 96). See also Capra (2007, p. 32f), Zwijnenberg (1999, p. 111).

to be mutually constituting.[16] It is her assertion that shape influences how one sees. When the shape shifts, so then does our thinking and vice versa (pp. 10, 37, 75, 100). Consequently, "our prevailing shape reflects our frame of mind" (p. 17).[17]

Through an array of compelling photographs, Farfel-Stark tracks three broad phases: the past, the present, and the future. After millennia relying on cycles and circles in simple planes, with belief in the compact nature of all things (2018, chs. 2 and 3), we gradually changed to rectilinear thinking, with grids and ladders that contributed to skyscrapers and an emphasis on making distinctions so that we live in a world of either/or (2018, ch. 4 and 5).[18] After this, already, she writes, we can see the shape of things to come: spirals, swirls, and the helix, linked in complex, three-dimensional webs, compatible with both/and thinking (2018, ch. 6). She even speculates that leadership itself is evolving from rotating responsibility conducted in tribal circles, through hierarchical leadership setting the leader apart as somehow extraordinary, such as the hero, with the next iteration she predicts to be open source, radically distributed leadership (2018, p. 120; see Voegelin, 1956).

I agree with what Farfel-Stark (2018) foresees. She foresees moving past the macro/micro distinction, the old hermeneutic circle, with its either/or, hierarchical structure, and in its place finding an integrated both/and image. This is not to *reject* the old way of thinking, since that will still contribute to our understanding. Nevertheless, we need more. She foresees focusing less on the parts than on the recursive, fractal patterns that emerge over time. We must add to our static models the dynamic models of process. Pressed to suggest a geometric shape to represent the new reality, she proposes the torus (2018, ch. 6). I happen to expect that a more realistic shape for the future will not be a shape at all, but rather (in the spirit of Leonardo) turbulence.[19]

## Leadership Studies as a Bevy of Dichotomies

A basic image in any investigation is the making of distinctions, of splitting that which appears to be compact into constituent parts. Making distinctions is the beginning of logic (Lloyd, 1992). Ken Wilber asserted that when "differentiation fails to occur, the result is fusion, fixation, and arrest in general. Growth becomes stuck at a particular stage; there is no further growth because

16. A version of this position is known as the Sapir-Whorf Hypothesis (Koerner, 1992).
17. Consulting Aristotle, Kant, Hegel, Dilthey, Flaubert, Heidegger, Cassirer, and Ricoeur, Saulius Geniusas and Dmitri Nikulin last year edited a book on *Productive Imagery* (or constitutive imagery) that addresses the imagination's causal role in shaping our social world (2018).
18. During World War I, a German barracks was camouflaged by trees, from the ground and from the air, but aerial photographers detected their whereabouts because they could see plain-as-day the rectilinear gardens the soldiers had planted in full sunlight in order to pass the time.
19. See below at chapter 10.

further differentiation fails to occur" (1998, p. 52). The first image I would like to emphasize therefore is radically simple. It could be anything, really, from a concrete object such as a rock to an abstract idea such as God. The first opportunity to use this image in leadership studies is the process of differentiating one thing to scrutinize, pulling it from out of its context because you want to pay attention to it and only to it. Out of a mélange of possibilities—the flux and welter of experience—you choose one thing to notice, so that you now have two: the object of your investigation, on the one hand, and its context, on the other. The system and its environment, the artist and her milieu, the tree in the forest, the ingredient and the pie—the focal and the subsidiary. That is a basic distinction.

As the story goes, when the professor told students they were going to study frogs, one student raised a hand to ask how they would know what are frogs and what are not frogs. In other words, how were they going to delimit their subject matter? It is not an unreasonable question for the uninitiated to ask. In leadership studies, new students frequently wonder what counts as leadership and what does not. When you enroll in a class on biology, you probably want to know: what is living? When you enroll in a class on psychology: what is the soul? How do you demarcate your attention and know where to look? To begin thinking at all, one must subdivide reality in some fashion, plucking one entity from out of an otherwise inchoate stream.

I would caution my reader, however, that differentiation in the mind implies a prior integration. Whatever you select to pay attention to, it did once belong to a tight fabric of everything else. This is true even of thoughts and ideas. The isolation one creates in the imagination for purposes of study is artificial and potentially misleading. At some point, a thorough understanding of the object of study will require you to understand how it fit into its context, e.g. what is its relationship to everything else? Did it emerge from out of its context? Does it in turn impact its context? Is there a sense in which the object that you study struggles against its context? Will it return back into the context and disappear, ashes to ashes, dust to dust? A theologian named H. Richard Niebuhr (1951) offered different ways of expressing the relationship into distinct themes. It goes something like this.

First, the act of differentiation allows you to explore the ways in which X is not Y. They are at least conceptually separable. For instance, leadership is not the same thing as society or culture or history. Second, one may ask how X produces Y or Y produces X. Often, as we shall see, it goes both ways (Cabrera & Cabrera, 2015, p. 63f). Culture (to pick one example) can be understood to produce leadership, but then leadership produces culture. At the very least, the two are **reciprocal**. The way I like to say it is that they constitute each other. Third, to some degree X and Y are *against* one another, held in some kind of tension, possibly competing against one another. Maybe they pose a contradiction. Whatever it is that you study engages in a struggle to become what it is and retain its integrity. Taking a giant step back, then, you and I can imagine X and Y participating in something that comprehends them both, which we might think of as Z. Whatever it is, Z can be imagined at a higher level of abstraction than both X and Y (see Cabrera & Cabrera, 2015, pp. 60–62). Two different species can belong to the same genus.

At this stage in the chapter, I want to reiterate that one of the most rudimentary and essential mental operations is finding and examining dichotomies and distinctions, no matter how they manifest as differences, oppositions, tensions, paradoxes, antinomies, or conflicts comprised of parts, pieces, subsystems, elements, components, modules, members, genres, species, facets, or properties. Differentiation creates an either/or (see Cabrera & Cabrera, 2015, pp. 56–60). Accordingly, we must recognize and analyze the two poles at the end of any dimension (north/south, us/them, good/bad). We must mentally see the parts in the whole or we get nowhere fast. Afterwards, we must figure out how the parts are related.

In leadership studies, we have been doing this for years now (see e.g. Alvesson, 2019, p. 32; Collinson, 2014; Cronin & Genovese, 2012). We differentiate the role of the leader from the role of the follower, seen together in a relationship. We differentiate the present from the future, or there is no awareness of the prospects of change. Even more fundamentally, we differentiate the present from the past, or there is no awareness of the possibility of change. We differentiate types of leaders and types of followers and different ways to lead (transactional/transformational, people-oriented/task-oriented, theory X/theory Y, and so on). We also judge leadership by its effectiveness and by its ethics, each of which is subdivided into better and worse. We find ourselves confronted in the literature by a slew of distinctions.

Before we are done, I will be introducing plenty more, to wit:

> leader/context; image/reality; surface/depth;
> focal awareness/subsidiary awareness; macro/micro; whole/part;
> agent/structure; static/dynamic; hierarchy/meshworks;
> social action/spontaneous order; imposed/emergent; episodic/recursive;
> *polis/psyche*; objective/subjective; reactionary/conservative;
> idealist/realist; *aporia*/coherence; entitative ontology/peregrinal ontology

Sorting into just two—making a dichotomy—is the simplest and purest example of differentiation. In principle, the whole can be comprised of more than just two parts (Cabrera & Cabrera, 2015, p. 13). Also, there can be more than one way conceptually to separate the whole (before and after, top and bottom, inside and out, and so forth). Once we make the key distinction, whatever it turns out to be, i.e. once the bifurcation becomes apparent, a logical question is how the parts integrate to make the whole.

## A Sample Dichotomy: Isaiah Berlin on Idealistic and Realistic Leadership

On the way toward a celebrated academic career, Isaiah Berlin spent a considerable amount of time analyzing and working alongside statesmen in Great Britain and the United States. Berlin also participated in the deliberations that led to the creation of the state of Israel, so he knew the Zionist leadership intimately. In addition, he devoted years of study to Russian intellectuals leading up to the Revolution of 1917.[20] This combination of interests and experiences gave Berlin a valuable perspective on leadership as it is actually practiced.

In 1954, while attempting to describe the Zionist statesman Chaim Weizmann, Isaiah Berlin drew an important distinction between two types of leader—each of which had enjoyed a measure of success and each of which he had seen up close (Berlin, 2001, pp. 186–194). After differentiating these two types of leadership, Berlin then identified a hybrid that seems to have emerged in actual practice.

The first type of leader we might refer to as an **idealist**. Frequently, this type comes from the margins of a group, almost an outsider (see also Berlin, 2001, pp. 143–161). (Napoleon was Corsican; Hitler was Austrian.) He (or she) works from a fantasy image of the people he will lead. He will talk of their glory and their destiny. His vision for them is simple, and his zeal intense. Part of his strength lies in ignoring or defying reality for the sake of that vision. This type of leader seeks to impose a pattern, if you will, as an article of faith. Followers feel lifted up out of the frustrations of their lives. The simple vision inspires followers largely because it offers a vantage point outside of the usual. Such leaders are romantic, mythic, different somehow from the ordinary:

> There is perhaps a quality which statesmen of this type [i.e. idealists] have in common . . . which comes to standing apart, at a certain distance, from the people with whose destinies they are engaged, and tending to see things in simple patterns, in contrast to the vision of those who see from within. . . . Outsiders romanticize and over-simplify more easily.
>
> *(Berlin, 2001, p. 145)*

The second type of leader we might refer to as the **realist**. Keith Grint would call him a *bricoleur* (2010, p. 24). This type of leader comes from the center or heart of the group and seems to be one of them. He knows what the followers face. From that intimate vantage point, close to their frustrations—as opposed to *imposing* a pattern, he *detects* a pattern—a pattern that takes into account real-world complexities and limitations. Whereas the idealist can come

---

20. For biographical information on Isaiah Berlin, see Ignatieff (1998).

across to others as unbalanced, if not fanatical, the realist retains a sense of proportion. His reassuring presence in times of anxiety says that we can cope.

The idealist insists that you shouldn't have to.

An idealist is served by ignoring the facts and displacing a follower's attention from the problem to the desired end-state, the goal. In the process, he embodies that vision and by his actions offers his life as a drama between the forces of light and the forces of darkness. The realist, on the other hand, has what Berlin called a "distaste for myths and drama" (Berlin, 2001, p. 193). He would rather work with existing forces to approach a desired end-state in patient deliberation, even though such a leader might appear to be compromising, idling. The realist rejects glamour as a falsification and a distraction, a mystification, rather than as a dynamic tool for social change.

In short, the realist tries patiently to disentangle the knot an idealist would sooner cut with a knife.

Each of these types has its strengths and weaknesses. Berlin witnessed the real world success of several idealists. He also saw their tendency to commit "monstrous cruelties" for the sake of the one truth they represent (Berlin, 2001, pp. 18, 23).[21] Their logic is not difficult to apprehend. For any given problem, they believe there is a right answer, in contrast to which all alternatives must be wrong. If alternatives are wrong, then it would be perverse to prefer them. The idealist is, in Berlin's words, a monist, which means that he knows the right answer and has the character to insist that others obey, to keep them from their folly, for their own good (see Berlin, 2001, p. 14).

Toward the end of his career, Berlin expounded on this temptation:

> It seems to me [he wrote] that once people say: "I am the agent of history—we should do this or that, because history demands it, because the class demands it, because the nation demands it, because the route we take is a kind of progressive *autostrada*, along which we are driven by history itself, so that anything which gets in the way, must be swept aside"; once you are in that kind of frame of mind, you tend to trample on human rights and values. There is a need to defend basic decency against this kind of passionate, often fanatical, faith.
>
> (Jahanbegloo, 1991, p. 147)

This authoritarian tendency is not necessarily because monism or idealism logically results in fanaticism. Those who champion the idea of transformational

---

21. Later, during a series of interviews, he returned to this theme. He said that "the idea of some ultimate solution of all our problems is incoherent" (Jahanbegloo, 1991, p. 143). Not only did he judge it to be intellectually incoherent, he also feared the practical consequences of this extreme position. "I believe that there is nothing more destructive of human lives than fanatical conviction about the perfect life, allied to political or military power. [The twentieth] century affords terrible evidence of this truth" (Jahanbegloo, 1991, p. 47).

leadership insist that the leadership they envision must be moral. The trouble, according to Berlin, is that human nature being what it is—a crooked timber, as he put it—the leader will be tempted to justify inhumane methods and make exceptions to basic decency.[22] This weakness is also its strength.

> The success of vehement, fanatical crusaders comes, very often, through the fact that, armed with a doctrine, or 'ideology' . . . they hurl themselves against apparently insuperable obstacles because they feel that they have nothing of value to lose: the 'cause', the ideology, is all that they hold sacred, they are remote from the sufferings of the human beings upon whom they inevitably trample, and, being morally proof against human considerations, they sometimes triumphantly break through against enormous odds.
>
> *(Berlin, 2001, p. 192)*

If one of the disadvantages of an idealist is fanaticism, as we have suggested, then one of the disadvantages of a realist is pedantry, a kind of absorption in the minutiae of an issue, getting lost in the nuances of the problem and never reaching concrete outcomes. The realist can become bogged down in endless process and in questions of method (see Berlin, 2001, p. 89, citing Herzen). Realists can seem pessimistic, if not boring. They certainly accept far less from a situation. Nonetheless, in the long run, realists get more of what they want (see Berlin, 2001, p. 139). They piece together more information. They constantly shift in response to circumstances. They can admit mistakes quickly, without losing face. What they are doing, in the words of Berlin, is improvisation (see Berlin, 2001, p. 140). He wrote:

> [With regard to this kind of practical leader] there is an element of improvisation, of playing by ear, of being able to size up the situation, of knowing when to leap and when to remain still, for which no formulae, no nostrums, no general recipes, no skill in identifying specific situations as instances of general laws can substitute.
>
> *(Berlin, 1996, p. 33)*

It is plain from his characterization of the two types that Berlin preferred realists. To paraphrase, he observed that leaders are most successful who possess (apart from luck) a combination of willpower and a capacity for non-scientific,

---

22. For an exposition of this temptation, see T. Price (2005). One should be careful not to assume that by making this distinction Berlin intended to contrast personality types. In fact, he was not describing personalities or psychological tendencies. His distinction is grounded instead on the *ideas* that the leaders held. Their leadership depends on one crucial difference. Idealists are monistic in their thinking, whereas realists are pluralistic.

non-generalizing assessment of specific situations ad hoc (Berlin, 1996, p. 38f). He added, "What makes statesmen, like drivers of cars, successful is that they do not think in general terms" (Berlin, 1996, p. 45).

Robert Lord (2019) takes this distinction between two types of leadership and recommends that idealist leadership take the *longue durée*, aspiring to much, but only eventually, whereas realist leadership concentrate on the short term, judging what might be feasible in the moment (p. 160). A good leader can be both.

Be that as it may, Berlin had described a simple contrast between two types of leader.[23] In the interstices between these types of leader, there is also a curious type that resembles the realist as one who devotes himself to his studies with care and precision. He also trusts and consults the intelligentsia, the credentialed experts from the world of academe. In this regard, he would seem to be an exemplary realist, cautiously learning from human experience, except that he then converts his learning to dogma. As a leader, he relies on the findings of science to reveal "the laws governing human behaviour" (Berlin, 2001, p. 50; see generally Berlin, 1996, pp. 40–53). He (this hybrid type of leader) believes that once he possesses such laws, he can then use them in an objective fashion to order the lives of other men. Like the idealist, he searches for right answers, to dispel superstition and hidebound custom. Such a leader is a monist in pursuit of an ideal. He holds that "all problems were soluble by the discovery of objective answers, which once found . . . would be clear for all to see and valid eternally" (Berlin, 2001, p. 51). For all of his respect and admiration, Berlin noticed in these leaders a temptation to social engineering. Their monism "justifies some of the most frightful forms of oppression and enslavement in human history" (Berlin, 2001, p. 18). These scientistic leaders, these social engineers, are in a sense wolves in sheep's clothing, idealists in the guise of realism.

Berlin's core distinction between the idealist and the realist resembles the more familiar distinction in the literature on leadership between transformational and transactional leadership. Crudely speaking, transformational leaders resemble Berlin's idealists; transactional leaders resemble Berlin's realists. Berlin's distinction certainly predates James MacGregor Burns' extended presentation of transformational leadership by almost a quarter century. The reader might want to dismiss Berlin's contribution as just an early version, a precursor. Any relationship between the two distinctions, however, is not clear. For example, transformational leadership intends moral uplift. Bernard Bass has written that transformational leaders "increase awareness of what is right, good, important, and beautiful" (in Ciulla, 1998, p. 171). The fanatical idealist

---

23. To this analysis, Aileen Kelly adds a word of caution. She notes that Isaiah Berlin understood that any simple "dichotomy, if pressed, becomes ultimately absurd." We are all hybrids. Leaders are both idealists and realists, to some extent, both monists and pluralists (Kelly, 2001, p. 8).

that Berlin feared is instead a "pseudotransformational leader" and not really transformational in the way that Bass meant the term. Whether this is a legitimate move conceptually is not the point here (see Ciulla, 1998, § III). Berlin staunchly opposed the idea that goodness is one, that a leader can credibly intend the right, good, important, and beautiful, all at the same time, because Berlin was a pluralist. He would have said that such a leader is fundamentally mistaken. One must repeatedly *choose* among good things.

I offer Berlin's analysis of leadership as an example of differentiating the phenomenon into two types, two images of leadership, and then in the comparison finding a hybrid. Like I said before, this kind of operation happens frequently in my field of study. Ordinarily, it is useful. We will return to it again later.

## Preparing for the First Extended Example

In the next chapter, I recount the story of a time when Martin Luther translated the Bible into his vernacular German. The story of Luther is often told as a classic confrontation between a hero (on the one side) and a volatile situation (on the other) in which a solitary figure overcomes the odds. Using the SFI, we can assert that Luther is usually the focus. Sadly, not everyone today knows the context. They have limited subsidiary knowledge of European history, the Protestant Reformation, and the significance of translating the Bible.

Luther did exert himself and can be credited with making a significant difference, yet at the same time he did so within a larger flow of events throughout Europe. What he did does not even make sense without some appreciation of the context. What I hope to begin to illustrate from the historical record is the relationship between leadership as we ordinarily talk about it and discernible changes in the prevailing society or culture. Luther impacted the culture, and culture impacted Luther. The two perspectives are seen to be complementary. The change process was fluid and shared—none of which justifies downplaying Luther's singular importance.

I would ask you to notice in what follows a dichotomy that pops up all the time in leadership studies: the tendency to focus on the leader as an image seen against an amorphous backdrop that other scholars study, using historical methods. In the social sciences we refer to this dichotomy as the agent-structure problem.[24]

---

24. For a closer investigation of the agent-structure problem, see chapter 5.

# 2

## LEADER IN CONTEXT

### Martin Luther Translating the Bible Into German[1]

### Introduction to the Chapter

The very life of Martin Luther (1483–1546) manifested turbulence, over and over. From his troubled youth in Saxony (Erikson, 1958/1962), through his contretemps against the Roman Catholic Church, and on into a bitter, even scurrilous old age, Luther trailed controversy, such that his name is readily associated with one of the most divisive eras in European history. The Western church and its polity cracked and then splintered into a dozen denominations—one of which continues to bear Luther's name. Obviously, he alone did not cause the Protestant Reformation in the sixteenth century, but it would be foolish not to acknowledge his paramount role.

Of particular interest here is his role in translating the Bible into the vernacular. In this capacity, Luther would be comparable to other translators across Europe who had an impact not only on the religious sentiments of the laity of Europe but also on the development of their discrete languages. This development was compatible with an emerging sense of national identity that was not resolved until the treaty (or treaties) of Westphalia in 1648, roughly one hundred years after Luther passed away. In this historical example, we find one of the ways that an individual's exertions and attempt at influencing others at the micro level helped to cause (or at least to accelerate) a large-scale change that registered at the macro level.

1. The author would like to acknowledge the assistance on this chapter of Rachel Wagner. A version of this chapter originally appeared 18 October 2017 online at *Voegelin View*, https://voegelinview. com/martin-luther-translation-bible-german/.

## Biographical Sketch of Luther

The basic facts about the life of Martin Luther are well known. After renouncing the study of law in order to become an Augustinian monk, Luther had demonstrated an aptitude for language, earning his doctorate in 1512, at which point he was appointed as professor of biblical studies at Wittenberg University in the region of Saxony. Further study brought him to question certain practices in the church, such as the issuance of indulgences. This criticism eventually drew attention from the authorities. Because of the printing press, his criticisms circulated quickly throughout Europe, so that he was summoned to account for his teachings—the most consequential of which was held in 1521. Luther's intransigence there influenced church authorities to excommunicate him and civil authorities to declare him outlaw, yet a sympathetic elector of the Holy Roman Empire spirited him away to Wartburg castle for his own protection. There, because Luther found himself with time on his hands for ten months, he began the project of translating the Holy Bible into German, while at the same time taking advantage of the printing press to continue his war of words with church authorities. (Luther was nothing if not prolific.) Eventually, he returned to Wittenberg to be among his growing number of allies, where he became embroiled in controversies for the rest of his life. Among his reforms was urging celibate nuns and priests to marry, including himself, becoming a father of six and something of an elder statesman to the Reformation until his death in 1546.

## A Man in Contexts

Luther emerged onto the world stage in the midst of preexisting tensions he did not create and could not control. From our vantage point several centuries after the fact, we may be tempted to construe the tensions as a simple dichotomy, i.e. an either/or conflict between Luther and the Roman Catholic church, but that would be an oversimplification of the times in which he lived. The cherished image of a lone hero confronting an enormous institution embroiled in corruption ("Here I stand. I can do no other.") fits a recurring narrative that apparently satisfies something deep in the culture, as we celebrate so many martyrs to individuality. One thinks of Socrates before the Athenian jury, for instance, or Jesus bar-Joseph before the Sanhedrin. One can summon up many such examples, such as Galileo Galilei struggling against the Inquisition or Mohandas Gandhi bringing the British Empire to its knees, single-handedly. It is an ennobling, yet frankly ridiculous story.

The character John Adams in the musical *1776* sardonically captures this tendency to valorize the hero:

> It doesn't matter. I won't be in the history books anyway, only you.
> Franklin did this and Franklin did that and Franklin did some other

damn thing. Franklin smote the ground and out sprang George Washington, fully grown and on his horse. Franklin then electrified him with his miraculous lightning rod and the three of them—Franklin, Washington, and the horse—conducted the entire revolution by themselves.

*(Stone & Edwards, 1970)*

To this trope of the solitary and heroic individual belongs the lone Chinese student standing athwart the communist tank in Tiananmen Square in 1989. It is the prophet Nathan pointing a finger at his king, declaring to David, "Thou art the man." It is a play about the martyrdom of Thomas Becket or of Thomas More. It is a film such as *Mr. Smith Goes to Washington* or *Norma Rae*. It is the One against the Many, the fragile new thing challenging the established old thing, i.e. the triumph of the underdog. Such a convenient and archetypal narrative plainly ignores the messiness of reality—a messiness that students of leadership ignore at their peril. The situation is always more complicated than the binary opposition we find it convenient to remember. Even so, the singular character of Luther lends itself to such a narrative. As Eric Voegelin wrote, "The spectacle of this one man, bending the course of a great civilization through the impact of his individual force, has never been equaled in its dramatic grandeur" (1998, p. 246).[2]

In order to tell the story of his leadership responsibly, let us accept the injunction of Wren and Marc Swatez (1995) to examine the historical context. In sixteenth-century Saxony, the peasants had grown restless at the reign of their princes, and their discontent would break out into rebellion during Luther's lifetime—the rebels often citing Luther as their inspiration. This was a societal tension Luther could not have created. As it happens, he was powerless to stop it, try though he might. The princes themselves were not always in agreement one with another. (Neither were the reformers whom Luther would inspire.) Lucien Febvre lays out much of the broken landscape that would become Germany (1929, ch. 5). He wrote of "contrasting Germanies; often mutually hostile Germanies" (1929, p. 115). Before Luther, "Germany was in a ferment" (1929, p. 196). For all its internal troubles, Saxony as a whole belonged to a loose empire that was torn among rival powers, including the following:

- the papacy (whose temporal authority was on the wane);
- the Hapsburgs;
- France; and
- England (personified by its willful king Henry VIII).

At this time, Western civilization was no monolith. All the while, at the gates of Europe there loomed the imminent threat of the Turk—a euphemism for

---

2. The movement itself nurtured a mythology of Luther as the singular hero as a way of "branding" him (Pettegree, 2015, pp. 168f, 180).

the Muslim forces under Suleiman the Magnificent. In short, the region where Luther emerged was already fairly quivering with the potential for conflict.

As for the church itself, Eric Voegelin (1998) asserted that "the schism came first, and Luther made a problem of it" (p. 220). In other words, Luther did not *cause* the rift that we know today as the Protestant Reformation.[3] The process of disintegration had begun long before he entered onto the scene. The church had become differentiated in space and time. That is to say, it varied by geographical territory (with the prime example being the split with the Greek Orthodox churches several centuries before, but made ridiculous during the so-called Great Schism of 1378 to 1417 when two or more rival popes started excommunicating one another), and this complex network of fractures varied down through the ages (Voegelin, 1998, p. 220f). The church wasn't everywhere and at all times the same. This was a fact—a realization brought home to Luther during his visit to Rome in 1510–1511, when as a young monk he expressed shock at the many ways that the culture there differed from what he had come to know back in his little hometown (Marty, 2004, p. 13). The undisguised differences in time and space revealed deep divides in the edifice of the church.

As José Ortega y Gasset has suggested in another context, superficial differences do not always need to cause alarm; instead, they may actually promise to strengthen a society. Yet sometimes the superficial differences one sees in everyday life are the result of a more profound societal rift, like cracks along the valley floor caused by shifts in tectonic plates far below ground. As Ortega put it, such "radical dissension necessarily terminates in the annihilation of the society in which it befalls" (1940/1946, p. 16). One could argue that it was into such a seismic event that Luther had stumbled. Voegelin offered a similar hypothesis: "The appearance of the 'great individual' does not cause the revolution, it is itself the symptom of a civilizational breakdown that may need only a suitable occasion for manifesting itself in the revolution" (1998, p. 247). We might say that society had reached an *aporia*, where things did not make sense.

A young and impressionable Luther would have first encountered evidence of such a "radical dissension" via his professors, when he heard about the theoretical confusions surrounding thinkers such as William of Ockham (who had died a hundred years before Luther was even born) (Marty, 2004, p. 6). Scholasticism was thought to have fallen into purposeless rancor. Thus, Luther inherited many of the issues his predecessors had struggled (and failed) to resolve *intellectually*. But here was more than an academic disputation. The Hussite Wars to the south had begun with the execution of Jan Hus in 1415; the obstreperous Lollards before that had followed the influence

---

3. Luther did not cause the rift any more than Martin Luther King Jr. caused segregation in 1963, despite being accused of doing so (read his famous "Letter from Birmingham Jail").

of John Wycliffe in England (Bobrick, 2001, pp. 58–70). John Stuart Mill (1859/1992) once remarked that "the Reformation broke out at least twenty times before Luther, and was put down" (p. 31). Luther therefore inherited many of the issues these heretics had struggled to resolve *politically*. Europe was splintering in thought and deed. Part of Luther's importance lies not so much in what he had said about all of this, but in the fact that he so profoundly experienced the sense that a disintegration was underway. Luther came to maturity suspended in a liminal time that Ortega would have formally called Discord (1940/1946).

Voegelin cites the controversy surrounding the sale of indulgences as an example of this burgeoning discord—a superficial difference of practice that was in his words "ripe" as a scandal at the highest levels of international finance before Luther posted his Ninety-Five Theses in 1517.[4] By Voegelin's calculations (1998), as a result of this "focal event" (p. 218), Luther became a celebrity within a month, and the issue over indulgences escalated quickly into revolution (pp. 228–231). That sequence of events could not have happened without certain prior conditions.[5] Luther was therefore born into a world in turmoil, only vaguely aware of a massive fault line under everyone's feet, and he left it many years later openly and irretrievably broken (Marty, 2004, p. 8f; Febvre, 1929, p. 302). As Voegelin put it: "The Reformation . . . begins with a release of pent-up forces and a crystallization of issues that were already present before 1517" (1998, p. 218; Eire, 2016, p. vii).[6]

In what sense, therefore, did Luther lead? In response to this volatile situation, Luther did not offer unique solutions. As George Sabine in *A History of Political Theory* (1947) noted, "The antecedents of all Luther's ideas both about church and state had been current since the fourteenth century" (p. 359). In that sense, he brought very little that was new, so we cannot ascribe this sort of originality to him. In fact, he would have denied originality. He claimed to be trying to restore lessons from the past. That is, Luther saw himself as confessing a faith that was rooted in the Gospels, written roughly fourteen hundred years earlier, and that found expression in the works of Paul and

---

4. It was ironic that the printing press which would give Luther such a powerful range of publication had also made the mass production of indulgences possible (Pettegree, 2015, ch. 3; McGrath, 2001, p. 16).
5. Luther had posted a different set of theses on the same church door several months before, on issues that Luther likely considered more provocative, without those theses causing the least disturbance (Pettegree, 2015, pp. 50–52). Thus it was not simply the posting of such theses that constitutes his singular act of leadership. Historians do not even agree whether Luther ever nailed these theses to the door of the castle church in the first place (Eire, 2016, p. 149f).
6. Alister McGrath (2001) chose this metaphor: "In the first two decades of the sixteenth century, Western Europe was like a dry tinderbox. It was merely awaiting a spark before it burst into flame" (p. 40).

Augustine. His movement's goal was to reform the national church by doing two things:

- taking it *back* to an earlier time of relative purity, even if that earlier time was to a large extent more of a fantasy;[7] and
- taking it *away* from foreign influences, such as Rome.[8]

In this regard, his was an ostensibly conservative mission of bringing forward from the past to an emerging situation.

Not only did Luther say nothing new, he also did very little that was new. Luther was by no means the first reformer. Figures such as Hus and Desiderius Erasmus had preceded him (Nestingen, 1982, p. 18). Their treatment by the authorities colored how he would be treated in his time and place. This is not to say that Luther was an ordinary character in a recurring drama. Something different was happening all around him, and it happened in large part because of him, but we need to put things into perspective. His emergence coincided with the printing press, for instance, and a surge in new universities across the landscape, thereby increasing the number of intensely curious readers (Voegelin, 1998, p. 218ff). As Alister McGrath explains, it was the rise of literacy that made the printing press economically viable (2001, p. 7).[9] Luther drew heavily from the humanists and mystics, who had laid a kind of groundwork (Marty, 2004, p. 19). When he did act, he did not act alone; Luther always had allies—powerful allies—both within the clergy and among the political class (Marty, 2004, p. 47f; Pettegree, 2015, pp. 18–25, 254 and ch. 7). Humanists, nationalists, and rank opportunists all tried to recruit him to their purpose (Febvre, 1929, ch. 6). Soon, he had attracted tremendous popular support: his superiors noted with dismay, for instance, that upon arriving in the city of Worms to be interrogated about his heterodox views, Luther was greeted at the gates by a boisterous and cheering crowd (Marty, 2004, p. 67; Pettegree, 2015, p. 135). In 1520, a papal legate who visited the region complained that nine-tenths of the people there supported Luther (Marty, 2004, p. 55). Marty writes: "Luther had

---

7. Martin Marty (2004) does point out that Luther himself did not believe that they were restoring a previous historical condition (p. 56). For him, the battle was perennial. At the same time, however, McGrath (2001) asserts that part of the motivation was to restore authority in the church to the people (p. 55).
8. Febvre argues that Luther was actually indifferent to questions of nationalism (1929, p. 169). If anything, he was altogether anti-political (1929, p. 172).
9. Increasing literacy in Latin (and not the vernacular) also precipitated a call for translation into the vernacular, as more and more people discovered just how limited their clergy's mastery of the language of the Vulgate made their understanding (McGrath, 2001, p. 35). It also made more people aware of the limitations of the Vulgate itself (p. 57). But keep in mind, notes Pettegree, that even then "a large proportion of the population could not even read" (p. 206).

become a celebrity with whom rulers had to reckon" (2004, p. 87).[10] Luther also had his imitators and hotheaded zealots (see e.g. Eire, 2016, pp. 187–199). We might say that in response to all of the pent-up discontent across the land, i.e. the grinding cultural tectonic plates, Luther was something of a catalyst, i.e. a precipitating cause, yet he was always responding to a welter of gradual, nearly imperceptible *underlying* causes. Part of his genius lay in his responses to the state or condition that so many others plainly felt. Today, we might say that Luther "leaned in" to the contradictions.

If Luther did not offer unique solutions, it may be because the problems themselves had been around for quite some time (Voegelin, 1998, pp. 220–228). His stance against indulgences in 1517 had been anticipated as early as 1482, in Paris (Febvre, 1929, p. 84). Luther was not exactly confronted with an entirely new problem. So why should he require a novel solution? Luther's attitude helps to explain why he was so surprised by the consequences of his efforts. His voice had resounded almost immediately, to a vast audience. Events overtook him. He was unprepared for the upheaval. Rivals, acolytes, and pretenders flourished. The institutions designed to ameliorate the crisis failed, sometimes spectacularly.

Making matters worse for subsequent interpreters, Luther did not profess a coherent system of thought about leadership and social change. He found himself embroiled in controversy, turning this way and that, reacting to opposition and taking advantage of a medium that put a premium on quick responses, rather than long, patient works of theoretical rigor. The fact that he did compose such lengthy works *in addition* to his partisan, polemical pamphlets and letters is a testament to his capacity for work, but these more substantive studies, such as his commentary on the Book of *Romans* (1908/1954), tend not to shed much light on his leadership. They were usually about other things that he regarded as more enduring.[11]

One could argue that especially in his polemical works, Luther's apparent inconsistencies and rhetorical excesses might have served as a turbulent surface for a calm under-layer, such that they were lapses in judgment or extravagances attributable to the heat of the moment. Otherwise, perhaps there was a persisting core to his beliefs. The problem for us today is that scholars continue to quarrel over what that under-layer might have consisted of, except to the extent that it was grounded in his religious faith. Thoughtful critics are tempted to give up and say that Luther was simply not altogether coherent. He was a man of contradictions (see e.g. Pettegree, 2015, p. 283). The possibility of this finally

10. As a result of Luther's position in the Peasants' War of 1524–1525 (consequently known as the Revolution of the Common Man), he did consequently lose support among the disappointed peasants (Marty, 2004, p. 98; Eire, 2016, pp. 199–214), although that came later in his career.
11. The tension Luther experienced between what is enduring and what is ephemeral is critical for understanding his historical significance, inasmuch as he dwelt fully in both.

did not seem to trouble Luther, who frequently held seemingly contradictory positions with glee, yet the turbulence and contradiction in his soul arguably mirrors the turbulence and contradiction in the world he inhabited. We are not able to shed much light today on this psychological question.

Nevertheless, I am aware of nobody who would contend that Luther had no impact on his historical context. On the contrary, he has been ranked as one of the most significant figures in European history[12] and certainly a founding influence on the German nation. His leadership is unquestionable, even if his thinking about leadership was never clear. As one biographer put it, "Between 1517 and 1530, Luther stood toe-to-toe with emperors and kings and contended with many of the forces that have shaped modern life" (Nestingen, 1982, p. 11). The world is different today because of him.[13]

In 1844, the social philosopher Karl Marx said of the Reformation in Germany that it "originated in the brain of a monk" (1978, p. 60), yet in 1852 he explained: "Men make their own history, but they do not make it just as they please; they do not make it under circumstances chosen by themselves, but under circumstances directly found, given and transmitted from the past" (1978, p. 595). In fact, he went on, "The tradition of all the dead generations weighs like a nightmare on the brain of the living" (1978, p. 595). Then Marx presents as exhibit A for this proposition the historical figure of Martin Luther, the monk in whose brain the Reformation supposedly began. As we pointed out earlier (and Marx here mentions openly), Luther was not issuing something new, so much as something quite old. Yet he did lead. He was not just a victim of his circumstances. Neither was he a puppet of his spiritual ancestors. How is that possible?

Perhaps as a way of seeing these lessons in a concrete example, we should consider his role in translating the Bible into the vernacular, which in his case was the German language.

## Translating the Christian Bible Into German

A social scientist would expect to be able to classify Luther's leadership. Howard Gardner's dimensions of leadership (Gardner with Laskin, 1995) would classify this one episode of translating the Bible in which Martin Luther exhibited **indirect** leadership, letting his exertions speak for themselves; although as we shall soon see, even in this particular undertaking he did exercise direct leadership within a widening circle of collaborators. His leadership, however, was within a narrowly drawn domain. That is to say that Luther in no way

12. *Time* magazine ranked Luther the seventeenth most influential person in human history (Skiena & Ward, 2013).
13. Febvre acknowledges that Luther was consequential, but only because of his immense failure (1929, p. 303f).

presided over society broadly, with the same scope of responsibility held by princes. That was not his kind of leadership. As he carried out the translation, he acted as a scholar and a churchman, a linguist and a poet. In all, his work was truly **visionary**, even if he was not the very first to have made the attempt. What then did he actually do?

For one thing, Luther had already chosen to write in the vernacular for many of his earlier print publications, before he even tried making a translation. This decision had been, in the words of Andrew Pettegree (2015), "bold" and "radical" (p. xii; p. 79). It gave him a tactical advantage of reaching beyond the narrow circle of intellectuals who were used to conducting disputations in Latin—a reach that in turn expanded the market for his books. Curiously, his opponents resisted for some time to do the same (p. 82).

Martin Luther did more than translate the Bible. For instance, he judged whether certain passages and even entire books should be included, in addition to helping determine the order in which those books would appear (e.g. Volz, 1963, p. 100). He also took an interest in how his book would appear, e.g. its font and layout (Pettegree, 2015).[14] He was not even the first person to translate the Bible into German (Volz, 1963, pp. 94, 104). That process had begun as far back as 1350 CE—130 years before Luther was born. He was also not the first person to translate the Bible into what is known as Low German, let alone into a couple of other regional dialects (Volz, 1963, pp. 102, 106). That remained for somebody else to do.

To the extent that he did work on translating the Bible into German, Luther did not work alone. Obviously, he was dependent on earlier versions of the Bible in Hebrew, with some Aramaic, Greek, and the Latin Vulgate from which to translate (Volz, 1963, p. 99).[15,16] He also became dependent on a coterie of scholars and editors, not to mention the printers who distributed his translation(s) far and wide, swiftly. Most important among his collabora-

---

14. Pettegree (2015) writes that "Luther spent his life in and out of print shops, observing and directing" (p. xiii). See also pp. 110, 141, 180.

15. A long time earlier (circa 405), the original texts had been translated into Latin, most notably by Jerome, which to the Romans was their vernacular. Not surprisingly, Jerome's efforts met with resistance (Bobrick, 2001, p. 15). Preachers had been making their own translations piecemeal in order to communicate with their parishioners, which should not be surprising inasmuch as the Apostles had addressed themselves to their listeners in their vernacular, going all the way back to Pentecost. As these Apostles wrote the books that were to become the New Testament, they translated from the original Aramaic into Greek, so the project of translating into the vernacular began contemporaneously with the church itself.

    As Augustine had once exclaimed, "By God's providence it is brought about, that the Holy Scriptures, which be the salves for every man's sore, though at first they came from one language, now by diversity of many languages . . . are spread to all nations" (Bobrick, 2001, p. 183, quoting *Fathers of the English Church*).

16. Martin Marty notes, however, that Luther did not rely on earlier *German* translations (2004, p. 72).

tors were Philip Melanchthon and Matthäus Aurogallus, but eventually there was an entire committee for the 1531 and 1534 versions (Volz, 1963, p. 97).[17] Some portions of the eventual publication, such as the *Apocrypha*, were not even translated by him at all (Volz, 1963, p. 96). It is also the case that he did not just sit down to do the work all at once and emerge sometime later with a finished product; Luther kept making edits throughout his lifetime—so much so that after his death there was some confusion about which draft was in fact the final and authoritative version (Volz, 1963, p. 103). A number of changes were made by other people after he died, but the casual reader was none the wiser. Pettegree (2015) estimates that between 1522 and his death, there would be 443 whole or partial editions in circulation (p. 188).

All of which is to say that Martin Luther did not retire to Wartburg castle in 1521 and emerge three months later with a fresh beard on his face and a German New Testament in his satchel. That is not how it happened. Yet something very much like that did happen.

Luther's translations soon had their rivals. Roman Catholic scholars tried to catch up with their own authorized versions (see Volz, 1963, pp. 107–109). Jerome Emser, for example, found so many errors in Luther's version that he decided to publish his own—also in 1522 (Marty, 2004, p. 74).[18] Nevertheless, it is widely held as a myth that it was simply Luther who translated the Bible into German.

What is to be gained by singling out this one man and his exertions, from out of the flow of world events? The problems he faced were not unique to him. Other men across Europe faced them also, and to some extent these problems had existed for some time before he was even born. Luther's response to these problems was not unique, either. Other men had translated the Bible into their own vernacular, going back to Pentecost, and translations were afoot in other parts of Europe as he began. He was not even the first to translate the Bible into German! Yet there was something original in his contribution. Although part of what made his story unique were the circumstances of his time and place (such as the printing press and the rise of nationalism), his response was— for all intents and purposes—original. We might think of it this way: poets rarely invent the languages they use, yet they bring a certain style to their compositions—a style that is both novel and fitting, like a composite that other men are compelled to notice and affirm, even as it is constructed of familiar elements. We might say that Luther may not have *created* anything new, but he *fashioned* a response in a creative way (Simmel, 1916/2005, p. 155).

---

17. James Arne Nestingen discloses that Luther also consulted ordinary people from town to help him understand certain specific terms and usages in the German, such as a butcher shop to learn about the terminology of meats (1982, p. 21).

18. This before the Council of Trent (between 1545 and 1547) pronounced the Vulgate to be error-free and the church to be its authoritative interpreter (Eire, 2016, pp. 378–384).

John Stuart Mill (1859/1992) once wrote, "The first service which originality has to render [unoriginal minds] is that of opening their eyes: which being once fully done, they would have a chance of being themselves original" (p. 65). One way that Luther led others from within his context is that he released others not so much to mimic him as to develop themselves after their own fashion, to take up the project of individuality. This would be true in two ways. First, it would be true in the narrow sense of interpreting scripture for themselves in the so-called priesthood of all believers, now that the text was available in their native tongue. Any literate lay parishioner had unmediated access to scripture. Second, though, it would be true more broadly that Luther released others to develop themselves in the sense of living their peculiar vocation, whatever that happened to be, just as he had been trying to live his.[19]

Lucien Febvre (1929) reminded his reader that Luther had struggled as a monk to conform with an ideal that did not suit him (p. 9). The cloister was not for him. The reformer was finally relieved to discover that there isn't just the one ideal.

I think we have landed on an important lesson here, but it pays to be careful. As Jaroslav Pelikan (1964) pointed out, it would be a mistake to construe Luther's significance as introducing individual*ism* into the Christian West (p. 20). A nuanced argument would emphasize Luther's abiding desire to uphold the unity of the church. It was not the case that Luther broke away as an expression of his individuality, to stand alone in his judgment of the world. He was not trying to exacerbate the splintering of Christendom. That move was to be made by other, more radical reformers (e.g. Eire, 2016, pp. 187–199). Luther had insisted on using the traditions of the church—and especially the traditions consonant with scripture—to criticize the institution, for its own good. It is still the church, no matter how mistaken or misled. So it is still the church throughout the variations of time and space that had seemed so disturbing; Luther ultimately embraced the variety that was routinely regarded by those in authority as a threat (again, so long as it was consonant with scripture).[20] For Luther, each Christian is both committed to the whole and yet free, bound to the church while at the same time liberated to engage in fulfilling its mission in changing circumstances. There is a unity to be enjoyed among the unlike expressions of the faith. That position entails a rhythm of conservation and criticism, valuing the church enough to hold it to account, to become its best expression in each contingent time and place.

---

19. This is partly what Max Weber was writing about in the third chapter of *The Protestant Ethic and the Spirit of Capitalism* (1904–1905).
20. Pettegree (2015) explains Luther's attitude toward the liturgy, for example, as strangely benign, because, he writes, "Luther positively encouraged variety" (p. 322). See also Febvre (1929, p. 244).

In short, even though Luther would not have spoken this way, he embraced the worsening discord in the church and the world as a generative opportunity, out of which something fresh (though imperfect) emerges. Luther certainly experienced the worsening fragmentation, as so many others had before him, but instead of treating it as some kind of collapse or irreversible split within the apparent unity of Christendom, he regarded it as an opportunity. The rift was actually a gift. The monolith of church and empire was no longer a reality (to the extent it ever had been), despite frantic efforts by guardians of both. Yet the significant conclusion to which Luther spoke so eloquently was that the monolith was no longer a desideratum. *The very idea* of a monolith was no longer a desideratum. He may not have appreciated just how far the fragmentation would go, but Luther exhibited it in his own life and endorsed it and gave it inertia.

This is the "map" for which Luther is primarily responsible.

In *The Shipwrecked Mind*, Mark Lilla (2016) cautioned similarly against blaming the reformers for advancing—not individualism, but **pluralism**.[21] Again, these men might have contributed to conditions that led to the emergence of pluralism later, but they were not themselves pluralists in the philosophical sense of the term. If anything, they were responding to a plurality of expressions of the church by bringing it all back under the aegis of scripture. Which is why it was so important to Luther that he share scripture with as many people as possible. To blame Luther for the "confusing, unsatisfying, hyper-pluralistic, consumer-driven, dogmatically relativistic world of today" is a convenient, but misleading myth (Lilla, 2016, p. 79; see Sartori, 1997).

The following adage is variously attributed to early reformers as a way of encapsulating the prevailing attitude: *In necessariis unitas, in dubiis libertas, in omnibus caritas*, which can be translated as "In necessary things, unity; in doubtful things, freedom; but in all things, charity."

Luther must have been thinking this way. Just as the one church abides in different situations differently, in Bohemia and Saxony and Rome and Britain, in a kind of **macro** diversity, so also the church requires a variety of stations and orders as vocations as a kind of **micro** diversity. In other words, it takes many types of people to make a church. Paul Althaus, writing in 1972, devoted the third chapter of *The Ethics of Martin Luther* to this question. Christians are each called to different tasks or roles, he wrote. We must not assume that every Christian must conform to one image of the best life. Such uniformity contradicts scripture itself (e.g. 1 Corinthians 12). But the diversity among Christians goes deeper than this inasmuch as any one person might occupy multiple roles—as employer, bishop, husband, and loyal servant of the prince, all at the same time. It was Luther, after all, who wrote that the individual human being

21. For a different and unrelated meaning of the term "pluralism," see Eire (2016, p. 45).

is both saint and sinner, *simul justus et peccator*. That is, he embodies the contradictions of a created world (see Febvre, 1929, p. 21), the tensions and antinomies that were to be explored further by such luminaries as Immanuel Kant and Georg Hegel. Each individual human being is the site of *aporias*. This insight is a profound leap for philosophical anthropology and central to this entire book.

Once again, therefore, we must not see in Luther's example any kind of championing of individualism (or pluralism) as a creed or doctrine at the expense of community and the complex interlocking web of relationships that constitute the good life. Individualism that masquerades as license and to hell with everybody else completely misses the point; we are bound to an ethic of duty. We are part of the larger whole. Nevertheless, what that looks like for one person in one situation will look very different from what that will look like for another person in a completely different situation. Not to be too facile about it, but Luther represents individuality, and not individualism.[22]

Let me take a giant step back. Philosopher Georg Simmel (1916/2005) wrote a penetrating essay in 1916 on art. Part of his analysis treats the issue of individuality. What is it? He wrote, "The essence of individuality is that the form cannot be abstracted from its content and still retain its meaning" (p. 48). You cannot empty it and then fill it up with something else and still call it the same thing. "The form . . . corresponds exactly and exclusively to the life of the respective individual. It lives and dies with him" (p. 49). Martin Luther as a whole was unique. There would never be another. The problem is that a strictly scientific way of knowing, according to Simmel, cannot abide this conclusion. It must categorize, classify, and otherwise sort any phenomenon—for that is part of its mission. It might put a person such as Luther into a grouping, as for example among Saxons or Augustinian monks, or it might isolate a trait or characteristic that a person possesses, such as courage (1916/2005, p. 67). It would certainly try to determine what "type" of leader he was, as we did earlier using Isaiah Berlin's taxonomy. In doing so, science occludes vitality, the life-force that made him what he was. That is not all, wrote Simmel. In addition, science tends to freeze time and examine a phenomenon as it might present itself in a fixed moment in the flux of time. Yes, science is certainly capable of dynamic or developmental models, marked in phases or stages to represent the predicted series of phenomena, though even here it tends to rely on the same basic method, albeit for successive moments. Stage #1 gives way to stage #2, which is turn proceeds to stage #3, and so forth—one right after the other (1916/2005, see p. 79f). Where, asks Simmel, is the unifying flux? Simmel took this a step further, however, to reject the idea of an atemporal reality, simply

22. One of the most astute spokesmen for individualism, Friedrich Hayek acknowledged that in Germany individual*ism* did not really make sense, even though they did possess a kind of cult of individuality with "deep roots in the German intellectual tradition" (1952, p. 26).

manifesting here and there, like a river that passes a succession of bridges. The person Luther is not the accumulated total of his experiences, manifesting here and there, so that he is the sum of these manifestations. The Ohio River is not the whole of it. Individuality is not some abiding reality, detached from the circumstances of life. Individuality is deeply historical, which is to say that the entire river is fully present *at each bridge along the way*. The fact that we do not talk that way reveals the limitation of the metaphor. For the individual human being, when I am present, I am fully present. This is entirely me, now.

I will insist on this insight later when I try to explain what Heidegger meant by leadership as a mode of being.

And so we might say that at Wartburg, even in his exasperating solitude, during a lull between open controversies, Luther was fully present, fully himself as he bent himself to the gargantuan task of translating the New Testament from the best Latin, Greek, and Hebrew accounts he could get his hands on. All that made Luther Luther was manifest in this work, not unlike a portrait in oils depicting a single occasion yet telling us something about the man as a totality (see Febvre, 1929, p. 97).

Luther's experience can be said to have inspired others—a surprisingly large number of other people, surprisingly rapidly—to do the same with their lives. And is that not precisely what is meant by leadership?

## Concluding Thoughts

Luther faced an objectively divisive condition, both in the intimacy of his soul and also out across Christendom. In an act of leadership, he saw it all not as a threat but as an opportunity. And the world changed.

By way of comparison, the Authorized Version of the Bible in English (frequently known as the King James version), which became the undisputed standard for centuries in the English-speaking world, was also not the first attempt to translate scripture into that language, but it borrowed far more from prior attempts and was done more intentionally by committee. The contrast is striking (Harter, 2017a). As Benson Bobrick (2001) pointed out regarding England, "Individual genius was not, perhaps, what was called for" (p. 259).

Leadership seems to have occurred in the process of translating the Bible into the vernacular, but isolating individual exertions becomes incredibly artificial. So many other things were also going on. This person and that person influenced what was to happen, and we can try to study their individual impact, even though as a matter of intellectual honesty we have to acknowledge the larger flow of events. The Bible was being translated into many languages at roughly the same time. It is not simply a matter of widening our historical lens to take in more data, to appreciate the full sweep of an era (even though that would be academically prudent). It might be prudent to expand the research laterally to include other people and their participation. It might also be prudent to expand the research to include what came before and after the episode of particular interest to us (Braudel, 1980).

At the very moment of leadership, no matter how narrowly drawn—even the wrangling over every jot and tittle in the text—multiple forces were at work, impinging on the social actors bent over their manuscripts. In fact, one reason Luther's example can be seen to be so compelling is that despite the crushing tensions he so evidently felt, his experience in Wartburg castle, hidden away at an undisclosed location, with time on his hands, safely hidden and at risk of boredom, he chose to undertake a task that was to have enormous implications—not only for the church, but also for the German language and national politics.

As Bobrick (2001) observes, Bible production "dominated sixteenth-century book production [such that] by the end of the century every European nation would have the Scriptures in its own tongue" (p. 86). Plainly, something in which Luther participated swept the whole of Western culture. And the original fears of the establishment turn out not to have been unfounded. Writes Bobrick (2001):

> In time the struggles of Charles V with a Protestant league of princes would end in a divided Germany, England would be split into two armed camps, and the Thirty Years' War (1618–48) would ultimately lead to the disintegration of the Holy Roman Empire.
>
> *(p. 103)*

As we now know, the Western world was to become different. Its culture was never the same. A mature analysis of such a colossal shift could profitably be told from either the micro or the macro perspective, but ideally both, inasmuch as they are complementary. There is little reason to adopt one perspective to the exclusion of the other, for that way lies reductionism and an imperfect understanding of social change.[23]

Of course, in order to study leadership responsibly, leadership scholars must broaden their mastery of the complexities within which leadership occurs—for example, knowing what might have contributed to it, what might resist it, what might be the institutional and cultural implications. Leadership arises within a

---

23. Manuel de Landa (2000) recently gave an example from the macro perspective when he wrote (p. 208):

> The Protestant Reformation, by championing the translation of the Bible into vernaculars, dealt a powerful blow to Latin's domination of ecclesiastical ritual and, more importantly, education. Thus, in one sense, the printing press aided some minor languages in their struggle against a major language. And yet . . . the printing press simultaneously aided locally major languages [e.g. French and German] in their struggles against potential local rivals.

Notice that he makes no reference to leadership of any kind.

broad, swirling, and indeterminate struggle to realize some kind of order. One might ask, speaking metaphorically, how does a lone swimmer influence the sea when the water is already being tossed by wind and waves, tides and passing vessels?

Luther himself, full of contradictions, tempestuous—leaping from paradox to paradox (Febvre, 1929, pp. 58, 199)—was a multiplicity, relieved not to be pressed into consolidating everything and everybody into one uniform and unchanging structure. Luther accepted the both/and that would appear to be constitutive of life, thereby incurring the wrath of institutional authorities and the disdain of philosophers ever since.

In order to make sense of their vexations, we might adopt the vocabulary of Richard Rorty. After Luther, people used different words and phrases, leading to the gradual disappearance of the old (1989, p. 6). In this, I do not restrict myself exclusively to shifting languages from Latin to German. I also mean the way that we talk in ordinary, daily conversation, and especially the metaphors that we find ourselves using. One must understand that for Rorty, the entirety of the vocabulary one uses daily originated as metaphor. As any given metaphor becomes more familiar, it becomes what we mean by "literal"—that is, we forget that it is only a metaphor. If you and I are willing to consider this possibility, then we should be amenable "to a picture of intellectual and moral progress as a history of increasingly useful metaphors rather than of increasing understanding of how things really are" (1989, p. 9; see also p. 50). Accordingly, language exhibits a spontaneous, unfolding, evolving order, with metaphors being thrown in among other metaphors, in our quest to make sense to one another. Luther's stature in this process is immense in large part because of "the accidental coincidence of a private obsession with a public need" (Rorty, 1989, p. 37). And so, having emerged from his private struggles not to conform, he had little reason to insist that his was the only vocabulary (Rorty, 1989, p. 39). He was saying, in effect, that there could be more than one. That is the point. For him, the Lord rejoices in many tongues and many psalms. Luther was not preaching the replacement of one vocabulary with another; rather, he was preaching that *there can be more than one vocabulary.*

For the sake of full disclosure, Rorty would have resisted the theological content of what Luther had to say. Yet Luther vividly illustrates a social dynamic that helps to explain how we got here today, for we have inherited a spontaneous order comprised of language and culture and practices, which it will be necessary in the next chapter to examine more closely. Luther demonstrates how this order (such as it is) came to be.

# 3

## STUDYING THE WHOLE WITHIN WHICH LEADERSHIP TAKES PLACE

## Social Action and Spontaneous Order

### Introduction to the Chapter

Most of us think that leaders create (or impose) order. But is that true? While leadership usually occupies the foreground of our attention, as a figure to the ground, there are nonetheless larger forces at work, often in the background. But then, that is true of any phenomenon we set out to study. A market transaction occurs within a shifting economic context. A storm occurs within a system of changing climates. A flower grows in a garden.

Martin Luther was a complex man living in a complex situation. It would be intellectually dishonest to pretend otherwise. So how does one conduct research into such a complex phenomenon and still come up with lessons of real value? This is a key question for leadership studies.

I look to Karl Jaspers, who—after reflecting on a long career as a scientist and philosopher—outlined a way for scholars to study complex phenomena, without ignoring the complexity. He advised setting limits to scholarship, creating artificial boundaries around the subject matter. Then, he said, proceed to examine things from three perspectives: (a) the encompassing whole (which I have been calling compact reality), (b) the constituent parts (as a result of differentiation), and (c) the dynamic relationship between them (as a process of integration). To confirm your findings, he advised, use multiple methods.[1] With such a pluralistic approach, you should be able to discern certain broad patterns. In this chapter, I intend to say more about the encompassing whole and less about leaders.

---

1. Klenke (2008) asserts that articles relying on mixed methods are increasingly popular in leadership studies (p. 156).

The "whole" within which leadership takes place goes by many names: it is known as the context or environment, often portrayed as society at large. What Jaspers was saying is that starting out you need a pretty big map. I have found the following map both lucid and useful. It has been attributed to Friedrich Hayek and goes by the name of spontaneous order.[2]

Hayek had a distinguished career as a social scientist, culminating in the Nobel Prize. Today, he is occasionally reviled as an apologist for greedy capitalists and for what has come to be called the neo-liberal delusion (see e.g. Monbiot, 2016; cf. Jemielniak & Przegalinska, 2020; Zamora & Behrent, 2016; Petsoulas, 2001).[3] Nevertheless, much of his best work is methodological, explaining what constitutes good scholarship. His treatment of three things informs my argument about how we might conduct leadership studies, namely complex phenomena, spontaneous order, and social action.

The following section begins with Hayek's conceptualization of complex phenomena and especially the spontaneous order that we refer to as society. These phenomena are too complex for anyone to know completely. Prediction is impossible. This alone makes leadership difficult, if not impossible to study. But then, as Robert Merton explained, social actions often have unintended consequences. One of those consequences is the spontaneous order itself. Nobody designed it. You could not design one if you tried.

Within that encompassing whole, human beings practice leadership. Concretely, the evidence shows us repeatedly that leadership might fail or make matters worse. To lead is to take real risks. So what can students of leadership learn about the context that will be of much use?

We know that leadership proceeds by episodes within the extended timelines of human history. Therefore, if we take Jaspers' advice, we go from studying (a) the spontaneous order in society, which at any given point in time is complex beyond understanding, to (b) the far greater complexity of history. Conceptually, we take an impossibly complicated configuration and then make things worse by setting that configuration in motion. This would appear to be the "whole" that Jaspers would have us examine as part of our studies into something like leadership. The following chapter attempts to explain what these terms mean, beginning with a closer look at Jaspers' advice.

---

2. According to Louis Hunt (2007, p. 61, n. 3), "spontaneous order" is a phrase coined by Michael Polanyi. Hayek first articulated the idea of "spontaneous order" at lectures in Cairo, Egypt, in 1955 (Caldwell, 2014, p. 14). Louis Hunt and Peter McNamara (2007) said, "The idea of spontaneous order is Hayek's best-known contribution to contemporary social science" (p. viii). Alternately, he championed the term "catallaxy" to describe the resulting order (1976).

3. On the relevance and significance of Hayek for leadership studies, see generally Peart and Levy (2013).

## Conducting Research Into Complex Phenomena

Thirty years after the publication of the *General Psychopathology* in 1913, Jaspers returned to write an introduction to a revised edition. In it, he addressed certain broad considerations of methodology in his field. I believe that his advice with regard to studying complex phenomena is apt.

To begin, he wrote, you have to delimit what it is you intend to study, because reality (on the one hand) and your mind (on the other) are each in principle infinite (Jaspers, 1986, p. 14).[4] Jaspers wrote, "The object of methodological research is always a selected object. It is not the whole of reality but something particular, a certain aspect or perspective, and not an event in its totality" (Jaspers, 1986, p. 10).[5] The directions of investigation that one can take are literally endless. It helps to be aware of these infinities, to be sure, but research can go astray quickly if the project is not bounded somehow. Prepare to answer the question: what exactly are you studying? In the previous chapter, we selected Martin Luther and his attempt to translate the Bible.

Next, Jaspers wrote, the nature of the phenomenon you wish to study determines the methodology you use. There is no method out there that is one-size-fits-all. Jaspers called the temptation to think that there is a single, authoritative method "the Impasse of Absolutization" (1986, p. 14; see Agamben, 2009, p. 7; James, 1909/1996, p. 219). Instead, he wrote, "it is important to master all the methods and points of view" (p. 14f). In fact, as Karl Jaspers mentioned, it would ordinarily be preferable to use more than one method so that they can complement, if not confirm one another. This second piece of advice pertains to how you intend to conduct your investigation.

Third, he wrote, anchor your work in experience, in concrete evidence. In the sciences, for instance, you would be advised not to get caught up in phrasings and formulations, definitional disputes and etymologies, unless they correspond to the facts or help you understand those facts (Jaspers, 1986, p. 16). This would be true also in the study of history.

One of the simplest ways of organizing one's thoughts is the relationship of parts to the whole, that is to say the elements within their comprehending reality (Jaspers, 1986, p. 10). Jaspers divided this schema into three elements (Figure 3.1).

You should expect to study the **parts**, i.e. the individual, discrete facts. In the human sciences, these facts come in two types—the subjective experience that somebody has, i.e. the lived phenomenology, and the objective manifestations such as physical events, expressions, performances, and overt actions

---

4. Jaspers, who made a name for himself in psychiatry before immersing himself in philosophy, held as a basic precept that "man is always more than he knows or can know about himself" (1941, p. 24).
5. On the selection of facts to study, see Poincaré (1914/1996, ch. 1).

Parts
↕
Connections
↕
Whole

**FIGURE 3.1**  Elements for Comprehending a Complex Reality.

(Jaspers, 1986, p. 11). Ideally, your study in the human sciences would have both.

You should also examine the **connections** among these parts. Jaspers organizes these connections into three types. There is what he called the genetic connection on the same plane of investigation, where you determine what emerges out of given conditions.[6] The second type of connection crosses the planes and seeks an explanation as to why something happens on another level, as for example that anxiety is a product of chemical imbalances in the brain. This second type of connection moves from neuroscience to psychology (Jaspers, 1986, p. 11). Leadership studies tends to promote itself as the second type of investigation in which we show how a leader's exertions (part) make a difference in society and therefore in history (whole).

Jaspers meant an investigator to include different types of connection. First, as we just stated, are the connections that parts have with one another. Beyond that, however, is the connection a given part has with the whole, the entirety. This is a different aspect of the inquiry.

Finally, as the third type of connection, you should be mindful of the **whole** in some sort of overarching schema. Jaspers adopted a version of the hermeneutic circle by which one understands the parts in terms of the whole (these pieces constitute a pocket watch) and also the whole in terms of the parts (see generally Mantzavinos, 2016). Jaspers' is a classic both/and approach that serves a pluralistic posture toward the sciences. Further, these wholes are nested into larger wholes, upward to infinity, just as the parts constitute wholes that are comprised of smaller parts, downward to infinity (Jaspers, 1986, p. 13; see generally Koestler, 1970).

The whole under investigation—whatever it is—can be divided into different configurations of parts. What do I mean by that? A poem can be organized in more than one way: by line (a sonnet is comprised of fourteen lines of iambic pentameter), by sentence, by stanza, or by image or idea. The human body can be broken down by subsystem (nervous system) or region (abdomen) or inner and outer, and so forth. Again, one must keep a study bounded so that it does not stray across limitless fields of inquiry in an undisciplined manner (Jaspers,

---

6. This type of relationship on the same plane of investigation is largely what inspired me to write this book, as I explain in chapter 5.

1986, p. 14). One must choose at which level to work, so long as you are mindful that reality extends further in every direction.[7]

Jaspers conceded that unifying all of this into a single investigation will be tricky (1986, p. 15). It is certainly artificial. Nevertheless, one must not elide the distinctions he was trying to make by casually holding that everything blurs into everything else and that it's one big wad of undifferentiated stuff—even if in one sense that is true (Jaspers, 1986, p. 17)! The distinctions matter. Then the way that these differentia are integrated matters. You must go through the process and not skip to the end. In effect, what you are doing is constellating the facts and methods (Jaspers, 1986, p. 17), so that the resulting product makes a credible contribution to scientific understanding. Many facts, many methods, in one bounded study—that should be the aspiration.

A succinct version of Jaspers' advice appears in a book chapter by sociologist Thomas Smith (1997), who identified three basic scientific questions: "What is the [whole] in question, what are the entities composing it, and how do the entities combine and organize to produce the [whole] itself?" (p. 55).

If as a result we find ourselves with some kind of theory about social action, probably the most we can hope for is an abstract pattern about how the whole (society) will tend to form, rather than any precise prediction about what will occur in distinct cases (Hayek, 2014, p. 441). That may have to suffice.

## What Is Meant by Complex Phenomena?

Let me begin this section by emphasizing Hayek's treatment of complex phenomena (2014). The term "complex" comes from being interwoven, entwined, or entangled—the full *plexus* (Szabo, n.d.). Hayek takes it as granted that there are degrees of complexity (2014, ch. 6 and p. 260f), but surely among the most complex phenomena are these three things: history, society, and the human mind. In leadership studies, of course, we deal with all three; but let us for the time being limit ourselves to society, for it is both within the context of society that leadership manifests and for the sake of society that the field of leadership studies exists. In society, then, not only are there more moving pieces, as it were, than in some machine or recipe, but the relationships of these elements, not only with one another but also with the environment, are many and profound.[8] A complex reality therefore requires a complex theory to help explain how it works. Hayek wrote that "a simple theory of phenomena

---

7. On issues regarding multi-level analysis, which has a long history in Leadership Studies, see generally Yammarino and Dionne (2019), Yammarino and Gooty (2017).
8. Elsewhere, Hayek (2014) endorses a version of Michael Polanyi's image of a polycentric order (p. 284f). Polanyi (1951) in turn credits mathematics for the polycentric problem (ch. 9, pp. 208–226). Nobody is in charge. Independent parts compete to steer the whole. Perhaps not surprisingly, neuroscience is telling us that the mind works the same way.

which are in their nature complex . . . is probably merely of necessity false" (2014, p. 263).[9] In fact, he went further. The complexity is so acute that no one can ever grasp it all (2014, p. 269f, citing Schumpeter, 1954). He wrote, "We have . . . in many fields learnt enough to know that we cannot know all that we would have to know for a full explanation of the phenomena" (2014, p. 275; see also pp. 269, 371, 436).[10]

The joke among university students in leadership studies is that the correct answer to any concrete leadership question is always "it depends." They have learned that there are just too many variables. In fact, we in the field of leadership studies keep adding to the list of possibly relevant variables:

- How structured in the task?
- How long have you been their leader?
- Are you taller than your followers are?
- What is your job title?
- How urgent is the task?
- Is this a crisis?
- Have any of you seen this kind of situation before?

The examples are too numerous to cite. In specific circumstances, when a leader is faced with a real-world dilemma, it turns out that "it depends" is the correct answer. Prediction is nearly impossible; the best you can hope for is some kind of principle attuned to broad, discernible patterns (Hayek, 2014, ch. 9). A leader can articulate the rule he or she is following in a given moment, but the leader is probably incapable of describing in any detail what sort of impact this will have on the social order (2014, p. 282). So many other things can happen. But then, if that is so, of what use is leadership studies? For that matter, of what real use is *leadership*? Hayek wrote, "The world is fairly predictable only so long as one adheres to the established procedures, but it becomes frightening when one deviates from them" (2014, p. 292). Your powers of prediction are apparently better when you "play it safe," yet isn't leadership about challenging established procedures?

There is no practical way for a leader to know everything relevant, i.e. the facts of the situation, the dynamics presently at work among your peers, the

---

9. Cabrera and Cabrera (2015) illustrate that the underlying rules for complexity can be quite simple, just as DNA is comprised of only four nitrogenous bases in DNA and color is comprised of cyan, magenta, yellow, and black (ch. 2). Hayek would not object to isolating the simple building blocks or rules, but then he would insist that they combine and interact in a bewildering variety of ways, so that a model of the whole—especially a model of how something complex evolves—will perforce be complex. The four basic colors do not begin to explain the portraits of Rembrandt.

10. Hayek took this position before the widespread use of computers, so that it might be the case that our capacity to do these things has increased exponentially since then. Nevertheless, he staked out the stronger position that complete understanding of complex phenomena would be impossible *in principle*.

values that people hold, and so forth. Perfect knowledge is impossible (2014, p. 200). **I accept this assertion as a premise**. Gerald Gaus looked into this claim and concluded that "expert prediction and guesswork are essentially the same" (2007, p. 156, citing Tetlock, 2005).[11] The question is how to operate in the world if this premise is true. Hayek wrote, "The recognition of this limitation of our knowledge is important if we do not want to become responsible for measures which will do more harm than good" (2014, p. 226). What Hayek is alluding to here are unintended consequences, of which there are many.

## Unintended Consequences

> No one who raises a cry ever knows what echoes his voice will awaken.
> —*Lucien Febvre (1929, p. 98)*

Martin Luther could not know in advance what his exertions would foment. His academic quarrel about indulgences in 1517 was a theological dispute that erupted into far more. Even his efforts to translate the Bible reverberated in ways he could not have anticipated as he sat alone at the desk composing a draft. The state of the Holy Roman Empire of which he was a part was a complex phenomenon that was becoming increasingly vulnerable in ways that few could predict. To his credit, Mats Alvesson (2019) reminds us that "leadership efforts can lead to almost any anticipated and non-anticipated outcomes and often lead to very little" (p. 37; see Collinson, 2019, p. 271).

Giambattista Vico (1744/2001) remarked many years ago that "providence uses people's limited goals as a means of attaining greater ones" (p. 489). He credited providence with driving history "without the knowledge or advice of humankind, and often contrary to human planning" (p. 127). Adam Smith (1776/1950) would make a similar observation regarding a market economy and the unbidden guidance of an "invisible hand." Something that none of us intended seems to bring about an order among us. Bohm (1980) would call it an "implicate order" that is emerging.

Rob Norton (2018) once remarked, "The first and most complete analysis of the concept of unintended consequences was done in 1936 by the American sociologist Robert K. Merton." Merton (1976, ch. 8) reported that—because of inevitable ignorance, occasional error, and a certain degree of indifference—not everything

---

11. Frederick Turner (1997) pointed out that even in a deterministic system, if we wanted to make a prediction about the real world, we are incapable of establishing causation, one way or the other. We have neither the time nor the processing capacity (p. xiv). Contributing to the difficulty, Alisch, Azizighanbari, and Bargfeldt (1997) remind their reader that complex social systems embody two principals: **positional heterogeneity** (no two social positions are identical) and **heterochronicity** (no two moments in time are identical) (p. 166). What works for me might not work for you, and what worked once may not work a second time.

one intends will come to pass. And many things that were not intended, will. Even when leadership works successfully in one context, that is no guarantee that it will work in another context. Leadership in battle, let us say, will not always resemble leadership in a small retail shop (see Gibb, 1947). Furthermore, the mere act of making a prediction known to other people can sometimes influence whether the prediction will come to pass! In addition, succeeding once at leadership might be precisely why you will later fail. Julius Caesar succeeded in crossing the Rubicon and driving Pompeii Magnus out of power, yet it was precisely because he was succeeding as a leader that conspirators resolved to assassinate him.

Consider what Merton and Barber had to say about the fundamental condition of sociological ambivalence (1976, ch. 1). Few things are as straightforward as they seem. First, they wrote, let us assume only one person playing one role (e.g. leader) in one culture. This is the simplest scenario.

## 1 Person, 1 Role, 1 Culture

Even here, under these conditions, the complexity of values, choices, and capabilities within that one social actor can be difficult to sort. Merton wrote elsewhere about the ambivalence of organizational leaders (1976, ch. 5). The job is largely defined by its internal conflicts, or as Merton called them "norms and counternorms" (p. 17). Strangely, he adds, anyone playing the role of the follower can be (a) indifferent to what the leader proposes, (b) in solidarity as well, and likewise (c) opposed—all at the same time (p. 16). This statement sounds contradictory, yet the point is that **people are contradictory**. To put it bluntly, we all walk around personifying complexity. The sooner we learn this, the better.

Next in the process of their little thought experiment, Merton and Barber introduced the complication of each person playing multiple roles, as for example that the leader (and follower, for that matter) is also an employee and a citizen and a parent (aka role conflict).

## 1 Person, 2 Roles, 1 Culture

A successful leader might resign his or her post in order to do a better job raising their kids (e.g. Stone, 2008; Nelson, Quick, Hitt, & Moesel, 1990). Role conflict adds to the unpredictability. Which role are you playing right now? (Do you even know?) Something of the sort pertains as well to multiple social identities, as investigated under the rubric of intersectionality (e.g. Appiah, 2014). At any given point in time, each person has multiple identities.

Next, consider the fact that within that one culture, it turns out that values frequently conflict; we have not completely appreciated the extent to which that might be true. (Isaiah Berlin had insisted that this is indeed the case.) There are just too many stakeholders with incompatible interests. Or they themselves possess conflicting interests, as for example when consumers want products that are both completely safe and completely affordable. You cannot have both. Nevertheless, this does not prevent them from *wanting* both.

Merton and Barber took this further. Even if we figure out what the relevant values might be within a single culture, however, and bring them into some kind of alignment, which is often thought to be the responsibility of leaders, there will be conflict with organizational structures that strain against the culture (and against one another in competition). For instance, we generally want people to be nice to one another, yet we also expect that under stress a supervisor at work must insist on following rules, even if doing so somehow hurts a subordinate's feelings. Besides, we might value the principles of democracy in the abstract, even though the workplace fits a more traditional, authoritarian structure. In short, structures and institutions make their own complex demands on leaders (see generally Douglas, 1986).

Finally, we can introduce the increasing likelihood in a global context of a leader trying to operate where cultures clash—so now how do you straddle two (or more) completely different worlds?

## 1 Person, 1 Role, 2 Cultures

Imagine the complexity with multiple social actors playing multiple roles at the intersection of many cultures. All of this, however, gets hopelessly confused because these things—people, roles, values, cultures—constantly change as well. Ambivalence makes a lot sense.

Hayek (2014) noted in 1967 that one of the reasons for our frustration in understanding a phenomenon such as leadership is the difficulty in trying to connect human actions with the orders they create. Let me say that again: the relationship between **actions** and **order**. We tend to assume that there is a causal relationship, i.e. that leaders bring about order. In leadership studies, we frequently hope so. But here's the thing: two completely different actions can create the same order, just as the same action can create two completely different orders. Furthermore, even if all actions have the same aim or purpose, that does not mean that the resulting order is what everybody intended—if, indeed, the result is not outright disorder. Besides, Hayek cautioned, the two are reciprocal; that is to say that over time actions create orders and *orders create actions* (2014, p. 288). The flow goes both ways. You push outward, but then reality pushes back (see Gaus, 2007, p. 154, citing Tanner, *Why Things Bite Back*). Or it shifts in an entirely unpredicted fashion.

Given this complexity and its fundamental uncertainty, what most people do on a daily basis is follow simple rules that seem to work most of the time. They say things like, "Honesty is the best policy."[12] Because even if folks do not

---

12. Robert Sugden (1989) wrote a compelling little article connecting this insight to game theory, in which he explained the tendency of orders or systems to perpetuate themselves over time in evolutionarily stable strategies (p. 91). Orders evolve, he wrote. Deviation from convention is

know precisely what their actions will bring about, they fear what might happen if they try something entirely new (Hayek, 2014, p. 292). Novelty raises the specter of disaster—a disaster for which they would be culpable. Sadly, however, sometimes playing it safe is precisely what jeopardizes the entire order. As Ron Heifetz (1994) alleged, you can be found culpable for perpetuating a doomed system. So, what's a leader to do?[13]

In the teeth of such complexity, therefore, making a decision can be fraught. This is why leadership *studies* exists, i.e. to assist participants in their deliberations. Except that in many ways leadership scholars are even more acutely aware of this inescapable complexity, which is why we hedge our bets and speak evasively, using qualifiers and dampening expectations. As well we might, out of intellectual honesty. "It depends." Still, is there not something we could be doing that would be useful? Consumers of books and articles about leadership want simple and clear answers. If scholars will not give it to them, plenty of charlatans will (Jemielniak & Przegalinska, 2020, p. 109).

Anyone hoping to write a circumspect and credible book about leadership that avoids this Scylla and Charybdis (both needless obfuscation and gross oversimplification) requires great care and a deft touch.

## Leadership in Context . . . What Context?

It is well established, yet still poorly understood, that the situation within which leadership takes place has an influence on its participants (see e.g. Kellerman, 2014; Vroom & Jago, 2007). Leadership never takes place in a vacuum. Call it the "circumstances" or the "environment" or the "context," leadership occurs within an encompassing reality. As far back as 1947, Cecil Gibb noted that "the first main point to be made . . . in leadership theory is that leadership is relative always to the situation" (p. 269; see p. 283). He explained that "leadership flourishes only in a problem situation" and that "the nature of the

---

increasingly punished, not by anyone in particular but by the nature of the process. Once everybody else has adopted the strategy of driving on the left side of the road, for instance, you probably should as well—but not because driving on the left is any more ethical or efficient than driving on the right. The system simply makes your choice for you, which is convenient. Rules of this type relieve us from having to think each morning in any depth about whether to drive on the left or the right side of the road.

13. Let us suppose you can figure this all out to the nth degree. The decision is entirely yours to do as you like. Herbert Simon (1990) explained that the ideal method for problem-solving in which you uncover all of the facts and learn all of the relevant dynamics and rank order your preferences so that you know explicitly what you want—even if you can do this, which Hayek doubts—it consumes so much time and effort to make one decision that everything else will suffer. You will never get anything else done. As a practical matter, Simon concluded, you must routinely satisfice. This capacity to foreshorten the process by accepting that which is "good enough" contributes, in his opinion, to our evolutionary successes.

leadership role is determined by the goal of the group" (1947, p. 272). Quoting C. Burt (1945), Gibb wrote that leadership occurs at the intersection of a dynamic mind with a dynamic social field (1947, p. 267f). This realization in leadership studies led to what Edwin Hollander called the situational approach, in which researchers examined the various ways that differences in the situation required different leadership functions (1978, pp. 30–38, quoting Alvin Gouldner and W.H. Cowley). Hollander's insight was subsequently adapted in leadership textbooks (e.g. Hughes, Ginnett, & Curphy, 2018).

One of the most obvious examples of the importance of the situation is the prevailing cultural norm regarding leadership itself; that is to say, it matters a great deal what people already recognize and accept as leadership, as opposed to what people in a given culture do not recognize or accept (Gibb, 1947, p. 268). When a personality does not fit the cultural norm, the attempted leadership will likely meet with resistance.[14]

I alluded to this earlier, but we can specify different kinds of contexts or domains, such as the political domain, the economic domain, the religious domain, and so forth—each of which interacts with all of the other domains (see e.g. Gaus, 2013, p. 68). An investigator can nevertheless restrict an investigation fruitfully to any one of them and set aside the rest.[15] Not only that, but we can usually discern multiple *magnitudes* of context as we broaden the scope outward, placing leadership within an organization, which fits within an industry, which fits within an economy, and so forth, into larger and larger circles. In other words, there is not just one macro. We refer to these magnitudes as "levels of analysis" (Rousseau, 1985).

Whatever we call it, context influences leadership and vice versa. Leadership would—in a manner of speaking—seem to be the smaller phenomenon, the micro. Context might seem to be the larger, encompassing phenomenon, the macro. Some studies examine the impact of the micro on the macro, whereas other studies examine the impact of the macro on the micro. That is, we can study the extent to which what happens at one level affects what happens at another level. In this chapter, we are trying to look more objectively at the macro, the whole, the context.

---

14. In preparation for the 2020 presidential elections in the United States, pundits are quarreling over what kind of personality we associate with leadership (e.g. Lewis, 2019; Koczela, 2019).

15. For a sample of books and articles illustrating this point, see e.g. Hartley, J., and Benington, J. (2010). *Leadership for healthcare*. Policy Press; Gunter, H. (2001). *Leaders and leadership in education*. Sage; Adler, N. J. (2006). "The arts & leadership: Now that we can do anything, what will we do?" *Academy of Management Learning & Education*. 5(4): 486–499; Peele, G. (2005). "Leadership and politics: A case for a closer relationship?" *Leadership*. 1(2): 187–204; Gordon, R. A. (1966). *Business leadership in the large corporation*. Univ of California Press; Campbell, D. J., Hannah, S. T., & Matthews, M. D. (2010). "Leadership in military and other dangerous contexts: Introduction to the special topic issue." *Military Psychology*. 22(sup1): S1–S14; Weems Jr, L. H. (2010). *Church leadership: Vision, team, culture, integrity*. Abingdon Press; Chelladurai, P. (2007). "Leadership in sports." *Handbook of sport psychology*. 3: 113–135.

## What Is Spontaneous Order?

Being mindful of the whole within which leadership takes place, as Jaspers recommended, presents us with considerable challenges. To begin, we must see it as more than just a backdrop for the exertions that would ordinarily interest us, like trying to report on a golf match held under windy conditions. Context is also more than an adversary to struggle against. When he wrote about spontaneous order, Hayek offered another way of talking about leadership's context.

The phrase "spontaneous order" has a technical meaning tied to a long, slow process, such as evolution. Many people today use the term "spontaneous" to mean sudden, abrupt, out of nowhere, more like a burst. Alternatively, it can now mean to be casual or "going with the flow." Nevertheless, I am hoping to stick to the original notion of something that emerges over time without any external design. Its emergence will, for the most part, be gradual and imperceptible.

Magoroh Maruyama gave a terrific illustration (quoted in Lawson, 2013, p. 76). Imagine a wagon train steadily crossing the plains of America. By chance, the oxen pulling one cart drown at a river. Their owner decides to settle there, since he cannot continue without oxen. The soil looks fertile, the water is fresh, the climate modest. As other pioneers pass that spot on their way west, some decide to stop there too and settle an adjoining plot of land. Soon, a blacksmith sees this cluster of farmers and decides this might suffice as a market for his services, so he too stops to set up shop. With the passage of time, more settlers turn this river crossing into a village. Nobody planned it. It happened piecemeal. As Johnson would say, it was created by footprints and not fiat (2001, p. 213).

A spontaneous order such as society occurs without anyone consciously designing it. Over time, the practices of individual participants create an overarching order that they come to accept—to the extent they even notice it at all. Johnson has called this "macro development" (2001, p. 99) and sees it in operation in slime molds, flocks of birds, and computer games: only a few rules for micro activity can generate complex structures. We have to remember that the participants did not at the outset intend this order. They did not gather in a meadow to vote on a social contract. No supreme authority stood on a mountaintop issuing decrees. Instead, spontaneous order emerged as the participants coordinated and otherwise adjusted to the actions of one another. Certain accommodations worked. Some didn't. Those that work create expectations for the next time. Soon, you find yourself with a routine that becomes taken for granted, a habit, requiring no further thought. Weave enough of these routines together and you get an order. Hayek insisted that participants do not have to have intended this encompassing order; in fact, they probably did not. They do not even have to be aware of its existence. They function well enough using what Michael Polanyi was to label **tacit knowledge** (see Hunt, 2007, p. 55). Nevertheless, it influences both their choices and the outcomes of their actions. And although it shifts and recalibrates with considerable resilience, it is also precarious. As with any order, it can collapse or shift into something different—again, whether the participants intended for this to happen or were even aware that it might.

One could think it is a paradox that one and the same order can be both resilient and precarious. With regard to **collapse**, which is the more dramatic event horizon, the order can simply end.[16] One of the results of its resilience is a gradual tendency for order to perpetuate itself, growing harder, less flexible, becoming increasingly rigid, if not brittle, a victim of its success. Since nobody designed it and nobody completely understands how it works, nobody can presume to preserve it against the thousand natural shocks that flesh is heir to. To some extent, it will resist pressures to change by accommodating them, for that is how it came into being, yet beyond a certain point it can lose suppleness, ignoring the many signals that something else is going on. Eventually, under sufficient stress, it quits working. One thinks for example of the Russian Revolution or the fall of the Roman Empire. I would contend that this is largely what occurred at the Protestant Reformation, no matter what Luther might have done. Much of the sort occurred in Iraq after the coalition defeated Saddam Hussein and the Ba'athist regime (see Sky, 2015; Muller, 2007, p. 209 notes 35, 36). Nobody really grasped just how extensively that prevailing order had permeated society, such that when it ended, people were scrambling to figure out what to put in its place (see e.g. Duncan & Coyne, 2015; Coyne, 2008).

With regard to **shifting** into something different, which is the more gradual or evolutionary process, its shape can morph into new patterns that result in a completely different kind of order while retaining a sense of identity. In a similar fashion, little girls grow up to be accomplished women without becoming entirely different people. The process by which this happens is gradual, albeit punctuated by significant events. An historical example might be the transition from one French republic into another. There is, on the other side of the evolutionary transition, still an order, and much of it persists from before, but you could not objectively say that it is still the same model or paradigm that it once was.[17] Critics of the New Deal from American history (Hayek among them) claim to detect a transmogrification from a more laissez-faire market economy before Franklin Roosevelt took office in 1933 to a more centralized, quasi-socialist economy since. In a similar manner, scholars have been trying

16. On the collapse of complex social systems, see e.g. Diamond (2011), Tainter (1990).
17. Management scholars sometimes refer to mission creep, but that is something different, because the spontaneous order that Hayek was trying to describe has by definition no mission. Alternatively, I suppose it could adopt a mission, as French society did under Napoleon, at which point it becomes a different kind of order.

to understand what has changed in Russia since the close of the Soviet Union. Spontaneous order is changing all the time.

Dariusz Jemielniak and Aleksandra Przegalinska have written a compelling book titled simply *Collaborative Society* (2020), in which they examine spontaneous order that has been technologically mediated, whether for profit (Uber), social change (Occupy Wall Street), amusement (Imgur), or mutual edification (Wikipedia). These phenomena tend to be open, emergent, cooperative, and highly suspicious of institutions and authority (i.e. **heterarchical**, as opposed to hierarchical or anarchical), yet nearly obsessed with process.

At this point, I would like to give a concrete illustration of some of the principles in spontaneous orders. The analogy is imperfect, yet when thinking about the board game chess, there are many rules that enable play but do not favor one player over the other. After centuries of evolution, they are unbiased, outcome-neutral, and largely negative (i.e. what cannot be done). Within those parameters of what constitutes fair play, each player has many options. There are literally twenty different first moves. The choice is yours. Thereafter, you will be constrained by prior decisions you have made and by what the other player chose to do, but there is still a bewildering variety of choices ahead of you.[18] You play until one of you cannot play without losing the king. As you become more adept, you reject certain moves as unwise. That is, you learn to ignore some of the choices. Even within the remaining choices, you and your opponent might create patterns that have been seen before and now have names, such as the Sicilian Defense. Nevertheless, sometimes the best play will have been unforeseen by the other person. In any case, the rules of the game are rarely questioned. To be fair, we have seen the introduction of the chess clock to hurry things along and the requirement of putting away your mobile devices during play. Unlike a spontaneous order that collapsed or shifted, the game of chess has persisted for quite some time. Although it might appear to be a product of design, its origins are rooted in cultural variation and experimentation going back 1,500 years.

If the whole we are expected to investigate in leadership studies is a spontaneous, hopelessly complex order beyond our powers to master, then what exactly is there to study? Are we entirely bereft? As I said before, Hayek believed that we can discern broad patterns and tendencies of the order to form in certain ways. Such things have been done before.

18. According to the online reference Wikipedia, "The number of legal positions in chess is estimated to be about $10^{43}$, and is provably less than $10^{47}$, with a game-tree complexity of approximately $10^{123}$." $10^{43}$ is 10,000,000,000,000,000,000,000,000,000,000,000,000,000,000 different possibilities. Talk about a complex phenomenon! Regarding chess and its complexity as a system, see Cabrera and Cabrera (2015, p. 44).

## The Relationship Between Social Action and Spontaneous Order

According to Hayek, millions of daily social actions sustain a comprehending social order and adjust as circumstances change—from donating baked goods to buying a car. These actions can be entirely selfish; it does not matter (Levine, 2018, p. 145). Leadership at the level of social action is understandable, even if the outcomes are inherently unpredictable. People will try to influence one another to do all sorts of things. When they gather into organizations, such as clubs and businesses, people will carry out organizational leadership. Here at the private level is considerable room for initiative, entrepreneurship, innovation, and risk taking (see Otteson, 2007, p. 30). Here too is the arena for leading people into competition against others (Otteson, 2007, p. 31). An underappreciated feature of social action within a spontaneous order is that others can refuse to follow.

Hayek also allows for the exercise of leadership within the structures that oversee the social order. Government is itself an organization that requires a degree of leadership in order to function. Somebody has to see that the roads are plowed of snow. Again, such leadership is unremarkable. It does not differ in any qualitative sense from leadership in other organizations, except that private organizations have private purposes whereas government serves a public purpose, such as managing the infrastructure and judging the occasional dispute.[19]

Leadership in social action for private purposes has the effect of shaping the public order, but that is not its purpose. It exists within and on behalf of what might be termed enterprising associations. A business tries to make a profit. A therapy circle tries to provide care to its members. Linus Torvalds created, develops, and defends Linux. Luther translated the Bible for the spiritual edification of his parish. Let us call this SA (social action) for the sake of SA. Ideally (for Hayek), leadership in government exists within and on behalf of spontaneous order, to keep things running smoothly, with a sufficient degree of fairness. This would be SO (spontaneous order) for the sake of SO. We will encounter an example of this with regard to the Common Law—that is, an ordering that keeps the civic order.

I hasten to admit that these are not the only possibilities. Frequently, social action has as its purpose the control or alteration of the prevailing order. We see this, for example, in the practice of electoral politics, when enterprising associations we call political parties campaign to put their people into office. We also see this when subversive groups rise up to protest and possibly overthrow a government. Jemielniak and Przegalinska (2020) include a chapter on social hacktivism.[20] Not long after his initial brush with authorities, Luther turned

---

19. I should mention that, even though the idea is controversial, privatization could be said to assume responsibility for some of these tasks.
20. Jemielniak and Przegalinska also identify ways in which social action for the sake of spontaneous order takes a darker turn, as for example lynchings and cyberbullying. They specifically mention

his energies against the empire and its sponsor, the Roman Catholic Church. This is SA for SO. It is true as well that those who represent the prevailing order often have as their purpose the control or alteration of social action. A lofty version of this activity can be found in George Will's *Statecraft as Soulcraft* (1984), but then a venal version appears in Nathaniel Hawthorne's novel *The Scarlet Letter* (1879) in which civil authorities give puritanism a bad name. During the Covid-19 pandemic, civil authorities issued orders for people to quarantine or shelter-in-place. Speaking simplistically, this is SO for SA. Perhaps not surprisingly, it is this last possibility that worried Hayek most.[21]

Despite the fact that order constitutes a tradition with "presumptive wisdom" (Boyd & Morrison, 2007, p. 90), this does not mean that by now it serves as a fixed and perfect guide to daily behavior. The ideal for Hayek is not to serve the past blindly. Frequently, people are ignorant of this presumptive wisdom, so they will continue to do things out of ignorance that disrupt the social flow. In addition, people will still look for excuses to gain an advantage, knowing the tradition. Moreover, sometimes, this presumptive wisdom has no clear answer to a puzzling predicament. There will always be gaps and conflicts. Accordingly, society must possess some mechanism to enforce and adapt this tradition. Widespread dynamism depends on an underlying legal continuity (Boyd & Morrison, 2007, p. 100; Muller, 2007, p. 199). The next chapter will speak to that. What Hayek dreaded most, however, was the wholesale rejection of that venerable and elaborate tradition for the sake of some bright idea. He hoped to instill in those with power a respect for that tradition, even if they will be called upon periodically to revise it.

Murray Rothbard—a controversialist who wanted to popularize the ideas of economists such as Hayek and more significantly Ludwig von Mises—noted that spontaneous order is not guaranteed. In fact, it faces many threats. How then to defend spontaneous order from such threats? In other words, what leadership at the level of social action helps to ensure that the spontaneous order we all enjoy is limited and not abused? For it was Rothbard's fear that those who command the levers of government will ruin the spontaneous order, out of willfulness or ignorance, by exercising an inappropriate leadership, SO for SA. In an article published in 1990, he listed a number of remedies, offering historical anecdotes to illustrate:

1.  If a leader tries to exert this kind of inappropriate leadership, you could, for example, withdraw and otherwise evade control, leaving the jurisdiction

---

internet vigilantes and the "dog poop girl" who was shamed in Korea for neglecting to pick up after her pet on a public train (2020, p. 182).

21. David Hume, one of the intellectual sources whom Hayek acknowledges, praised Henry VIII's sweeping reforms of the church in the sixteenth century, especially his suppression of monasteries, although Hume admits that these extraordinary exertions (SO for SA) had beneficial, unintended side effects (quoted in Yenor, 2007, p. 114). They were the kind of leadership that Hayek tended to resist.

or taking your business underground. This is at best a temporary solution. Luther was spirited away into hiding.[22]

2.  You could organize acts of defiance, refusing to capitulate, in which case you will plainly suffer. This tactic might work, as it did in India under the inspiration of Gandhi, but not always and not without tremendous cost. Luther eventually did emerge to champion the cause in Saxony, saying publicly "Here I stand, I can do no other."[23]

3.  You could try to persuade the powerful about the merits of spontaneous order, hoping they will restrain themselves and defer to spontaneous forces. When he posted the Ninety-Five Theses, Luther was hoping to correct the institution in the secluded halls of academe. Not only is this tactic unlikely to succeed, since you are asking the powerful to limit their influence, but even if it works for a while, you will have to do it all over again when you are faced with somebody new in a position of power. Power is a recurring temptation. Besides, if the masses do not understand what the government is doing by limiting itself, for their own good, they might clamor for the powerful to intervene on their behalf in ways that thwart the good. That pressure can become intense.

4.  Alternately, you could try to persuade the masses, either by means of agitation and coercion (which makes you no better than the threats that worry you) or by means of education. It is probably fair to say that by implication, Rothbard endorses this fourth option.[24] Luther himself finally embraced this last alternative.

I hesitate to describe the relationship between social action and spontaneous order as micro and macro, as though they are magnitudes within a single structure, such that social actions fit underneath the prevailing order, like subordinates on an organizational chart. Social actions are not like the parts of a pocket watch designed to work together in order to keep time. That model misperceives the relationship in significant ways. We do not all belong to a single organization run by the government. If we did, that would be the definition of a totalitarian order. Instead, we belong to all sorts of different organizations with various missions. It may be true that to serve our various (and sometimes contrary) purposes, we participate in another type of organization that preserves the boundaries we require in order to fulfill our private purposes. Somebody has to print the money. Somebody has to keep

---

22. A contemporary example is cryptocurrency, which is expressly designed to avoid government oversight.

23. A contemporary example are the protests of government restrictions during the Covid-19 pandemic.

24. Rothbard fails to mention the remedy provided by James Madison and his colleagues to create a government in which ambition and self-interest is made to serve the public good, constrained by an elaborate system of meaningful checks and balances (Munger, 2007, p. 183f).

the peace. Somebody has to provide for the common defense. Nevertheless, the spontaneous order described by Hayek is not a single, monolithic, and unified hierarchy. It exists largely to provide vast pockets of liberty within which the citizens can operate on their own behalf, with discretion and not direction. This qualifier is important for understanding what Hayek was trying to do. He was no anarchist, opposed to order. He was trying to circumscribe a necessary order for the sake of preserving the maximum degree of individual liberty. Today, David French makes the same point in another context. He writes, "The government is responsible for securing . . . liberty; the people are responsible for advancing . . . virtue" (2019, p. 13). That is well said. We will come back to this image of the spontaneous order or **catallaxy**, especially in the next chapter on the Common Law.[25]

Perhaps Hayek should get the final word:

> The recognition of the insuperable limits to his knowledge ought indeed to teach the student of society a lesson in humility which should guard him against becoming an accomplice in men's fatal striving to control society—a striving which makes him not only a tyrant over his fellows, but which may well make him the destroyer of a civilization which no brain has designed but which has grown from the free efforts of millions of individuals.
>
> *(Nobel Memorial Lecture, 1974)*

## Preparing for the Second Extended Example

The following chapter extends the topic of spontaneous order as it pertains to an institution quite familiar to Hayek: the Common Law. Not only is the Common Law a product and example of spontaneous order, it is also an integral part of the administrative structure that preserves the spontaneous order for the rest of society. In the course of describing the Common Law, we will also have reason to consider where there is room within the institution for the practice of leadership. In many ways, the Common Law exemplifies what Hayek was writing about.

---

25. Polanyi (1951) also cited the Common Law as an example of spontaneous order (e.g. p. 198ff). Perhaps because he was a scientist, he expended more effort showing that science is a spontaneous order. He also mentioned doing jigsaw puzzles (p. 43f). de Saussure (1959) offered language itself as being paradigmatic of spontaneous order (ch. 2).

# 4

# THE EMERGENT ORDER
# OF THE COMMON LAW[1]

*Leges sine moribus vanae.*

—Horace (Book 3, Ode 24)

## Introduction to the Chapter

At the county fair, Alfred conveys a mule to Blake in exchange for three shillings and a goose. Blake takes possession of the mule, leading it back to his shire, where he turns it loose in the paddock. The mule trots away in a straight line and slams head first into the far rail. Staggered, it shakes its head and then trots in another direction, but again it doesn't stop short of the rail. It collides at full force and appears stunned by the impact. Blake has seen enough. He hies back in the twilight to the fair in order to find Alfred, whom he finds with the goose under his arm.

> "What's the idea of selling me a blind mule?" he begins.
> "Oh, he ain't blind," replies Alfred calmly.
> "Then why does he run headlong into my fences?" asks Blake, furious.
> "That mule . . . he just don't give a damn."

For thousands of years across the planet, people have been engaged in all sorts of activities such as commerce. They find themselves embroiled in controversies about what is remediable. Who owns the apples on the branch that overhangs the border fence? What if my dog gets into your chicken coop? How do you and I establish ownership of a creek bed that gradually shifts as a result of

1. The author acknowledges the critical contributions of Michelle Kundmueller.

seasonal floods? Can I exact some kind of satisfaction if you insult my honor? Does the landlord inherit a stranger's belongings? The ways that people interact are nearly endless. The ways that these interactions can go wrong are also vexingly endless. Jerome Hall once put it this way: "There are thousands of rules of law, millions of human beings, and an infinite number of facts and interpersonal relationships" (1949, p. 37). There must be some method for resolving these conflicts and preserving the civic order. That method is likelier to persist if it hews to some shared sense of fairness, without which people resort to other means of redress.

Something called the Common Law is an institution dating back over a thousand years and currently in use by roughly a third of all people on the planet (see JuriGlobe).[2] It has been an integral part in turn of feudalism, absolute monarchy, colonial administration, and industrial democracy. It is also one of the greatest of all cultural achievements. "So venerable," wrote Sir Frederick Pollock in 1890, "so majestic, is this living temple of justice, this immemorial and yet freshly growing fabric of the Common Law" (p. 111). Nobody created it. Nobody controls it. It is an incremental, self-correcting system that exemplifies what it means to speak of an asymptotic order that emerges according to a discernible, complex form we call justice. As humanity develops, the Common Law carries forward the accumulated wisdom of the past while adapting to changing circumstances, making it an extraordinarily resilient institution.

It is my contention that the Common Law exemplifies spontaneous order. It is paradigmatic (Agamben, 2009, p. 17).

In the popular imagination, law emerges by edict or legislation and appears in a law book somewhere. Actually, that image of the law represents barely the tip of the iceberg. The entire register of enactments for any regime—its regulations, crimes, codes, and ordinances—is grounded in a far more elaborate and elusive sense of the law that nobody pronounced and that does not appear in any book. It is too vast to be encapsulated by a library, yet it governs our daily lives. Likewise, in the popular imagination, many believe that laws are the product of deliberation and political will. But that type of law is dependent on the broad ocean of law known as the Common Law. The term "common" has several uses. It means a law common to all human beings, or at least common to everybody in a particular jurisdiction, common even unto the king, originating out of the experience of common people about ordinary things.

As a place to begin, *Black's Law Dictionary* (5th ed., 1979) defines the common law as "the body of principles and rules of action, relating to the government and security of persons and property, which derive their authority solely from usages and customs of immemorial antiquity." The Common Law is to be distinguished from other types, such as statutory, criminal, equity, and canon

---

2. Friedrich Hayek (1973/2012) went so far as to allege that it is coeval with society itself (p. 72). He wrote that "law existed for ages before it occurred to man that he could make or alter it" (p. 73).

law. Judgments grounded in usages and customs since time immemorial make for an elaborate cultural artifact that on the one hand seems so vast and intricate that it requires specialized training to master. On the other hand, it is actually grounded in ordinary common sense, requiring no specialized knowledge whatsoever. It is both.

## How Does the Common Law Work?

The standard definition does not capture what makes the Common Law important to consider as a cultural institution. First, it originates in custom—custom so old that nobody remembers a time when it was not the custom. Or as Sir William Blackstone (1765–1769) famously put it:

> Whence it is that in our law the goodness of a custom depends upon its having been used time out of mind; or, in the solemnity of our legal phrase, time whereof the memory of man runneth not to the contrary. This it is that gives it its weight and authority: and of this nature are the maxims and customs which compose the common law. . . .

Being so well established, such a custom can be said to enjoy the assent of the people as a whole, and not only of the litigants. The assent goes all the way back as an intergenerational consensus.[3] That is to say, it fits the judgment of ordinary people today, including those who are not parties to the specific dispute, but also accords with the judgment of our forbearers, no matter when or where they flourished. Every fishmonger, vassal, and stonemason. This sense of universal and longstanding custom is a more enduring basis than any vote. It is more widespread than any decree. Courts look back, not out of deference to anybody in particular, but instead to tradition. Thus, the Common Law is not based on logic, decree, or even God's will. "The common law is not a brooding omnipresence in the sky," wrote the Supreme Court Justice Oliver Wendell Holmes (in dissent) in 1917 (*Southern Pacific Co. v. Jensen*). Instead, the basis of the law is experience. It enjoys the weight of widespread and enduring practice.[4]

3. A medieval jurist named Henry de Bracton explained that much of the content of the Common Law comes from the Roman Empire, although a lot derives from the Anglo-Saxon and Germanic tribes (see Hogue, 1966, p. 23; Plucknett, 1956/2010, pp. 294–300). By the twenty-first century, of course, the Common Law has integrated a variety of cultures and is no longer "euro-centric"—despite the fact that most examples in this chapter will have been drawn from distinctly Western sources, inasmuch as the institution itself took form in Great Britain.

4. Rulings in one Common Law jurisdiction are understood to reflect universal precepts, so that a court in Auckland should arrive at an equivalent outcome to one in Tallahassee. The ruling pertains only to the parties in that particular dispute, but it should resemble the law elsewhere. Thus, judges may consult far-flung jurisdictions when formulating decisions.

According to Arthur Hogue (1966, p. 197), Blackstone was to identify seven tests of custom before it could be validated as law. That custom must be:

- ancient,[5]
- continuous,
- peaceable,
- reasonable,
- certain (or ascertainable),
- compulsory, and
- consistent with the overarching web of other prevailing customs.[6]

Originally, these customs were local and varied, a patchwork of isolated villages. One adhered to the practices that obtained where the courts reside. This array of different, even contradictory, customs demonstrated respect for the importance of community and the way people do business. One might say that it carries some legal weight to argue that "that's not how we do things around here." Friedrich Hayek contended that this is because it is manifestly fair to base judgments on the reasonable expectations of the litigants (1973/2012, p. 82), and the reasonable expectations of litigants would be based on that which is customary where they live and work. Besides, in the highly decentralized Middle Ages, there was not yet a central civic authority to insist on uniformity (Plucknett, 1956/2010, p. 314).

Does this fact of a variety of local customs contradict the idea of a universal law, valid for every jurisdiction and every age? On the contrary, it speaks to the historical process by which the customs of so many localities evolved, showing us the process by which the Common Law matured. As far back as the Roman Empire, the goal was to accommodate local rules while providing a sufficiently abstract system to permit some commonality throughout the empire (Kaczmarczyk, 2018, p. 57, citing Schiavone, 2012). In some instances, the process was accelerated by political authorities hoping for some consistency throughout the realm, but in many instances the people themselves adapted their customs to fit their neighbors. This might have been in part to allow for integration between villages—so that a peddler could straddle them both, for example, for purposes of trade—but it also might have been in part to benefit from learning from each other what works and what doesn't work. As transportation and communication networks improved, making these villages less isolated from

---

5. Cf. Plucknett (1956/2010, p. 307f).
6. Hayek (1973/2012) postulated that these customs were not first verbalized, but instead evolved out of practice. "The experience gained by the experimentation of generations embodies more knowledge than was possessed by anyone" (p. 119). These customs persisted only because they happen to work, even if nobody is aware of them (e.g. pp. 19, 70, 80). Strangely, to articulate them is to subject them to critique and undermine their effectiveness (p. 60).

one another, people could share their experiences across jurisdictions. Localities gradually discover by means of experience which customs might need to be revised, even from the experience of their neighbors, so that over a long period of time people everywhere tend to align many of their customs anyway, without any external authority having to impose uniformity. As Hayek noted, "in the course of time all the separate individual sets of values become slowly adapted to each other" (2014, p. 353). The Common Law reflects this tendency and certainly to some extent contributed to it.[7]

Because it is accepted practice—whatever this custom might be—and has been for a long time, disputes are supposedly few. The people can be trusted to be reasonable. When disputes do arise, many are resolved without recourse to the legal system. Maybe the parties walk away or come to reconcile. Or they take it into the back alley for a fistfight. Or they negotiate a cash settlement that leaves each of them whole. These remedies, known as "self-help," tend to reinforce the existing system. They are an acknowledgement that the people can work things out to each other's satisfaction. The Common Law vests ordinary people with considerable discretion to manage their daily affairs.[8] At the same time, the Common Law existed precisely in order to limit certain modes of self-help, such as vengeance and feud—modes that disturbed the king's peace (Hogue, 1966, 147).

When the courts must get involved, however, judges consult precedent—again, in deference to longstanding practice. In this way, down through the years the decisions accumulate. Not only do they accumulate, increasing in volume, but they converge or solidify around certain familiar precepts. After all, it is a staid principle of basic fairness that similar cases should reach similar outcomes (*a similibus ad similia*). An individual judge might see things differently now and then, but gradually the principles should cohere.

Eventually, some scholar can assemble all of these findings into a single volume and constellate what has heretofore been decided. A well-respected example was Samuel Williston's 1920 hornbook *The Law of Contracts*.[9] We might think of these texts as crystallizations of long-standing jurisprudence. Since

---

7. Still, it is important to insist that custom prevails. Local custom still governs. Common Law does not exist to extinguish variation and run roughshod over local practices. Strange as it may sound, the Common Law respects how things are done in the jurisdiction where the case arises, but it has the tendency to bring these customs into alignment, albeit at an abstract level. For example, the remedy for a breach of contract might be the same in different parts of the world, yet where one defendant pays restitution in dollars another pays in pounds. Adherents of the Common Law will reject the excesses of cultural relativism, while at the same time being sensitive to cultural differences.

8. We should also notice that the Common Law relies on a process in which the participants sit down and deliberate and do not resort to some other method, such as trial by combat or ordeal (Hogue, 1966, p. 19). At one time, in specific jurisdictions, these were considered viable alternatives.

9. One of the earliest compilations under the authority of Justinian, the so-called *Corpus Juris Civilis*, dates from the sixth century (Hogue, 1966, p. 22). Unlike other continental legal systems, however, the United Kingdom did not simply import Roman law (Hogue, 1966, pp. 186, 242). I mention

1878, the American Bar Association has repeatedly supported these projects, in part to assist the legal profession in its work and in part to expose the extent to which the law remains inconsistent or unclear (Hogue, 1966, p. 251).

On occasion, the legal system will overrule itself and conclude that it had been mistaken, but doing so is extremely rare. In fact, decisions are expected to adhere to a doctrine known as *stare decisis*, which means that in the absence of compelling reasons otherwise, a prior decision should govern subsequent cases on the same issue.[10] So not only does the Common Law seek to reinforce existing customs out there in the world, it embodies the dignity of custom. It is itself customary.[11]

This process of cohering, converging, solidifying into accepted doctrine—a tendency to come together, as it were—is offset by a remarkable capacity to diversify and adapt to changing circumstances (see Hogue, 1966, pp. 8–12). What the law knows to be some precept (let us call it precept A) must undergo differentiation as nuances become hard to ignore, so that over time you find yourself with $A_1$ and $A_2$. This process of differentiation from case to case acknowledges subtlety and shades of meaning, a process which continues until you find yourself hundreds of years later with $A_1, A_2, A_3 \ldots A_n$. For instance, wrongfully taking property that does not belong to you can now be theft, conversion, robbery, burglary, shoplifting, fraud, embezzlement, larceny, looting, and piracy. This process of increasing complexification is one way that the Common Law grows. In short, it grows both inward (as it congeals) and outward (as it proliferates). It grows like cauliflower.[12]

---

it to illustrate the practice of periodically composing digests of the law. Another example of significance to the Common Law specifically, and to the development of American law, are *The Commentaries on the Laws of England* of Sir William Blackstone, published between 1765 and 1769 (see Stacey, 2003). His work drew from the prior exertions of Henry de Bracton (1569) and Edward Coke (2003).

10. *Stare decisis* is not rigid. As Benjamin Cardozo once explained, "Back of precedents are the basic juridical conceptions which are the postulates of judicial reasoning, and farther back are the habits of life, the institutions of society, in which these conceptions had their origin" (1921, p. 19; see also Hayek, 1973/2012, p. 82, quoting Lord Mansfield; Plucknett, 1956/2010, p. 347). The precedent may have been wrongly decided. Customs might have changed. A judge is not expected to operate in blind obedience to prior rulings. Before he was elected president, Abraham Lincoln (1953–1955) had criticized an infamous decision by the Supreme Court of the United States (*Dred Scott*) by saying that a bare ruling that defies history, logic, and the seamless web of the law is not dispositive ("Speech at Springfield, Illinois," June 26, 1857).

    Nevertheless, once a judge confronts a precedent, the burden is upon him or her to explain any departures from it. Of course, in a few instances, there is no precedent at all, so *stare decisis* would be of no help then. On the principle of precedence generally, see Plucknett (1956/2010, pp. 342–350).

11. The Common Law not only derives from social custom and is itself customary, it also tends to reinforce social custom and become a significant contribution to the way people conduct their business hereafter. That is to say, it participates in defining what is customary.

12. Hogue (1966) allowed as how during the Middle Ages the Common Law also grew by absorbing other categories of law, such as feudal custom and the law merchant (p. 5). In this way, huge chunks of precedent were added at one go.

As things in the world change, such as new technologies, the law seeks to overlay familiar doctrine, but the shrewd advocate will argue that the old way will not work in this instance. Existing rules no longer apply. Is a telephone an invasion of privacy? Courts invite advocates to persuade them by using analogy: Is this novelty more like a familiar case X or like a familiar case Y? Which precedent should govern? For instance, the driver of an automobile might choose to use the car as a weapon and not simply as a mode of conveyance. Does that difference tell us which precedent applies here? Is there any kind of significant difference between a weapon and a dangerous instrumentality? How about failing to secure a massive Angus bull that wanders onto a dark road at night? Is that also a dangerous instrumentality? Are these cases similar? How so? The advocates are expected to state their case.

Arthur Hogue (1966)—on whom I have come to rely extensively in this chapter—offers a vivid example of how the Common Law was to work (p. 16). In a case dating back to 1255, a certain stranger to Northumberland by the unlikely name of Gilbert of Niddesdale accosted a hermit, beat him up, and stole a penny. Gilbert was subsequently detained by the poor man's neighbors, so the hermit asked them for his penny back. The neighbors informed him that first he had to assert his right to the property by punishing the thief himself. The local custom at the time was to behead a thief, which the hermit reluctantly did. Apparently, his neighbors subsequently let him take back the penny.

Now the Common Law has evolved since 1255; a beheading would not be necessary today. But such was apparently the custom at the time, in that locality. The rationale for the custom—that is to say, the underlying principle—is quite understandable. If you won't assert your right to property and take steps to protect it, then why should your neighbors do this for you? You have some responsibility to care for what is yours. This is a principle that we can accept today. In light of changing circumstances (such as a widespread police system) and changing mores, nobody would be obliged to uphold the precise manner of doing this as once prevailed in "merry olde England." The principle on which a decision is made gets refined through the years, yet the basis for it was in fact the prevailing custom. The court system may abstract from the concrete details in order to find the more generally applicable law. As customs and circumstances thereafter change, so too will the law. Protect your own property, yes. Behead a thief yourself over a penny, no.

## Who Is the Leader Under the Common Law?

The so-called body of the law comes together, crystallizes, while also differentiating and shifting or evolving to meet the situation. Occasionally, it prunes itself. That is to say that the Common Law is a dynamic cultural institution at the macro level. Who in the process deserves to be called a leader is unclear. Could it be the valiant advocate, i.e. the barrister celebrated in story and song, with sword in one hand and shield in the other, as for example in the dramas *Inherit the Wind* or *To Kill a Mockingbird*? And if so, the advocate for which side? Or, is the leader a persuasive juror, as in *Twelve Angry Men*? But if a juror, why not the jury foreman?[13] Let us not overlook the sheriff, the bailiff, the plaintiff, the defendant, a courageous witness (not to mention the medieval offices of steward, beadle, and reeve). . . . Which of these social actors is the leader? The exercise of identifying a leader becomes tedious (if not impossible) when so many people are involved in such a vast enterprise.[14]

So perhaps a better question is this: which steps in the legal process constitute leadership? That is thinking at the micro level, which is often the bailiwick of leadership scholars. But again, the process as a whole offers plenty of opportunities for somebody to lead.[15] Everybody is expected to do their job, even if the outcome turns out to be the same as so many cases before this one. To that extent, maybe the entire legal apparatus grinds through leadership at a macro level, leaving individual exertions to contribute this and that to the overall system. Isolating one episode and calling that leadership is artificial. Besides, we find ourselves with a line drawing problem: Is it leadership to argue a case? To interrogate a witness? To file a pleading? So many activities constitute the whole that maybe those of us in leadership studies might take a giant step back from narrowing our investigations into discrete parts. The legal system is not simply the context within which leadership takes place; the Common Law is itself leadership. That is a different way of talking. Consistent with the theme of this book, therefore, we can say that we find leadership here at the macro level, without the necessity of Great Men.

The Common Law exhibits distributed leadership over time to form a stable, yet adaptable institution for resolving conflict based on rulings in individual cases that depend on established principles that evolved over a millennium. The law is "common" because it applies to all people—including rulers—and because it derives from the accumulated wisdom of all people, high or low.[16] In contradistinction to traditions that rely on sacred texts, wise lawgivers, or the momentary will of the people, the Common Law entrusts ordinary people over

---

13. See e.g. Curtin (2004), Bevan, Albert, Loiseaux, and Mayfield (1958).
14. Some individuals down through the ages such as kings Henry II (1133–1189) and John (1166–1216) did have a disproportionate impact on the Common Law, although they were known for far different things. Henry II energetically and competently administered his estates, solidifying the Common Law throughout the realm. His son John was so inept that his barons were emboldened to press upon him the first *Magna Carta* in 1215 (see John, 1215/1995). Each had an impact on how the law evolved (Hogue, 1966, ch. 2). Was one of them a leader and the other not?
15. The bestselling author John Grisham has at one time or another found myriad ways to make heroes (and villains) out of just about everybody engaged in the legal process.
16. Much of the history of the Common Law is the struggle by the kings of Great Britain to impose a uniform judiciary over the entire realm, which solidifies its usage, while at the same time being pressured by barons, financiers, and the church to submit the royal office to the same rule of law.

time, in the aggregate, to manage their lives. To put this into the vernacular, under the Common Law together we lead ourselves (see Voegelin, 1991, p. 57).

Hayek (1973/2012) developed the idea that there is a useful distinction to be made between commands issued for the sake of some purpose and rules within which participants are free to pursue their own private purposes (p. 125). A basketball coach designs a play that the participants for his team are expected to execute, but a referee makes no such demand. The referee wants to see that the play (whatever it is) is performed according to general rules of the game, such as no traveling, no double-dribble, no fouls, no going out of bounds with the ball, no more than five players on the court for one team, etc. We do not want referees to favor one team over the other, let alone choosing in advance which team should win. Their rules must be "negative, end-independent, and abstract" (Petsoulas, 2001, p. 30).

Government is instituted in part to serve as that impartial referee to guarantee the operation of a system of justice, no matter who in fact wins or loses (Hayek, 1973/2012, p. 141). We might think of it as a category error (and a very popular one at that) to believe that government exists to determine outcomes and otherwise subordinate individual lives and property to some shared or common purpose. We as individual human beings do not exist to help the government accomplish some overarching aim, regardless of how lofty it is, except to the extent that its aim is to empower people to seek their own aims. A day of voting therefore is not some referendum on the direction voters want the nation to go. Nations do not "go" anywhere, unless they are by definition totalitarian.

Even a constitution, regarded by many to be "supreme," governs the government itself and not the society that promulgates it (Hayek, 1973/2012, p. 134). If anything, a constitution will declare to that government, "This far and no farther." It is the people in their private capacity who determine what they are to do with their time and talent and treasure, so long as they do so within the bounds of what Hayek called "universal rules of just conduct" (see e.g. p. 113).

Imagine a public beach of uniform quality one mile wide and a hundred yards deep. It may be perfectly legal for families to locate their chairs and umbrellas in a single line perpendicular to the shore, one directly in front of the other, at regular intervals, but that will never happen. Beachgoers spread out for all sorts of reasons and collectively form an array without any direction from some person in authority. Instead, they come and go as they please, coordinating loosely in an ad hoc fashion so that some may frolic, some may sleep, and some may gawk. Tensions here and there may flare up, but we generally expect everyone to sort themselves out, so that they can all enjoy their day at the beach. Nobody rushes out with a tape measure to ensure that their umbrellas are symmetrically aligned.

In another meaningful sense, therefore, the Common Law has had the effect of limiting the scope of leadership, inasmuch as ordinary understandings of leadership describe it as interpersonal influence based largely on expressions of the leader's will, whereas the law is something explicitly impersonal. It merely sets boundaries within which individuals exercise their freedom.

## Professionals, Experts, and Ordinary Folks

Saying that the Common Law entrusts ordinary people is likely to provoke puzzlement from any lay person who has had dealings recently with a court of law. Most ordinary folks who have had to get involved in a legal proceeding today sense that the system belongs to experts—that is, to professionals such as lawyers and judges. These experts are the only ones who seem to understand what is going on and how it all works. (And maybe they should, given how many years they devoted to its study!) Saying of the Common Law that it "exemplifies distributed leadership" can strike a lay person as naïve.

In response, I would argue, first, that these professionals are far more constrained than it might appear (see e.g. Cardozo, 1921, p. 136f). They do not enjoy much discretion in what happens (not if they want to keep their license). They are officers of the court carrying out pre-prescribed roles, not unlike the clerk, the bailiff, and the janitor who keeps the courtroom tidy. Yes, just because there are many roles does not mean there are not differences in responsibility, authority, and expertise. Distributed leadership does not have to mean that everybody is similarly situated and of equal rank. Nevertheless, the attorneys are not given much latitude to shape the future.

My second response to the suspicion that only the experts get to lead goes like this. Unlike statutory law codified by a legislature, the Common Law is unwritten, except in the opinions of judges in concrete instances. In those decisions, they seek to explain how established precepts from previous cases govern the community's effort to resolve a particular conflict.[17] By now, of course, after a thousand years of court cases from around the world, there is a vast collection of their rulings. Somebody has to serve as the curator of all that wisdom. Nevertheless, being the curator of that storehouse of rulings does not necessarily make them the leader.

Does that mean the judge in a given case is the leader? Only in a manner of speaking, inasmuch as Common Law comes from the good sense we expect of any reasonable person, no matter what the jurisdiction. The term "common" derives in part from a sensibility that all reasonable people share, whether its source is divine or natural law. The judge therefore is not to be regarded as a font of wisdom with special powers to know the right thing to do. A judge cannot impose a private opinion, no matter how learned. Ideally, the Common

---

17. It is a misnomer to refer to the Common Law as "judge-made." Judges do not make it. If they try, they will be reversed on appeal. The purpose is instead to interpose between litigants something decidedly *im*personal (Ortega, 1940/1946, p. 29).

Law keeps the law from becoming too esoteric, as though it were the exclusive domain of highly specialized experts. Instead, the judge can be said to embody the accumulated sense of justice as it would be enacted in ordinary life by reasonable people. The Common Law springs from the wisdom we share as human beings. The judge is there in large part to articulate what we all know to be fair.[18] As Hayek put it, one *discovers* and does not *invent* the law (1973/2012, p. 78).[19] A judge certainly may not "pronounce any rule he likes" (p. 100).

Too many lay people know of instances where that did not happen. Indeed, the system is not perfect (see e.g. Voegelin, 1991, p. 60f). It doesn't help that theater and the media find high drama in such miscarriages; except that in one sense these failures are exceptions that prove the rule. Where else do you obtain the judgment to critique an outcome, if not from the common reservoir that we expected the judge to share? So, yes, the system is imperfect. That is one of the costs of distributed leadership. Not everybody gets it right. Happily, the Common Law is especially adept at self-correction. It just takes a long, long time and regrettably too many miscarriages along the way.

As a concrete incident arises in the life of ordinary people and they go to court, the judge compares the facts to established principles. If a principle derived from previous rulings on similar cases disposes of this case, the judge is expected to uphold that principle and do nothing more. Whereas the great majority of cases do fit existing principles, which are validated by widespread usage, now and then a judge must exercise prudence and not simply impose the law in a mindless, cookie-cutter fashion.[20] What results in those situations is not a pronouncement from a higher authority, as though the judge consulted some secret and transcendent truth; instead, it is more of a hypothesis, i.e. a tentative finding that is subject to appeal and that is to be re-tested in similar situations arising later (see Cardozo, 1921, p. 23). Despite the understandable desire to get the right answer, once and for all, the Common Law demonstrates considerable humility . . . and patience, with due respect for tradition. As Cardozo wrote, "The work of a judge is in one sense enduring and in another sense ephemeral. What is good in it endures. What is erroneous is pretty sure to perish" (1921, p. 178).

18. This principle explains why the courts have adopted the fiction of the Reasonable Person. What would a reasonable person know? What would a reasonable person expect? Courts frequently use this device to frame the question they are assigned to answer (see Cardozo, 1921, p. 89; see generally Vaihinger, 2014).
19. See also p. 151, quoting John Locke, 1676.
20. Cardozo (1921, p. 30f) identified four methods for resolving these types of cases: analogy (how is this situation like another preexisting precedent?); history (in what direction is the law trending?); tradition (what would ordinary people here expect of me, based on past practice?); and the common good (what seems right for me to do morally?). Ideally, of course, all four methods will point toward the same outcome. Not surprisingly, perhaps, Hayek rejected the fourth method as a departure from the Common Law (1973/2012, p. 83); it was, in his opinion, not a judge's place to make such a determination.

Occasionally, some new legal concept comes into existence in order to answer the demands of an evolving society. How for example is data mining an example of unreasonable search and seizure? Other courts will tend to cite those attempts that accord with their own interpretations, until a discernible principle finally gains acceptance. Deference to precedent is always subject to contrary rulings, so that out of the differences that emerge the institution itself will eventually gravitate toward the most suitable. That is because the law is not some mysterious absolute to which the best-trained minds have access; rather, it is the discovery of what seems to work *by means of experience.*[21]

The Common Law is not altogether distinct from other kinds of law. To a great extent, these other kinds of law rely on the Common Law. Even statutory law requires the Common Law to interpret meanings and resolve ambiguities (see Cardozo, 1921, pp. 14–16; Plucknett, 1956/2010, pp. 328–341). It is not too much of a stretch to say that in Common Law jurisdictions, statutory law (and even a constitution) *presupposes* the Common Law. Often, courts must try to discern what in fact legislators intended when the plain language is not clear, though they must also sometimes try to intuit what the legislatures *would have* intended in a situation that was never explicitly considered during their parliamentary deliberations. Despite the attempt by lawgivers to make pronouncements, once and for all, there is still a residual role for the Common Law to give meaning to legislation in the contexts of life. Hall wrote, "There is always, in the nature of social fact, a peripheral sphere of uncertainty where the meaning of rules is vague and in a state of flux" (1949, p. 40). The Common Law is amply suited for this task.

We can think of it this way. Statutory law tends to be deductive, whereas the Common Law emerges from actual practice, on a case-by-case basis, as courts reason from the particular to the general. In this fashion, the legal order resolves ambiguity and tests its boundaries. The Common Law is also limited to the parties in any given dispute, which has the added benefit that errors and less-than-optimal rulings do not redound to others. Any harm is restricted to a small number of people, primarily the litigants. Court decisions are not *diktats* to the entire community.

The idea of leadership often suggests a leader in possession of a vision for others to follow. His or her authority would derive from political power, for example, or prophetic afflatus. The Common Law entrusts ordinary people to (a) fashion their own visions in the pursuit of happiness and (b) try to influence each other, within certain constraints, in an incremental process that pays special regard for individual differences and life's changing contexts.

---

21. The expectation that the law is a science and that the system should be able to arrive at the right answer in every instance, as though submitted to some kind of perfected algorithm, is to misperceive the nature of the law and hews to a vision of the process by which a community orders itself that relies too heavily on Enlightenment thinking . . . and not a little impatience.

A student in the field of Leadership Studies might be forgiven some confusion at this point. There does exist in the literature a tendency, dating back thousands of years, to portray leadership as the assertion of one's will onto other people, *by means of* other people, for their mutual benefit. Within this literature, leaders are to learn the mechanics of influence in order to bring about their vision of a better world. Everything the Common Law stands for would seem to ignore or contradict that literature. Thus, if leadership is presumed to mean the one, then how can the other be construed as leadership?

A couple of points of clarification would be in order. First, the existence of the Common Law does not preclude leadership as a private and wholly voluntary activity. The law is only a part—and, by design, a *limited* part—of the social order. Within the constraints of the law, teachers may still teach, parents may still parent, coaches may still coach, managers may still manage, even commanders in the military may still command. Nothing prevents this. Furthermore, leaders may make attempts to influence the law itself. This is not prohibited either. Of course, advocates in a court of law struggle to win over decision makers, both judge and jury, to the merits of their case. Jurists may explain their reasoning in an attempt to persuade other jurists of their opinion. Law professors may argue in an academic setting for new or different legal principles. Journalists may do so in the media. Legislators may suggest statutes. The Common Law ultimately depends on many discrete acts that fall within the definition of leadership. Nevertheless, these exertions are to be bounded—that is, subservient to a system no single person may control. We can all participate, and more of us probably should, even if none of us should ultimately wrest total power. I would go a step further to claim that the best way to prevent anyone from wresting total power is for all of us to exercise leadership and not to suppress or frustrate leadership.

Having said all of that, I do see something pernicious in certain versions of leadership. And I am by no means the first observer to feel this way. Writing in 1850, Frédéric Bastiat lambasted the arrogance of many prominent Enlightenment figures, quoting a number of its foremost heroes, such as Bossuet, Fénelon, Montesquieu, Rousseau, Raynal, Mably, Condillac, Saint-Just, Lepelletier, Louis Blanc, and most incisively Robespierre (1850/2007). Small wonder, he wrote, that Napoleon took them all seriously and simply replaced the superiority of the intellectuals with himself as the master (1850/2007, p. 41). Out of this cultural milieu, intellectuals seem to have agreed among themselves that there is a qualitative difference between themselves and the *hoi polloi*, the great unwashed, the masses, or what a later social critic called the *booboisie*.[22] Woodrow Wilson, before he became president of the United States of America, alluded to the voters as clay to be molded by leaders (Wilson, 1952; for pas-

---

22. Mencken (1923/1956, pp. 59–63).

sages using the same metaphor, see e.g. Bastiat, 1850/2007, pp. 24, 39). More recently, one national politician was caught referring to voters as a "basket of deplorables" (Reilly, 2017).[23]

Ever since the Enlightenment, many critics have weighed in on the presumption of the intellectuals.[24] There is something of an opposition between the two approaches: if the law is "made," i.e. a product of design, then it is a fair question about who is qualified to do so, but if instead it is not made and simply grows organically, then the attempt to *make* law borders on being presumptuous. That is to say that the Common Law does exhibit a strong anti-Enlightenment and anti-positivist temper. This is no accident (see e.g. Stacey, 2003, p. 45; Hayek, 1973/2012, ch. 2). The system is intended to be organic, belonging to everyone, distinctly *not* dependent on abstract Reason or the findings of intellectuals. It is no accident that the Enlightenment tends to be associated with jurisdictions dependent on some version of Roman law, as for example France, whereas the Common Law tends to be associated with Great Britain and its commonwealth. Also, the Common Law system stands for some version of the natural or divine law as somehow inherent in the people.[25] The Enlightenment has an ambiguous relationship with such claims. A more precise way of characterizing the opposition (without trying to delve too deeply into the breadth of the Enlightenment) is between the Common Law and the archetype of the lawgiver.[26] The Common Law needs no lawgiver. That might be a more promising way to see it.

Hayek (1973/2012) explained that Enlightenment thinking made a number of errors. Among these is the belief that an expert can master the ongoing

---

23. In fairness, she was referring to half of the voters for her opponent and not to the entire populace.
24. See e.g. Aron, R. (2001). *The opium of the intellectuals.* Routledge; Bauman, Z. (1987). *Legislators and interpreters: On modernity, post-modernity and intellectuals.* Cornell University Press; Benda, J. (1927/2009). *The treason of the intellectuals* (R. Aldington, trans.). Transaction; Crossman, R. & Engerman, D. (eds.). (2001). *The god that failed.* Columbia University Press; Desch, M. (ed.). (2016). *Public intellectuals in the global arena: Professors or pundits?* University of Notre Dame Press; Furet, F. (1999). *The passing of an illusion: The idea of communism in the twentieth century* (D. Furet, trans.). University of Chicago Press; Hollander, P. (2017). *From Benito Mussolini to Hugo Chavez: Intellectuals and a century of political hero worship.* Cambridge University Press; Hollander, P. (2006). *The end of commitment: Intellectuals, revolutionaries, and political morality in the twentieth century.* Ivan V. Dee Publishers; Hollander, P. (1981). *Political pilgrims: Travels of Western intellectuals to the Soviet Union, China, and Cuba 1928–1979.* Oxford University Press; Scruton, R. (2015). *Fools, frauds, and firebrands: Thinkers of the new left.* Bloomsbury; Sorel, G. (1999). *Reflections on violence.* Cambridge University Press; Wolfe, T. (2016). *The kingdom of speech.* Little, Brown & Co.
25. Robert Stacey adds that by the time the Common Law had evolved to the time of Blackstone, it also relied heavily, if indirectly, on Christian tradition. This however is a controversial claim (see generally Storing, 1987). Eric Voegelin asserted, "All legal cultures experience their primary source of order as located in transcendent reality, though the expressions of the experience differ widely" (1991, p. 79). The extent to which this may be the case regarding the Common Law exceeds the scope of this book chapter.
26. Brent Cusher has written on leadership and the process of lawgiving (2015, 2014, 2013, 2010).

details of a dynamic, complex system with sufficient dexterity to control its outcomes. That is simply not possible, as evidenced time and time again by engineers, military commanders, businessmen, and physicians. (Why then would we expect more from leaders?) Instead, we seem to have evolved systems that work better than anything experts could design (p. 37). He wrote that "we can preserve order of such complexity not by the method of directing the members, but only indirectly by enforcing and improving the rules conducive to the formation of a spontaneous order" (p. 51). This is clearly what judges do. What then of the lawgiver? Looking back, even the most celebrated lawgivers, such as Hammurabi, Lycurgus, and Solon, were simply formalizing laws that were already in existence: *rendering* them, as it were, and not fabricating them because they somehow knew better (p. 81). We misperceive the role of the law-giver otherwise. Judges discern in concrete cases what lawgivers discern in the abstract as general principles.

It seems likely that leadership plays some part in creating, maintaining, adapting, and destroying social systems. I am not going to deny this. Those of us who teach and study leadership can probably think of examples of each. There is no reason to restrict leadership to any one of these activities and not include the other three. Each can be the result of leadership. And in many instances (though not all), such leadership is clear and justifiable. But then what we must conclude is that nearly all of it is leadership. And if nearly all of it is leadership, then what exactly does leadership mean as a distinct concept? I am making the claim that leadership *at the macro level* is social participation for the realization of a better future. Period. Full stop.

It is this way of thinking about leadership that accords with the cultural institution we call the Common Law.

## Concluding Thoughts

Hayek celebrated the Common Law as an example of spontaneous order, even though in actual fact it is more of a hybrid system that preserves many of the best features of spontaneous order. This chapter used broad principles and discernible patterns, just as Hayek had promised, to describe how that system works. In this conclusion, let us isolate several lessons that will continue to inform our study of leadership under these conditions.

First, the Common Law makes it difficult to know who the real leaders are, because it is more of a group effort. The Common Law is an institution that enacts leadership. Furthermore, contributions to the system have been made down through the centuries, so that something of the leadership of those who came before us survives. Nevertheless, it is also in our powers today to refine that system, less by spontaneous means, which Hayek nearly venerated, and more by deliberate and purposeful effort, so long as the development aligns with the system as a whole and promises to carry on its mission into the indefinite future. The Common Law is less about leaders and more about those who are willing to participate. We might call them social agents.

Second, the Common Law aspires to represent a perennial wisdom handed down through the ages—a wisdom that does not require special powers or esoteric knowledge. The system for administering the Common Law, which we might call its structure, is admittedly too complex for most laymen, which is why we need lawyers, but its content should not be. That content should always be reasonable, compatible with the expectations of ordinary folks conducting their personal lives. Reasonableness is its watchword.

Third, thousands upon thousands of individual cases in hundreds of jurisdictions, each one with its accompanying story, together constitute a civil order that was bequeathed by no lawgiver. It emerged over a long period of time and has assumed a wholesome shape without evidence of design. That is to say that the institution or structure must be seen as a manifestation of history, a cultural domain that flows through us as agents, shaping us as much as we shape it.

# 5

# MACRO/MICRO PERSPECTIVES
## A Basic Dichotomy Holding Us Back

### Introduction to the Chapter

The chapter on Martin Luther reminds us that the simplistic map depicting a leader versus his context requires greater subtlety. Leadership studies could afford to expand its scope laterally to include rivals and allies and institutions. More is going on than one person's exertions against some amorphous fog. In addition, it reminds us that the leadership episodes we like to study take place within a longer timeline of complex antecedents and consequences. Furthermore, Luther exemplifies someone who bumped up against *aporias* and after years of struggling against them suddenly saw them in a fresh light, not as a threat but as an opportunity. His insight altered the course of history.

The chapter on the Common Law describes a cultural institution where leadership takes place without any individual person necessarily serving as the leader. It also illustrates the dynamics that go into what Hayek called spontaneous order, an order that nobody designs and probably nobody fully understands. At any given moment in time, society is changing in myriad ways, without central coordination, yet the very thing that we seek will emerge on its own after multiple iterations. By means of social action, when people are simply going about their private lives, communities can gradually create a sufficient expectation of justice. The cutting edge of that institution, where innovation and growth occurs, takes place where litigants compete with one another over *aporias*. The way forward is to be found through seeming contraries.

Broadening the investigation into leadership means appreciating the complexity inherent in social life. Any episode we choose to study participates in a turbulent flow of events. Not only is paramount reality more complicated than it might seem, but it also changes constantly, often in ways that nobody could predict. At each point in time, on a large scale or a small scale, contrary forces are at work shaping the course of history in a kind of shifting tension. That tension is not only a condition of the world out there; it is part of who we are as perplexing creatures. Each of us embodies that condition.

Luther came to accept that fact. In fact, he celebrated it. But then he had faith that it was all part of God's plan. Strangely, Hayek also embraced the idea that something benign could come about without our need to control it. Order can emerge on its own. Nobody has to impose it. The causal mechanism for a better social world depends on each of us doing what we think best, from our individual perspective, as we make little adjustments to one another. Yet neither Luther nor Hayek thought that this better world was inevitable. These private choices that supposedly contribute to the greater good must reflect or carry forward our common sense. If in our private lives we apply the accumulated wisdom from the ages, then everything will eventually work itself out. It is a paradox, but life would appear to be constituted by antinomies.

In leadership studies, we neglect this possibility. We isolate our narrative around a singular human being who possesses a singular vision for the future. Conflict and ambiguity, whether out there in paramount reality or in here in the heart, soul, or mind of the individual, is regarded as a problem to be overcome—if, that is, we even acknowledge its existence. Yet people have choices. They can feel torn about what to do. Leaders experience doubt. It may be the case that the group can go in more than one direction. They probably already are! Sometimes, you have two equally acceptable alternatives. In addition, of course, sometimes you have two equally bad alternatives, and you are stuck having to choose the lesser of two evils. I am here making the plea that life is inherently, even necessarily, conflictual. Leadership takes place within that condition and—let's be honest—contributes to it. Maybe, that is a good thing. But not always. . . .

To the extent that we are interested in social change and more narrowly in the agents of social change, we must also account for the possibility of confusion and menace. Not every social actor is a hero. Ernest Renan, for example, looked bitterly at the historical convulsion known as the French Revolution (1789–1799). The events themselves are disturbing and strange. Many who would ordinarily be regarded as criminal or insane were to play key roles in the mayhem. But then they were not entirely responsible for the uprising; Renan argued instead that the uprising was responsible for their behavior. He called it an orgy, a cyclone, and a whirlwind. He referred to these characters—instrumental though they undoubtedly were—as "straw blown by the wind" and buffoons "dragged along by the dizzy hour" (1892, quoted in Vernon, 1978, p. 120ff). He wrote, "They were sublimely ignorant" (1892, quoted in Vernon, 1978, p. 120). Their status derived from the unexpected opportunity for their vices to be put on display and celebrated by the mob. That's about it. Renan did not want to credit them with leadership. In fact, it would be peculiar to attribute the uprising to any existing structures at the time either, inasmuch as the prevailing structures were taken by surprise and thrown down. So what then? If not unwitting (and witless) agents or structure, some third thing perhaps? Whatever we might surmise (and I would guess that writers such as Fyodor Dostoevsky and René Girard could offer dark suggestions), the social action on display in Paris did not in and of itself form spontaneous order. If anything, it delivered the opposite. So, was it "leadership" for a villain to roam the streets killing people wantonly or for a lunatic to shout unintelligible encouragement? If we are serious about studying leadership, we should probably consider these reprehensible exemplars, too, and not avert our gaze.[1]

Having said that, however, I have not recoiled from considering the possibility that leadership serves an emerging Good, whether we call this end-state synchrony or justice or harmony or an implicate order. It goes by many names. Mats Alvesson, whom I respect highly, diminishes this approach to leadership as Disneyland-inspired and grounded in religion (2019, pp. 31, 39)—as though that is a bad thing. Something seems to be informing our efforts and guiding us toward a future that few, if any of us, could have foreseen. Much as social scientists are understandably reluctant to consider occult forces, it is not unreasonable to see something of this implicate order in the way that an acorn becomes an oak and a community forms around a market (à la Hayek). I do not presume to know what that ultimate image looks like; I do not enjoy privileged access to its contours. I certainly do not consider it inevitable that we shall successfully realize this ideal—whatever it is. Many have tried and failed. The quest for order often suffers from unintended consequences, as I have been saying. Nevertheless, something in the human mind that the ancient Greeks labeled *logos* works in attunement with an unseen order. What that might mean is for each generation to discern together, as they carry forward into a new world the perennial wisdom that lies within them as a resource.

If you have a map, you can walk the territory to confirm its accuracy. When given a map of the future, however, you cannot do that. Not yet. By the time you have reached the future in order to check the accuracy of the map, it is too late. You are already there. For that reason, something in you in the present moment will have to tell you whether the future map is actually desirable, or even intelligible. Today, you must judge the vision of tomorrow according to your imagination (Harter, 2015). How do you know as a leader (or, in my case, as a scholar) which is the way to go? How do you know which is best? I hold that there is something transcending a person in the moment, something toward which we struggle. We need one another to bring it about, but somehow even the promise of it resonates.

---

1. Psychologist Ernst Kretschmer purportedly once wrote, "There's something strange about psychopaths. In normal times we write expert evaluations on them; in times of political unrest they rule us" (quoted in Bair, 2003, p. 437).

Implicit in this project is a differentiation between leadership as a micro phenomenon, at the interpersonal level, and society as a macro phenomenon. I pictured Luther (micro) changing the face of Europe (macro). I pictured the Common Law as a macro phenomenon establishing a context for leadership as a micro phenomenon. I teach leadership as something you do to make a difference in the world. Focus on the micro to change the macro. That tiered (and tired) image—while instructive—prevented me from conceiving leadership as something else. Let me explain how I got here.

## The Original Challenge

My motive for undertaking this particular investigation began with a challenge— a challenge that gradually shifted how I think about leadership more broadly. It started in the winter of 2015. While reading *How Institutions Think* by Mary Douglas (1986), I came across a statement that was to vex me. She wrote, "Social facts must be explained by social facts" (p. 34). It is a simple assertion. But is it true?

One afternoon a couple of years ago, the members of a faculty search committee where I work were sitting around puzzling why we rarely see sociologists apply to teach in our university's leadership program. One hypothesis stuck with me. Perhaps (we thought) sociologists are not academically interested in the exertions of individual social actors; instead, they study groups, communities, and other collectives. They see no reason to study leadership, any more than literary theorists need to study spelling. What they study in literary theory might be *comprised* of words that are to be spelled, but these scholars operate at a higher or more encompassing level. In other words, it is a division of labor to let somebody else worry about how words are spelled.

At my own university, circa 2020, the faculty subdivides biology into molecular biology and chemistry, on the one hand, and organismal and environmental biology, on the other. Different magnitudes call for different academic disciplines. I get that. In a similar fashion, the mechanical engineer might want to master the intricacies of metal fatigue, while an automotive engineer considers the entire car. It helps the mechanical engineer to know the conditions under which the metal will be expected to operate in a motorcar, just as it helps the automotive engineer to know the limits under which the metal in an engine can operate. Still, the two engineers are concerned about different, even if interdependent, things.

What the search committee was using at the time was an image of a hierarchy, arranged by magnitude, in which leadership studies occupies the micro level and sociology occupies the macro level. In the abstract, such an image (macro/micro) serves its purposes, but then it can be used inaptly, as I intend to demonstrate. Be that as it may, however, this was the image by which we were operating at the time, as we sat around our conference table shooting the breeze.

When using this image (macro/micro), each magnitude has its own integrity, such that you can restrict your research to one magnitude or another—not *forgetting* the fact that the magnitudes may be interdependent (because they are), but *bracketing* that fact for the purpose of concentrating your attention. (Phenomenologists call this act of bracketing *epoché*.)[2] So perhaps sociologists understand intellectually that leadership helps to explain what happens at the macro level for which they are responsible, yet they are trying to explain the macro level *on its own terms*. In which case, they probably are not really doing leadership studies at all. That's what we suspected. Our hypothesis about why sociologists do not apply for jobs in leadership studies (inasmuch as they are responsible for the macro whereas we are responsible for the micro) has a certain surface plausibility, even if it happens not to be true. Nevertheless, I had to find this out for myself.

Because I teach in the field of leadership studies, I consider the extent to which we explain social facts by referring to psychological factors and individual exertions. Isn't the point of leadership studies to ascribe social causation to discernible leaders, to those we refer to as agents? We seem to exist as a field of study in order to show that the micro can explain the macro. Constantine instituted the Christian church. Abraham Lincoln freed the slaves. Peter the Great modernized Russia. So forth and so on. We simply want to understand how that sort of thing happens. That is how I always imagined it.

In the literature, however, I started to find examples of only three out of four basic permutations with regard to leadership studies:[3]

- **smaller** level explanations of the **smaller** level, micro-to-micro (e.g. Bass, 1990, pp. 354–360; Manz & Sims, 1989; McGregor, 1966; Blake & Mouton, 1964; Carnegie, 1936);
- **smaller** level explanations of the **larger** level, micro-to-macro (e.g. Isaacson, 2010; Wills, 1994; Bass, 1990, p. 197f. citing Max Weber; Rustow, 1970);
- **larger** level explanations of the **smaller** level, macro-to-micro (e.g. Osborn, Hunt, & Jauch, 2002; Merton, 1949/1968); and
- **larger** level explanations of the **larger** level, macro-to-macro (literature example not found).

Would it be possible (I asked myself at the time) to examine leadership strictly at the larger level? What would that even look like? The chapter on the Common Law which you just read was a halting step in that direction.

---

2. See generally Patočka (2018).
3. Yammarino and Gooty (2017) explain these permutations (p. 234).

## Durkheim Explains Why Social Facts Are Explained Only by Social Facts

To prepare myself for the challenge, I traced Douglas' admonition about using social facts back to Emile Durkheim (1858–1917), a titanic figure from the early days of sociology. If anyone insisted that the larger level explains the larger, it was he. In his groundbreaking classic *The Rules of Sociological Method* (published in 1895), Durkheim repeated the same admonition as Douglas had stated. In the preface to the first edition, for example, he wrote, "We separate the psychological [micro] from the social [macro]; . . . we refuse to explain the complex in terms of the simple" (1895/1938, p. xxxix). In the following pages, Durkheim said it again, this time as a general principle: "The determining cause of a social fact should be sought among the social facts preceding it and not among the states of the individual consciousness" (1895/1938, p. 110; see pp. 141, 144f).

Raymond Aron called it the "principle of homogeneity of cause and effect" that a social phenomenon can be explained only by a social cause (1967, pp. 17, 22, 24, 37, 77, 78). Likewise, Donald Levine traced this principle back further to the Baron de Montesquieu and Auguste Comte and the **Postulate of Societal Realism**, which states that "society is no more decomposable into individuals than a geometric surface is into lines, or a line into points" (1995, p. 165f, translating from the *System of Positive Polity*, 1848–51; see also p. 178; Levine, 2018, p. 154).[4] Levine notes that to his credit Durkheim did not just declare this postulate dogmatically. Instead, he demonstrated in his research the "superiority of explanations that adduce strictly social causative factors" (1995, p. 171).

In order to drive home the point he was making, Durkheim added that "every time that a social phenomenon is directly explained by a psychological phenomenon, we may be sure that the explanation is false" (1895/1938, p. 104). That is a strong claim. Some anthropologists criticized Durkheim's approach as unnecessarily reductive (e.g. Kroeber & Kluckhohn, 1963, p. 325, n. 25). Robert Merton (1976) later softened the position a bit, when for example he admitted that a thorough understanding of a social phenomenon would include psychological considerations, such as the social actors' motivations, but he was just not doing that when he was practicing sociology (p. 147).

Durkheim pointed out that scientists in emerging fields of study have always had to do what he was doing—which is to say that, at some point, they had to recognize that the object of their investigations (whatever it happens to be) has a nature of its own (1895/1938, p. lviii; see pp. 101, 103, 124; Levine, 2018, p. 103). It was a matter of differentiation. (We have seen much the same thing

---

4. The alternative favored in leadership studies is the **Postulate of Methodological Individualism** (Levine, 2018, p. 145): "Social phenomena are best explained by analyzing the propensities of the individual actors that constitute them."

in leadership studies for the past fifty years, as we have tried to guard our turf.) Durkheim admitted in the preface to the second edition that until the science of sociology developed further, it would be difficult to determine what, if anything, at the micro level could be said to influence what happens at the macro level (1895/1938, p. liv). Perhaps leadership studies as a distinct field of study exists to close that gap. That remains to be seen. Regardless, leadership studies *per se* did not exist at the end of the nineteenth century.

For Durkheim, therefore, the social is a force separate from and superior to the individual social actor (1895/1938, p. 90). As such, its antecedent must be found in the nature of society itself (1895/1938, p. 102). Individual exertions cannot explain the social, although Durkheim did say they might "facilitate its explanation" (1895/1938, p. 111)—a locution that, in the English, is not altogether clear. The relevant factor for him, as a sociologist, was that which makes the individual behavior truly "social" (1895/1938, p. 112, n. 21).[5]

Durkheim explained that a social fact is not a "social fact" simply because everyone is the same in some regard. Calling something a "social fact" is not a conclusion about how widespread something is throughout a given population, whether it be a belief, practice, or value. Whatever that "social fact" turns out to be, he wrote, "it is to be found in each part because it exists in the whole, rather than in the whole because it exists in the parts" (1895/1938, p. 9).[6] Each human being has a belly button, for instance, but we would not call that a social fact. A social fact is social because it has an objective status and a coercive impact on individuals (1895/1938, p. 2). One thinks for example of law and language (see e.g. 1895/1938, p. 30). They exist whether a particular individual is thinking about them or not. Their rules tend to influence behavior, even if nobody is present to enforce them. The macro is seen to influence the micro and not the other way around, no matter how many individual human beings exhibit this "fact." In other words, Durkheim insisted that what would be of interest to him was exclusively that which flows from macro to macro and consequently flows from macro to micro. He was not saying things could not flow otherwise (see e.g. 1895/1938, p. 108); rather, he was saying that such a phenomenon would not be of professional interest to a sociologist. Social facts are not, as he put it, products of the will; "they are [instead] like molds in which our actions are inevitably shaped" (1895/1938, p. 29).

Like a clever lawyer, Durkheim did move back a step to make a fallback argument. He argued that exertions of the will that do result in changes to society, such as Martin Luther's efforts to translate the Bible, actually prove the

---

5. Not surprisingly, perhaps, Durkheim took it one step further, arguing that the social milieu can be differentiated between the general milieu (as the larger construct) and specific or sub-milieus. Then, he made the exact same claim as he had made about individual social actors, to the effect that the general milieu can explain the specific milieu, but not the other way around—and for exactly the same reason (1895/1938, p. 116).

6. Any resemblance to what Arthur Koestler (1970) called a *holon* is no accident (see Donaldson, 2017).

existence of social facts inasmuch as the social facts serve as the "opposition" to these exertions, the condition that will have had to be overcome—rather like the water through which we swim. The swimmer does not create the water. The swimmer has to churn through the water, account for the water, and ultimately prevail against it. No water, no swimming. I guess one could say that Durkheim chose to study the water and not the swimmer.

What this schema of Durkheim's generates is an image of society as a flow, a series of transformations (1895/1938, p. 134). "A" transforms into "B" which in turn transforms into "C." The resulting series "A-B-C" constitutes the arc of development of special interest to sociology (1895/1938, p. 139).[7] In my imagination at the outset, therefore, leadership studies investigates the micro phenomenon, *as opposed to* the macro phenomenon of social change. We get the smaller phenomenon; they get the larger. Is that it? These are simply separate magnitudes. Sociologists had their work to do. I have mine. To intermix them seems to be a category error (see Ryle, 2009). One of them is a social role; the other, a theater where that role is enacted. Emile Durkheim, as we just saw, insisted that sociology would not be interested in the exertions of individual social actors. In sociology, social facts can be explained only by other social facts.

It follows that in his opinion sociologists would not concern themselves professionally with the study of a phenomenon such as leadership. One is macro. The other is micro. The rationale for insisting on this distinction had something to do with establishing the identity of the academic discipline known as sociology, i.e. as a step toward an academic division of labor. Let somebody else investigate leadership.

Thus, even if the one influences the other, they must be kept separate conceptually. For example, if you were to conduct a multi-level analysis, as is often done in the social sciences, you must first differentiate the levels from one another. Leadership and society are not the same thing. Maybe leadership scholars should keep their nose out of other people's business.

I was not so easily deterred. Something about Durkheim's explanation did not make sense. I had to go back to the underlying image of a dichotomy between the macro and the micro. It clearly has its uses, but was it also limiting the imagination?

## Reconsidering a Basic Dichotomy: Macro/Micro (and Also Meta)

This macro/micro distinction is one of the most familiar dichotomies in nearly any field of study. As stated in the preface, the macro is large in scale, whereas

---

7. Be forewarned, Lucien Febvre (1929) quoted André Gide that "the most troublesome problem arises from the necessity of describing as 'successive' states that interweave and are simultaneous" (quotation marks supplied) (p. 229).

the micro is small by comparison. I would take it one step further. The micro is a magnitude or level within the macro. Another way of saying this is that the macro encompasses the micro. Cabrera and Cabrera (2015) use the image of a container (p. 61). The macro *contains* the micro.

In the spirit of pondering dichotomies, I need to add another magnitude or level known as the **meta**. The prefix "meta" is not used to signify that which is simply higher and bigger than the rest. Yes, it *encompasses* the macro/micro model, but only in a manner of speaking, because it stands outside of the entire model altogether. We might say that macro and micro are like concentric circles along a single dimension outward; meta belongs to a different dimension. Micro might be like a room in a house; macro, like the house. Meta is like standing at the curb looking up at the whole house, thinking of it as a house, and comparing it to other houses on the street. Meta means beyond—not separated from the rest, off on its own, but referring back to the whole structure, an Archimedean point of reference. One must step outside of the schema in order to judge whether it works.

Meta has the sense of being reflexive, just as metaphysics is asking what we are doing when we are doing physics (see generally H. Lawson, 1985). "What exactly are we doing when . . . ?" By going meta, we learn to stand outside of our framework to ask about the process of framing. We quit using the maps and their insets and start asking how maps are made. That is meta. From that vantage point, we are no longer bound by the rules of the game. We *transcend* it. This is a typical move in philosophy, of course, as one turns the mind upon itself: a thinking about thinking. Heraclitus once noted: "The way up and down is one and the same" (fragment CIII, translated in Kahn, 1979, p. 240f). To a great extent, therefore, we need to be more meta about the study of leadership.

Sociologists resort often to the macro/micro distinction (see e.g. T. Smith, 1997, ch. 5; Rousseau, 1985). They talk about them as **levels**. In 1988, Norbert Wiley tackled the whole idea of using "levels" in the analysis of social phenomena. Wiley was engaging in some meta-analysis about multi-level research in sociology. He described something he referred to as "structural closure." A structurally closed level does not depend on causal influences from a lower level (1988, p. 260). What happens at one level must be explained at that same level, an assertion echoing Durkheim and Douglas, as I already mentioned. There is however a risk in working toward structural closure, he noted; there is a temptation to switch from structural closure to level-imperialism, which is the belief that any one level is *the only level there is* (e.g. Carnap, 1934/1995). Alternatively, to put it differently, that changes at other levels in the hierarchy can be explained solely from any one of the levels, as though one were sufficient. This position is untenable and frankly unnecessary (Yammarino & Gooty, 2017, p. 237). We can reject it as reductive. For example, I refuse to accept that all social change of any note must be explained as leadership, despite what Thomas

Carlyle famously wrote in the nineteenth century (1841/2011). Wiley argued instead for connections among "somewhat autonomous and irreducible" levels (1988, p. 260). What happens at one level affects what happens at other levels.[8] He called it Emergence and Feedback, in a never-ending process. I have come to agree with his way of thinking.[9]

Acknowledging these connections from one level to another does not negate the utility of thinking at levels. One might use levels to describe tiers in the process of abstraction, as you move in your imagination from species to genus. Socrates and Alcibiades were both men, for example. The category "men" is a generalization from the specific instances. One might use levels to achieve a point of view, gaining critical distance, searching for patterns—not unlike standing on the balcony to watch everybody waltz, as Ron Heifetz (1994) famously recommended (see also Cabrera & Cabrera, 2015, pp. 64–66). One might use these levels to extend one's thinking in any one of several directions, as for example looking at a larger field than the original phenomenon of interest to you or looking at the historical context.[10] What, for example, is macro to the macro, i.e. even bigger? Or micro to the micro, i.e. even smaller? Each of these uses can contribute to understanding.

If you want to understand the zebra, it helps to understand its place within the herd and also what it eats—and what eats the zebra. To be brief, the zebra is an organism that participates in larger systems. Quickly, I decided that, when it comes to studying leadership, having to choose between micro and macro perspectives is a false dilemma (see Yammarino & Dionne, 2019, p. 48). My original image was inadequate. **Leadership studies is not a micro level.** What then is it?

## The Agent-Structure Problem

> The observer may choose . . . between the flowers or the garden, the rocks or the quarry, the trees or the forest, the houses or the neighborhood . . .
> —*Singer (1973, quoted in Moul, 1973)*

My question about where leadership fits within the image of the micro and the macro is a variation on a long-standing dispute in the social sciences known as the agent-structure problem (see e.g. Kaczmarczyk, 2018, p. 52, citing Berger &

---

8. Contrary to Durkheim, Yammarino and Gooty (2017) caution against trying to explain social phenomena from a single level (p. 232). I am looking not so much at multi-level analysis as at the dynamics of cross-level relationships (p. 234; see also Lee, 1997, p. 24).

9. Klenke (2008) cited Olivares, Peterson, and Hess (2007) regarding a different set of "levels" that exceed sociology's mission, but hew closely to the study of leadership: *mitwelt* (the interpersonal), *umwelt* (embodied experience), and *eigenwelt* (reflective introspection).

10. Wiley calls these not "levels" but "continua" (1988, p. 255).

Luckmann, 1966; Crossley, 2011; Wendt citing Ruben, 1985). The problem was imported into leadership studies by the redoubtable James MacGregor Burns. Burns called the agent-structure problem one of the most widely studied approaches to human change (2003, p. 215). Caroline Brettell (2002) refers to this tension between agent and structure as "a leitmotiv in the history of the social sciences" and "a master metaphor of Western thought" (p. 442). Levine (2018) agreed that the "opposition between the individual and society dominated nearly all of Western social thought" (p. 114). Nevertheless, Burns called for leadership scholars to transcend this simple dichotomy (2003, p. 216). I agree.[11] But first, we should probably re-state the problem.

One of the most cited versions of the agent-structure problem is an article by Alexander Wendt, who wrote in 1987 that two seemingly opposite propositions appear to be both true and useful:

- Social actors shape social structures.
- Social structures shape social actors.

We encounter a dichotomy (agent/structure), one that presents us with a dilemma, and it is this: specifically, in the flow of history, which shapes which? The former assertion that social actors shape social structures is, in the extreme, compatible with a position known as **atomism** in which the individual human being is the unit of analysis;[12] whereas the latter is, in the extreme, compatible with what is known as **holism** in which the collective is the entire unit of analysis.[13] Norbert Elias remarked that few controversies are as unattractive (1970/1978, p. 73). Jepperson and Meyer (2011) complain that in sociology the overall murkiness about the problem is striking (p. 55). Sharon Hays (1994) notes, however, that our "conceptualizations of structure, agency, and culture *do* shape what one chooses to study as well as the results of one's research" (p. 70). Therefore, we have to resolve it somehow.

Levine (2018) listed a few likely alternatives to consider in making sense of the apparent either/or (p. 199):

11. As the agent-structure problem pertains to leadership studies, I recommend Yammarino and Gooty (2017). See also Fairhurst (2001).
12. Atomism has been referred to as mechanicism and sociological nominalism (Levine, 1995, p. 49). We might speak of the Postulate of Methodological Individualism to the effect that: "Social phenomena are best explained by analyzing the propensities of the individual actors that constitute them" (Levine, 1995, p. 129). Atomism also goes by the name of individualism, which is further subdivided into **ontological** individualism and **methodological** individualism (see Jepperson & Meyer, 2011, p. 56). I do not believe, however, that this latter distinction is relevant to my argument.
13. Holism has been referred to as organicism and sociological realism (Levine, 1995, p. 49). We might speak of the Postulate of Societal Realism to the effect that: "Society is a supraindividual phenomenon with determinate properties not reducible to individual propensities" (Levine, 1995, p. 153).

- Agency and structure are simply **irrelevant** to one another.
- Agency and structure begin with completely **different definitions** for the nature of the problem, so of course they proceed toward different answers.
- Agency and structure are **competing** forms for understanding the same social phenomenon.
- Agency and structure are **collaborative** forms, each converging on the same problem from different angles.
- Agency and structure are **complementary** forms that address different aspects of the same problem.
- Agency and structure belong to a hierarchical **architecture**, with agency nested within structure (the classic macro/micro).

Nick Crossley (2011) has a different reaction, and I tend to concur with him. He considers the whole agent-structure problem, dating back at least as far as Thomas Carlyle (1841) and Herbert Spencer, to be misleading (p. 5), perhaps a false dilemma. The two are expressions of the same thing. Neither one exists without the other. They are instead "mutually implicating" (2011, p. 128). Each of them—agent and structure—is subject to processes of interaction. Crossley seeks to transcend them by putting his focus on the interaction itself. Agents modify structures, and structures modify agents. They shape each other in response to what has gone before (2011, ch. 3 and p. 126). There is no pause, no time out. In the study of historical episodes, he writes, "We never start from a stop position" (2011, p. 31). What we ought to notice, in his opinion, is the never-ending flow, the intermediate dynamic between and among these (2011, p. 123). Social reality is, in his words, "intersubjective and co-constituted" (2011, p. 130). Influence shapes further influence, in a kind of cascade (2011, p. 177). Tony Lawson (2013) gives a simple example when he writes that "early developments of structure cumulatively restrict later ones" (p. 75). One cannot speak of influence as a process without this time dimension in which the past shapes the present, for both agents *and* structures.

Any pattern that does emerge of the sort Hayek promised to us resembles networks that cluster into what can be called worlds, such as the art world or science. Nevertheless, these structures (both networks and worlds) "entail inter-active dynamism" (2011, p. 137). Crossley writes that "it would be disingenuous to assume that the structures derived are anything but snapshots of a relational figuration which is always in process and constantly evolving" (2011, p. 128).

The question about the agent-structure problem originated in the scholarly literature toward asking which of these two (agent or structure) is "primitive"—as in prior and irreducible (Dessler, 1989, p. 445). Do you begin from the micro or the macro? Wisely, theorists have by now sought a both/and solution,[14] giving

---

14. Caroline Brettell mentions Anthony Giddens and Pierre Bourdieu in particular (2002, p. 438). Don Levine tracks this suggestion of a both/and solution back to the 1960s in the work of Walter

each unit of analysis co-equal status, such that agent and structure are mutually constituted (Wendt, 1987, p. 339; see Lawson, 2013).[15] To affix one as primitive to the exclusion of the other is a form of "level essentialism" (Jepperson & Meyer, 2011, p. 68) or what I have labeled elsewhere as reductive.

Leadership studies tends to make the agent primitive. That is why we want to know what Martin Luther did. That is why I originally assumed that leadership studies begin with the micro phenomenon. We rarely credit structures with having causal properties. To the extent that anything can be said to shape the leader, we ascribe causation to other agents, such as parents, teachers, role models, and predecessors. Otherwise, as Wendt points out, we leave the causation of leadership itself (in his words) opaque and untheorized (Wendt, 1987, p. 343).[16] Leaders make things happen, we say. But what makes leadership happen? This "atomistic" tendency on the part of leadership scholars has been countered in the literature lately, yet it still plays a role in the conduct of research. It persists in popular literature and leadership education. Leadership takes the foreground; structure (as context) operates in the background.

Those of us in leadership studies have had to re-think this approach. For one thing, social structures are remarkably deep, hidden, powerful, and durable (Hays, 1994, p. 62). The Common Law is a superlative example. Much of our time is spent obeying them and perpetuating them, even when we are unaware of them. Maybe *especially* when we are unaware of them. We frequently behave like automatons or puppets when it comes to these structures, as Hayek observed. Even the choices we would like to believe that we can make are shaped by social structures (1994, p. 64; see also Popper, 1966, p. 90). We might say that even when you have a choice, you rarely change anything. The

---

Buckley and Werner Stark, who in turn asserted that it goes all the way back to Plato (Levine, 1995, p. 49). Yet even as recently as 2016, Jaspal, Carriere, and Moghaddam were calling for even further integration (p. 265).

15. Hays (1994) presented a continuum, placing atomism at one end and holism at the other, with two alternatives lying in between. There is the option I just described in which agents and structures constitute each other (a simple both/and), which she called **structurally reproductive agency**. She preferred something she called **structurally transformative agency**, which emphasizes the role of agents to transform structures, as for example during social revolutions (p. 64). What she was apparently trying to indicate was that agents can do more than make superficial adjustments on a day-to-day basis to the structures in which they find themselves, so that over time, in small ways, their choices can alter structures incrementally and often unintentionally. Instead, she was more amenable to the intentional and deep transformations associated with what we know as leadership. As one might put it, holism treats people as puppets, structurally reproductive agency treats them as unwitting servants of social systems, structurally transformative agency is about the possibility for leadership, and atomism treats people as mythological figures who can do just about anything.

16. The reverse is also a possibility, wherein holistic theorists treat leadership primarily as an effect of the system (Wendt, 1987, p. 346). As Durkheim and others might put it, the structure calls forth its own reproduction and transformation (Wendt, 1987, p. 347). Originally, I had wanted to know what leadership from this holistic perspective might look like.

structure grinds ahead. However, I do not think that leadership scholars are trying to downplay how difficult and rare leadership might be. I think that, if anything, leadership scholars do regard social structures as formidable. But why adopt a spirit of antagonism in the first place? That is what I would like to know.

David Dessler, for example, points out that structures are not only the context or environment in which leadership takes place, like the backdrop for action, they are also the means by which action even occurs (1989, p. 444; see Giddens, 1993, p. 169). Martin Luther King Jr. worked within the church structures of his day, for example. Furthermore, structures are frequently the outcome of leadership as well as the medium through which action takes place (1989, p. 452). Václav Havel is reported to have claimed that despite the presence of two different "intentions" (the intentions of life and the intentions of the system), life is manifested in systems (Přibáň, 2016, p. 42, citing "The Power of the Powerless"). Structures exist before, during, and after. They are context, means, and product. Maybe Alvesson is right: "Leadership can often be seen as less of the ultimate source of influencing than a lubrication mechanism, making [structures] sometimes functioning more smoothly" (2019, p. 38). All of this, without even addressing the causal properties of structures themselves (see Douglas, 1986). What then would it look like to develop theories and conduct research giving both agent and structure their due? Is that even possible? Here, the SFI (subsidiary-focal integration) that I explained earlier makes a significant contribution.

If you recall, SFI asserts that we come to understand by means of a focal awareness on parts that we gradually integrate with subsidiary knowledge into a generalized pattern. We swing the flashlight here and there while using our imagination to piece it together. Why not adopt a similar strategy for leadership? We can focus on agency, as we have for many years, and we can also focus on structures, as sociologists and political scientists have been doing. But then *we can also focus on the integration itself.* That is, we can push to the forefront the agent-structure problem, integrating everything. Wendt resorted to a traditional method of doing so: posit a hypothesis and then go test it, repeatedly. That way, you begin with some piece of subsidiary knowledge, and then turn the flashlight to check whether you were correct. If the chair in the beam of light is facing to the right, then you can hypothesize that there is a corresponding table and that the table is further to the right of the chair. Having done so, you swing the flashlight over in that direction and find a table . . . or not.

This integrative vision of the agent-structure problem means that we can say—and indeed have been saying—that agents and structures are conceptually distinct yet mutually constitutive (Wendt, 1987, p. 360; see Sinek, 2017, p. 165). What we uncover is the interplay of two activities and not just one. First, we examine the mechanics at work in a specific, concrete situation, such as Martin Luther translating the Bible. This is often the work of historians. Without this, we are engaging in unfounded speculation. Second, we infer the existence of laws that would appear to govern similar cases. Without this, we are simply compiling stories with no apparent meaning. That is to say, we want to know *how* something happened and in addition *why* something happened. These are not necessarily the same thing.

Jeffrey Berejikian (1992) has given us an example about how this works. He began by contrasting two ways of explaining the roots of revolution. One was based upon a holistic vision of society; the other was based on an atomistic vision. We might use these briefly to illustrate how one might analyze Martin Luther's exertions.

On the one hand, at the time of the Protestant Reformation, Europe was undergoing large-scale structural shifts toward nationalism. Since uprisings are a permanent feature of history, always ready to erupt, what they require is (a) some sense of cohesiveness among the disenfranchised as a group (and not isolated acts of defiance) and (b) a little slack in the systems of control so that the rebels gain space to take action.[17] The German princes and their reform-minded allies in the clergy gave the people a sense of shared identity, and the church found itself surprisingly vulnerable in its efforts to quell the dispute. Earlier, it had successfully crushed similar outbreaks, but now it could not. Its methods were ineffectual. Not only did structures seek to constrain the rebellion, structures such as the nascent publishing industry contributed to it (Carlsnaes, 1992, p. 256). Indeed, Luther's extensive training and status came because of the very institution that he sought to question. Without institutional support of some kind, there could be no Reformation. Without institutional opposition, there would have been nothing to reform. So the energy for rebellion accumulated and found at least a little momentum, centered on the example of Martin Luther—a German with political sponsorship who survived the efforts of the church to silence him. If it were not Luther, it would be somebody else. If it were not Saxony, it would be some other place. If it were not 1517, it would be some other time. So much for a cursory example of the "structural" version of what happened. As Dressler asserted, "Structural theory alone does not provide and is not capable of providing a complete explanation of action" (1989, p. 444).

On the other hand, from the atomistic perspective, individual social actors of different kinds each found something in the moment to make rebellion more likely than not. What are the risks? What are the rewards? The words of Martin Luther, as well as his example, influenced people, one at a time, to cast their

---

17. William Moul complains that from this point of view, a student of social change becomes vulnerable to the ecological fallacy in which the nature of individual human beings is inferred from broad-based participation in a group, such that we think that all rebels think a certain way and feel a certain way, just as all priests and bishops think and feel the same way or all Germans think and feel the same way (1973, p. 496). On the ecological fallacy generally, see Firebaugh (2001).

lot with the uprising. Each of them weighed the alternatives, considered their interests, then did what they thought was best. There were peasants and friars and clerks and publishers and soldiers and butchers and scholars, each in distinctive social positions, with their distinctive wants and needs. The rebellion was like a drama played by a variety of different, independent actors. Luther had the lead role. He was the star of the show. At various points along the way, he could have chosen otherwise. Therefore, the focus of the plot is the fact that he chose *intellectual* rebellion. Moreover, the Roman Catholic Church unwittingly populated the drama with clumsy villains.

Richard Vernon (1978) interpreted Georges Sorel to have made a similar distinction between (a) revolution as an enterprise by individual social actors working in collaboration to overthrow the government, on the one hand, and (b) what we might call spontaneous disorder, when a society shifts without anybody necessarily trying to make it happen. It just does. In the former version, we imagine sketchy characters in a smoky back room, bent over maps and plotting. We remember scenes from Dostoevsky or Solzhenitsyn, where young men practice the dark arts of insurrection. In the latter, people are going about their business, like nothing happened, yet the system is so far from equilibrium that it doesn't take much for the whole thing to rotate like an axle toward something new. These shifts, these phases of discontinuity, Sorel argued, are usually the more substantive historical events, to be understood only in retrospect. Acts of rebellion come and go. Men intent on mayhem think that their late night machinations will make a difference—an uprising, perhaps, or a bombing, or an assassination. Quoting Sorel, "The historians of the future are bound to discover that we labored under many illusions" (p. 30). What looks prospectively as high drama and noble sacrifice could very easily look in retrospect as criminal foolishness. Often, true revolution is (in a kind of mirror image of Hayek's spontaneous order) an unintended consequence of micro behaviors designed to accomplish other things (Vernon, 1978, p. 27). The whole incident takes on a life of its own.

William Moul (1973) insisted that in fairness, you have to conduct your research at both the micro and the macro level because the objective is to understand why and how things happen. If you begin with a premise that limits the alternative explanations, then you have jumped to a conclusion already. The structural explanation itself must *compete* with the individual explanation. Otherwise, you presuppose what you were supposedly trying to find out (1973, p. 496). The issue is less about the unit of analysis (part or whole) and more about the type of variable that explains certain behavior (1973, p. 495). That is to say that for Moul, the two approaches are not so much complementary as conflicting, but in a good way. We should want to understand their relative impact on historical events.

When doing this, however, we must get beyond the tension of a moment. Walter Carlsnaes (1992) advised against frameworks in which the agent and the structure are locked against one another at a crucial stage in time. Too often we imagine a lone figure standing before a claque of menacing authorities. Agents are continuously acting. Structures are ceaselessly exerting pressure. What we should want to know is less whether one or the other can be said to have "won." Instead, we should want to know how they shaped one another over time, back and forth, such that we arrive at our current situation. Prior decisions by individual social actors helped to transform the Roman Catholic Church into something different from what it had been in Bavaria at the time of Jan Hus. By the time Luther came along in Saxony, the church could not crush the uprising and burn the heretic. The context was different and the structure had changed. Leadership is the product of a long sequence of interactions. Carlsnaes called the process a social **morphogenesis** (1992, p. 260; see generally Archer, 2013). And the power of this additional element of the passage of time guides leaders to shape structures for the sake less of immediate victories, like a one-time effort such as meeting weekly quotas, than long-term liberty, to render the structure itself more responsive, more amenable to future efforts to realize our goals.[18] We must consider, as Fernand Braudel called it, the *longue durée*.

None of which allows us to say in any sense how leadership manifests at the macro level, at the structural level. We in leadership studies would seem to have carved out for ourselves the micro part of a both/and, which I now find unduly constrictive and inapt. I just do not believe we can afford to leave it there. Again, we should be interested in the interactions, the dynamics of change. Leadership studies should be less about the first floor micro or even the second floor macro. It should be about the staircase that connects them. Regrettably, we tend not to talk that way. In the next chapter, I intend to offer a way to forward.

---

18. I believe this is precisely the conclusion drawn by Herbert Simon in *Reason in Human Affairs* (1990), James Carse in *Finite and Infinite Games* (1986), and Richard Rorty in *Contingency, Irony, and Solidarity* (1989).

# 6

## BEING AT THE CENTER OF TENSIONS

*Las Meninas*[1]

### Introduction to the Chapter

During a speech on leadership at the United States Military Academy at West Point, William Deresiewicz (2010) concluded in this fashion:

> I started by noting that solitude and leadership would seem to be contradictory things. But it seems to me that solitude is the very essence of leadership. The position of the leader is ultimately an intensely solitary, even intensely lonely one. However many people you may consult, you are the one who has to make the hard decisions. And at such moments, all you really have is yourself.

Do we know this to be true? And if it is true, how do we as leadership educators instruct our students as to the meaning of this claim? For it seems that to instruct them well, we ought to expose our students to what practicing leadership feels like. In this instance, how might we prepare students for the experience of solitude or loneliness or social isolation?

The social sciences investigate leadership as to what is likely to be the case, yet the arts are uniquely equipped to give students an opportunity to discover what it must be like. Whether or not the adage that "it's lonely at the top" turns out to be true can be verified by means of surveys, interviews, memoirs, and so forth (see e.g. Wright, 2012; Pratt, 2001; Sala, 2001; Bell, Roloff, van Camp, & Karol, 1990); yet this chapter contends that students of leadership will more

---

1. The author acknowledges the gracious advice of Nicole Marie Garcia, Robert McManus, Anu Mitra, and Oliver Thomas.

readily appreciate the experience vicariously through the arts, in a different way of knowing.

Educational psychology explains how important the telling of stories can be for leaders and leader development (e.g. Gardner, 2006). Neuroscience tends to confirm this finding (e.g. Swart, Chisholm, & Brown, 2015). Stories enrich the imagination, giving the student as a prospective participant in leadership a wider and probably more complex array of narratives. This should be true whether those stories appear as history, fiction, theater, or film. The use of narrative generally in leadership education has been documented elsewhere (e.g. Warner, 2011; Denning, 2007; Harvey, 2004). These findings apply not only to written accounts, but also to artifacts such as those offered in the visual arts, including paintings (e.g. Jarvis & Gouthro, 2015; Ricke-Kiely & Matthias, 2013; Nissley, 2002; Jacobson, 1993).

As to the adage that leadership is potentially a lonely or isolating experience, perhaps educators might resort to examples from art to help students imagine it. For purposes of illustration, this chapter selects one masterwork for consideration: a painting titled *Las Meninas* by Diego Velázquez (1656). Interpretation of the painting will be based predominantly on the work of José Ortega y Gasset. Through his eyes, we can more readily see that this unusual portrait contributes to the vicarious experience from a particular point of view. In the end, it is itself a lesson to recognize that leaders do occupy a particular point of view, for that is the existential nexus from within which leadership emerges. All of the possible dichotomies we have been talking about in this book converge on the human individual, who lives in a world of both/and. For leaders, these dichotomies are more pronounced and urgent.

## Finding the Pin-point Impulse

Anthropologist Ruth Benedict (1934) wrote that many if not most cultural practices originate in some fairly mundane impulse—to eat, to woo—or in a common experience such as menstruation. She wrote, "They are pin-point potentialities, and the elaboration that takes place around them is dictated by many alien considerations" (1934/2005, p. 35). By means of culture, human beings surround the "pin-point" with a lot of seemingly unrelated, peripheral accoutrements. Mealtime becomes more than the consumption of nutrients. We watch television networks dedicated to food, we ask about the provenance of our foods before purchase, we stand thoughtfully contemplating a menu. We are told to drink only certain wines with fish. We prepare food using elaborate procedures and the latest gadget and perhaps pride ourselves on plating. We observe rituals before eating such as prayer. We have generated a slew of norms about how to conduct oneself during mealtime. "Ask to be excused from the table," we say. "Use the correct fork. No elbows on the table!"—so much that has nothing to do with physiological necessity, yet we come to associate all of it with eating.

So yes, men are lustful, Benedict wrote, but that alone does not explain the institution of marriage. Men can be pugnacious, but that alone does not explain war. There is a whole set of other things that contribute to any given cultural phenomenon.[2]

It is with this lesson in mind that I would argue that the version of leadership that I am putting forth in these pages is an attempt to set to one side all of the cultural baggage that we commonly associate with leadership and get back to the pin-point impulse, the relatively simple origin around which so much else accretes. Leadership is actually grounded in the mode of being with other people to improve the present. It is an expression of the vitality of life to surpass itself.

- You detect a boundary.
- You bump up against an *aporia*.
- Then, you seek ways to work past it.

Thus, we will have narrowed our scope to a pin-point, the act of stepping across boundaries in search of resolution. The impetus for leadership can be found here, in what Plato called the *metaxy* (Rhodes, 2013).

Everything else about leadership deserves to be parsed out—held up to the light and shaken. Why do we associate leadership with competition, for instance, with celebration, with glory, with men, with sexual success and monetary reward? Why have we in our culture combined leadership with the idea of distinction? None of these are necessary elements of leadership. They are contingent. In my own culture, they have grown up like kudzu over a long period of time. And I am not here to question whether the combinations are a good idea or a bad idea. But if I am charged with studying leadership, then at some point I ought to differentiate leadership from everything else that comes with it culturally. Thus, rather than complicating leadership in these pages, I am actually trying to simplify it. The problem, of course, is that to do so I must gain some distance from the culture wherein I write and teach.

As a question of methodology, Benedict went on to suggest that maybe instead of studying the pin-point impulse out of which cultural practices arise, as I have done here, we might flip things around, beginning with the institution as an entirety. Maybe the impulse—whatever it is—does not explain the institution so much as the institution explains the impulse (1934/2005, pp. 232, 236, 243). The institution exists. Describe the institution. Out of that

---

2. Niklas Luhmann (2008/2010) made a similar argument from within sociology regarding, sex, love, and marriage as distinct pin-points. Complicating the study of culture is the fact that frequently the participants hide behind these accretions in order to deny the "pin-point impulse" around which they formed (see Benedict, 1934/2005, p. 125). A taboo might prevent us from being honest about what is really going on.

institution, seek the impulses (plural) that participate in it. A fancy dinner might feed the body, yes, but it also exhibits wealth, for example, or cements friendship, or gives lovers a chance to become acquainted. A lot more is going on than the gratification of a single desire. The same could be said about the institution we call leadership. I have tried to isolate the pin-point impulse while ignoring the cluster of other impulses that also manifest by means of this institution—impulses such as pride, greed, aggression, sexual desire, paranoia, and so forth. In leadership, a lot of stuff is going on.

Stripped of these other impulses, my version of leadership probably seems rather thin. The problem is that these accretions, as we are calling them, vary across cultures. In one culture, the leader is he who sacrifices the most (potlatch), whereas in another culture it is he who emerges from out of trances, while in yet another culture he might be the one who by stealth and treachery most cunningly robs and steals from his neighbors. Anthropologists such as Benedict can multiply these examples. And that is why I choose not to focus here on the particular accretions in Western culture and instead focus on the pin-point impulse, thin though it might be, as the commonality in every culture, the constant, the recurring element. I do not think that Benedict would disapprove. She wrote, "As we become increasingly culture-conscious, we shall be able to isolate the tiny core that is generic in a situation and the vast accretions that are local and cultural and man-made" (1934/2005, p. 245).

In order to do this, I have chosen a representation of a single point in time, a moment that captures the experience of being at that nexus, where dichotomies converge and are felt and become somebody's responsibility. In a world of either/or, each of us occupies the in-between, for that is the very definition of *metaxy*.

## The Painting *Las Meninas*

The enormous canvas by Diego Velázquez (1656)—previously known as *La Familia de Felipe IV*—presently hangs in the Museo del Prado in Madrid. It has been the object of considerable analysis—not only an object of investigation in the visual arts generally as a painting, but also in history broadly understood, philosophy, and optics. Gertje Utley catalogues many of the interpretations derived from this one work:

> Although for some Velázquez's *Las Meninas* served no greater purpose than the apples did for Cezanne, others looked to the painting as a model of artistic excellence, as a national cultural icon, as an artistic ready-made imbued with culturally accessible referents, as a stage for political comment, or as a template for philosophical reflections on creation and perception.
>
> *(2003, p. 197)*

This *tableau-vivant* includes a self-portrait of the artist pausing briefly while executing a painting in the royal household. Vividly, the light streaming from the right-hand side of the room illuminates a little blond girl dressed elaborately and standing at the center of a small gathering. This compelling creature is the princess Margarita. Her impassive face lies at the center of two lines crisscrossing at diagonals (Foucault, 1966/1994, p. 12). One line, sweeping from the upper left, i.e. from the face of the painter, down through the girl toward a small boy or dwarf and a sleepy dog at the bottom right; the other line, sloping from the heads of two darkened adults in the upper right, again through the girl's face, downward to the base of an enormous canvas dominating the far left side. The girl appears to be the responsibility of two young ladies-in-waiting who bend toward her. But something about the composition defies a simple description of her as the focal point of the painting. She is not (see Luxenberg, 2003, p. 31).

Above her head, in the back of the room, are two independent sources of light on an otherwise darkened wall. Just above the girl's left shoulder one can see a chamberlain in a doorway, coming or going, the light from another room outlining his pose. His name was José Nieto Velázquez (no relation). Above her right shoulder is a framed image of an indistinct couple, presumably a married couple. Why it is illuminated is hard to tell from such a distance, until one realizes that it is a mirror. The couple in the mirror is illuminated because they stand on this side of the room, on what is the near side of the room, where the viewer is standing, so that it appears to reflect back two people who do not appear in the foreground, yet must be there somewhere, where the light is plainly streaming in. Who are these people? Why do they not appear in the foreground?

The couple in the distant mirror is the king and queen of Spain, Philip IV and María Ana. They are the parents of the illuminated little girl. They stand where you the viewer are standing. It is from their vantage point in the tableau that you look into the room. The painter Velázquez is looking at you. Thus, the painting is not intended to portray the scene from his point of view, from the point of view of Velázquez. The child is looking at you. Others in the room appear to be gazing at you as well, and why not if indeed you are the sovereign? The room tends to extend back into darkness, making the little girl the focus of your attention, for—whatever else you are—you are her parents. It would be natural that she should be the object of *your* attention. But again, she does not stand at the exact center of the scene. She is not the focus of the painter's attention, either.

The chamberlain in the back is responsible for managing the daily schedule of the royal couple. At the time, he exercised a kind of power enjoyed by clerks and functionaries who help a sovereign get things done, so that he represents the continuing responsibilities of the office. He might be reminding the king and queen of some appointment. The light behind him serves as a summons to another world, another stage, where the sovereign must govern. The mirror, on the other hand, is illuminated, but the faces of the royal couple are too far away, too indistinct for identification. It was only by inference that one realizes who they are.

Of significance is the fact that the painter himself is taller and positioned higher than anyone else in the room. He is supposedly seen to possess a cherished key of the royal chamber (Stratton-Pruitt, 2003, p. 1, quoting da Costa, 1696). Even a shard of light on his sleeve points like an arrow toward his face. If as you lift your gaze up from the girl, you scan across items competing for your attention, and the highest is Velasquez—not the best illuminated figure, mind you, but tall. Yet it is the backside of the canvas to the left on which he is about to paint that dwarfs the gathering. It is enormous and dark. Nothing of the image on the front of it can be seen. The canvas looms over everybody, without the benefit of direct illumination. In some ways, it is the most significant object in the room, almost a *repoussoir* figure, regardless of whether you are not immediately drawn to notice it. The back of the canvas is more of a presence that one feels. As Estrella de Diego has written, "The right question would be then what the canvas represents, and not what is represented on the canvas" (2003, p. 162).

One can derive at least two lessons about leadership from this painting. For one thing, it depicts a constellation of powers in the royal household, in which the painter gives himself a rare status as an intimate of the court, in a position to assess and record what he witnesses on that giant canvas. The suspicion that in this painting he was overstepping his bounds is well-documented (see e.g. Brooke, 2003, p. 68; Stratton-Pruitt, 2003, pp. 128f, 139, 143, n. 9; Alpers, 1983, p. 33; contra Ortega, 1972, pp. 84–106). For present purposes, however, the second lesson to derive involves the peculiar fact that the viewer of the painting occupies the same position as the sovereign. The viewer gets to experience part of what it must be like to serve in that leadership capacity. As Alisa Luxenberg put it, the "ordinary viewer [gets to] step into the royal shoes" (2003, p. 13). She calls it a "you are there" experience (2003, p. 14). The image will "literally draw in the viewer in such a way that his position seems privileged" (2003, p. 19; cf. Stratton-Pruitt, 2003, p. 135).

José Ortega y Gasset (1975), writing on phenomenology and art, noted that it is often the case that the most important feature of a painting is that which is *not* depicted. What you do notice, if you really look, is the empty space or outline for what is missing, like a puzzle piece that has not yet been placed (1975, p. 53). With regard to *Las Meninas*, that empty space, the missing puzzle piece, is the subject of the painting, i.e. the sovereign. And the space where it is missing is where you are presently standing, not somewhere within the frame of the painting. That absence says something.

Ortega devoted the final chapter of that book—originally published in 1946—to urging viewers to consider the point of view of the artist. In this case, of course, it was Velázquez. Ortega argued that to understand a painting, such as *Las Meninas,* one really ought to come to some kind of understanding of the man who painted it and of his environs. What was the context? What was going on in his life at the time? When Ortega wrote a preface to the book for his German readership, he offered a brief autobiographical account of his own intellectual life, helping the reader see things from *his* point of view as a philosopher, but then he switched things all around and said, in effect, that in order to understand an artist one must understand his audience, his viewer. So according to Ortega, in effect, you and I are to move from (a) the painting, such as *Las Meninas;* to (b) the artist, such as Diego Velázquez; to (c) the viewer, which in this case is the sovereign and which is you. The strange thing is that Ortega also wrote of Velazquez that he is "the painter least concerned with the spectator" (1972, p. 95).

The painting is therefore about two things, neither of which appears in the painting (Searle, 1980, p. 480). One is the sovereign and one is the canvas with its back to us. Ortega noted that Velázquez had done this at least once before, earlier in his career, when a painting titled *Christ in the House of Martha and Mary* depicts none of those three persons (1972, p. 102). To the extent sovereign and canvas are represented in the painting at all, the image of the sovereign is distant and blurry, whereas the canvas shows us only its backside. How then can a painting which represents two things not in fact represent them to us, but leave it for us to infer? They are, in the words of Ortega, compresent—like the far side of an orange. They are present without being immediately perceived. Which means that we are not meant to view the painting from the point of view of the artist. His point of view lies elsewhere. The mirror firmly fixes our point of view as the sovereign and not some second artist in the room painting Velázquez painting. For the philosopher John Searle (1980), this presents us with a double paradox. Nevertheless, as a viewer the paradox is not insuperable, because it certainly appears to be a scene that the sovereign would have experienced as he stood there, playing at least these three roles: model for a portrait, parent, and leader.

## Seeing Behind the Image, in a Retrocession

In his history of Western painting, José Ortega y Gasset traced a line from (a) an emphasis on the object itself, no matter how fanciful or idealized, to (b) an emphasis on the eye of the painter and his experiencing of the world, back further into (c) the mind of the painter, where the artist forms an image based in part on interior thoughts and memories and psychological constructs, such as archetypes and symbols (1972, pp. 24–32). Ortega used the simple analogy of looking through a window onto a garden (1972, p. 68). You can focus on the garden, or you can focus on the window pane, but not both at the same time. The high Renaissance had presented viewers with the following two layers: the object being portrayed on the canvas and its idealized (often religious) significance, its meaning. The former is a "window" onto the latter—an image we referred to earlier as an icon. Velázquez comes along presumably on behalf of realism to show us the thing itself—the horse or the soldier or the room— without trying to convey anything more. The surface that you see has no depth. Many critics accept this interpretation of his work, as though nothing lies beyond the windowpane. They admire the craftsmanship of the window and fail to recognize the beauty of the distant mountains beyond.

But then Ortega speaks against this interpretation, and he specifically cites *Las Meninas* as evidence. The objects arrayed in the room are both more and less than an exact image of a moment in time, somewhat like a photograph in its verisimilitude. To be sure, the painting does not necessarily point elsewhere, to some distant mythic or holy dimension, as it would have in the Renaissance; it does not somehow imply transcendence. But then it *does* point somewhere other than the artist's point of view. That is to say that it is not merely a representation of what the artist would have seen, either. That would be impossible, inasmuch as the artist is one of the objects. We are unable to see things from his point of view. As Ortega put it, "Velazquez' technique is a continuous progress in a negative skill: that of dispensing with more and more" (1972, p. 99). Which leaves us in a peculiar place. The painter supposedly "least concerned with the spectator" gives us an image from the spectator's point of view, and it is a view shared by the spectator with the sovereign, the leader, which is why one can say that the experience for us is vicarious.

So, to what extent does the painting suggest a retrocession into one's mind, behind the eyeballs to some interior dimension? Ortega explored this dynamic in some detail in his *Meditations on Quixote*, where he wrote about considerations of surface and depth, as we had reason to mention previously. One does not perceive directly what is deep, just as you cannot see the forest for the trees, yet you do have the capacity to conceive it. He wrote, if you recall, "Everything has within it an indication of its possible plentitude" (1914/1961, p. 32). It is impossible to take in at a glance the entirety of a thing. But to see beyond it, to extract the lesson or the significance of a thing, one must also see it. We must work with both the surface *and* the depth. The surface implies depth, just as *Las Meninas* implies the sovereign, and also implies the unfinished painting on the outsized canvas to the left, and likewise implies the larger world for leadership beyond the little door at the back of the room. "Impressions form a superficial tapestry from which ideal paths seem to lead us toward a deeper reality" (1914/1961, p. 74). One might say that the "presence" presupposes the "essence," but you cannot have the one without the other.

Ortega then explained the process in this way. In the first moment, one focuses on the object at the center, as it presents itself. In *Las Meninas*, this would probably be the illuminated *infanta*. Next, one scans the vicinity, looking around the object at its place within its context, how it is related to other things, such as the painter and the dog and the mirror. In doing so, you make the other objects the focus of your attention, one at a time, as you place the original object into the periphery, even if momentarily. Here is a practical application of Meeks' SFI, as I explained it previously. Then, your mind conjectures about what is compresent, for it is art's fate and even to some extent its mission to omit something of significance, inasmuch as the constellation · of objects arrayed before you belong to a comprehending reality (1914/1961, p. 88f). And so you infer the rest. Which is to say that a structure, such as a painting, is more than an assembly of parts, an aggregation of this and that and some other thing; it is also the relationships among them (1914/1961, p. 90). And *Las Meninas* portrays a fairly complex configuration of relationships.

Accordingly, the vacancy in the painting that you or I as the spectator presently occupy indicates (without expressly showing) the leader's place in the tangle of relationships within which he lives and upon which he operates as sovereign. We reach that vantage point by an act of imagination. And it makes sense to us only because we can relate to the experience.

## Genuine Solitude

The sovereign is not literally present on the canvas. The sovereign occupies a point outside of the tableau, so there is already a sense of separation from the world being depicted.

The sovereign's attention (like yours) is drawn in different directions—to the process of being painted, to be sure, but also to the other characters in the room, to the doorway in the back, to the mysterious mirror, but most imminently to the child, for how could a parent not dote on his or her child? And yet the child is all dressed up in a complicated costume, and on her face she has a look of boredom or displeasure. She is cosseted, wrapped in her wardrobe and surrounded by ladies-in-waiting. One can feel a kind of remoteness even from her.

The foreground is well lit, but then not too far back the enormous room falls into shadow. A considerable space opens out beyond the *infanta*, where nothing is completely visible. It is a void. At the back, the paintings already hanging on the wall are obscure—too far away and frankly too high up from the floor to appreciate. The image in the distant mirror is indistinct and easy to overlook, even though it is you. That is to say, you as sovereign are far away. And the open door draws your attention elsewhere, to a place you cannot presently see.

The painting also connotes the weight of expectation. So many people are looking to you: the painter, of course, who might make anybody self-conscious, but also the daughter, who might wish you could liberate her, and then the retinue, not to mention the chamberlain caught trying to do his job keeping you on schedule. About the only figures oblivious to your presence are the dog and the dwarf kicking him. And again, the looming canvas serves as a kind of expectation that you are being preserved for posterity. The expectations on you as a leader are not bound to the moment of being painted. They will continue. And you have to be mindful of this.

Not to make too much of this, but the daughter is an heir, whose life will extend your influence as a parent. In her case, the legacy will include the political implications of her eventual marriage, which will not be trivial. So there is not only the implication of influence through space (beyond these walls) but also through time. Velazquez could not know this then, but the little girl would become Holy Roman Empress, German Queen, Archduchess consort of Austria, Queen Consort of Hungary and Bohemia, and an elder full-sister of Charles II, the last of the Spanish Habsburgs. Nevertheless, in this very moment and at this very time, all of that responsibility, though compresent for a sovereign, is also in one sense far away, one might say "occluded" without being ignored.

Michel Foucault mentioned this dimension of time when he observed that the painter is the one who must transform a changing reality into a fixed image. In the flux of circumstance, he must appraise the scene and settle on an unmoving representation (1994, p. 5). Yet Velázquez also wishes to represent the flux by means of this fixed representation; in other words, he is to capture not only that which is in motion but also the motion itself. He does this in part by representing a tension, inasmuch as tension is not a stillness or a lack of turbulence; rather, a tension is the point at which competing forces grapple, holding each other in a strained equipoise. The present would not exist in its current form if these competing forces had not created it. And so the painter places the spectator at the point where you can experience the tension.

One of the tensions implicit in the painting is the tension between the reality to be depicted (the sovereign) and the portrait—a tension Velázquez holds in his gazing. Another tension is between the unseen window on the right through which the scene is brought to light in a kind of beneficent flow, as opposed to the opaque surface of canvas on the left, where everything must be brought to a standstill (Foucault, 1994, p. 6). The lighting unites everybody in the scene, whereas the painting must separate the subject from everything else. It is the painter, as part of the unified scene, who must cut out most of it, in order to isolate the one thing he is there to portray, the sovereign—despite the irony that in fact Velázquez has depicted it all *except* that which he is there to portray (Foucault, 1994, p. 10).

Back of these tensions, however, is a more troubling tension between what can be seen and what can be said (Foucault, 1994, p. 9f), for the one and the other are in one sense correlative (that is King Philip we see in the mirror and that is Margarita we see in the foreground), yet image and speech belong to entirely different ways of knowing. That in the mirror is not precisely Philip, any more than here before us is precisely Margarita. She is a two-dimensional image intended to represent her, and the mirror image of Philip is intended to *represent a representation* of him. We quickly reach a point at which our language fails us. Or this: in the hazy mirror is the sovereign, by all indications the most important figures in the room, yet the image of the royal couple is staid and unreal, especially when contrasted with the solid and dynamic figure of the subordinate on the stair, who seems more real (Foucault, 1994, p. 10f).

The sense of expectation and responsibility reveals another tension. As Svetlana Alpers pointed out, "At court, as in a picture, order is produced by acts of representation" (1983, p. 39). The representation of the sovereign to the assembly imposes a kind of order onto the room. At the same time, however, the painting shows us some limitations of leadership. Corresponding to what one must do as leader, as the object of so much attention, then, the painting suggests many of the things one *cannot* do. As the subject to be painted, of course, you cannot really move. Not much, or you disturb the painter's reverie. You cannot intervene directly to stop the dwarf from kicking your dog. You cannot plop yourself onto the floor to play with the princess yourself—nor are you needed, apparently. You cannot leave with the chamberlain, wherever it is he is going, but you cannot completely ignore him either. And the most obvious thing should not go unsaid, you cannot focus on yourself. It is not permitted. Everything is arranged around you. You have a prominent place to occupy, and it requires a considerable lack of self-regard.

In this sense, a point of view serves as a vertex, from which two or more geometric rays extend. These rays must be held together somehow: top and bottom, left and right, light and dark, near and far, now and later, etc. But since the person occupying that point of view serves as the vertex, he (or she) cannot be depicted—or at least cannot be depicted by the person occupying the vertex, inasmuch as Velázquez successfully depicts himself at a vertex that we cannot share. In another irony, though, the subject of the painting—that is, the sovereign—does share the vertex with you, the spectator, for it was necessary to do so if vicarious learning is to take place. You and I step into the vertex, into the tensions that constitute leadership. And one of the most perplexing vertices in leadership is the point from which multiple, competing roles extend—as model, parent, and ruler.

Thus, to others, you are a representation. You are an object to be painted, for example, but then you are also a parent, you are the factotum's boss, you are an image on the unseen canvas, you are a figure in the mirror. You are a cluster of different, in some cases competing, representations in the eyes of other people. You are present in the painting only to the extent that you are this cluster, held by different persons with different agendas and different perspectives. One might say that you are a disembodied composite of everybody else's representation of you. But then, by the same token they are forever nothing more than representations to you—unless, that is, you exercise your critical powers to interpret what you see. Which brings me to my final point.

## The Lesson Within the Lesson

Much as the painting can be used to illustrate an experience of solitude known to leaders, the exegesis of it is also a lesson for prospective leaders. That lesson brings with it a kind of critical distance. One cannot accept the image superficially. One cannot say simply it is a pretty picture or a vivid example of Spanish realism. One must examine it and think about it. One must enter in to participate in the painting, closing a distance, while at the same time staying aloof, pondering its meaning. This implies another kind of solitude—the necessity of holding the world at arm's length, so you can study it and seek out its hidden meaning and its possibilities.

For a leader cannot accept the world as it presents itself. (The image is not an idol.) A leader must read into things and piece many parts together, minding the relationships that will extend beyond what you presently know. To be sure, a leader cannot ignore what presents itself and live in a fantasy constructed in his or her imagination, detached from paramount reality; yet the leader must employ a power of critique, asking not only what is really going on but also what might need to change. The compresent, in other words, should include that which does not yet exist, though one day might. For a leader must see around corners, no longer seduced as so many of us are by what is set before us. As Ortega put it:

> There are men who decide not to be satisfied with reality. Such men aim at altering the course of things; they refuse to repeat the gestures that custom, tradition, or biological instincts force them to make. . . . [For such a person] his life is a perpetual resistance to what is habitual and customary. Each movement that he makes has first had to overcome custom and invent a new kind of gesture.
>
> *(1914/1961, p. 149)*

In fact, this was one of Niccolò Machiavelli's most profound insights, which is that non-leaders are too caught up in the surface of things—in the appearances and simulacra of ordinary sensation—whereas a leader must extricate himself mentally, seeing past the surface as a field of potential illusion, and hold himself apart. He must create a space from which to assess his world. With that practice, however, he removes himself from a level of participation or immersion the rest of us enjoy, in merriment and pleasure, which it is his burden to preserve for the rest of us, whether we recognize it or not.

To this extent, I would argue, the leader abides in a kind of solitude, not removed from the world and from other people, as though somewhere far away, but in its midst, from a singular vantage point that cannot be delegated to anyone else.

## The Individual Still Matters

Please do not take the wrong message from what I have been trying to say in this chapter. Yes, the image of the lone leader standing athwart history, yelling "Stop!"—that's unduly limiting and more of a cartoon. A nuanced understanding of leadership requires reaching beyond the one we call the leader to consider the impact of all that is not the leader, for leaders operate within a vast, complex, and unpredictable context filled with rebels and rivals and cops and confessors, cultural norms, institutional practices, and legal expectations. Leaders function in relationship with all of that. It also requires reaching beyond the moment—and even beyond the discrete episode—toward the *longue durée*. The episode we prefer to study has a long and revealing history. Finally, we should investigate what it might mean to speak of leadership as an undertaking, a dynamic activity in which social actors of many types participate.

In all of this, however, the individual human being matters and matters a great deal. Individuals take risks. They establish critical distance from reality, presuming to judge the present. They imagine possible futures. For all of the noise in spontaneous order, the clamor of opinion in daily life, the give-and-take of dialogue—ultimately, at some point the individual person must venture away from external influences and instead venture forward into one's own solitude . . . to ponder, to reflect, to dream. Otherwise, your ideas are not your own. You are an extension of somebody else's design, a subordinate at best. The order celebrated in these pages requires engagement, each person bringing his or her perspective. And if the opportunity arises to lead, the impetus has to come from somewhere internal. The journey out of the clutches of convention toward the unfamiliar, to the unmapped—that's a lonely quest. And upon one's return, as Plato pointed out, you will be subject to a variety of forces arrayed to dismiss you, abuse you, and maybe even destroy you. Maybe.

None of that happens unless the hero first goes away. This "going away" can be literal, or it can be figurative. One can mentally step outside of one's circumstances in order to garner a fresh perspective. This entire book has been dedicated to that rhythm of leaving, of differentiating oneself, of undertaking the hard quest alone, and then returning, of integrating oneself, of bestowing a boon on others. There is a loneliness inherent in this rhythm, a courage to step away on one's own, driven by an existential imperative and a courage to come back as a changed man or woman presuming to upset the order everyone has adapted to. *Las Meninas* depicts that rhythm as a tension, a being in-between, caught in that metaxy where you cannot make an either/or decision and be done with it. You must sustain the tension in service of others, holding these tensions loosely. You must do so in your mind, in your relationships, in your organization, and frankly in the world at large. Leadership as a mode is crossing those apparent boundaries, back and forth, with a sovereign independence.

Theories of synchrony and morphogenesis, turbulence and hierarchy all must contend with the paradox of collective phenomena in which individuals participate uniquely. As conceptualizations, they account for the old familiar tension between freedom and order, holding at arm's length the twin hazards of complete withdrawal and complete absorption, anarchy and totalitarianism, isolation and groupthink, dissipation and rigidity. But to hold the tension is not to identify a fixed point and cling to it stubbornly, refusing to go one way or the other. The *metaxy* is not a literal place. Rather, it is to operate within the tension, moving fluidly within a tolerable range, making progress like Daedalus toward the far shore. This is the experience that Velasquez would have had trouble depicting as oil on canvas: to be many things to many people, to move in and out of situations that call for different things, without trying to be a chameleon. You alone preserve that continuity that constitutes your identity. And the work required to establish that character is a lonely business.

One could argue that by refusing to break their pose and accommodate their daughter, the king and queen in *Las Meninas* are teaching her—again, vicariously—the solemn necessity of being self-possessed, holding themselves amid the fuss and competing claims on their powers with dignity, being sovereign in a deeper sense. They seem to be saying to her: "No, we will not leave with the chamberlain. No, we will not sweep you up in our arms. No, we will not intervene to stop the dwarf from kicking the dog. We could do any of those things. But leadership does not mean doing whatever you want." Just as a *polis* must find its identity, so also must the individual—finding an order that coheres. But it coheres in part within a fluid context. That's the trick. A pliable coherence, sensitive to the tugs of desire and duty, while at the same time bringing forth a new thing.

By the end of this book, I will have described what I call **aikido politics**, wherein the leader represents the calm center, the fulcrum around which life spins and whirls, where the tensions of the universe converge and are held loosely. In order to occupy this space without whirling apart, however, one must be conscious of the play of forces—and not only be conscious, but feel them deeply, for leadership is at its root an *experience* within those tensions.

## The Existentialism of Ortega

The painting that we have been discussing conveys a lesson that was to be adopted and developed as a school of philosophy known as existentialism. Maybe it would be too generous to call it a school. It is at the very least a posture (as opposed to a pose, which connotes being false). As we have seen, Ortega wrote on the painting described in this chapter and on art in general, but he was also an existentialist philosopher. I believe this is no coincidence.[3]

---

3. For a more thorough analysis of the extent to which Ortega was indeed an existentialist, see Villaseñor (1949). Perhaps not surprisingly, a number of the scholars cited in these pages were

Ortega insisted that ultimately each of us is alone. Despite all of our under-standable desires for relationships and community (e.g. 1958, p. 76f), we also possess a drive to withdraw, to ponder things for ourselves. We may have been raised to think all sorts of things. We absorbed conventional instruction and found practices to fit the prevailing systems. We listened and watched and negotiated a way of being in the world. He wrote that "ordinarily we live installed, too safely installed, within the security of our habitual, inherited, topical ideas" (Ortega, 1958, p. 78). Yet at some point, if we are fortunate, we discover that these are all hand-me-down truths, somebody else's creed, inau-thentic to our lived experience. As he wrote:

> If I allow things around me or the opinions of others to influence me, I cease to be myself and I suffer otherness, alteration, confusion. The man in a state of otherness, outside himself, has lost his own genuine character and lives a false life.
>
> *(1958, p. 91)*

Nobody else can live my life. Only I can. And that life is a drama, an unfolding narrative that hasn't been written yet. We are en route, incomplete, pilgrims-on-the-way. Nobody can walk the path of another person without being false. So each of us must choose—literally, moment by moment—whom to become. And when we discover that the solutions to life's predicaments that we inherited are inadequate, we fall back into a primal condition of bewilder-ment (see 1958, p. 26). Now, on a small scale, these dips into liminality can be annoying and a little wearying, as we struggle to make up our own mind about the best way to go forward. As Ortega observed, we are constantly adjusting (1958, p. 37f). Periodically, however, the experience is so deep, so profound, that it constitutes a crisis.

On such occasions, we often retreat behind society, insisting on things we no longer believe, largely because we have no idea what is supposed to take its place (1958, p. 92). Or worse, we suspect that we do know and we don't like it. In either case, we dread the unsettled condition. Better to persist in a false mode. And so we trade our God-given prerogatives for sheltered anxiety.

Velasquez conveys the entangled existence of the royal couple. They live in luxury, thriving on power, surrounded by sycophants and precious works of art. They have a beautiful daughter. Yet precisely because they occupy this tension, the place of radical isolation, they are more alone that most. They are not even in their own portrait, except as fuzzy images on the far wall. They are everywhere constrained and tugged. And it is this reality that should haunt the

---

existentialists of one stripe or another, e.g. Buber, Nietzsche, Jaspers, and Heidegger. For the sake of seeing both sides, let me note that Norberto Bobbio wrote one of the more compelling cri-tiques of existentialism in 1944, published in translation four years later.

viewer. Often, the person in the room with the least amount of discretion is the leader (Alvesson, 2019, pp. 32, 36). I am not suggesting that a leader somehow leads the least authentic life, although there is certainly that risk. I would argue that for some, that life is precisely the most authentic one could live. Some are called to plant their feet squarely in the midst of the maelstrom and hold their place. We often appreciate that in a leader. We often seek that in a leader.

Ortega noticed that an individual's existential crisis may be frightful and dramatic, yet the severity of the crisis is so much worse when entire generations participate in rolling on an axis away from established ways of doing things. If we all feel lost and desperate for authenticity, then truly we inhabit a turn of historical significance. And it was just this sort of axial change that Martin Luther suffered in his person. He was to contemplate the meaning of the times. Where others cried alarm, he learned to bellow with joy. A crisis is an opportunity. You just have to find it. And in such epochs, sometimes the person least equipped to lead is the one trying desperately to hold it all together. And so we return obliquely to Isaiah Berlin's dichotomy between the idealist who longs to break free and the realist who picks through the confusion slowly (perhaps too slowly?) with bricolage. Which is the "mode" one should adopt?

What Ortega was arguing for is contained in one of the chapter headings in *Man and Crisis* (1958): "Truth as Man in Harmony With Himself" (ch. 7). Ortega was less concerned about the content of that outcome than he was about its congruence (1958, p. 115). For a life should fit like well-tailored clothes. Ortega was especially exercised by the fact that at some point the full weight of culture—its elaborate, abstruse, nitpicky, convoluted structure—would become unwieldy. Like trying to swim in armor, one has to shed what no longer serves a purpose. In little things, you can make amendments. But in big things, you have to start all over again from scratch. And that's overwhelming.

It is interesting to mention that Ortega wrote extensively in this book of the idea of a generation. Generations come and go, making their changes, shifting the culture to suit them. Every once in a while, however, a generation works together to transform society completely. Ortega was not saying that one person, acting alone, will remake the world. He wrote of a generation, in dialogue, collaborating across the disciplines, in all walks of life, fashioning together the next ethos. Like Lincoln, he knew that if the people aren't vigilant, a strongman, a man of action, will step into the confusion promising some kind of answer.[4] (For Ortega, that strongman was Generalissimo Francisco Franco, who ruled Spain from 1939 to 1975.) Crisis becomes an opportunity for him and his cronies, while the chance to remake the world will have devolved. And for that reason, sometimes in leadership studies we have to study the strongman, because sometimes that's who leads.

---

4. Back in 1904, Lewis Terman wrote, "Leadership in certain individuals implies a want of self-reliance in the others" (p. 421).

Let me be clear. Ortega was not *in favor of* revolution, that axial movement toward a different way of doing things. He was not defending any generation in its headlong destruction of the prevailing order. It happens, to be sure, and a sober scientist must acknowledge that fact and try to understand it, but revolution exacts a considerable price. Ortega ultimately favored at least a semblance of continuity, a continual process of reform (see Ortega, 1940/1946), rather than putting off the necessity of change until it becomes unbearable and everything bursts. He wrote:

> Revolutions, so incontinent in their hypocritically generous haste to proclaim the rights of man, have always violated, trampled on, and broken man's most fundamental right, so fundamental that it may stand as the definition of his being: the right to continuity.
>
> *(1961, p. 80)*

So in a sense, Ortega was also posing two types of leadership: the strongman and the revolutionary. Both emerge under certain conditions. They are alternative ways of dealing with crisis. And in my opinion the empirical study of leadership must recognize both and not toss them aside as something other than what they are. Nevertheless, the ethic of existentialism, in which the goal as Ortega sees it is coherence or harmony, suggests where his sympathies lay: in a patient, deliberate process of becoming, from within the turbulence of the metaxy.

# 7

# LEADERSHIP AS A MODE OF PARTICIPATION IN HISTORY

## A Peregrinal Image

### Introduction to the Chapter

Karl Jaspers advised scientists to examine not only the whole and the parts of whatever they are studying, such as the fish and its innards, but also the relationships that constitute that whole. We must detect the patterns that formed, sustain, and alter that order. This will be especially difficult for studying the spontaneous order we know as society, because it is simply too complex. As Renan observed, some events such as revolutions are far more chaotic than others. Yet even in relative calm, much of it is not even known to participants. After words of caution against presuming to have mastered all of the details for any given social order, this does not mean that we cannot learn something of value. Our hopes for complete powers of prediction may have been dashed by Hayek and a lifetime of rueful experience; yet we should be able to arrive at broad principles and patterns.

This chapter addresses how we might talk about the way that people participate in the social order. What, in effect, are their modes of participating? For it stands to reason that leadership must be one of those "modes of participation." If it is not, then there is very little for us in leadership studies to talk about.

Certainly at the beginning of leadership studies, we relied on what philosophers refer to as an entitative ontology, the being of separate things—in this case, leaders. We identified them, described them, put them into categories like sorting loose buttons in grandma's tin, and studied their traits and behaviors, but always as though the object of our study was the leader. We do tend to study "entities." Today, most scholars recognize that we have had to move beyond the "leader-centric" approach. In many instances, though, we are still stuck in the entitative ontology. That is, we look not only at leaders (as distinct entities) but also at followers, groups, organizations, cultures as things, as units of analysis, participants or players in leadership (again, the agent-structure problem). Or levels. Even the relationship between the leader and followers can be regarded entitatively. We study static objects and their relationships. We rarely question this ontology at its root. Maybe we should complement our entitative ontology with something else, something more representative of the dynamic structure of reality.

The following section relies primarily on a series of lectures given by Martin Heidegger who was explicating a book written by Aristotle. Even though Aristotle was writing thousands of years ago, it offers what I consider a fresh ontology—an ontology that comports with the necessity of situating leadership into the flow of history. Later in this chapter, therefore, I would like to say a few words about history as the ur-context.

## Leadership as a Mode of Participation

In leadership studies, we emphasize the agency of individual social actors such as Martin Luther. We have bent ourselves to the project of categorizing leaders and their practices into types.

According to a lecture series from 1931 by Martin Heidegger (1981/1995), we might say that "to categorize" is to have gathered and unified in such a way as to display or make manifest as a being—that is, we mentally assemble an array of qualities or sensations into a whole and give it a name. We might point and say, "That is a lamp," as a way of differentiating the lamp from, say, a toaster or a bird. In that way, we use our literal powers of logic to bind together and make accessible (1981/1995, p. 3). Logic enables us to say what something is, as opposed to some other entity. Logic makes possible the process of assigning symbols (such as words or names) to units of experience, which then has the utility of being kept in the memory or communicated to others. This is what is meant as an **entitative ontology**. To categorize therefore is to utter the symbol and expect it to mean something distinct from other things. One would expect to be able to do this for leadership, differentiating leadership from other things, yet we seem frustrated trying to do so with precision (see generally Rost, 1993). Why is that?

Here is one reason. Dian-Marie Hosking (1995) sought to differentiate an entitative ontology with a relational one, to the effect that "things" exist only in relationship with something else, so that the object of our studies is the relationship and not the entities in some kind of isolation.[1] My first book took this approach (2007a). Technically, in my opinion, this is still "entitative" in that we

---

1. Freise (2018) lucidly explains that speaking of objects and speaking of relationships are two different paradigms—complementary, yet different (pp. xviii, xxvii). He credits Kant with struggling away from what he calls a substantialist ontology (p. xiv). Surprisingly, the natural sciences have made this transition, whereas the humanities seem to have moved the other direction, away from their birthright of studying relationships (p. xvi).

were simply expanding the scope of what is an entity. It would be the case that the "entity" could be a group, team, organization, nation-state, or species. It is still based on a static model of reality. What I am doing here next, however, is different. John Caputo (1986), quoting the German mystic Meister Eckhart, refers to this alternate ontology quaintly as "peregrinal," having to do with a pilgrimage, being in transit, moving and not stationary, en route, literally coming through the field (p. 199).[2] We want to speak less of *things* and more of *actions*. Or as Caputo put it: we speak of that which is underway.[3]

> A new logic . . . will succeed where ancient metaphysics was shipwrecked: it will be a logic of action and movement, not merely a logic of a changeless structure, of transtemporality.
>
> *(Patočka, 1998, p. 15)*

Leadership studies expands our vision in two directions: laterally, to show how the object of our investigations is connected to its environment; and vertically, to show how it develops. No less an authority than Albert Einstein apparently thought that physical objects are not static matter, but forms of volatile energy (cited in Holquist, 2002, p. 6). How much more a sociological form such as leadership?

Think in terms of the way in which people engage in social action. Let us use the term **mode** for a distinctive way of participating. A horse exhibits a variety of gaits: they walk, trot, canter, and gallop. These are modes of locomotion. Caring is a mode that humans exhibit (Gilligan, 1982). To what extent can we say that leadership is a mode?

Since Caputo was explicitly trying to capture Martin Heidegger's peregrinal approach, we should consult the man himself. Heidegger actually attributed his approach not to Eckhart but to Aristotle. What Aristotle was doing in the book of interest to Heidegger (book $\Theta$ of the *Metaphysics*) was to elucidate the terms we often use for dynamics and energy. Aristotle was beginning his discussion of these phenomena by saying they are not categories. One cannot gather or unify units of experience in order to display or make manifest by asserting what it is, with emphasis. Pointing to an example may not be adequate. These phenomena are different in kind. They are a different way of talking about reality. Dynamics and energy are not about what something is. Instead, they are about what happens (Heidegger, 1981/1995, p. 6f). Because this is the case, wrote Heidegger, we need a different way of using logic (see also Freise, 2018, p. ix).

We might say that our goal is to examine activities and not things, events and not objects.

---

2. Apparently, peregrine falcons were not raised from the nest but instead caught fully-grown before being tamed; hence, their lives were already underway.
3. See generally James (1909/1996, chs. 6, 7); see also de Saussure (1959, ch. 3).

Although there is one reality in which we all participate, it is a reality we experience in at least two different ways or modes. For our purposes, we will treat leadership here in only one of these ways—as it pertains to phenomena we have since called change, motion, power, influence, and so forth. The implication, it seems to me, is that one should not expect to define such phenomena in the same way that one defines an object such as a lamp, a toaster, or a bird. We have to choose our **mode**.

Therefore, we might say that "beings" can be talked about and understood in multiple ways (Heidegger, 1981/1995, p. 21). What follows is one of those. It has certain advantages.

The problem is that we mix them up together and draw unfounded conclusions. In ordinary conversation, as well as in scholarship pertaining to leadership, we certainly experience change (as in movement, transformation, alterations, influence, and so forth) and then ask what brought it about. We ask this when we want to understand how change occurs (Heidegger, 1981/1995, p. 41). If we want to take responsibility for bringing about change ourselves, as prospective leaders, we need to understand how change occurs. One of the words we use to name that which brings about change of any sort is *power*. In leadership studies, we seek the art of making change, which in turn depends on an understanding of how power works (Heidegger, 1981/1995, p. 60). We speak in terms of that which brings about change and that which is changed, such that we talk in terms of *that which* is active (and uses power) and *that which* is passive (Heidegger, 1981/1995, p. 47). An entitative ontology lies at the heart of the agent-structure problem that we mentioned in a prior chapter. We say that there are agents and there are structures. This entitative way of talking can prove to be problematic, if not misleading. Heidegger asks his reader to follow Aristotle toward a different way of talking.

Perhaps it is strange that we do not experience power directly, as a thing in itself, in the same way that we do not experience *causality* directly, unless we have already presupposed the very thing we are trying to study (Heidegger, 1981/1995, p. 65). Power is an inference. We undergo some experience, let us say, and then infer that an unseen "power" has become manifest as change. A company enjoys a turn of fortune, so we ascribe causation to the new CEO; a brigade meets with newfound success on the battlefield, so we praise the unit commander. What we infer is that this thing—this person or this position— has power, which we now know to be true because circumstances are different from what they had been. It only makes sense that leaders should want to acquire whatever it is that makes circumstances better. Understandably, they look to us in leadership studies to disclose the secret ingredient that works. "What is power?" they ask. "And how does it work?" From there, the mission for prospective leaders becomes obvious. Machiavelli was right: the objective would be to obtain and use that power.

But consider a different possibility. From this other "mode" Heidegger was trying to explain, things (leaders) do not "have" power or "use" power. Instead, power is what constitutes things (Heidegger, 1981/1995, p. 86). We flip it around, in other words. Force creates and interrelates all things. Nobody has it. It has us. We want to understand power, but not to use it as though it were a tool, like a hammer; instead, we might seek ways to participate in it. We want to plug in to a vibrant, pulsating network of distributed energy that nobody created or possesses. This is a different way of talking.[4] It certainly changes how we talk about what Luther did.

This idea of force can be broken down into two types, according to Heidegger: forces without discourse, such as gravity, and forces with discourse, such as interpersonal influence (Heidegger, 1981/1995, p. 99). Leadership falls into the latter category. Everything depends on whether the participant possesses a soul. If he or she does, that soul responds to what is known as *logos*, which Heidegger referred to as the ruling structure (1981/1995, p. 103). Psyche (or soul) and *logos* correspond. You can in fact have one without the other (1981/1995, p. 106), but *logos* governs discourse that leads to interpersonal influence (1981/1995, p. 105). At the heart of discourse is purpose (or *telos*); a billiard ball striking another billiard ball has no purpose and no discourse, yet a human being trying to communicate with another human being does, no matter how vague or obscure that purpose might be (Heidegger, 1981/1995, p. 114). *Telos* > *logos* > discourse.

At this point in the lectures, Heidegger made an interesting observation with regard to purpose. Purpose presumes a choice, a seeking of one thing rather than another. That is, discourse has a direction *toward* something (its purpose) and *away* from everything else. That purpose represents two things: (a) some image, which we in leadership studies call a vision, and (b) the work required to realize or render that image, i.e. to produce something consonant with that image (Heidegger, 1981/1995, p. 117). Just think about path-goal theories of leadership. That process of production requires raw material. In short, to bring about change, there must be something to be changed. To make a wooden table, the wood must change (Heidegger, 1981/1995, p. 118). You must hew it, split it, lathe it, sand it, stain it, and so forth.

The articulation of a purpose implies some forthcoming activity. To state a purpose is to say that something must be done. Again, the focus is on the activity.

Now, lest we draw the conclusion that the raw material for leadership is the *follower*, as the wood is raw material for a carpenter, Heidegger suggested that instead the raw material for social power is the present, the exact configuration of circumstances in which we find ourselves at the moment, for it is this that

---

4. I will return to this distinction later when I talk about cities, roads, and traffic.

the leader hopes to change.[5] The literary critic Walter Benjamin (1968) cited Marcel Proust regarding the incurable imperfection in the very essence of the present moment (p. 151f).[6] That's a lovely way to say it. To be even more specific, in deference to Heidegger's lecture, it is the boundlessness of the present, the radical indeterminacy of what is. It comes down to choice. We can go this way or that way. A leader responds to an image in his or her imagination and points the way (Heidegger, 1981/1995, p. 119). Which means that the leader understands in some fashion that there even is a choice. (As Hayek reminded us, it often happens that we do not realize there is a choice. Part of Luther's genius was to perceive in the exasperating conflicts of his day an opportunity for renewal, a flowering of individual piety.)

We cannot credit with leadership a person responding to a situation in the only way he or she knows how. That is not leadership. Leadership is the result of the leader entertaining two or more possibilities and making a choice (Heidegger, 1981/1995, p. 121; see Martin, 2007). So, there is the activity of imagining and choosing. That process resembles the earlier schema about moving from a compact reality through a process of differentiation, toward integration.

This means that even before pointing or gesturing toward one direction or another, the person we credit with being a leader will have produced *in the mind* a vision of a preferred future, a view toward some outcome to be produced, in opposition to other possibilities. That vision is bounded, separating X from Y, i.e. what is to be the case from what is not to be the case. The vision introduces boundaries to a boundless present, beginning in the mind (Heidegger, 1981/1995, p. 124). Accordingly, if we were to track the leadership process back to its roots, its origin, we would find the purpose chosen by the leader, and that purpose is a response to the relationship of forces that constitute the present (Heidegger, 1981/1995, p. 129). An abstract way of saying this is that leadership is a response to the present—a response originating in some goal or objective intended to create boundaries that shape or determine the future, resulting in action—which in the case of ensouled beings is communication (Heidegger, 1981/1995, p. 129). That response on the part of the leader derives from wanting to pursue or to flee, to go after or go away from, to encounter or to avoid (Heidegger, 1981/1995, p. 131). The image dictates which is to be the case. In most cases, the image to be rendered or produced in the real world is some intricate combination of the two, both toward and away. The leader pursues happiness, for instance, while at the same time fleeing stress; yet (in the interest of full disclosure) it is often the case that happiness in the future requires exertion in the present, such that leadership is a going forth and withdrawal, a search and an escape, in subtle combination, toward this and away from that at

5. Alvesson rightfully criticizes leadership studies when it makes the follower the raw material (2019, pp. 29, 31).
6. Or *l'imperfection incurable dans l'essence même du présent*.

one and the same time (Heidegger, 1981/1995, p. 131). It is rare that it is purely one or the other. In either case, though, it involves motion, change, and activity. What actually leads is force, persuasion, energy.

This is not to suggest that leadership is infallible. The image in one's mind might be flawed (an internal problem). The conditions might be inauspicious (an external problem). The way forward might be blocked for some reason. This is why saying of somebody that she has "power" turns out to be maladroit. Everybody who lives has the impulse to strive. Luther had insisted that this was the case. Each of us is stirred, restless, churning. We have energy to lend. Our lives are already underway. History flows on. Everything else in a social context is context-dependent. Therefore, leadership as a process is more of a "mode" of being (Heidegger, 1981/1995, p. 147), regardless of the actual outcome. It is purposeful striving with a boundless present to bring some kind of desired outcome into being, to produce (to lead toward), to elicit from out of one's circumstances a preferable future. That exertion is work. Power, as Heidegger put it, is "that from out of which change and transition occurs" (Heidegger, 1981/1995, p. 184) and "that whereby something is 'in process,' at work, in full swing" (Heidegger, 1981/1995, p. 193).

In these passages, we come very close to my definition for leadership.

Taking a giant step back, we might see power as a sum of excitation that remains constant (MacIntyre, 1997, p. 18). Useful analogies might include the brain's electrical activity or a power grid or the water cycle, always in motion, restless. Yammarino and Dionne (2019) offer their own version of a peregrinal ontology at a macro level in their discussion of dynamic networks (p. 48), which I will come back to in a subsequent chapter. As usual, Ortega found an elegant way of expressing this peregrinal ontology as it pertains to humanity. He said that human beings might have a body and a soul, each one an entity in its own right; nevertheless (as he put it), "man is not a thing, but a drama—his life" (1958, p. 73).

To draw a conclusion to this section, therefore, leadership might be explained as a mode of being in response to the boundless present, purposefully forbearing some things and resisting others, pursuing some things and fleeing others, toward a desired future consonant with an underlying structure in our souls that we share with other human beings—a structure we exemplify or invoke when we engage others in discourse. An awkward definition, to be sure, yet it does present a novel understanding of leadership.

## Flow: An Image for History

Earlier, we spoke of complex phenomena as though they exist at a fixed time, like a snapshot of reality, which is most certainly not the case. Complex phenomena come into being, change, and in some cases cease to exist. Each of these phenomena—e.g. a market, language, or society—has a lifespan or story.

Complex phenomena participate in history, just as leaders participate in complex phenomena.

For leadership, implicit in the study of patterns within the whole of society and the relationships among its parts would be the notion that things happen across time. We cannot rely exclusively on a static model of reality (Lord, 2019). The very idea of leadership presupposes a dynamic model and some way of imagining the lapse of history. Spontaneous order as a whole emerges and operates within history. Questions of leadership contrast (a) where we are today with (b) where we hope to be tomorrow. We want to know how the order works. We would like to think that leadership is an integral part of that narrative (Lord, 2019, p. 151).

Ordinarily, the leadership process that we study formally consists of episodes. These episodes would be of an indeterminate length. Leadership taking place during Pickett's Charge took place during the Battle of Gettysburg, which took place during the American Civil War, which took place during the whole experiment known as the United States of America, which is taking place as part of Western civilization, which is taking place as part of human history. Fernand Braudel (1980) created a time scale to portray an array of possibilities, from the abrupt incident through intermediate phases outward to the *longue durée*, bounded at the extreme by that which is timeless.

By selecting a single episode, of whatever length, a scholar obviously rips it out of context from a long and complex, interwoven fabric of other episodes—a turbulent cascade of influence and counterinfluence flowing this way and that (see Arendt, 1958). Any attempt to isolate an episode for study is by necessity artificial and to some extent misleading (Wren & Swatez, 1995).

It is nevertheless understandable to study episodes instead of anything longer because the further into the future one is trying to track leadership's impact—after all of the intervening events—the harder it gets (Stroup, 1997, p. 132). If the measures are too far apart, you miss the intervening activity. It could be that between measurements, the system changed and changed back. That often happens in systems that reassert themselves or go through cyclic patterns (Horsfall & Maret, 1997, p. 184). Also, it could be that things accelerated far more than the leaders ever dreamed, tumbling out of control.

Picture if you would a particle in a flowing stream. In the language of fluid dynamics, history is the streamline. Leadership is the pathline for the particle. You can trace its path as it scoots along, influenced by the stream. But then picture that particle leaving an ink trail in the water. In a turbulent stream, the ink trail (or streakline) does not follow the pathline of the particle because it is also carried along separately by the streamlines. Once it has been secreted, it belongs to the stream to determine its trajectory, because by that point the particle will have separated. In a similar example, picture paratroopers dropping from a plane. They will not land along the flight's path, but because of prevailing conditions, they will drift some distance downwind. As Polanyi (1951) stated,

"There is no rational criterion by which the accidental fulfillment of a prediction can be discriminated from its true confirmation" (p. 20f).

Social change is the streakline. Studying a leadership episode is like watching the particle squirt its ink without examining the streamlines or the fact that because of the turbulence of the streamlines, the pathline and the streakline are not the same. Historians use the study of episodes over time to engage in flow visualization.

Once the American Civil War ended in May 1865, not everybody in the field received word of it right away. It took some time for hostilities to cease. However, just because the war ended did not mean that the institution of slavery—though formally abolished—would abruptly discontinue. Already by November of the same year, the state of Mississippi adopted its notorious Black Codes, in essence restoring slavery by subterfuge: "black children were forced to work as 'apprentices' for white planters, usually their former masters, until they turned eighteen" (Phillips, 2006). This occurred after the war to end slavery. The streakline of emancipation was caught in some nasty undercurrents.

Which is why Jaspers' advice to set boundaries on one's research makes sense, but also raises concerns about what might have been overlooked. Jan Patočka reminded us, "Individual phases of our experience . . . are not isolated, they are always in a context" (1998, p. 165; see Tolstoy, 1959, p. 174). Nevertheless, a dynamic model of any length has advantages over a static model. At the very least, we can say that it complements the static model.

If we must be satisfied with broad patterns in our understanding of complex phenomena, as Hayek indicated, and if we aspire to a dynamic model of reality, probably the broadest is the pattern of **flow** to represent what happens through time.[7] In daily life, we presuppose that events have antecedents and consequences, so that if patterns emerge and then recur such that we find ourselves within some kind of order, they do so by a dynamic process. That process can be represented as a flow, with at least a rough, linear direction. The metaphor of flowing is part of the etymology of the term "influence," which is a term of considerable import to students of leadership. Other English words within that family include flux, fluid, fluctuate, fluent (and affluent). They all implicate change or motion along a surface—usually in the same direction.

Morihei Ueshiba, the founder of the martial art known as Aikido, urged a similar imagery in his meditations. He wrote that Aikido "originates with the flow of things—its heart is like the movement of the wind and the waves. . . . [Likewise] you must be able to let yourself soar like a bird and sport like a whale"

---

7. Machiavelli (1532/1991), for example, relied on the metaphor. Havre, Hetzler, and Nowell (2002) recently applied the metaphor of history as a river to offer "a macro-view of thematic changes in a corpus of documents over a serial dimension" (p. 9). They contend that the metaphor "is familiar and easy to understand and that it requires little cognitive effort to interpret the visualization." Daniel Little (2010) agrees that the metaphor is intuitive, yet limiting (p. 9).

(2018, pp. 38 & 44). He wrote that "your body should be in tune with the movement of the universe" (2018, p. 74). At the end of this book, I will draw further from the writings of Ueshiba to illustrate something I call aikido politics, but for now the emphasis is on the imagery of flow, movement, and change.

The question logically suggests itself: What if the object of our study were not leadership per se, but change? What if leadership is only an incident or activity to which we might be able to attribute some change, an incident in which leaders participate? Admittedly, other factors contribute to any change witnessed in the real world; leadership is not the only cause. We cannot say that social change is entirely a function of leadership, y = f(x).[8] The phenomenon of change itself turns out to be the real star of the show (see e.g. Dopfer, Foster, & Potts, 2004, p. 268). Maybe we talk about leadership only because it betokens agency, which in turn thrusts us into that hoary dispute about which factor is primitive: structure or agent. Better to speak of participating in leadership.

How then do we imagine that flow? Here, we revisit the question raised in a previous chapter about the role of metaphor and analogy. What purpose does the imagery serve? For purposes of clarification, I am content to use the idea of flow for its explanatory powers and not to suggest that history obeys the scientific laws of fluid dynamics.

Toward that end, please think of a straight line representing the flow of time, from the past to the future. Most of us learned how to draw timelines in elementary school. A system that flows unvaryingly along that line is in a steady state. If, however, that line bifurcates, so that two (or more) branches emerge, you now have two (or more) lines to follow through time.[9] As the line or lines continue to change, they might change in some kind of pattern in which the changes repeat themselves predictably, such as splitting in half every thirty minutes. This is an example of periodic behavior. In nature, we discern the seasonal rhythms of the earth (winter, spring, summer, and fall). In certain remote jungles, fireflies flash in sync, simultaneously, and then go dark together. In society, anthropologist Lévi-Strauss studied the patterns of descent from one generation to the next in just this fashion. By way of contrast, this line (or lines) could change in some non-repeating fashion and exemplify aperiodic behavior. At that point, we must consider the possibility of chaos—a topic of considerable relevance to my overarching argument.

8. Rex Kline (2017, p. 175) goes further, pointing out that interposing a mediating variable to account for indirect causation is still artificial and potentially limiting, even though to a large extent that's what my book is doing. X → M → Y (in which M represents the mediating variable) is simplistic. How do we even know what X (leader behavior) is? Or Y, for that matter? What is the time lag (see also Lord, 2019, p. 152)? How do we know there aren't other relevant variables at work? And can we say that the appearance of such a sequence is the result specifically of causation as opposed to something else?
9. Bifurcation could mean an actual split into two flows, or it could mean a moment when a flow can go in either of two directions, but not both.

Human history is replete with such lines. You have population growth, geographic dispersal, life expectancy, infant mortality, Moore's Law, and so forth. Some of these "lines" do disappear, never to be seen again. The dodo bird is gone forever. Other lines appear to have reached a steady state. Then there are those that exhibit periodic or aperiodic behavior (or some combination of the two).

These lines do not exist in isolation from one another. What happens along one line impacts other lines. When the population of predators in a specific area increases, the prey nearby are likely to decrease.[10] The result of all these interwoven "lines" is complex by any standard. History can be characterized as one flow comprised of many entwined or interlacing flows. The horizontal flow represents the lapse of time, but then one can also depict the influence of one line upon another line as a kind of **turbulence**, tumbling into one another, as they tend to increase or decrease or otherwise alter one another, exerting pressure.

Historian Carl Gustavson once lamented the tendency of amateur historians to ascribe events to a single cause, as though it were completely linear, because circumstances are always far more convoluted than they first appear (1955, p. 55). He wrote,

> It is impossible . . . to predict specifically the precise direction that social forms will take, what obstacles they may meet, and how a conflict of forces will result. Too many variables are involved, too many human elements are present.
>
> *(1955, p. 80)*

In ordinary conversation, we often treat history as just one thing, an arrow notched into uniform increments of centuries and years, so that all things at any given "point in time" share a date. They all participate in the same steady flow of time. Yet we regard this flow as comprised of different flows. We can speak intelligibly of a history of China or a history of Africa, because—even though they shared the same planet and the same moments in chronological time—they ran separately from each other for thousands of years. Furthermore, some lines seem to speed up or slow down. Even today, in a global context where Chinese people and Africans visit and interact routinely, we can still speak of a history of China and a history of Africa. In principle, of course, we can conceive of these distinct histories comprised of even smaller ones. We can talk about the history of a city or of a lake. Each plot of ground can be said to

---

10. One of the more infamous examples of trend lines supposedly influencing one another is the correlation between hemlines and the stock market (see Mabry, 1971). A picturesque example of intermingling lines is a compelling photograph from February 20, 2015, posted by the NASA Earth Observatory and titled: "Suwannee Blackwater River Meets the Sea."

have its unique history. (When you buy a house, a title search establishes the history of its ownership.) Even a thunderstorm has a life span.

Subdividing history by geographic region is only one way to do it. For our convenience, we can also subdivide history into geologic time scales such as eons, eras, systems, periods, epochs, and ages. Think, for example, of such historical phases as the Bronze Age or the French Revolution. Or the Protestant Reformation. One can also describe a history of certain cultural pursuits, such as warfare, art, and religion. Again, these various tributaries intermingle (and occasionally disappear altogether), but the point is that we are able to conceive of simultaneous histories in the plural.

Among the variables with which we must contend are the **interpretations** that people give to their experiences. Interpretations are themselves events within the flow of history (Voegelin, 1987). When Augustine tried to make sense of the fall of Rome, he offered a unique framework for understanding how its ruin might fit the traditional narrative of the everlasting kingdom established by the Risen Christ. That effort of his took place within history and participated in shaping how readers understood their circumstances. Later, as the *philosophes* of the Enlightenment offered a different image of progress, that too took place within the flow of history and altered how people viewed themselves and their activities. Not long after, Karl Marx would publish another just-so story that was to have a long-term impact on the choices that people made. In short, historiography itself has a history (Nisbet, 1969). And each interpretation has the potential to shift how we subsequently behave. An interpretation is an event. History and its interpretations are mutually constituting.

Interpretations change based in part on each person's place within the context. This notion echoes back to the Cabreras' rule about point of view (2015, p. 52). What I imagine about what is happening is largely determined by where I stand. There are other aspects as well. It matters a great deal, for example, where I was raised. It might make a difference which social class I belong to—what ethnicity, religion, sex, or enclave. My interpretation is, as Dana Meadows (2008) pointed out, based on where within a given system I find myself. This is only natural. The same staircase looks different from the top than from the bottom. Therefore, in this book I am offering an image of a single reality with multiple vantage points, yielding multiple versions of what we are looking at. To an extent, what we experience of the shared or paramount world is relative to our position within it. Each version has the potential to alter that reality as more and more people adopt it.

These experiences are frequently rendered as **narratives**. Neuroscience is telling us that human beings appear to be hard-wired for stories (Swart, Chisholm, & Brown, 2015). And since history itself is a human enterprise, of course it unfolds as a complex saga comprised of episodes, characters, and story arcs, both tragedy and comedy. True, the narrative flows in one direction, but at least it gives meaning to the intricate braiding of so many variables. More importantly perhaps, it gives meaning to who we are as part of that saga. We orient ourselves in life's implacable onrush. Again, some things remain constant. Of the things that change, some unfold according to recognizable patterns, while others are completely unpredicted and even jarring. The threads of existence extend and tangle, fascinating the observer and contributing to our understanding of what might be possible. Going forward, the story is not yet written. We get to write it. What then is it we wish to write?

The *experience* of the flow of time is not insignificant. That inward flow is by no means steady and predictable. Time as we experience it can speed up or slow down, intensify or grow slack. Just as a practical matter, we know the difference between a long languorous afternoon in the sun and the morning hubbub at the market. We can even jump around, so to speak, by remembering the past or anticipating the future. Perhaps the most famous novel on the iridescence of time is Marcel Proust's multivolume *In Search of Lost Time* (1913–1927). This capability to step out of the flow of time gives to human beings a considerable evolutionary advantage. Philosopher Eric Voegelin (2002) was to place this capability of "no longer forgetting (*anamnesis*)" at the heart of his analysis of social order. Psychologist Jordan Peterson (2018) has emphasized our capability to imagine possible futures as paramount in our success as a species. It is because of this capacity to experience time differently that we can speak meaningfully of anything like a period of crisis, for example, or "the times that try men's souls" or "the fullness of time" (see e.g. J.E. Smith, 1969). This is a far different way of imagining 9:45 a.m. (EST) on Tuesday, February 26 in the year 2019 (CE).

In a forthcoming chapter, we distinguish the **subjective** experience of chaos from the **objective** condition of chaos. I am doing the same thing here, distinguishing the experience of time from the objective condition of time. I do this not to dismiss what philosophers refer to as the phenomenological. For how we experience reality, one another, and ourselves regardless of objective conditions—this determines our responses.

Fortunately, as Voegelin informed us, "There is a science that investigates the questions of patterns in history" (1990, p. 95). In fact, the patterns are what *constitute* history (1990, p. 113). It follows that, because leadership occurs in episodes that are themselves part of a longer and more intricate flow of events, the study of history would seem to be implicit in leadership studies. I would like to go further than this. Because of the importance of the flow of time, we can talk about events in a different and more accurate way—a way that captures the fluidity of history.

It is the difference between talking about cars and highways, on the one hand, and traffic, on the other (see de Landa, 2000). One of these is entitative and, in one's imagination, tends to be outside of time. A car is a car is a car. The other is peregrinal and tends to depend on the vicissitudes of time.

A word of caution. Sometimes, people assume that an order, no matter how complex, has both stability and structure. Consequently, if they are correct, we should not expect to study Hayek's spontaneous order under the rubric of time. Nevertheless, Hayek did not hold that order requires either stability or structure (Petsoulas, 2001, p. 56). On the contrary, order persists over time and persists in large part because it constantly adjusts to a changing reality, the way the Common Law evolves. Spontaneous order is comprised of change.

## Braudel on History Among the Human Sciences

In leadership studies, we tend to ascribe social change to leaders. We tend to emphasize what individuals accomplish. To the extent that we seek verification for our claims in history, we tend to focus on incidents, events, discernible shifts, or what we might call discontinuities that leadership helps to explain. Therefore, for purposes of our scholarship we isolate a war (if not a battle) or a revolt or a migration and try to show how our models explain what happened and why it happened in precisely that way.

Fernand Braudel, a distinguished French historian, pondered history's uses and its place among the human sciences, including sociology, economics, and politics. Specifically regarding this tendency of ours to emphasize individual exertion as the causal force in history, he wrote, "We do not believe in this cult of demigods, or to put it even more simply, we are against [the] proud and unilateral declaration: 'Men make history.' No, history also makes men" (1980, p. 10).

This is not to say that historians do not frequently examine the extraordinary exertions of individuals. He concedes that proposition: "To the narrative historians, the life of men is dominated by dramatic accidents, by the actions of those exceptional beings who occasionally emerge, and who often are the masters of their own fate and even more of ours" (1980, p. 11).[11] However, this framework of humans making history, all by itself, will not suffice. It may be the case that the attention of historians is often drawn to episodes of upheaval and change along a relatively digestible timeline, beginning on one date and ending on another date. A crisis such as a peasant uprising or stock market crash often induces us to place that perilous situation within a longer context, in order to discern its origins and its meaning. In other words, discontinuities on a small scale invite us to see things from a larger scale (1980, p. 6), for is this not what Augustine did upon the fall of Rome? "Resounding events often take place in an instant, and are but manifestations of that larger destiny by which alone they can be explained" (Braudel, 1980, p. 5). As scholars we are drawn from explaining individual episodes by means of a longer, intermediate length of time.

Braudel went to great lengths to present a schema of history along a continuum, ranging from the abrupt at one extreme to the *longue durée* at the other.[12]

---

11. For a popular example, see Goodwin (2018).
12. Lord (2019) recently suggested another gradient ranging from milliseconds to millennia (pp. 154 & 164f).

At one extreme, which we can call the very short term, we have events or "surface disturbances" with identifiable social actors, "short, sharp, nervous vibrations" heavily dependent on those who experience it (1980, pp. 3–5). Think for example of what comes to mind when somebody refers to Arab Spring, Woodstock, or crossing the Rubicon. This is traditional history, "proportionate to individuals . . . headlong, dramatic, [with a] breathless rush of its narrative . . . explosive" (1980, p. 27f). Here, we expect to find leadership.

Most historians can then place that abrupt event within an intermediate range of somewhere between ten and fifty years. These are phases to be experienced within one lifetime, a chunk of time that has its own unique traits, such as the *fin de siècle* or the Age of the Robber Barons. But, Braudel noted, there are time scales that extend far longer. When one is talking about historical phenomena that last for a century or more, you are considering what he called the *longue durée* (see Editors, 2015). At this extended duration, one is now probably considering what we might call a structure, which Braudel defined as "an organization, a coherent and fairly fixed series of relationships between realities and social masses" (1980, pp. 27, 31). To cite one example, Braudel himself wrote about the history of merchant capitalism. To talk about this in a meaningful way, you need to incorporate more than a few decades.

This *longue durée* extends outward even further to become "a history slower than the history of civilizations, a history which almost stands still . . . a dialogue which never stops repeating itself" (1980, p. 12). We might even wish to describe the outer limit paradoxically as an unaltering history, a geographical time/life, the changeless condition, or at least imperceptibly slow cycles within which human life operates, because no matter what happens, the flowers still bloom and the tides turn (1980, pp. 3–5). In the lull after a bombardment, when the doughboys stood to go over the top during World War I, they could often hear larks in the distance singing, just before they gave a shout and clambered out of the trenches into No Man's Land. In such a world, the larks still sing, as they did thousands of years ago for Neanderthals. Such broad time scales can become important to understand. "In the living world there are no individuals entirely sealed off by themselves; all individual enterprise is rooted in a more complex reality, an 'intermeshed' reality, as sociology calls it" (1980, p. 10).

It is this intermeshed quality that convinced Braudel to call for a dialogue across the disciplines. Even within history, no single framework completely explains what happens. Not only are there different time scales, there are also different causal forces that can be studied, even though no one of them alone unlocks the secret—not genetics, not geography, not economics, not religion (1980, p. 10)—not memes, not the forces of production, not the will to power. He wrote that "there is no problem which does not become increasingly complex when actively investigated, growing in scope and depth, endlessly opening up new vistas of work to be done. . . . There is never any problem, even, which can be confined within a single framework" (1980,

p. 15). For this reason, scholars need one another. Braudel was calling for dialogue. Quoting Lucien Febvre, he stated, "What a wealth of precious suggestions on method and on the interpretation of facts, what cultural gains, what a step forward in intuition if intellectual exchanges between these diverse groups were more frequent" (1980, p. 17). He called such a dialogue a "necessary convergence" (1980, p. 25). Together, we might "define a hierarchy of forces, of currents, of particular movements, and then tackle them as an entire constellation" (1980, p. 34).

In response to the argument that findings which would be amenable to all of the sciences would also be pretty generic and bland, he bites the bullet. *So what if* all we arrive at are "elementary truths, aphorisms amounting to no more than common sense (1980, p. 46)"? That in itself would be something. We can then grow from there, together, at the very least cross-pollinating as we go. Braudel noticed that some academic centers had already started to create what are called complex studies (such as area studies, gender studies, and race studies), which are attempts to launch those interdisciplinary conversations around a selected topic. In my opinion, leadership studies can be one of those. However, if that turns out to be so, we face two risks. First, we simply bring into our house all of the squabbles that already exist out there among the disciplines, as they jostle for supremacy. Braudel wrote that "each social science is imperialistic, however much it may deny it" (1980, p. 56). Second, leadership studies itself might become imperialistic with regard to the other disciplines, claiming for itself a kind of preeminence we do not deserve.

Braudel understood that an academic field of study has to establish itself—its credibility and identity. He did not believe that the disciplines could be collapsed into one another, blended beyond recognition. Each has to defend its integrity. "The wish to affirm one's own existence in the face of others is necessarily the basis for new knowledge" (1980, p. 25). Still, that does not preclude collaboration. As a historian, Braudel noticed the extent to which the human sciences rely on the two extremes in his little time scale and ignore the intermediate: they focus on the flashpoint, the event (the strike, the bankruptcy, the invasion, the invention) or they focus on the timeless, the perennial (1980, p. 50). Here, in his opinion, between the oh-so-brief moment and that which is enduring, historians have a lot to contribute.

One of the obstacles to interdisciplinary dialogue and collaboration that Braudel noticed is the fact that each discipline uses its own schemas, with their own lexicon. In the human sciences, one finds a diversity of schemas. Braudel wrote that "research is a question of endlessly proceeding from the social reality to the model, and then back again, and so on, in a series of readjustments and patiently renewed trips" (1980, p. 45). The idea of a schema is a very old form of reasoning used in every human science; we all have them. We might call them maps, schemas, grids, and so forth. We use these as a template to overlay and hopefully approximate reality (1980, p. 59). In other words, failures in practical affairs allow us to check the validity of our schemas, since failure raises the question whether they are any good (1980, p. 56).

Let us be honest: if science is based on the ability to predict, we in leadership studies are a long way from being a science (1980, p. 8f; see generally anything written by Barbara Kellerman). However, with so many models out there, even within the disciplines, how do we come together? Braudel did two things: he offered his time scale (short, intermediate, *longue*, perennial) as one schema that historians use, and also he suggested that the rest of the human sciences go back and see how their schemas fit this one. We should consider how his differentiation informs the work that the rest of us are doing.

I asked myself the same question, though not so deftly as Fernand Braudel.

Georges Sorel once differentiated two conceptions of history that writers about leadership often confuse (Vernon, 1978, pp. 7–9; see also Turner, 1997, p. xv). One is to recapture what the participants were thinking and hoping and trying to do, in the moment, from their vantage point. He called this **genetic** history, to identify the genesis of what happens. The other conception of history looks more broadly, from the vantage point of the present, knowing what we know now. We understand things today that the participants did not. Hindsight, they say, is 20/20. Sorel called this second conception **retrospective** or scientific history. We often study episodes of leadership using both.

What does it mean to be in the flow, to occupy a position within a complex reality that is churning all around you? It pays us as leadership scholars to appreciate the subjective experience. But it also pays to step back, so to speak, to adopt a more objective view of things. Doing both in turn is a form of that hermeneutic circle, another both/and. It is my contention that leaders actually do both. They feel the full weight of the predicament, immersed in things up to their elbows, while at the same time drawing away in their imagination to see things dispassionately, as part of a longer trajectory. In that way, they have the opportunity to look ahead and scout out alternate pathways.

## What This Means

Jaspers advised us to include in our studies the whole within which the phenomenon takes place. Leadership takes place within the complex phenomenon of society, within which we can detect only broad principles and patterns. Furthermore, society participates in a larger, comprehending whole that we refer to as history. The broad pattern we find in history is the metaphor of flow. Here we return to the idea put forth by Jaspers that not only should we examine the part and the whole, but also the relationship between them. What we find in the interstices requires a dynamic model and not just a static model.

Heidegger relied on Aristotle to come up with language for this purpose, the mode having to do with energy, power, motion, and change. When it comes to interpersonal influence, things are happening all around us. In the midst of unrest, leaders generate or adopt ideas about the particular direction we might go, and when a vision finds resonance with or is attuned to the underlying structures of consciousness, others might follow. The flow does not stop regardless, but it can be diverted, if (that is) there is something being communicated that elicits a corresponding response.

Leadership is a mode of participation. It is one way to engage reality in time.

# 8

# DIALOGUE AS A MODE
# OF PARTICIPATION

### Introduction to the Chapter

In the previous chapter, we considered a different way of talking about leadership, as a mode of participation, entering the flow of history. That way, we avoid the agent-structure problem. We say that agents and structures constitute one another over time. We say that leadership is about the dynamics that prevail between the agent and the structure and about the mode that shapes them into some kind of order.

This chapter looks at a prosaic example of spontaneous order as it emerges by means of this mode of participation, a way of being together. Whereas the Common Law that we examined earlier is an enduring institution with broad applicability and its roots in the distant past, a **dialogue** is by its very nature ephemeral and limited to those who participate. They create something that never existed before. When it ends, often late at night, it vanishes. Klaus Krippendorf (2018) calls it "the fastest evolutionary process I know" (p. 82). Even then, in its traces one detects a process of ordering taking place, a little cosmos that has long-term implications for the *psyche* and the *polis*—as well as being good for its own sake.

In the chapter on Martin Luther, if you recall, I cited historians. That was by design. In the chapter on the Common Law, I quoted jurists and legal scholars. In a chapter on dialogue, too many academic disciplines have addressed what the term even means. The phenomenon does not belong to any of them. In that respect, dialogue as a phenomenon resembles leadership as a phenomenon: their study is an interdisciplinary affair. In deference to Jaspers' advice, therefore, we shall have to limit our investigation in some fashion, or the whole analysis becomes unwieldy.

Nevertheless, the fact that so many disciplines have taken up the topic indicates its widespread significance. More than one discipline has even undergone a "dialogical turn" in which dialogue is not only a phenomenon to be studied, in the board room or the classroom or the therapist's office; it has also become part of that discipline's own method for studying whatever it is that they set out to study (see e.g. Levine, 2018; Freise, 2018). Dialogue fits what Jaspers had recommended as a way of conducting research pluralistically. Interdisciplinarity is largely a dialogue across disciplines. Dialogue has the character of engaging one another across boundaries.[1]

By broad consensus, dialogue's first great exemplar was the ancient Greek philosopher Socrates, whose practice of dialogue was recounted by his pupil Plato. After an extended description of what I mean by the term "dialogue," we must turn to Plato. By the end, dialogue shall be revealed to be a complex phenomenon of spontaneous order that is both radically indeterminate and yet also guided toward an emerging or implicate order. In my opinion, this section based loosely on the dialogues of Plato is the lynchpin of the entire book.

## What Do I Mean by a Dialogue?

> Speech, the *logos*, in its fundamental reality, is the most human of conversations, a *diálogos*. . . . Dialogue is the *logos* from the point of view of the *other*, the neighbor.
> —*José Ortega y Gasset (1975, p. 20)*

The term "dialogue" literally refers to the coursing or flowing of *logos* with or through others. Ordinarily, *logos* indicates speech, as in monologue, but its root includes the idea of some pervading structure we might recognize as the truth. David Bohm was to refer to this truth as an implicate order (1980). Dialogue is a kind of interpersonal flux in the experience of the emergence of that order, as we approximate the truth in our little, temporary *cosmos*. One might think of it as bringing forth or rendering the truth into language, into symbols. The ancient Greek term *logos* is (like so many Greek terms) wonderfully ambiguous that way and thus quite versatile. It can also be confusing.

The term "dialogue" is also elastic. Some writers, such as Mikhail Bakhtin, will contend that nearly any expression, including warfare, science, and art, can be understood as participation in a dialogue (see Holquist, 2002, ch. 2, titled "Existence as Dialogue"). However, that usage goes too far for my purposes. In an abstract and metaphysical sense, yes, I concur with him, but it does not

---

1. Kaczmarczyk (2018) schematizes four methods for dealing with the presence of many different approaches in any academic discipline (p. 71f). My version is more whimsical than his:

   a.  prove that yours is the best or the only approach (e.g. Carnap, 1934/1995);
   b.  forge a synthesis or grand, unifying theory (e.g. Goethals & Sorenson, 2007);
   c.  allow for separate approaches, but stay in dialogue with one another (e.g. Harvey & Riggio, 2012); or
   d.  do just empirical work and do not talk about it.

help us at the outset to rely on such a broad understanding. We need to narrow it down a bit, as per Jaspers. In the same way, the Dutch psychologist H. J. Hermans, H. Kempen, and R. van Loon (1992) wrote of the dialogical self, whereby the mind confers with itself (see also Voegelin, 1990, pp. 58–64). In the same vein, Manolis Dafermos (2018) defines consciousness itself as having "dialogic structure and orientation" (p. A4). That is another way to extend the idea of dialogue more than is presently necessary. Again, even though I embrace this use of the term as well, i.e. dialogue as the ground of consciousness, it would be best to hold that thought in abeyance.

The following characterization of dialogue has been influenced most by five, disparate writers:[2]

- Martin Buber (1878–1965), an Austrian-born Israeli philosopher;
- Mikhail Bakhtin (1895–1975), a Russian literary critic;
- Hans-Georg Gadamer (1900–2002), a German phenomenologist;
- David Bohm (1917–1992), an English physicist; and
- William Isaacs, an American management consultant.

For present purposes, dialogue is a particular way that two or more persons engage one another. It is a mode of being together. Unlike monologue (asserting), transference (seeking to direct the other), subordination (seeking direction from the other), and withdrawal (walking away from the other), dialogue is active engagement with the other (Kaczmarczyk, 2018, p. 64). The participants participate in constructing an experience where they value things such as truth and meaning and rely on one another to figure out what that is. In a similar fashion, Karl Weick (1995) is known for his work on processes of meaning making. No participant presumes to declare the truth once and for all time, like issuing a command or preaching the gospel. That is a different mode (Simms, 2015, p. 72). Rather, dialogue is **intervocal** (Feld, 1998). Dialogue is comprised of an exchange, back-and-forth, in which the participants share responsibility for what transpires and therefore hold one another accountable.

Xiaojing Wang (2018) distilled five key elements of dialogue:

- One must regard the other as another subject and not as an object.
- Each participant enjoys equal rights within the dialogue.
- Not only will a dialogue consist of many voices, it will allow many ways of talking.

---

2. Presiding over my remarks, I hope, is the spirit of American sociologist Donald Levine (1931–2015), whose scholarship and example inspired me most to practice dialogue as a way of teaching and more so as a way of life. Evidently, he touched many others the same (see obituary by Allen, 2015). He once wrote that "the climax of liberal learning appears in the experience of genuine dialogue" (2006, p. 218; see e.g. Matusov & Miyazaki, 2014).

- Each participant tries to think about what the other is saying.
- The conversation is in principle never-ending, unable to finish.

*(p. 142f)*

1. Imagery. Common metaphors for dialogue include the talking circle and sitting around a table. The image of the circle does two good things. It helps put the focus on one another, face-to-face, oriented toward one another (Kaczmarczyk, 2018, p. 59). It also equalizes status, such that nobody enjoys prominence. As William Isaacs (1999) put it trenchantly: like a circle, dialogue has a center but no sides (p. 19). Nonetheless, the image of the circle fails to capture dialogue's dynamic character. Dialogue is not a static phenomenon any more than leadership is, so we have to imagine its form in three dimensions, in another mode using our "peregrinal ontology" as mentioned in a prior chapter, which means that dialogue is often depicted in the literature as a framework *through which* meaning can be said to flow (Isaacs, 1999, p. 19).[3]

For Mikhail Bakhtin, patterns of flow are unpredictable because they are generative (Olshansky, 2002–2018). Participants end up saying and doing things that they never would have in isolation. Part of the charm of dialogue is its wayward trajectory, where new thoughts and ideas emerge, spawned by the give-and-take. That trajectory is highly contingent on who happens to speak that day and what they happen to say (see also Simmel, 1908/1950, pp. 51–53). Participants can be understood to fill in the empty space between them, without realizing the designs of any one of them. As Bakhtin (1986) wrote, "Any concrete utterance is a link in the chain of speech communication [such that] thought itself—philosophical, scientific, artistic—is born and shaped in the process of interaction and struggle with others' thought" (p. 91f). And despite its linear structure of utterance and response, interspersed by significant pauses, like any "fluid" it will undergo turbulence before it ends.

2. Dialogue and decision making. Some people use the term "dialogue" to refer to conversations that have a shared purpose, and although in one sense that is accurate, it would be a mistake to treat group decision making as dialogue. Decision making by its very nature seeks to close around some conclusion, i.e. an answer to a problem (see generally Edwards, 1954). By way of contrast, dialogue is radically indeterminate, wide-open. It goes where it goes, constrained primarily by a mutual regard for truth and meaning. Otherwise, it has a life of its own. Any decision that spins off from dialogue is incidental, a happy spark flung out by centrifugal force. The essential dichotomy here is between a search for closure (which is not emblematic of dialogue) and openness (e.g. Isaacs, 1999; Bohm, 1996b; Buber, 1965, p. 7; Simmel, 1908/1950, pp. 51–53).

---

3. On the imagery of flow, see generally Csikszentmihalyi (1990).

Do not misunderstand. An open mind is not an empty one. Dialogue does not expect the expert to pretend to be ignorant, as though we should all know and not know the same things. Experts should speak about what they uniquely understand. That is part of what they contribute. They must be prepared to speak in such a way that everybody else can be made to understand. Nobody gets to close off discussion by saying, "You wouldn't understand." But then each participant is expert with regard to his or her own reasoning. The guiding role in dialogue is less about those who know and more about those who seek to know, the explorers rather than the experts (Kaczmarczyk, 2018, p. 65, citing Znaniecki, 1984).

3. Mutual regard, but remaining individuals. The mystic philosopher Martin Buber, best known for his work *I and Thou*, subsequently explained in some detail what he had meant by dialogue (1965). To him, dialogue is in the best sense communion, a sacrament, in which you get to retain your point of view, knowing it to be limited. The experience of dialogue means that everyone appreciates his or her own limitations, so that they work together voluntarily to overcome them (1965, pp. 6, 35), not by sharing *knowledge*, which is a different activity, but by sharing the predicament (1965, p. 8).[4] The first step is to turn toward one another, figuratively speaking, to make the other participants in the room the object of your attention (1965, p. 22). William Isaacs suggests that dialogue will seem more like a romantic dinner in this regard than a chat in a public space when the subway screams by (1999, p. 234). In order for this mutual regard to happen, participants must move beyond being mere onlookers (watching) or observers (paying attention), by becoming aware (Buber, 1965, p. 8ff). Being an observer who is detached from the predicament would be an appropriate mode for a scientist, yet that is a different mode (1965, p. 12).

Scientists observe nature from a detached point of view. By way of contrast, dialogue may be informed by what science discerns, but it exists for another purpose. It is not about something to observe. Rather, it is about something to do (Simms, 2015, p. 51). That activity is called hermeneutics, which is about interpretation. Other participants serve as companions and partners in this activity (Kaczmarczyk, 2018, p. 60). Dialogue is shared hermeneutics.

Buber anticipated an objection. By becoming aware, he wrote, you are not merging somehow into one another, blurring toward some fantastical "group mind" in which everybody thinks alike (1965, p. 25). Not only is that not the goal, but such a tendency would probably be suboptimal. Nevertheless, some sort of unification or binding does occur, so that dialogue emerges on a gradient between mere collectivity, in which people assemble like passengers waiting to board a train (on the one hand), and groupthink, in which people

---

4. Matthias Freise (2018) explains that in psychotherapy the analyst helps the patient recognize and work within his or her limitations, but not from a God's-eye point of view. The analyst is also limited, a fact which his or her own experience being analyzed should have disclosed. Together, they work from within their limitations (p. xxii).

squander their individuality (on the other) (1965, p. 31). If we need similes, the one extreme is like a pile of rocks, whereas the other is like a slab of butter. Dialogue is like neither of these. Participants are unified in their sociability (Simmel, 1908/1950, pp. 51–53).

Tellingly, Buber welcomed into dialogue especially those who would oppose him, his adversaries. Participants have to differ. What is not permitted at the table is indifference or worse, contemptuous dismissal (1965, p. 34). By the same token, of course, adversaries risk polarizing a group, creating sides (Isaacs, 1999, p. 5). Therefore, participants can begin in opposition. They should bring their disparate opinions and ideas. Moreover, they should be willing to assert them. In this way, the group collaborates to "ripen the issue" (in the terminology of Ron Heifetz). Daniel Pinnow (2011) wrote, "A good leader must be able to deal with contradictions and conflicts. More than that: they must ensure that they are openly expressed and resolved" (p. 161).

The group must avoid rigidifying from there, which so often happens in the real world. As Levine insisted, disagreement is a condition of dialogue. One must acknowledge "that the hearer offers a constant challenge. . . . This condition is inherently stressful and difficult to realize" (2006, p. 218). Participants are neither separate (on the one hand) nor subsumed by the group (on the other), neither independent nor dependent. They are *inter*dependent, in a catallaxy.

4. Focus on the present. Buber explained that group processes are sometimes about the past (as for example reconciling after wartime) and sometimes about the future (as for example making strategy). Dialogue brings an emphasis on the present—what you are thinking right now and why, what the other person is thinking and why, questioning who we are to each other, in the moment (1965, p. 15). What people undoubtedly discover, if they are being honest, is that their present state of mind is predominantly a product of past thinking (Isaacs, 1999, p. 51). Should it be? The past does encroach on the present. But then so does the future. Whatever is said is uttered with some anticipation as to what others might do in reply (Bakhtin, 1992, p. 279f); so, we come to realize just how tightly our present is determined by the past and the future, in a perpetual rhythm. Dialogue tries to help everyone refresh their thoughts and opinions, so that together we can turn aside from the past and the future long enough to create meaning under these unique conditions (Isaacs, 1999, p. 165; Bohm, 1996b, p. 3).

Dialogue is not designed to reject the past. That would be impossible and unwise. It does bring to consciousness the literal influence (or influx) of the past. Sometimes, participants learn about one another's traditions and heritage—not so much to reject them as to understand and honor them without being bound by them. Gadamer even characterized dialogue as participation in the unfolding of tradition (Simms, 2015, p. 75f). In addition, dialogue is not unmindful of what awaits us out there when we go home to our families and jobs. It does try to put the moment into perspective, without the temptation to forget what is happening right now, in this direct encounter, as I look you in the eye.

5. Differentiate, then integrate. People will disagree about some things. Otherwise, there is no profit in the exercise. Nevertheless, they have to agree on other things, such as the language we expect to use and certain rules of conduct. Otherwise, the participants will fail to engage. The task in dialogue is to enact a rhythm that consults both the similarities and the differences (Bohm, 1996b, p. 4)—not for the sake of accomplishing some pre-determined purpose, but instead for its own sake.

This is not to say that dialogue has no purpose. Rather, the purpose emerges from out of dialogue (Isaacs, 1999, p. 51). In that sense, it resembles spontaneous order. The participants literally evoke it, bringing it forth by means of their words. To impose a purpose beforehand is to misunderstand what dialogue means. Communication that has a predetermined purpose tends to shape what is said and therefore what is thought. Obviously, if a participant has a point of view or private agenda, the objective will often be to defend his or her side in the ensuing debate. Participants who do not already have a side to defend will nonetheless listen for certain things and ignore everything else, as they figure out what the sides are and which side they are on. By way of contrast, in dialogue, wrote Bohm, "nobody is trying to win" (1996b, p. 7). It is not about winning.

One manual on conflict management (Fisher, Ury, & Patton, 1981) tells the story of an old man watching two kids throw a Frisbee back and forth. At one point, he hollers out: "Hey! How do you know which one of you is winning?" Clearly, the old man did not grasp what was going on.

Implicit in any purposeful communication is a thought process of **differentiation**. We ask ourselves, as a group: What are we trying to do, as opposed to what we are not trying to do? What constitutes success, as opposed to failure? What information is relevant and what is irrelevant? What do we know to be true or false? Dialogue does not ignore or pass over this important step in the process; differentiation is obviously real and even useful. Participants should expect to bring their differences to the surface. Then dialogue moves from differentiation toward integration. Just to be clear, though, it is less a process of moving toward convergence and more a process of moving back and forth between divergence and convergence, repeatedly. Maybe the hardest step is taking a divergence and widening it further. Let me explain.

Once the differences bubble up and participants hear them out loud, the real work begins. Participants must become conscious of the process that produced them. They must make explicit the underlying assumptions driving these differences (Bohm, 1996b, pp. 22–27).[5] In effect, they are widening the differences by showing just how far apart the assumptions are that produced the different positions. In doing so, the group may as a result suspend the assumptions, at least temporarily, in part to test them and find out whether they are meaningful

---

5. According to Karl Simms (2015), Gadamer was to refer to these as prejudices (see p. 76).

and in part to go in search of alternate assumptions (even new ones) that might yield results that are more satisfactory. Maybe there is a way to transcend the opposing viewpoints, perhaps by finding that they are simply alternate ways of doing the same thing. Maria Andrianova (2018) even defines dialogue as "the ambition to look at a problem from multiple points of view and strive to value these various positions equally" (p. 2; see Levine, 2018, p. 3).

The principle of suspending judgment is critical to dialogue, although to be clear it does not mean surrendering one's position. It does mean that by making these assumptions explicit and then suspending them, participants are likelier to adopt a posture of **fallibilism** (Bohm, 1996b, p. 44); they consider the possibility, in other words, that they are at least to some extent wrong. Not that they *were* wrong and now at last are right, thanks to everybody's participation in the process. No: *even now* they could be wrong. At any given point in time, they could be wrong. We could all be wrong. Dialogue helps everybody recognize that fact and learn to live with it. Again, participants work within their limitations.

6. Proprioception. In dialogue, therefore, participants help each other become more aware of the processes of thought that led them to where they are. Bohm calls this operation **proprioception**, which is a way of witnessing one's own mind at work (1996b, pp. 27–29, 83–95). In a group setting, this means bringing the different assumptions together into one place and generating other assumptions to join them, as though dumping them onto a table and sorting through them. The group does this work together. The mind of each individual participant has to be capable of this operation, which neuroscience tells us tends to occur in the cerebral cortex, at the front of the brain, not unlike projecting them together onto a screen and seeing them temporarily as equally viable for purposes of comparison. What are our options? What do we think of them? An inability to do this work means that you cannot entertain alternatives and do not understand that there even is a choice.

Bohm encapsulated his vision of dialogue as "the collective way of opening up judgments and assumptions" (1996b, p. 53; see Simms, 2015, p. 70). But be careful. As Bakhtin reminded his readers, a dialogue is limitless, unbounded, open ended (1992, p. 170). Once open, nobody knows where it will take you.

Now, if you were to infer that for Bohm, the root problem is how we think, you would be close to his position, yet he set aside an entire chapter to explain that thinking is not so much a **problem** as a **paradox** (1996b, pp. 70–78). A problem is something that one solves, for that is what you do with problems. The thing is that you cannot conclusively "solve" your thinking, as though there exists some remedy to make things all better. Thought occurs within a paradox that is insoluble. You are thinking about thinking. You are using as an instrument that which you hope to examine, not unlike using a microscope to see itself. That is a paradox, an unavoidable paradox (Bohm, 1996b, pp. 79–82). Yet, just as the paradox is unavoidable, you can transcend it. Dialogue helps, largely because it lifts each participant out of his or her individual or private thinking and gives everybody a different vantage point.[6] To borrow a metaphor, you can see your own eye, but only with the aid of a mirror. Dialogue is like that mirror, which serves the purpose of gaining critical distance from one's own thinking.

After gaining that critical distance, you come to appreciate more fully the extent to which you are limited. Perhaps you come to appreciate more fully the extent to which somebody who disagrees with you is not necessarily wrong (see Simms, 2015, p. 120; Taylor, 2002, p. 141). Gadamer referred to this process as a fusion of horizons. I have my horizons, limiting me. I cannot see beyond my horizon. We are always encompassed within horizons. As we engage one another, I do not abandon my horizon and adopt yours. Instead, we use one another to see further (Simms, 2015, pp. 77–80).

What dialogue accomplishes, in a manner of speaking, is seating each participant as judge of his or her processes of thinking, interjecting what neuroscientists call executive function into the reflexes that predominate (Bohm, 1996b, pp. 83–95; see especially pp. 93–95). Everyone escapes the gravitational pull of one's beliefs, even if only for the duration of the conversation, inasmuch as doing so grants perspective.[7] Michal Kaczmarczyk (2018) derives three key qualities of legitimate dialogue. First is critical self-assessment, motivated by some combination of doubt, curiosity, and the ethical position known as fallibilism. Second is attention to the adequacy of the reasoning on which such thinking is based. Third is openness to the perspective of the other, in the hope of fusing horizons with one another (p. 62). So the focus is on two things: one's previously unexamined justifications and the alternatives presented by other people.

Sitting here reading these words gives you an opportunity to consider what Bohm was trying to say and hopefully convinces you that what he said makes sense. Dialogue sounds wholesome, you might say. You can think something abstractly, escaping that gravitational pull in the moment, and sometimes the impact will be profound. Some things you read will dramatically alter your worldview. But abstract thought is also frequently pale or ephemeral, like only reading about yoga. You can read a book and say that you understand yoga. To understand yoga, however, it helps to do it. Such tacit knowledge based on experience fixes it in the mind more thoroughly, with nuance and rigor. So for Bohm, the temporary escape from the gravitational pull of your own thinking is certainly salutary, but it is probably not enough. You have to experience it for yourself (Bohm, 1996b, p. 90). You have to go out and do it. Only then do you understand how hard and also how rewarding it can be. Dmitri Olshansky has written that "Bakhtin had no fear of intense, even violent confrontation. The carnival is not some country fair. It is a place of radical creativity, intense sexuality, grotesque spectacle, and constant inversion of natural order" (2002–2018). It helps to immerse yourself, up to the elbows.

---

6. Hans-Georg Gadamer called this a process of self-forgetting that is "experienced, not as a *loss* of self-possession, but as the free buoyancy of an elevation above oneself" (1976, p. 55).
7. On the ethical imperative to gain critical distance, see Harter (2017b).

We might say that abstract thinking is more like being a tourist and tacit knowledge is more like emigrating.

Having said this, I realize that my emphasis has been on the workings of the individual mind, i.e. how it functions separately. I have been selling dialogue here as an astringent for any one person's ability to think well. It will work for you, I say, because it does this and this for you. David Bohm was very careful to *avoid* giving the impression that the point of dialogue is individual improvement, so it is only fair that I add his admonition that dialogue is a way of participating in a larger reality. One surrenders a degree of individual autonomy, even if only for an evening, for the sake of being a part of the boundless. You quit being an isolated atom, bumping up against other atoms. You no longer have the luxury of sitting back like an audience member passing judgment on life's pageant. What *you* think in the moment is secondary to what *we* hope to think together. During dialogue, you and I build something together and share responsibility for it. What comes of it later is anyone's guess (see e.g. Csikszentmihalyi & Sawyer, 2014). In the present, dialogue is like group singing or amateur theatrics in an ensemble—in the same way that a string quartet shows up at the same place and works through a piece requiring each of them to act in concert for there to be music. A dialogue is like a jam session.

Reading the score is akin to abstract thought; actually playing the music yields tacit knowledge. Playing alone as practice is necessary; playing together should help you improve, but it also results in a performance that has its own value. For Bohm, dialogue as a way of being with other people has intrinsic value. Isaacs (1999) wrote:

> Dialogue is properly a gift relationship. . . . When we speak together in dialogue, we are speaking in a way that seeks to contribute one to the other. A conversation where the people are essentially trying to extract something from others moves away from dialogue.
>
> *(p. 393)*

So ultimately, rather than a course in self-improvement, dialogue is a ritual benefaction.

## Plato at the Heart of It All

The most famous dialogues were written thousands of years ago in ancient Athens. The practitioner is often regarded as the first philosopher. His pupil then took up the spirit and certainly much of the content of these dialogues in order to compose some of the most significant works of literature in human history.[8]

---

8. Kryštof Boháček (2018) reminds us that Plato wrote different kinds of dialogue—many of which bear little or no resemblance to what we ordinarily mean by the term. In *The Apology*, Socrates delivers three speeches at his trial. In several late dialogues, Socrates pays little or no role whatsoever. In the earlier dialogues, however, we see Socrates conducting what amounts to an

My access point to Plato is the political philosopher Eric Voegelin. One may ask why it would not be sufficient to rely on the words of Plato himself, yet his words are mediated already through translators, and Plato himself was mediating the words of Socrates. The interpretations of what Plato was trying to say are many. It was no exaggeration when Lord Whitehead (1978) wrote, "The safest general characterization of the European philosophical tradition is that it consists of a series of footnotes to Plato" (p. 39). I am relying on Voegelin not only because for several decades now I have found his voice to resonate, but more importantly because Voegelin's interpretation of Plato in particular discerns an emphasis less on *psyche* or *polis* and more on dialogue itself as the supreme ordering dynamic, as a *paideia*. Freise (2018) made the same assertion, to the effect that ultimately neither *psyche* nor *polis* is real, as in tangible, i.e. the focus of our consciousness (entitative). Instead, the most real is the encounter with one another (peregrinal). Dialogue is the process by which *psyche* and *polis* are being ordered (p. xxiv).[9] A.E. Taylor (2001) made a similar claim that for Plato philosophy is "the friction of minds employed in the joint pursuit of truth" (p. 149). It is less about arriving at answers than about conducting life deliberately together. Doing so is itself an ordering activity. Dialogue is, like leadership, a mode of being in the world.

Dialogue turns out to be a special kind of communication in which participants constitute themselves. I mean this in at least two ways. First, the participants constitute themselves **together**, in a shared order that is limited to the participants and also limited to the time during which they communicate. They create what Eric Voegelin called a "little cosmion," i.e. a temporary emergence of interpersonal order that evaporates when the dialogue ends and everybody goes home.[10] Krippendorf (2018) captured this ideal by saying that dialogue is a process of self-organizing (pp. 80–82). Second, the participants constitute themselves **separately**, as they participate with others in the dialogue, for each participant orders himself or herself in part by communicating with others. That is, we grow and sharpen our minds, increasing our knowledge and awareness, while practicing certain virtues such as deference and patience. We become something different (and presumably better) as a result of participating with others. Thus, when the dialogue ends, we bear the imprint of that order and take it with us into our daily lives. In this way, dialogue occupies an intermediate position between the *psyche* and the *polis*, as the dynamic mode between the micro and the macro which promises to edify them both. To the extent that either

---

interrogation of some hapless companion. I would not want to suggest that every Platonic dialogue is exemplary of what I refer to as dialogue.

9. In a similar fashion, Johnson recently wrote about the sidewalk rituals that constitute the city, as an example of emergent order (2001, p. 96, citing Jacobs, 1961).

10. Voegelin wrote, "The idea of personal membership in a community of the spirit, irrespective of family ties, was still in its infancy; it had just begun to express itself, in the fourth century, in the form of philosophical schools" (1957, p. 118).

*psyche* or *polis* is corrupted in some fashion, as they undoubtedly are (for Plato was not naïve), dialogue offers a place to escape and participate in something good, shielding oneself from the corrupting influences of reality.

In the *Timaeus*, Plato told a myth about creation in which the demiurge seeks to radiate his goodness as the "supreme principle which governs the coming-into-existence and the order of existence" (Voegelin, 1957, p. 200). This divine force imposes order on a preexisting substratum that possesses its own energy and to some extent resists being brought within the divine order, which implies that in the absence of the demiurge, this substratum qualifies as chaos in the popular sense of the term. That which conforms to the divine force, however, becomes a cosmos. Goodness—as that supreme principle (*arche*)—brings into being (*genesis*) an ordered existence (*kosmos*).

In a similar fashion, participants in dialogue bring their good intentions together in a shared act of creation, to elicit some kind of order out of the many forces at work in their individual lives. Each participant is beset by distractions and agendas, let alone trying to operate within a larger culture that intrudes into their thinking. They are embroiled in private appetites and superstitions, let alone the drama of living. They bear within themselves a degree of chaos. Simply bringing a variety of people together introduces further chaos—an amplification or coupling of chaos, as it were—unless participants quickly constitute themselves.

For Plato, Socrates functioned as the exemplar of a human demiurge who sought to radiate goodness. He was a true servant of the divine who sought to bring order to the souls of others and through them to the city of Athens (Voegelin, 1957, p. 8). To do this, he had to enter into the field of contending forces (Voegelin, 1957, p. 11). This agonistic field of struggle is itself the cosmion Socrates wished to create: not a formal place or process, not an institution, but a temporary arena where participants by their own consent bring their disordered thoughts and ideas to struggle with and against one another, for the sake of eliciting order. For Socrates, not only is dialogue of this kind an "agonistic field," but there is also an agonistic field *within* the individual soul, where disordered forces struggle on a micro level. Plato contended that "the psyche is a society of forces" (Voegelin, 1957, p. 125). That is to say, wrote Voegelin, that "dialogue is the symbolic form of the order of wisdom" (1957, p. 12).

Continuing with the mythology of Plato, dialogue is itself a judgment on the surrounding chaos, a rebuke of sorts to a disordered world. The participants withdraw from the bewildering flux for the sake of radiating good order. What we find are really two complementary motives. One is negative, in the sense that it is a turning-away-from (from busy-ness and unworthy activities, for example). The other is positive, in the sense that it is a turning-toward (Voegelin, 1957, p. 13). In the *Phaedrus*, Plato went so far as to refer to a state of erotic mania that obviously cannot be sustained indefinitely, despite the possibility that at this heightened level of animation, which we know as love, the participants embody the highest good (Voegelin, 1957, pp. 137, 140). Their communion is a manifestation of the ordering force of the cosmos. Moreover, dialogue, for Socrates, was the supreme form of lovemaking. (Or is it that lovemaking is the supreme form of dialogue?)

The participants therefore constitute themselves as a little cosmion, with a shared purpose of radiating goodness. Otherwise, as I have said before, it is radically indeterminate. As Voegelin put it, they "create existential community through developing the other man's true humanity in the image of his own" (1957, p. 13). Therefore, the one God whom they share draws likeminded people together, each of whom bears the imprint of order and willingly shares it with others, for their mutual edification, in a spirit of love.

In the *Phaedrus*, Plato describes a myth in which our souls, even before we are born, frolic in the wake of some divinity, like pilot fish, such that upon being born we seek each other out and happily recognize a preexisting bond. Through dialogue, as we each incarnate the divine, we bring that divinity into the world. God manifests in our communion (Voegelin, 1957, p. 19).[11] It will be brief. It will be incomplete. It is always at risk of collapsing into disorder. Its long-term effect is indeterminate.[12] Nevertheless, we embody the divine and go home edified, increasingly motivated to go find others and imprint order onto their lives—not through coercion, but through persuasion. Perhaps over time, as this dynamic continues, order radiates outward, into the lives of more and more people, gradually transforming society. That is the long-term hope. Nevertheless, so long as the dialogue lasts, the participants are bound to each other in a manifestation of the good (Voegelin, 1957, p. 43).

One of the themes in Plato's *Republic* is the rhythm of going up and going down (Voegelin, 1957, pp. 52–62; see also p. 116f). The participants in the dialogue themselves talk about going up and going down literally, and Socrates uses the same imagery in his famous Allegory of the Cave, but the underlying meaning of this imagery has to do with living in such a way that you do both. You ascend to contemplate the good, but then you must descend, back to your mundane lives, in part so that you can go attract others to the good. Otherwise, if the lovers of the good spend all of their time isolated in their little cosmion, the *polis* will be governed in default by the unenlightened (1957, p. 116). This whole pattern speaks to the ephemeral character of dialogue as a temporary mode of being, which must eventually disperse and give way to other modes.

---

11. This is a claim also made by Buber (1965).
12. Voegelin wrote that "it is beyond the powers of man to overcome the transitoriness of the flux and to create eternal Being. The eternal Form in Becoming is a fleeting moment between creation and dissolution" (1957, p. 123).

## Objections to Dialogue

We already mentioned the apprehension that dialogue would result in a hive mind in which the participants lose their individuality.[13] We stated that if done correctly, dialogue rejects any such thing. Also, dialogue is not presented here as the only means by which groups of people can conduct business. It is intended to be a choice. Other means, such as decision making, adjudication, negotiation, preaching, and teaching, small talk, and performances, also have their place.

For a person eager to accomplish things, dialogue can seem pointless, especially when it has no defined purpose. Busy people do not believe they have the time. A more substantive objection comes from a different angle. Those who regard truth as a fixed thing, capable of being enunciated, are likely to see dialogue as a sideshow, if not a threat. Either we know what is true (so why bother?) or there is no such thing as truth (so why bother?). It cannot be in the proper sense a quest for truth, many would argue, if the abiding spirit were one of openness and fallibilism. Taken to an extreme, dialogue resembles post-modern relativism, in which everybody has his or her own truth. In response, Dafermos (2018) points out that post-modernism rejects dialogue as pointless. Why is that? Dialogue does consider there to be such a thing as truth, against which we can measure our thoughts and ideas. What it questions is the belief that truth is a set of propositions to be derived by means of logic and evidence, like a possession that one hews from the dirt. Perhaps truth is a way of living and not an answer in the back of the book (Dafermos, 2018, p. A14). Even once somebody in dialogue speaks, rendering or manifesting the truth, whatever that might mean, that is by no means the end of the matter. What did the others hear? Many are the implications that nobody can readily assimilate. More dialogue is always required. If I were to concede that truth is something toward which dialogue directs itself, truth is also inexhaustible, nuanced, complex. The quest for truth never ends, not unlike the evolution of the Common Law that grinds steadily onward. Just because you cannot discern the boundary of an object does not mean it has none. You can approximate it. Nevertheless, epistemologically, according to Dafermos, it ought to be done socially (2018, p. A12).

Charles Taylor (2002) used Gadamer's hermeneutics to address the concern that we are incapable of understanding one another—a claim that sometimes pops up among post-modernists. At some point, wrote Taylor, we are each human and rational beings. If I try to make myself understood, I may not succeed, but if we keep trying there is hope. The breakthrough comes when

---

13. Steven Johnson referred to "swarm logic" (2001, p. 74)—but actually he meant something more like spontaneous order, in which each participant does his own thing. He even says that the key to swarm logic is local information and "street-level assessments" and not some top-down, authoritarian command. That mistaken way of thinking, he called the Myth of the Ant Queen (2001, ch. 1).

I quit assuming that you are wrong and instead see that what you are saying is a viable alternative (p. 141). That moment comes with a cost. But then, as Catherine Zuckert mentioned (2002), dialogue is not just about the content. It is also about becoming better acquainted (p. 203)—even with yourself! As she explained, with dialogue we are not describing a technique but a "way of being" with other people (p. 213).

Another objection to dialogue refers to the existence of power differences in any group (Dafermos, 2018, p. A13). To declare everybody equal is to ignore social reality. Genuine equality of status is impossible. To this, proponents of dialogue reply in at least two ways. First, dialogue does not pretend those differences do not exist. Dialogue is not a utopia. If anything, it makes those differences explicit and addresses them openly. In that sense, even the powerful must account for themselves—for their power as well as for their utterances. Second, the ideal of suspending one's assumptions makes equality of status for the duration of dialogue an aspiration. Nobody doubts that one basketball team might have more talent on its roster, yet you still have to play the game according to unbiased rules. Life is not fair, either, yet we still work toward fairness. Fairness is, if nothing else, a heuristic. In short, the presence of power differentials does not render dialogue useless.

Yet another objection arises from the increasing commodification of other human beings creating such an enormous divide that the idea of treating other people as persons is more difficult than ever, especially as social media puts greater distance between ourselves and those we interact with (Dafermos, 2018, p. A12; see Jemielniak & Przegalinska, 2020).[14] To which proponents reply that *of course* this is one of the reasons that dialogue is needed so desperately. Dialogue is a means of transforming our detachment and isolation into some degree of intimacy. Nobody said it would not be hard to do. This objection is actually an argument for dialogue, and not against it.

## Who Is the Leader of a Dialogue?

Participants in a dialogue can play multiple roles. Not everyone is necessarily the same. Socrates initiated and ultimately guided his dialogues by the asking of questions. David Bohm allowed for there to be an organizer and facilitator. William Isaacs outlined four significant roles, i.e. initiator, consensus builder, questioner, and thoughtful bystander. Don Levine foresaw a role for the classroom instructor to model dialogic behavior. At its simplest, there will be the one who speaks and those who listen.

According to an entitative ontology, each of these could be construed as the leader, yet they are not all the same function. Besides, the roles could shift

14. Jemielniak and Przegalinska caution that online dialogue can be exploited as free labor, when somebody hijacks thoughts and ideas to profit themselves or to use against participants later (2020, p. 194).

around, so that the leader at one minute could become a follower in the next. From a peregrinal ontology, however, we are not trying to isolate a leader so much as we are to detect the process of leadership, no matter who does what. As we saw in a previous chapter, leadership is a distinctive mode, which I would argue is necessary for participants in dialogue. Dialogue can be understood as the same leadership mode shared by all, no matter where that mode is embodied.

Frankly, those of us who practice dialogue have had the experience in which we forget ourselves, so caught up are we in the enthusiasm of discovery. We do not notice who said what. We no longer care. Everybody is animated. Trying to figure out people's roles at that point is inapt. By the same token, we have had the experience in which falling silent is itself a phase of grace, when we pause to ponder the moment and nobody does anything overt. Where lies leadership then?

If you recall, we stated that leadership might be explained as a mode of being in response to the boundless present, purposefully forbearing some things and resisting others, pursuing some things and fleeing others, toward a desired future consonant with an underlying structure in our souls that we share with other human beings—a structure we exemplify or invoke when we engage one another in discourse. That desired future takes shape in the collective imagination the more we talk. Whatever the content, the process of dialogue itself constitutes spontaneous order and exemplifies the good life. We can think of it as dialogue for its own sake, as we become more transparent to one another, more intimate, humble in our fallibilism and perpetually open. The difficulty lies in making the transition from discussion and debate, during which we talk at one another (at best), to mutuality, regarding one another less as an object and more as a Thou.

"In what consists the care of the soul, we know: a constant conversation of the soul with itself and with others" (Patočka, 2002, p. 137). I would like to give Buber the last word: "All the regulated chaos of the age waits for the break-through, and wherever a man perceives and responds, he is working to that end" (1965, p. 39). In a manner of speaking, then, dialogue comes into being as participants take response-ability for the present. They will have adopted a mode for leadership together.

## Preparation for the Next Chapter

I am indebted to Michael Holquist for his extensive account of the scholarship of Mikhail Bakhtin. In its broadest sense, Holquist wrote, dialogue suggests that meaning is relative to people in different positions at the same time (2002, p. 21). Not only do you and I have different points of view, we have different experiences. We bring different knowledge, opinions, and stories to the same place. Dialogue therefore is an event that is shared. Or as Holquist put it: "Being is a simultaneity; it is always co-being" (2002, p. 25). In what should now be a familiar construct, dialogue includes three centers: there is me, there is you, and there is the space we share. Dialogue serves as the means by which we structure that space. He called it the "architectonics" of ordering the parts into a whole (2002, p. 29). Furthermore, the process never stops.

When you ignore or stifle the other person (or persons), you ruin the process. For when you do, it is no longer dialogue. Doing the same thing at the macro level, in the *polis*, makes you a tyrant (2002, p. 34). Doing so at the interpersonal level makes you at the very least a jerk. But we can take this to a micro level: you can ignore or stifle other possibilities within your own *psyche*, where you are advised to consult multiple points of view in order to build a coherent and adaptable self. When you suppress some aspect, some interior voice, from the dialogical self, you build in vain. Something will not be quite right. Therapists exist to help you restore the little lost voice. Just as a piece of paper has two sides, therefore, so consciousness has at least two perspectives (2002, p. 36). What one can see, the other might not, and vice versa. That is why we need so many points of view.[15]

Apparently, Bakhtin took this entire dialogical approach to an extreme. According to Holquist (2002), he believed that "nothing is anything in itself" (2002, p. 38). Later, Holquist continued in this vein when he wrote that for Bakhtin, "nothing exists in itself and we live lives of buzzing, overlapping, endlessly ramifying simultaneity" (2002, p. 195). What he was alluding to is the connectedness of all things, the compact reality that our minds are so quick to lacerate conceptually, making distinctions and simply stopping there, clinging to the integrity of the part yet oblivious to the whole. At the social level, this manifests as drawing boundaries and policing for impurities, both literal and ideological (see Horvath, 2013; Douglas, 2003). It seems that, often in the preservation of the integrity of the part, rather than the whole, leaders lead the way (e.g. Kellerman, 2004, ch. 9). That's a shame.

In order to capitalize on this dialogical way of thinking for leadership studies at the macro level, I would like to shift my investigation toward the mathematized sciences. Here, we encounter dynamics that are dependent on communication among the parts. The quality and extent of this communication is a variable in the creation of something larger called synchrony. My guide in this adventure will be Steven Strogatz. The applicability of the mathematics of synchrony to the study of dialogue and leadership will then be addressed, followed by a brief description of a sociological approach to questions that Strogatz has been raising—an approach known as **social morphogenesis**. In other words, as he will show us, we can witness phenomena like dialogue among inanimate objects, animals, human tissue, and computers. What is going on there?

---

15. My previous book on the lectures of Michel Foucault (2016) elaborates on this ideal of a prospective leader cultivating this dialogical capability in the mind by consulting one's conscience and letting the leader-in-you confer with the philosopher-in-you.

# 9

# OSCILLATIONS, CHAOS, AND SYNC (OH MY!)

## Introduction to the Chapter

Our story thus far. This book set out to answer a question about leadership studies as the investigation of agency in social change. What are the dynamics in which leaders participate? And how is that manifest at the macro level?

In order to give ourselves a concrete example, this book considered the impact of Martin Luther's efforts to translate the Bible into the vernacular. What we found is that his exertions took place within a context that has its own significance. Not only did he struggle against a very complex institution, but he used that institution for his purposes and helped to build up his own, as an informal partnership of Wittenberg University, the publishing industry, the Saxon princes, and a slew of like-minded reformers. At that point, we were confronted with the tension between the leader as a social agent and his context, with its various institutional structures.

Luther's story revealed that leadership belongs to complex phenomena. It is a complex phenomenon in its own right. There is no way in principle to understand completely what happened. The complexity exceeds our powers of understanding. If with hindsight we have difficulty tracing the impact of leadership, as a practical matter, then leadership in the heat of the moment cannot possibly foresee everything that could happen next. There are too many moving parts. Moreover, whatever a leader does will likely have unintended consequences.[1] Despite this incapacity to design a world of complete and utter comprehensibility, one does find that spontaneous order will evolve toward a

---

1. Polanyi (1951) pointed out that scientists of all people are incapable of predicting the direction of science itself for many of the same reasons (p. 110).

number of broad patterns and principles. Leaders would be advised to appreciate the complexity without surrendering to it.

As students of leadership, we have been charged by Karl Jaspers to delimit our investigations, making plain what we study and what we do not study. Within that boundary, we were advised to differentiate the parts and the whole, but then also to consider the dynamics between these two, for it is these dynamics we ultimately want to understand. We want to learn about the mutually constituting forces of social action and emergent order, as they shape one another.

This book then offered as an example of spontaneous order the long-standing institution of the Common Law, in which no single person rises as the leader. Instead, the complex web of unwritten expectations carries forward customary practices, adapting these expectations to changing times, but always reinforcing certain deep and unspoken precepts about prosperity, fairness, and peace. Within such an order, liberty becomes a goal in part because it is by means of our ingenuity at the immediate, local level that we respond to changing conditions and make incremental improvements, validating the tradition without deferring to it blindly.

After considering the ambiguous role of the lone hero (Luther) and the complex phenomenon of a long-standing, pervasive, and distinctly impersonal institution (Common Law), we turned to the obvious question about which of these is primitive: the agent or the structure, the hero or the institution? By now, of course, we recognize this as a false dilemma. The two work together over time to shape one another, in a never-ending cascade. Neither is primitive. So how do we talk about the relationship between these two entities?

Heidegger (1981/1995) outlined a peregrinal ontology, by which we consider not the entities as distinct things (neither agent nor structure), but instead the flow of activity, as one event bleeds seamlessly into the next, i.e. the course of changes or movement across time. Leadership can be imagined as a mode of participation within that flow, a way of engaging with others in the transformation of the present into a future that more closely accords with our deepest sense of order—a sense we share with one another. From this way of imagining, we implicate history as the complex flow where leadership manifests. That is, we begin to realize a model of leadership within the dynamics of emergent order that takes place all around us and never rests.[2] Rather than having to choose between leader and context, agent and structure, we can speak of leadership as a mode.

The chapter you just read offered a concrete example in which people constitute themselves, creating a temporary order of limited scope among participants. Dialogue can be a sociological form, with a loose but discernible structure. But what dialogue illustrates is the necessity of participating in a

---

2. The term "emergence" means "the process by which patterns or global-level structures arise from interactive local-level processes" (Mihata, 1997, p. 31; see generally Johnson, 2001).

distinct mode, with a distinct attitude of openness toward the spontaneous order that emerges among the participants. Dialogue does not work without it. You can seat people in a circle and invite them to talk, but dialogue depends on the mode by which they conduct themselves in that setting. For leadership scholars, dialogue is a way of witnessing the process that on a large scale formed the Common Law. Dialogue is a nimble, almost ephemeral activity compared to the majesty of the Common Law, yet they each demonstrate the processes of leadership in which participants seek to manifest their shared sense of how human beings ought to live together.

Going all the way back to the example of Martin Luther, we can see that the main characters in that momentous drama missed an opportunity to engage in anything like dialogue. In fairness, Luther did adopt a mode of reaching out to engage others in their preferred idiom. He wrote in Latin as he tried to engage scholars in a debate. Even his method of delivery—posting theses on the church door—fit the practice of the day. You could argue that he was trying to establish a dialogue. Later, he wrote in German to his parishioners. His method of delivery here was quite different, as he assiduously cultivated the popular press that was only then coming into being. It is true, unfortunately, that he ended up lashing out as things got out of hand, forgetting his temper and abandoning the spirit of amity. At one point or another in his weakness and desperation, he condemned the Roman Catholic Church, the uprising peasants, the Jews, and just about everybody. By then, we can see that his leadership waned to a vanishing point. What he is known for—and what changed the face of Europe—were his efforts within that mode of leadership that we were talking about. We can set aside the rest as a failure, even an embarrassment to his legacy. We have to make that kind of distinction. It is not the man Luther that we in leadership studies set out to judge. It is his leadership. I do not know of a simpler way to say it.

From a broader perspective, which we have been calling the macro, people do work together. They rise up, organize, march, migrate, coordinate, collaborate, and otherwise act in concert. How does that happen? We might call this phenomenon **social synchrony**.

## The Experience of Synchrony

I accept Brian Eno's contention that the imagination can aid the work of science and that science enriches the imagination. They are mutually constituting. A scholar who exemplifies that symbiosis is Steven Strogatz. His 2003 bestseller *Sync* promises to enrich the imagination of leadership scholars interested in the question of how we are to investigate leadership at the macro level. A brief tour of his book follows.

Strogatz specializes in applied mathematics and more particularly in the phenomenon of synchrony or "sync"—which is an example of spontaneous order in which oscillations in different entities or objects fall into a conjoined pattern. Now, before we start, not everything that occurs in tandem deserves to be called synchrony. Male fireflies each light up at twilight according to some internal cadence, whether anyone else is there or not. They will blink on and off regardless. Likewise, when you drop two tennis balls at the same time, they should fall side-by-side and bounce in a similar fashion. They were designed that way. There is no reason to puzzle over their behavior. Either of these oscillations (the blinking and the bouncing) can originate from within, like turn signals on a car, or they can originate from without, like the tides being tugged by the moon. Seeing two identical things behave in exactly the same way at the same time is not strange. "Well, of course," we say, "they were each separately responding to the same cause." Alternatively, in some instances, the appearance of synchrony is only a coincidence, happenstance, a matter of luck. We can readily think of examples in social settings where people act in ways that appear to be conjoined or collaborative, from one person to the other, but instead are internally caused, externally caused, or happenstance.

What fires the imagination of Strogatz is when two or more oscillations come together on their own to form a shared pattern, like flipping a toggle switch simultaneously. They become "phase coherent" (2003, p. 134). Synchrony does not appear to be the result of either internal or external causes. Neither is it happenstance. So, what gives?

His description begins simply. In order to avoid distractions and clutter, let us begin with two and only two identical entities exhibiting a pattern in which they oscillate unerringly in tandem. Synchrony occurs when these two entities "couple" by communicating, however that is being done (2003, p. 3). Neither of them individually nor some external force made this happen. The pattern emerges *from their interactions*. Even when their separate oscillations begin in seeming disarray, over the course of time the pair will align or attune with one another. As his book unfolds, Strogatz complicates this rudimentary schema, proceeding in this fashion:

> from the most primitive form of coordinated behavior—a pair of identical rhythms in sync—through ever more intricate choreographies in time and space: from two oscillators to many, from identical oscillators to diverse ones, from rhythms to chaos, from global coupling to local interactions in space.
>
> *(2003, p. 232)*

What if the number who participate is unlimited? What if they are not alike? What if their in-built oscillations vary widely? What if only some of them can communicate?

The remarkable thing is that he finds empirical examples of synchrony in physics, chemistry, biology, computing, psychology, and ultimately in mathematics. Like Leonardo, Strogatz suspects that synchrony is one of those underlying, unifying dynamics that works across the disciplines—not exclusively as a metaphor or analogy. Though if an analogy, it is a remarkably deep one (2003, p. 214).[3]

Throughout his book, the author acknowledges the difficulty in accounting for complex phenomena, which is why he begins with a radically simplified model and develops from there (2003, p. 35). By no means did he intend to ignore the incalculable complexity of the real world. Like Jaspers, he just has to set aside or bracket reality for the sake of having a manageable problem to solve. The mathematical theme for all this, he writes, is spontaneous order. How does it work? Where does it come from? It would seem that these systems synchronize themselves and are self-organizing (2003, p. 21). Even inanimate objects can organize themselves (2003, p. 109). No leadership required. At first, the whole idea of complex adaptive systems sounded like voodoo or mystification; but then (as Strogatz generously allows), plenty of physical laws explain behavior that can seem impossible (2003, p. 152; see e.g. Laszlo, 1996, p. 71). Non-local causation is now part of physics. Accordingly, he trusts mathematics to shed light on the mystery he calls synchrony. In the simplest version of the model the two oscillations (whatever they are) become "absorbed" into behaving as one (2003, p. 23).[4]

---

3. The Cabreras were to call this a far transfer (2015, p. 115f). They cite the example of Charles Darwin transferring lessons he had learned from geology.
4. **Stochastic resonance** is a type of synchrony, when a weak signal (trigger or infusion) can be amplified and optimized by the assistance of preexisting noise (see Gammaitoni, Hänggi, Jung, & Marchesoni, 1998). This is not the synchrony of equivalent oscillations operating in parallel, like two fireflies or two neurons of comparable strength; instead, it is a conversion of noise—which is louder, more diffuse—to magnify the signal. The imagery of stochastic resonance is particularly apt for leadership. You participate in a preexisting activity (noise) and work with it to achieve your purpose (signal).

  Given a number of independent oscillations such as fireflies or neurons, one might think that statistically, they would occur at rates according to the familiar bell curve distribution. At the beginning, in fact, they will tend to, with most of them clustering around a kind of average rate and a few outliers at both ends running extra fast or extra slow. For a while, the variation in their rhythms tends to cancel each other out (Strogatz, 2003, p. 174); but after multiple iterations you might notice an increasing unity that at some threshold or "phase transition" snaps the entire collection into uniformity (2003, p. 54). An unstable equilibrium thereafter holds them in place (2003, p. 61).

  Strogatz progresses in the book toward the challenge of chaos. Chaos is by definition deterministic. It is not random and does not admit an uncaused cause. Nevertheless, it will be, in his words, "erratic [with] seemingly random behavior in an otherwise deterministic system; predictability in the short run, because of deterministic laws; and unpredictability in the long run, because of the butterfly effect" (2003, p. 188). At first blush, therefore, it seems unlikely that chaos can be part of synchrony. Strogatz assures us that indeed you can have coupled chaotic systems (2003, p. 193). By this point, we reach ideas too abstruse for someone like me to master and probably beyond what is necessary for our purpose. Suffice it to say that leadership is a seemingly chaotic process of bringing unlike participants into some kind of sync within a chaotic context that flows in a turbulent manner toward an unforeseen future. For his part, Strogatz then alludes to "the study of nonlinear systems composed of enormous numbers of parts" (2003, p. 209) and to complexity theory.

Karl Jaspers, if you recall, had urged investigators to examine the parts, breaking things down and looking closely at the micro phenomena. Leadership studies has been doing that. At the same time, Jaspers urged stepping back to look at the encompassing whole. Strogatz tells the story of synchrony as an attempt to see the big picture. "The whole system has to be examined all at once," he wrote, "as a coherent entity" (2003, p. 182). From this enlarged vantage point, one can see global patterns that signify the presence of a network defined by its relationships among its hubs and nodes (2003, p. 231; Jokisaari, 2017; see generally Barabási, 2003). The structure determines the dynamics as least as much as the dynamics determine the structure (Strogatz, 2003, p. 237).

Just to get our bearings: we know from leadership studies that agents influence one another. We already saw in these pages that agents and structures influence one another. Taken together, agents and structures influence the dynamics that will occur between and among them, just as the dynamics influence the agents and structures that will emerge. I have been trying to say that leadership is a mode of participating in these complex, mutually constituting dynamics.

Looking back, we saw that dialogue exists as a circle where every participant faces one another, in direct contact. Plainly, human society is too vast and intricate to allow for such immediacy. The structure will have to be more complex. Accordingly, we find the emergence of sub-groups, plenty of indirect communication such as rumor, and attempts at one-directional broadcasts to reach the widest audience without opportunities for feedback. As Strogatz explains in his book, these more complex structures are be analyzed by using network theory. He consults network theory to understand social phenomena such as fads. A fad is a type of synchrony. How do large-scale populations with irregular connections transition toward synchrony?

Large-scale networks are usually comprised of clusters (e.g. families, neighborhoods, political parties, and the like) (2003, p. 240). These clusters link loosely, if at all, with the rest of the network. Yet the vulnerability to abrupt and massive change across the network depends on weak connections across clusters, where only a few people (known as brokers) have access to wildly disparate clusters—groups that would otherwise have little traffic between them. Some individuals belong to two very different clusters simultaneously. They straddle disparate worlds. Their role in social synchrony is key. The presence of these "links" determines how likely it is that a society will be able to transform quickly and completely. These weak connections enhance the likelihood of leadership. These leaders are in fact mediators—about whom there will be more to say in chapter 14.[5]

---

5. Jemielniak and Przegalinska note the presence online of "hackerspaces" where participants with varied knowledge and skills interact, often anonymously, to trade in processes of peer production (2020, p. 121). These are literally social networks with fluctuating structures of authority on behalf

Structures among clusters that are linked loosely across the network turn out to be especially adaptable, open to local conditions and extensive experimentation within clusters, but swift to collaborate efficiently when required (2003, p. 248f). This "small-world architecture" also requires only a few simple rules to permit it to survive (2003, p. 251; see again Cabrera & Cabrera, 2015; Johnson, 2001). It is not necessary to impose an elaborate regime.[6] At this point, we should recall the structure of the Common Law.

Think of it this way. Leadership at the micro or retail level in which change is attributable to a solitary person is ultimately unreliable as a model. Experts say that it is insufficiently robust (Strogatz, 2003, pp. 15, 258). Perhaps a broader, more impactful form of leadership lies in creating and sustaining these architectures—as in taking responsibility for the network. Rather than focusing on the process by which change occurs, perhaps we should focus on the process by which systems emerge to facilitate and process change. This is not a trivial distinction. You can lead at the micro level, but can you lead at the macro level? Think of it as a choice: you can champion a cause or you can tend the structure. You can be an activist reacting to the system or a steward of the system. Strogatz is interested in the social structures that undergo emergence. Something of the sort was what Heifetz (1994) referred to as a holding environment. Abraham Lincoln (1953–1955) wanted to end the practice of slavery. However, he admitted that he needed to secure the union as a paramount task. Only once emancipation was compatible with his macro aims of winning the war did he issue his famous proclamation (see Harter, 2015, ch. 8). Michael Polanyi, writing about scientific research, wrote, "The function of public authorities is not to plan research, but only to provide opportunities for its pursuit" (p. 111). We might contemplate the leadership that makes these networks flourish.

We find two levels of leadership, therefore: the retail and the wholesale. In a Common Law jurisdiction, attorneys operate at both levels. They must vigorously represent the interests of their clients and try to help them prevail (retail), though at the same time they are officers of the court, with an enduring loyalty to the law itself and to its faithful administration (wholesale). These roles are, like so many things, mutually constituting, just as athletic coaches try to win, but only while upholding the integrity of the game and sportsmanship. Or college professors who teach their classes in areas of specialization and also govern their institutions by serving on committees and taking turns as department chairs, deans, and provosts.

---

of users' liberty. Challenging the role of agency, however, online bots have been conducting business and influencing users for some time, using the virtual order that prevails to limit the liberty of living human beings (2020, p. 191).

6. Strogatz differentiates structures from leadership. With regard to structures, de Landa (2000) will differentiate these so-called meshworks that Strogatz is here describing from more rigid structures known as hierarchies, about which there will be more later.

Many a battlefield commander depends on an elaborate superstructure of logistics, intelligence, and weapons manufacture. Leadership lies in both (a) using the system to achieve certain ends and (b) managing the system itself. What Strogatz implies is that leadership at the macro level where you oversee the network's capabilities is at least as important, if not more so. But beware: the network must not be commandeered to run as though it requires leadership at the retail level. You do not run the whole company in the same way that you run a shift on the factory floor. There is a time and place for that kind of leadership, which Hayek would have called the enterprise—issuing orders, trying to win, serving a mission. However, there is also a responsibility of self-restraint to construct and enforce a relatively supple field in which leadership at the micro level can operate under the fewest necessary rules. You need both coaches and referees, barristers and judges, agents and structures.

Strogatz understood as an empirical matter that the rules by which a society orders itself are elaborate and (to a great extent) unknowable (2003, p. 261).[7] He was not naïve. Yet even here, we notice what looks like sync. Part of what makes social synchrony difficult to model is the enormous diversity of its composition—the people, the relationships, the norms, and institutions. It matters who all is participating (2003, p. 264). It also matters how they are connected. Is this a mob gathering at City Hall or an online chat group (see e.g. Jemielniak & Przegalinska, 2020)? Are there already people nominally in charge? Strogatz hesitated to transfer his findings from synchrony directly to social systems, as though human beings are cogs in a machine, yet he saw something of the same patterns there.[8]

We know from network theory that nodes are competing for connections because connection means survival (Barabási, 2003, p. 106). Linkages improve one's competitive advantage. They also improve the *network's* competitive advantage.[9] One of the findings that Lincoln intuited at a young age (1838) is that a social actor connected to many other people, such as neighbors, friends, and coworkers, is less suggestible.[10] The many voices one hears tend to cancel each other out. In that configuration, no single person exerts disproportionate

---

7. Johnson (2001) disagrees, arguing that the rules themselves can be quite simple.
8. Albert-László Barabási (2003, p. 222) was not so reticent:

> Network thinking is poised to invade all domains of human activity and most fields of human inquiry. It is more than another helpful perspective or tool. Networks are by their very nature the fabric of most complex systems, and nodes and links deeply infuse all strategies aimed at approaching our interlocked universe.

9. For similar reasons, armies compete to occupy rural crossroads and urban intersections.
10. Put in terms of systems thinking, "at critical levels both excessive [parts and interactions] can diminish adaptive fitness" (Elliott & Kiel, 1997, p. 75). Fewer people and fewer interrelationships among them thereby increase the adaptability of the whole. Interestingly, chaotic systems are in one sense easier to influence, if you are a prospective leader, because all it takes is a nudge toward a more stable orbit. Stable systems are less easily nudged out of their orbit (Bird, 1997, p. 144).

influence (2003, p. 266). Perhaps this is why controlling spouses, cult leaders, and totalitarian regimes try to restrict the networks of their followers and instead isolate them, so that the proportional impact of the "leader" is that much greater (see Arendt, 1970). A less malign version of this dynamic is the role in any social network of hubs or brokers, because hubs are by definition so widely connected. If a hub switches from A to B, its impact on the network is that much greater because of a greater reach. Therefore, anyone seeking positions of influence might aspire to become a hub, widely connected, and perhaps prevent followers from doing the same. That strategy has a limited impact over the entire span of the network, however, compared with the hub that *helps other nodes become hubs* themselves (see also Manz & Sims, 1989; Heifetz, 1994). If you think about it, a hub's access to multiple other hubs expands its efficacy while diminishing its uniqueness, i.e. its relative status. (By the end of my book, you will recognize this lesson again.)

Strogatz notes that in sparse networks such as small businesses and small towns, where connections are already few, the hubs enjoy a disproportional share of influence. Here, some version of the Great Man will probably prevail. Leadership studies is right to study these phenomena. As those connections throughout the network become tighter and more extensive, though, the need for a Great Man diminishes (2003, p. 268; see also van Vugt & Ahuja, 2011). In fact, a large, tightly woven network will probably be in a position to resist attempts by the Great Man to impose a singular vision.

The image of the network captures the "peregrinal ontology" we introduced in a previous chapter, as some kind of energy passes from node to node. A network is a pulsating field of exchanges and encounters. Mathematics can help to determine the optimal structure of these networks, not unlike finding the best way to manage traffic flow (2003, p. 270). People on their own will make seemingly independent decisions that—taken together with everybody else—constitute social patterns, even without mathematics (Johnson, 2001). Some patterns are more durable and successful at helping participants achieve their myriad goals. (Traffic engineers do not tell you to go to the grocery; they are responsible for finding the best way to facilitate your desire to go to the grocery at the same time that your neighbor wants to drive to the airport.)

Strogatz points out that some stable patterns are stuck, resisting growth or improvement. Systems do have resilience, which might seem like a good thing until you stand back and try to wrench it completely into a new pattern. The stable system itself resists modification (2003, p. 271). Margaret Archer teaches us that they have "morphostatic mechanisms" (2013, p. 1). In actual practice, of course, many patterns emerge and then dissipate, crystalize, and disintegrate.

Synchrony is more likely when the variation with regard to oscillation within a system is less (Strogatz, 2003, p. 272). This only makes sense. If we are all relatively similar, the chances that we will sync increases, like fireflies and tennis balls. But that would teach us the wrong lesson if a leader tried to render the followers similar, if not identical, in order to combat fluctuations and diversity—all for the sake of synchrony. As Strogatz words it, a healthy social system has to tolerate a degree of "noise intensity" to keep from falling into groupthink and totalitarian sameness. At those magnitudes, "synchrony becomes a symbol of all that is subhuman" (2003, p. 273). We might say that in subhuman synchronies, columns of fungible soldiers goosestep in cadence through the streets.

What Strogatz considers optimal in the long term (which he called a supple form of sync) is precisely what Hayek had noticed in the spontaneous order he liked to refer to as a catallaxy. It must tolerate, if not encourage diversity, with an openness to change, without evaporating into formlessness (i.e. anarchy).

At the macro level, we can describe and to some extent measure this structure. Strogatz then shows that the same basic patterns of synchrony occur at the micro. They are not restricted to large-scale phenomena. Let us take a look at one of his examples. Insight, he wrote, is a burst of synchrony in the brain (2003, p. 277). In the "neural commotion" of the nervous system, synchrony occurs and subsides repeatedly. He then wrote that "synchronized neural activity is consistently associated with primitive forms of cognition, memory, and perception" (2003, p. 279). Furthermore, "consciousness may be the subjective experience of these states of synchrony passing by in our brains" (2003, p. 283). These mental events are more likely to survive in the long run the greater the synchrony up front, when learning (2003, p. 280; see Medina, 2009). Another way to say this is that you are likelier to remember that which synced up to begin with. Why is that? Because that synchrony is likelier to recur later as memory. It persists outside of direct consciousness until an opportune time. It becomes subsidiary (SFI). The experience of no-longer-forgetting, of restoring a previous synchrony, we should call *anamnesis* (see Voegelin, 2002). Some psychologists call these patterns beneath consciousness archetypes (e.g. Peterson, 1999). Johnson wrote of emergence (2001).

The same worry that we found with a stable equilibrium at the social level, i.e. that the whole can become too rigid and insular, pertains to the *psyche* as well. Some orderliness in the mind is desirable, obviously, yet it is possible to become fixated at a suboptimal level, such that opportunities to think afresh and learn something new become more difficult, if not rejected out of hand. As one might say, "I've thought that through to my satisfaction." At that point, the mind lapses into ideology and dogma. Instead, the *psyche* requires its own supple form of sync with a fundamental openness to being corrected, which philosophers call **fallibilism** (see Rescher, 1998), which is something we had reason to mention in the chapter on dialogue. The implications for the practice of dialogue should be obvious. To my way of thinking, and I honestly believe this to be a significant claim, dialogue is precisely the flow that keeps the *polis* and the *psyche* supple.

Strogatz concludes his book by offering nonlinear mathematics as a powerful analytical tool for the study of social order (2003, p. 286). He turns to the imagery of fluid dynamics as his paradigm "where the roiling of a turbulent fluid intermittently gives birth to coherent structures like helices and plumes, rather than degenerating into a bland, uniform smear" (2003, p. 287). It is not that the turbulence itself evidences leadership. Turbulence has many fathers. It is the generative capacity of turbulence where opportunities for leadership arise. Turbulence (which is often construed as a crisis) can be the context most conducive for the emergence of leadership.

The mind has to capitalize on its internal turbulence, using it and remaining open to its vicissitudes, without neglecting the encompassing order that emerges. The brain must, in his terms, synchronize chaos (2003, p. 288). We saw this previously with regard to SFI in an early chapter. In Strogatz's experience, there is something fascinating about the possibilities. He has found this dynamic of synchronization "beautiful and strange and profoundly moving, in a way that can only be described as religious. . . . [T]he spectacle of sync strikes a chord in us, somewhere deep in our souls [and] touches people at a primal level" (2003, p. 289). I concur. Strogatz's testimony foreshadows my book's conclusions.

## The Processes Behind Social Synchrony

The study of synchrony at the level of mathematics and physics, though difficult, can prove to be useful. Nevertheless, we in leadership studies do have to remember that social phenomena are qualitatively different from what they study in the natural sciences. Even if there is such a thing as social synchrony, as Strogatz claims, we are still talking about people with free will and about their inter-relationships, which are immaterial realities. That fact alone complicates things (see generally Searle, 1984). Another limitation of the work being done by Strogatz is that it eschews the causal mechanisms that make it happen (see also Back, 1997, p. 47; Polanyi, 1951, p. 19). Each individual science has the burden of undertaking that piece of the puzzle. Biology has to explain biological processes. Chemistry has to explain chemical processes. How does social synchrony come about? Tony Lawson sees language of emergence, self-organization, and synchrony as "a placeholder [in] the absence of any account of processes whereby unprecedented phenomena occur" (2013, p. 62; see generally Johnson, 2001). He continues, "It does seem *prima facie* mysterious that a novel form of entity, etc., and so order, should ever be possible, whatever the context" (2013, p. 62). The mathematics of the thing is insufficient to explain where it comes from.

Strogatz confesses to being in thrall to the experience of synchrony. Something about it fascinates him. This makes sense given that his task was not to explain why it occurs. It probably does seem mysterious. Yet as Douglas Porpora argues, "Social systems do not just spontaneously and mystically self-organize" (2013, p. 36). Sociologists go deeper into the mechanism, penetrating the mystery. We might say that their job is, in part, to investigate the causal mechanisms behind spontaneous order, as set forth by Hayek. One specific approach to doing so is known as social morphogenesis, to which we now turn.

The ideas surrounding social **morphogenesis** were ascribed originally to Margaret Archer. Her studies into the dynamics of social change take experiences of the sort described by Strogatz and try to analyze them in a systematic fashion through a sociological lens. By doing so, she brings us that much closer to seeing leadership at the macro level.[11] In other words, social morphogenesis promises to explain the processes by which social synchrony occurs.

The goal is to describe the processes by which society changes (Hofkirchner, 2013, pp. 129–132; see Donati, 2013, p. 206f).

(a) Some processes simply **reproduce** what already exists, leading to persistence of the same basic form. Think for example of electing a politician's successor into office: "Meet the new boss/same as the old boss" (Townsend, 1999).

(b) Some processes lead to **growth**, generating more of the same, such as larger markets, more nation-states, more laws, etc.

(c) Some processes **replace** what exists with something else, as might happen upon conquest or revolution (a discontinuous process, aka REVO).

(d) some processes **transform** what exists into something else (a continuous process, aka EVO). Evidence of these processes might be a new product, a new paradigm, a new social structure, and so forth (Porpora, 2013, p. 30f).[12]

Any useful theory must answer three questions (Donati, 2013, p. 228):

- How is **variety** produced in the first place?
- How is a winner **selected**?
- How is it **stabilized** in a process known as elaboration?

11. The term "morphogenesis" itself refers to a process that might be more properly called morphogenetic/morphostatic mechanisms or M/M. The former is the generation of a new shape or form, whereas the latter is the prevention of changing the existing shape or form (Porpora, 2013, p. 25). Both processes exist in any social system of any complexity. They tug and pull against one another.

A word of caution: do not let the term "mechanism" here fool you. Archer differentiates M/M from genuinely mechanical processes. For her, social change is qualitatively different (2013, pp. 8, 15), for reasons of particular interest to leadership studies. She wrote that "many metaphorical borrowings by social theorists need to be stripped of their over-hasty appropriations from complexity theory in natural science and some practitioners of the latter need to restrain their buccaneering" (2013, p. 15).

12. In the *psyche*, for purposes of comparison, we remember, learn, change our minds, or refine our understanding. It is the same basic array of four possibilities.

The process occurs over time (Porpora, 2013, p. 28). Any change arises out of **antecedent** conditions, such as expectations, customs, and rules. It consists of **behaviors** within that context. And it results in **consequences**.

antecedents → behavior → consequences

What happened previously influences what can happen now, and what happens now will influence what can happen tomorrow (Lawson, 2013, p. 75). Throughout this three-stage process, morphogenesis is comprised of three distinct, yet interdependent elements known as social **structure**, **agency**, and **culture** (together referred to as SAC) (Porpora, 2013, p. 26; Hofkirchner, 2013, p. 147). Many scholars unnecessarily collapse these three into one another, though we might imagine them better as imbricated, i.e. layered and overlapping, like tiles on the roof. At each stage, all three exist, even if they are each undergoing change (Porpora, 2013, p. 26f). For example, there are preexisting structures, a preexisting culture, and social actors shaped by both structure and culture before anything of interest to us happens (Lawson, 2013, p. 72). Then something new does happen. When the change under investigation concludes, there will still be structures, social agents, and a culture, and they will be different somehow. We might construct a two-dimensional table to capture the permutations (Table 9.1).

During the change process, social agents dip into reflexivity. This is a key phase in morphogenesis because it recognizes the creativity human beings possess to make choices (Archer, 2013, p. 8f; Porpora, 2013, p. 29; Forbes-Pitt, 2013, pp. 105, 115; Hofkirchner, 2013, p. 137). Many social theorists have erased agency by characterizing individual human beings as "parts" or "nodes" without a history, without personality, and without unique notions about the good (Forbes-Pitt, 2013, p. 106). Network theory, as we saw, tends to do that. This "dip into reflexivity" is the time for **cognition**—for operations such as contemplating, strategizing, and imagining. Nevertheless, the process dies if social actors do not communicate about what they are thinking (shades of dialogue!). Of course, **communication** does not result in actual change until social actors get up out of their seats and **cooperate** (Hofkirchner, 2013,

**TABLE 9.1** Permutations for Analyzing Social Morphogenesis.

|  | Antecedents | Behaviors | Consequences |
| --- | --- | --- | --- |
| Structures |  |  |  |
| Agency |  |  |  |
| Culture |  |  |  |

p. 137; see Donati, 2013, p. 218). That is, human beings can be seen to move through a progression.

- Cognition (reflexivity/ideas)
- Communication (recursivity/actions)
- Cooperation (stabilization into a new norm/relations)

Part of the problem for scholars is that free will on the part of one person makes the outcome radically uncertain. When two persons communicate, they double the uncertainty. Into this uncertain process with all of its moving parts, morphogenesis insists that at any given point in time, there are multiple mechanisms vying to bring about or prevent change (Archer, 2013, p. 13; Maccarini, 2013, pp. 50, 55).[13] The change process does not take place in a vacuum. Morpho**genesis** as a causal or generative mechanism with positive feedback works against morpho**stasis** with negative feedback (Porpora, 2013, p. 25). Furthermore, more than one of each is unfolding everywhere you look. Leader A is trying to get everybody to choose X, yet leader B is urging the same people to choose Y. These social actors are trying to change some things but not others.

What we find is an elaborate and bewildering array of causal mechanisms at various stages of unfolding, both large-scale and small, for and against change, for (and against) totally unrelated goods, dependent on different types of people with multiple, conflicting wants and desires who can at any point change their minds—all simultaneously generating noise. The leader presumes to marshal resources to bring one of these arcs to completion. As often as not, these "arcs" cancel each other out, resulting in no change and pent-up frustration instead. Johnson wrote that effective leaders have to "reach around" the noise (2001, p. 175).

So, social change will be difficult if not impossible to predict because of (a) randomness, which occurs even in natural systems; (b) our own fallibility and bounded rationality as observers; (c) the sheer complexity of the system, both in breadth and depth; (d) unintended consequences; (e) the fact that every

---

13. Archer says that society presents us with "a complex array of empirical manifestations, since multiple mechanisms can and do interfere with one another's exercise and resultant outcomes" (2013, p. 13). What we end up with, if we look closely, is a process that is "uncontrolled, non-teleological, non-homeostatic, non-adaptive and therefore unpredictable" (quoted in Maccarini, 2013, p. 48). With so much going on, there is no way to predict what the hurly-burly of their force and counterforce will generate (Maccarini, 2013, p. 50). Maccarini states that "explanation [of social phenomena] involves multiple rather than single trajectories. Multiple processes overlap and intersect one another and explaining 'social facts' involves a particular logic, situating outcomes in terms of their location in intersecting trajectories with their independent temporalities" (2013, p. 55). For instance, it may be that two strong social forces clash and hold one another in equipoise, more or less canceling each other out, leaving some third, weaker force to operate uncontested and seem for all the world to be the strongest (Lawson, 2013, p. 68; see also p. 72).

change alters the context for subsequent change, so that no two episodes can be identical; and (f) each social actor's ever-changing free will/reflexivity.

Social morphogenesis as a way of studying social change does not pull any punches. It is designed to account for the complexity we should expect to find. In a manner of speaking, though, it displaces the criticism of synchrony implicit in Archer's work. That is, she had complained that what the mathematicians and their ilk had been neglecting was any scrutiny of the causal mechanism, when in fact she isolates the "mechanism" in the indeterminate activity of social actors, within the context of a specific structure and culture. There lies her black box. Perhaps as a sociologist she cannot penetrate further, but it does sound a lot like she has not exactly bagged the hare. She seems to have left it for somebody else to do.

I humbly suggest that leadership studies step into the breach.

## Using a Morphogenetic Toolkit

Martin Luther stands as a champion of what Archer calls reflexivity, which in his case was the untrammeled conscience of the believer in discourse with God and man. He had chafed under the forced synchrony of a dysfunctional social order, so that when he finally asserted himself openly, he found entire nations respond to his example—not in apish imitation, but with the same spirit of liberation. A new synchrony at a higher level of abstraction cut swaths through Western Europe.[14] Structures fell or transformed. Culture certainly cauliflowered, elaborating into national identities. Most importantly, social agents became more aware of their agency. Lutheran theologian T.A. Kantonen wrote that a central doctrine of the Christian faith is personality-construction (1941, p. 111). Within a few generations, philosophers started to experience this newfound sense of individual responsibility with a heavy sense of dread (see Pelikan, 1950).

The Common Law as an institution evolves according to a process of stabilization without stasis—a phrase used by Archer in her explanation of a morphogenetic society (2013, p. 18).[15] Its treatment of each participant as a distinct social agent with powers of reflexivity allows for a degree of liberty consistent with social order, in which everyone is to be treated in an equivalent fashion, so that there is no separate system of justice for the rich and powerful. Its history describes a slow-motion synchrony toward a surprisingly resilient integration of structure, culture, and agents capable of adapting to a variety of causal

---

14. Roman Catholics and other students of history would undoubtedly treat this era as a turn away from wholesome unity and instead a time of lamentable confusions (e.g. Voegelin, 1998), which is not incompatible with the possibility that Europe was passing through an era of morphogenesis. Such historical passages are by their very nature liminal and disruptive.

15. In a parallel development, see Lazego (2013, ch. 9).

mechanisms. It certainly exhibits a deliberate attention to antecedent conditions embodied in customs and precedent. Social conflict and creative legal advocates generate variety, which the courts exist in order to select such that over time certain broad precepts stabilize into guiding norms in a recursive process that never ends.

Dialogue expresses reflexivity in concourse, where the intimate features of cognition are brought into conversation. In the words of Maccarini (2013), dialogue is meta-reflexivity, where participants help each other think about their thinking (p. 40). Here, synchrony is not the overt purpose; instead, a dialogue can be understood as a reticular network, relatively small in scale, yet designed to frustrate the emergence of domination (Maccarini, 2013, p. 49). The synchrony (if any) emerges out of the process. Dialogue is an environment conducive to fresh ideas that nobody in isolation would have thought of. Having said that from within an entitative ontology, we must remember that dialogue is an activity, a mode of openness where variety produces more variety (e.g. Archer, 2013, p. 14), where we can see "diversity rather than division" (Archer, 2013, p. 20). Archer (2013) would support the idea that dialogue is an example of interactive heterogeneity (p. 15). Wolfgang Hofkirchner (2013) might characterize dialogue as "a series of concatenated spaces of possibilities" (p. 135). No matter how you say it, dialogue generates variety, but then Pierpaulo Donati (2013) insists that dialogue is also the regulative element of morphogenesis (p. 228), because over time dialogue tends to bring about stabilization (p. 218). I would go so far as to suggest that dialogue is the smallest unit of social change—where participants are few in number, the outcome is wide open, the results are ephemeral, and the whole thing ends in a matter of a few hours.

Implicit in dialogue is the risk of experiencing turbulence, which is both threatening and generative. Leadership that stimulates and contains this experience as a way of being in the world contributes most to morphogenesis. Its antithesis is some version of leadership that rejects being questioned and rejects openness and novelty, that shuts down reflexivity, conversation, and any emergent order that competes with the regime for the hearts and minds of the people. Perhaps the most vivid example of this negative leadership on a large scale is government by terror, the polar opposite of morphogenetic dialogue (see de Vries, 2005; Arendt, 1953). We might picture it as a forced synchrony, a relatively simple coupling grounded in widespread anxiety.

Archer and her colleagues return again and again to the words of caution that society is always more complicated than will appear from any single vantage point. Structures are more elaborate, cultures are more embedded, and agents are surprisingly undetermined. Not only that, but there are simply more of them than we are able to canvas. Structures have substructures and competing structures, just as cultures do. Of course, each agent among millions is a quivering point of uncertainty. Each of these three (structure, culture, agency) is undergoing multiple causal mechanisms at any given point in time, some of them gaining strength and some of them dying.

The point is that society is the arena in which multiple forces contend—making alliances, changing tactics, waxing and waning, riding coattails, working behind the scenes, catching lightning in a bottle, engaging in the long, slow march through cultural institutions (Gramsci), letting no crisis go to waste (Emanuel), changing the story, congealing and splitting up, kissing and making up, banishing, ridiculing, outlawing, sneaking in the back door, and every other sort of dynamic. Synchrony does not seem to be much in evidence. To the extent it ever does occur, it will be limited and rare. It also might be frightening to behold. Yet it would seem that to succeed, leadership must entail at least some degree of synchrony, some type of like-mindedness. Maybe we should be surprised that it *ever* occurs?

## The X Factor

I want to say that the primary reason we can never obtain certainty about the future has to do with the introjection of forces that could not be predicted. Some have attributed supernatural powers to a sovereign divinity outside of time and space (e.g. Pelikan, 1987, ch. 4, citing Gibbon, Tertullian, and Jerome; Toynbee, 1957, ch. 38).[16] Some acknowledge sheer randomness in the universe, also referred to as chance or vicissitudes (e.g. Peirce, 1884/1992, ch. 15). Quantum physics can seem enigmatic for just this reason (see Lord, 2019, p. 151; Laszlo, 1996, p. 28). I prefer to talk in terms of **free will** (see Ciulla, 2019, p. 110), or what Giambattista Vico (1744/2001) called **conatus**, Immanuel Kant (*Third Antinomy*, 1819) called **spontaneity**,[17] and Hannah Arendt (1958) called **natality**. Bob Price (1997) acknowledged that subjectivity, whatever it means, "is an objectively real, emergent property of biological and social life" (p. 14). Think about the paradox: subjectivity is objectively real. One sees it exemplified in human choice, the variety of opinions people have about the same things, and changing, unique circumstances that elicit different responses from the same person at different times (Levine, 2018, p. 103).

Page Smith once insisted that history is not a predictive science, inasmuch as the ability to predict depends on a closed universe. He wrote, "If we know anything . . . it is that history is open, full of extraordinary potential and inexplicable turns and changes" (1964, p. 227).[18] I rely heavily on the idea that humans possess a creative nature, without which leadership looks completely different.

16. According to Laszlo (1996), even Sir Isaac Newton fell into this camp, but never got around to publishing his complete thoughts (p. 25), so we are left with a truncated version that leaves out God.
17. Polanyi (1951) more recently cited this antinomy as the clash between causes and reasons to explain the same event (p. 26).
18. Alternate explanations obviously do exist. See e.g. Gustavson (1955, p. 63f).

I do not have to prove that in some abstract sense human beings are in fact free from determination, so long as we experience ourselves in this way. From this vantage point, leadership would appear as an expression of our liberty—a proposition I find supremely satisfying.

None of which is meant to reject the impact of the social on these individual displays of spontaneity, for we know that, despite the myth of the lone genius, creativity (like leadership) can also be studied as the product of social forces. Another both/and. In fact, it is broader even than that simplistic binary model, for we can adopt different "focal settings" such as genetics, group dynamics, and history, without having to settle on any one magnitude to explain it all (Montouri & Purser, 1997, p. 14). "Systems can open up possibilities for parts which the parts in and of themselves might not be able to have" (Montouri & Purser, 1997, p. 6). The same is true of leadership, without our having to reject the spontaneity of each individual participant. This insight into the complex interactions among various causal forces does not remove the unpredictability; if anything, it compounds it (Montouri & Purser, 1995; Laszlo, 2010, p. 10). Yes, the leader must operate in some fashion independently of his or her environment (Montouri & Purser, 1995, pp. 74, 79). Even so, that environment affects the leader, having contributed to that moment of independence and helping to make sense of it. Society is in one sense a foil for leaders, a whetting stone necessary to develop the leader. It is also a leech, poised to take advantage of the leader's initiative (Montouri & Purser, 1995, p. 76). The philosopher might say that society is part of the ecology of a leader's consciousness.

Montouri and Purser (1995) shrewdly compare the "lone genius" myth to being more like a Ptolemaic view of the universe (everything revolves around the genius), rather than a Copernican view in which multiple bodies orbit around one another (p. 81). As a result, we can study the conditions that contribute to leadership, helping to elicit creativity from out of the spontaneity of participants, so that we encourage "freedom of expression and movement, lack of fear of dissent and contradiction, a willingness to break with custom, a spirit of play, as well as dedication to work, purpose on a grand scale" (p. 84, quoting Barron, 1963). Hayek would concur: spontaneous order emerges within considerable latitude.

On the surface, synchrony appears to be the opposite of turbulence. We might suspect that leadership ultimately manifests as synchrony, but that conclusion overlooks the possibility of leadership manifesting as turbulence. Maybe both are true. Leadership is about both synchrony and turbulence. Let us look at turbulence in the next chapter.

# 10

# TURBULENCE AS THE SHAPE OF THINGS TO COME[1]

## Introduction to the Chapter

People collaborate, cooperate, and coordinate all the time. In many instances, leadership is not required. When leadership does occur, sometimes it manifests as continuity and sometimes as change. Sometimes it represents continuous or evolutionary change (EVO), but it can also represent discontinuous or revolutionary change (REVO).

To be thorough, leadership of different types can be going on simultaneously, working in parallel or contrary to one another. Somebody on one side tries to preserve the status quo. Of those on the other side who seek alteration, some want to go one way, but others want to go another way. These "causal mechanisms" of social morphogenesis and morphostasis crisscross, emerge and vanish, negate and amplify—conceivably all of it the product of leadership at multiple levels on behalf of multiple, often-competing interests. To the five-year-old mind, it presents a bewildering confusion.

One of the most engrossing depictions of this kind of turmoil is Aleksandr Solzhenitsyn's cycle of gigantic novels known as *The Red Wheel* (1984–1991), where he tells the story in fiction of the Russian Revolution, beginning in the first days of WWI and Russia's hapless prosecution of the war. We are exposed directly and indirectly to generals and colonels, the Tsar and his wife, Rasputin, activists, artists, laborers, farmers, charlatans, and oblivious noblemen. It becomes evident that for Solzhenitsyn the absence of the statesman Pyotr

1. The author would like to acknowledge the assistance on this chapter of numerous friends and colleagues, not least of whom were Ryan Fisher, James Kelly, Peter Monaghan, Paul Robinson, Carly Wever, Austin Wood, and Henry Wilson, in addition to the CSS Research Workshop at my university.

Stolypin has its own relevance, like a void and a personification of what might have been. Characters keep mentioning that none of this would have happened if only he were still around. (After multiple attempts on his life, Stolypin was assassinated under mysterious circumstances in 1911, three years before the beginning of the war.)

In these novels, we listen to quarrels and misunderstandings. We see how a factory's labor unrest jeopardizes the military's war effort, while the effete intelligentsia hold dinner parties and lean out of their windows to watch the riots far below in the streets. Solzhenitsyn is careful to give credence to opposing sides, on the presupposition that different sectors can be led by conscientious men and women, even if the circumstances are such that they find themselves on a collision course. Of particular interest (to leadership students) is Solzhenitsyn's characterization of a younger Vladimir Lenin in Zurich, watching this all happen from abroad and seeking to participate from afar, exacerbating the conflict, in order to launch his own bid for supremacy (which as we know he succeeds in achieving by 1917). In these works of fiction, the turbulence of pre-revolutionary Russia is palpable and dispiriting.

Events can seem turbulent, but in order to make sense of turbulence itself, we need to figure out what it is. Mathematicians and physicists are in the vanguard trying to understand the phenomenon. Their approaches are disciplined, with a strict vocabulary and accepted methods. Even the best of them do not presume to understand the phenomenon completely, not as it manifests in the material world, yet they know more than most of us in leadership studies.

## The Terms "Chaos" and "Turbulence"

Most laymen use the terms "chaos" and "turbulence" in a non-technical fashion. In my opinion, scholars have to be sensitive to this common usage. Ordinary language results from a long and intricate process of unmanaged communication in a variety of situations, becoming part of its own spontaneous order, and it often deserves more respect than experts will give it. Even if our purpose here is to correct popular usage, first I would like to acknowledge its existence.

If you recall, I have mentioned the book by Farfel-Stark (2018) more than once. In it, she tries to predict the shape of things to come by locating the shape of how we are coming to imagine. She notices that civilization has developed from circles to right angles to three-dimensional networks. What, she asks, is the shape of things to come? It is my contention that what comes next is not a shape at all. Instead, it is turbulence. If I had to predict, I can foresee our culture, institutions, and artifacts increasingly adopting the counter-intuitive character of turbulence. By this I do not mean formlessness, an empty or anarchic miasma of randomness, with everything tossed together higgledy-piggledy, wildly shifting from one reality to another like a bad cartoon. Turbulence has a more precise meaning.

Turbulence has a street level meaning as a first order construct. It also has a technical meaning as a second order construct thanks to mathematicians, physicists, and engineers. In addition, it can be used as an analogy, drawing from one familiar area of knowledge to help explain another (Vico, 1744/2001, p. 76). Not only that, but the term can have metaphorical value. Finally, the similarities or overlap across domains such as fluid dynamics and human history may be deeply suggestive of some broad applicability for the same concept.

Toward the end of his life, Leonardo da Vinci brooded over the tumult of a deluge, sketching its endless swirls. His depictions of eddies, vortices, swirls, and spumes could be instructive, fascinating, and ominous. In his notebooks, Leonardo also tried to describe in words what he could see and imagine. The physicist Fritjof Capra, writing in 2007, credits Leonardo with being ahead of his time on this topic: "Such detailed studies of vortices in turbulent water were not taken up again for another 350 years, until the physicist Hermann von Helmholtz developed a mathematical analysis of vortex motion in the mid-nineteenth century" (p. 175). Leonardo was open to the possibility that the reason for analogies of this sort is that some basic principles were at work across the phenomena and at every magnitude (Kemp, 2004, p. 4; contra Clark, 1939, p. 111). He attempted to penetrate the surface phenomena to "the geometrical substrate of God's design" (2004, p. 85).

Sir Isaac Newton is reported to have anticipated the integral role of chaos in basic physics (Gleick, 2003, p. 136f). A conventional history of the science of chaos, however, often begins with the mathematics of Henri Poincaré and is then applied to the natural world via Edward Lorenz. More recently, turbulence was the topic of Werner Heisenberg's doctoral dissertation, although he admitted many years later that he still did not understand it (reported in Ball, 2014). Not long after James Gleick made it sexy in 1987 by writing a bestseller, Margaret Wheatley introduced chaos theory to leadership studies in 1992 with her popular book *Leadership and the New Science*. Its latest champion in the literature is probably Mary Uhl-Bien, as I had reason to mention before (see e.g. Uhl-Bien & Marion, 2008). Turbulence as one manifestation of chaos is a term used by others in the social sciences to describe certain irregularities, in markets, for example (e.g. Mantegna & Stanley, 1996), economics broadly (e.g. Dopfer, Foster, & Potts, 2004), politics (e.g. Rosenau, 1990), organizations (e.g. Polley, 1997), and psychology (e.g. Bion, 1976/1994), so there is already precedent for its use in the social sciences (see Turner, 1997, p. xxvi).

Many if not most attempts to apply the concept are at best metaphorical. Writers use terms such as chaos, uncertainty, turmoil, and turbulence to denote disorder without really attempting to master the mathematics and science. Most of us in leadership studies are satisfied with the metaphors and analogy. For many, chaos is simply a lamentable condition to account for and—with due leadership—to overcome. This is the spirit in which Peter Drucker wrote about turbulence (2006). Alternatively, we have Peter Vaill (1989) and Margaret

Wheatley (1992) to thank for telling us we need to consider the generative properties of chaos as well.

The word "turbulence" has a revealing etymology. The redoubtable *Oxford English Dictionary* (2016) notes: "from [the] Latin *turbulentus* 'full of commotion,' from *turba* 'crowd.'" Turbulence shares a common root with the word "disturbance" as a tumult. In both cases, something at some level enjoys a predicted form or flow, a discernible pattern, which meets with unanticipated upheaval. Inherent in the meaning of the term is the imagery of fluid dynamics.

## For Our Purposes, Then, What Is Turbulence?

In physics, the concept of turbulence pertains to certain properties of flow, as for example in fluids (gas or liquid). Stated crudely, turbulence is a word often associated with irregular fluctuation in the properties of flow, such as velocity or direction. The underlying imagery is of changes to something already in motion. Changes to a body in motion are to be expected.

We can say this much. First, turbulence can be regarded as a disruption or disturbance in a steady or "laminar" flow. Second, turbulence is unpredictable. One might even say that turbulence *is* unpredictability. Third, turbulence has a cascade effect of trailing eddies in its wake, churning up the flow in multiple directions. That is to say that turbulence appears to have causal properties. Fourth, turbulence can be said to have a history. On this last point, let me explain.

When discussing the duration of turbulence, I want to identify four possibilities: (a) Perhaps the disturbance that we notice in a given flow eventually dissipates without further infusions of energy to keep it roiling along. The flow ultimately settles back down by means of negative feedback loops into a laminar state. (b) Turbulence can also go the other direction and trigger an amplification that quickly overwhelms the system by means of positive feedback loops. A small disturbance can quickly throw off the entire trajectory. (c) Not only that, but—speaking from an entitative ontology—the turbulence itself can be said to move, like the Great Red Spot working its way across the surface of the planet Jupiter. We talk this way about weather phenomena on earth; the hurricane, for instance, is considered a thing with a name and properties and its own life span. (d) In yet another scenario, turbulence can be found recurring in the same spot where a steady flow encounters some kind of obstacle, such as a bridge's pier. What appears to be moving steadily (the river) no longer does so when it reaches this spot. The wake created by this obstruction exhibits a never-ending turbulence. To summarize, we see that sometimes turbulence settles down, sometimes it amps up, sometimes it moves from one place to another, and sometimes it persists or recurs in the same spot.

Before going too far, in my opinion, we should differentiate the **subjective** experience of chaos, when we are bewildered, overwhelmed, and confused, from the **objective** condition of chaos. We often construe things as chaotic when we do not understand what is going on. What seems chaotic may not be chaotic. Watching any team sport such as rugby for the first time can be baffling. Consider also the frenetic activity surrounding an anthill. Let us not be over-hasty rejecting the subjective experience. For one thing, if I base my behavior on my interpretation of the circumstances, whether they are what I believe them to be or not, then that will still be pertinent to understanding my involvement in leadership. If I think it is a crisis, I will act as though it is a crisis, whether it is one or not.

What this notion does, however, is open out onto an awkward realization that participants can interpret events differently. These interpretations will vary depending on the vantage point occupied by each individual (Cabrera & Cabrera, 2015). Our perspective always limits us. None of us enjoys a God's-eye point of view. In one sense, therefore, turbulence is in the eye of the beholder.

It is my position that turbulence characterizes the liminal phase of any change process, from unfreezing the fixities associated with the status quo to refreezing the new fixities on the other side. In between (in a space also known as the *metaxy*) is turbulence. Leaders undergo personal turbulence and ask followers to undergo turbulence, such that the organization or society churns, even if only a bit. This is part of the price of leadership. It is also frequently part of what makes it exciting. Turbulence is sometimes evidence of creativity and innovation, as well as its engine. Therefore, the *experience* of turbulence is conceptually built in to leadership. Nevertheless, does it help us in any way to analyze leadership?

## Leadership and Turbulence

> Great leaders typically emerged during economic crises, social upheavals, or revolutions; great leaders were generally not associated with periods of relative calm or quiet.
>
> —*Hughes, Ginnett, and Curphy (2018, p. 484)*

Leadership can be responsible for preventing, limiting, or even ending turbulence. It can also be responsible for making it more likely, if not actually inciting turbulence or making it more pronounced. It would be a mistake logically to construe the presence or absence of turbulence as evidence one way or the other of leadership.

In the previous chapter, we looked at the phenomenon of synchrony, in which two separate phenomena somehow on their own start to oscillate in tandem, with a unified rhythm. For many, leadership is about achieving social synchrony, bringing people into alignment, so that they work well together, heading in the same basic direction without too much supervision. To an extent, that is correct (Donaldson, 2017). By the same token, the quest for synchrony can backfire. Sometimes, in order to reach our goals, we might have to tolerate a degree of turbulence. I say this for three reasons.

First of all, no matter how strict the order a leader intends to impose, there will always be small fluctuations. In addition, contrary to certain management philosophies, there probably should be fluctuations, even in the most stable process.[2] To borrow language from the study of mechanics, every system needs a little play in the joints. After a certain point, turbulence is ineradicable. The goal of most managers is to keep these fluctuations within tolerable limits, often by checking a CUSUM chart as part of statistical quality control. George Box reassured his reader in 1957 that "a cycle of variants which does not significantly effect (sic) production can be run almost indefinitely" (p. 85). In leadership studies, one thinks of the work of Ron Heifetz in this regard (1994). If the fluctuations exceed certain limits, however, then leaders are expected to investigate; but if they can shrink the amplitude of these fluctuations, then so much the better. This is all pretty standard stuff.

Second, beyond the persistence of some ineradicable turbulence in stable systems, we know that things change, necessitating adaptation along the way. This in turn entails turbulence afresh. We know that there will be internal changes, such as the death of a trusted employee, as well as external changes, such as a new competitor in the market. In either case, the change process entails a degree of turbulence. This is especially true for large-scale changes. Turbulence also accompanies the early stages of system integration, as well as the late stages of system disintegration. Not to belabor the point, but turbulence in one part of a system often generates turbulence in other parts, as the totality continuously adjusts. Even the most stable system, however, participates in a larger world where turbulence happens all the time. Nobody controls the entire thing. Accordingly, even stable systems must learn to adapt to an unstable milieu.

Third, I would take this a step further and suggest that turbulence is constitutive of what it means to be vital. A turbulence-free environment is sterile and, for all intents and purposes, certifiably dead. So why is turbulence for so many writers on leadership portrayed as the enemy, a menace to good order and something to be remedied? Leadership entails turbulence. A softer version of this position is to accept it as a necessary evil requiring leaders to cope. As stated, though, a number of writers celebrate the generative possibilities of turbulence (e.g. Wheatley, 1992; Vaill, 1989). As with so many dichotomies, of course, we are not bound to choose one over the other. There may be a happy medium somewhere in between, i.e. a steady degree of turbulence.

---

2. Writers on organizational leadership have been addressing the significance of chaos and turbulence since the 1990s (e.g. Losada, 1999; Thietart & Forgues, 1995; Freedman, 1992; Wheatley, 1992; Senge, 1990).

Alternatively, we may find that the ideal degree of turbulence shifts over time, so that a leader might tack one direction one day and tack another direction the next. It turns out that turbulence is not the enemy; sometimes, it is your friend. And sometimes, effective leadership requires that you reach in there and provoke the system into turbulence yourself. Let me give an example from aeronautics.

Research teaches us that when a fixed wing aircraft tilts upward, the flow of air across the top of the plane wing separates and no longer passes directly over the wing control surface. This separation has an adverse impact on the ability to control the plane, because it was designed to use downward pressure from that flow. Without that flow going across the top, those controls become useless. For this reason, designers have attached little devices to the surface of the wing called vortex generators. These devices create a small amount of turbulence before the flow separates, so that some of that turbulence sweeps downward along the surface of the wing enabling the controls to work (Donaldson, 1950; see also McFadden, Rathert, & Bray, 1952). No turbulence, no lift. No lift, no control. Turbulence is part of how planes stay aloft. The trick is calculating the right amount of turbulence and directing it where it needs to go. Thus, even though turbulence represents unpredictability or chaos, it is not such that it cannot be calculated and put to use within very specific parameters. That is the paradox facing leaders as well.

Rather than being an unmitigated evil or an unbridled good, turbulence is simply a reality that must be anticipated, used, and to the extent possible managed, despite its inherent unpredictability. The idea of synchrony that we looked at in the previous chapter suggests that two or more objects oscillate together, in lock step. This might sound to the layman like the goal of leadership. On the contrary, social systems—even when aligned for a shared purpose—necessarily experience a degree of turbulence. It is ineradicable, it accompanies change, and it is constitutive of vitality. Under certain conditions, then, leaders become like those vortex generators, causing just enough turbulence to keep the entire operation aloft. I see three ways that leadership participates in turbulence.

1.   Leadership as part of **negative** feedback loops.

In the literature on leadership, leaders are often understood to be "disturbance-handlers" who respond to the experience of disruption by fixing it or at least minimizing it, somehow domesticating the situation (e.g. Drucker, 2006). Bass and Stogdill credit Henry Mintzberg (1973) for including this function in his taxonomy of managerial roles (1990, p. 33). If this turns out to be the case that leaders sometimes quell disturbances, then at the macro level the *collapse* of turbulence or even the *absence* of turbulence might evidence leadership at the micro level.[3] In his taxonomy of social power, James Hillman (1995) reminds us that maintenance is often neglected as a leadership function, because it is not so readily evident. It is certainly not sexy. Some writers just toss this function aside as something other than leadership; it is management, they say, so let us not talk about it. From this perspective, I want to ask whether leadership is somehow conceptually opposed to turbulence, as diplomats are to war?

Before going forward, one might ask: how is an absence of something evidence of the presence of something else? One can conceive such a thing, as for example the unusual longevity of an economic boom or the prolongation of peace between two adversaries. The fact that conditions have not deteriorated when we have every expectation that they would have by now can possibly be credited to the people in charge. One thinks of Sherlock Holmes in Sir Arthur Conan Doyle's short story *Silver Blaze* (1892):

> "Is there any point to which you would wish to draw my attention?"
> [asked the inspector]
> "To the curious incident of the dog in the night-time."
> "The dog did nothing in the night-time."
> "That was the curious incident," remarked Sherlock Holmes.

The absence of that which you would expect to happen just might warrant further investigation. It was the eminent historian Edward Gibbon who wrote that "instead of enquiring why the Roman empire was destroyed, we should rather be surprised that it had subsisted so long" (1830, p. 642). Sometimes the absence of turbulence is evidence of leadership. And let us not forget that the mission of leadership sometimes is not to quell turbulence out there in paramount reality, so much as it is to ease the turbulence participants feel, i.e. their subjective turbulence.

2.   Leadership as part of **positive** feedback loops.

They say of the best preachers, they comfort the afflicted and afflict the comfortable. A classic both/and. Leadership might be responsible for the absence of turbulence, but it might also be the reason for it. The presence or absence of turbulence would not—in and of itself—be determinative. Social occurrences have many causes, and in fact a single social occurrence can have multiple causes (e.g. Mill, 1872/1988, ch. 3), so we must not make the mistake of assuming that evidence of turbulence is always attributable to leadership.

---

3. I am reading the latest issue of *National Review* in which David Harsanyi (2019) complains that those who rate U.S. presidents tend to prefer those who stir things up rather than those who preside over periods of relative calm. The so-called experts notice the turbulence, whereas the constituents prefer peace, prosperity, and predictability.

Edwin Hollander remarked that "leaders are credited or blamed for out-comes over which they alone had little effect" (1992, p. 46). Social change itself is not necessarily because of any leadership whatsoever. To be candid, real social change on a large enough scale can rarely be attributed to any one social actor, no matter how praiseworthy. Lincoln did not free the slaves all by himself. Martin Luther did not launch the Protestant Reformation all by himself. In sum, we frequently speak of leadership as stirring things up, injecting novelty, amplifying discontent, agitating, serving as a positive feedback loop exerting pressure to overcome the system's inherent resilience for the sake of transforming the system into something else—presumably into something better. That image, however, like the one about negative feedback loops, is limited.

Just to complete the picture, it is often the leader's mission to precipitate turbulence in paramount reality, such as transforming a business, or it is the mission to disturb participants' *subjective experience*, or both.

3.    Leadership as part of **both** positive and negative loops.

Ronald Heifetz offered his own version of a both/and solution to the question of leadership and its impact on turbulence. In *Leadership Without Easy Answers* (1994), he examined a related phenomenon familiar to the mathematized sciences, namely disequilibrium. He noted that systems respond to stresses by trying to preserve and if necessary reestablish equilibrium. Yet they evolve only by means of disequilibrium (1994, p. 28). The systems that adapt (and therefore endure) will undergo both. They move toward and away from disequilibrium at the same time. Leadership, in his view, "contains" the disequilibrium, allowing enough to foster development without totally giving over to anarchy. There is, in other words, a tolerable range of disequilibrium—which we might think of in terms of a tolerable turbulence. Neither too much nor too little. With the passage of time, therefore, the responsible leader nudges the system one way or the other, in order to sustain an adaptive balance. For instance, when a stressor threatens to overwhelm the system entirely, a leader might need to become more authoritarian (1994, p. 122). Heifetz called this "regulating distress" (1994, p. 139). A leader must know the limits of the system's tolerance. Too hot, you must cool it down. Too cold, you must turn up the heat. His is another way of talking about both positive and negative feedback loops. Leadership is neither all of one nor all of the other. Thus, the leader is managing the degree of turbulence, including the subjective experience of chaos.

## The Sense of Fitness Emanating From the Hippocampus

The physicist David Bohm (1996a) wrote about the sense that we have of fitness. Somehow, we recognize when things fit. Bohm held that, at their root, art, mathematics, and science all derive from a longing for a universe that fits together, that ultimately makes sense.[4] Something in the soul wants every "either/or" out there to resolve itself as a both/and. Some of us even reach up to nudge a crooked picture frame back into level or mindlessly line up the silverware on the table for no apparent reason. Human beings are capable of seeking some kind of encompassing order, despite the evidence. We are eternally optimistic . . . or desperate. By way of contrast, pluralism as a creed can seem off-putting, like giving up too easily. Surely, if we are patient and diligent, the order will reveal itself.

What pleasure, therefore, when an apparent chaos reveals a hidden pattern, e.g. when you solve the puzzle or finally see that the duck is also a rabbit! Yes! Satisfying—in the way that "happily ever after" is satisfying. Many of us are counting on karma to make it so. If not in this life, then later. Part of the charm of reactionary populism is its sense of restoring that which was familiar. I get it. I have walked the rubble where my childhood home used to be. My parents have passed away. Two sisters are gone . . . too young. Too young. I keep losing things that once made up my world, including my hearing, my eyesight, my stamina. A part of me wants everything to be restored, because once upon a time it all seemed to fit.

As it turns out, I was wrong about that, but what did I know? I was a kid. I do know the feeling when things fit. More accurately, I know the feeling when things do not fit (see Ortega, 1940/1946). I have had clothes that chafe and music that jars. I have developed free-floating anxiety to accost me every so often and shout, "Something's not right! Something's not right!" Writing poetry, I can sit back and judge when the meter does not scan. I get fussy when the cranberry juice is not exactly where I expect it to be in the fridge. Over time, I have developed quite a palate for fittingness.[5] People who know me will point out that in some areas of life, not so much. I get things wrong. Maybe I just do not notice.[6] That does not mean I am entirely bereft of that same desire. I have had to consult my inner sense of fitness while writing this book!

Bohm gave us a way of talking about the capacity of our energies to move us toward a world that fits—toward harmony and balance. Sewage pipes are meant to fit into one another. Jigsaw puzzle pieces fit. We want our psyche as well as our polis to be just as harmonious. We want to be able to step back and say to ourselves, "There." One does not require God or even metaphysics to name this attraction we experience an "implicate order," an unseen order that will have to emerge because of multiple iterations. As often as not, we fall under the spell of the god Apollo. And you can be damned sure that Apollo's clothes fit.

---

4. Geoffrey Cupit (1999) argued that fittingness is the definition of justice.
5. This sense of fitness is thought to reside in the hippocampus, working in conjunction with something called the substantia nigra/ventral tegmental area (SN/VTA) in the midbrain (see Kumaran & Duzel, 2008; Kumaran & Maguire, 2006). Bohm had said that apparent contradictions indicate that something about the present is not working (1996a, p. 116). Something does not fit. We have an instinctive sense of this (1996a, p. 110).
6. Given the plasticity of the human brain, there is hope for me yet (see Herdener et al., 2010).

In the same manner, even children can readily judge unfairness. Disturbances in the available order do something at the emotional level. They accompany bouts of cognitive dissonance. We know that the brain readily compares an undesirable present with an ideal future (Peterson, 1999, p. 50). We are beginning to unearth the neuroscientific validation of Heidegger's philosophical hypothesis about leadership as a mode of being, as described in a previous chapter. We continually overlay mental maps onto our experiences. When they do not fit, the brain allows a degree of anxiety to stimulate us to do something about it—to get up and leave, for instance, or stay in the situation and change it, or possibly reconsider the maps we were using to begin with, a possibility which makes us especially uncomfortable.

Dissonance can quickly lead to disorientation, once the fixities are gone. Notice, though, that the sense of fitness relies on an entitative ontology. Only "things" are thought to fit; what they constitute together is a discernible whole, a comprehending thing. Here in these pages, though, we are trying to escape the gravitational pull of our entitative ontology. So perhaps in accord with the spirit of fitness we might speak in terms of resonance, a kind of auditory resolution. Not a thing, but an event. Some musical chords are plainly means to an end. We have all had the experience listening to a song such as Chopin's *Prelude in E Minor* (op. 28, no. 4) when the tensions finally resolve themselves and we can sigh audibly with relief.

To some extent, therefore, turbulence is the experience of disturbances or disruptions in the hippocampus when motion or activity or the prevailing narrative seems to violate the laminar flow of expectations. At such moments, we will have stumbled upon an order the brain does not recognize . . . at least not yet. For most people, the experience of turbulence is construed as bad. For the expert—and for the leader—the experience can be stimulating. It wakens us to possibilities. What I am urging is for leaders to lean in to these possibilities. No fight or flight. Rather, **look harder**. Activate that part of the brain that explores the unknown (Peterson, 1999, p. 52). This posture toward the future has become known in the popular literature as a growth mindset (Dweck, 2016). Over time, after a series of such turbulent experiences, one develops a richer, more versatile set of maps. Furthermore, the amygdala learns to becalm itself in turbulent situations (Peterson, 1999, p. 55). In leadership studies, we used to call it grace under pressure.

Is it any wonder therefore that when certain maps seem to recur, they become trusted by the brain that this is just how the world works. We have seen it all before. Maybe there is, as I have been saying, an underlying or transdisciplinary motif here. And it begins with a sensitivity to—and tolerance in the neurosystem—of turbulence, so that we might consequently do things in paramount reality to bring our situation into alignment with our inner sense of harmony.

Something about the idea of an "infinite game" (to quote James Carse) violates our need to bring it all to a conclusion and settle accounts. "You mean it all just keeps going?" Well, yes, I hope so. You may cash out, as it were, and good luck to you on the other side, but the whole messy pageant continues in your absence.

After a series of turbulent encounters, however, one has to wonder if the brain's chemical reward for figuring things out is possibly inducing you to jump to conclusions, to see things that are not really there. It feels so good to be right that maybe you are being too quick to claim the reward. For the operation to work neurologically, you have to follow the trail; you have to enter the dark heart of the forest. You have to go into *aporia* and not casually wave in its general direction, saying, "Been there. Done that." In other words, after enough turbulence the brain starts to consider the possibility that some things will never "fit."[7] You cannot bring about complete harmony and finally realize implicate order in all its fullness. Maybe in this vale of tears, that would be expecting too much. Which is not to say that it is not there. The absence of complete order does not disprove the existence of a possible order. Nevertheless, after a point the quest for order has to accept the extent to which that order will not manifest. Indeed, it may be the case that we just do not see the order that is there, which was Hayek's insight about spontaneous order, but even so there is some consolation in the thought that maybe things were meant to be that way. Maybe turbulence is constitutive of life itself, of both society and history. It is by means of turbulence that both the Common Law and dialogue function. Maybe turbulence is not a threat but a gift, keeping us aloft, propelling us toward the far horizon. Maybe it is not the world that is broken so much as it is our image of what brokenness means. This, I would argue, is the beauty of Luther's breakthrough. He did not find an order on the other side of chaos. His critics are right to point this out. Instead, he embraced the chaos, and with it the liberty to seek and create order with other people, rather than submit to institutions, let alone to the dictates of logic.

This realization made Luther dangerous.

## Turbulence in and Among Open Systems

Perhaps we might look at turbulence from a systems perspective. A system in crisis, unable to sustain its regularity, like water that cannot continue to flow unobstructed, has three possible outcomes. It can struggle to restore its order. It can revert to a simpler order by abandoning the one that no longer seems sustainable, moving down in complexity. Or it can graduate to a new order, i.e. a more advanced or sophisticated order that transcends the crisis, moving up in complexity (Harter, 2007b). As Edgar Morin put it, the system can (a) retain

---

7. Rorty (1989) considers the psychological need that the world ultimately fit together as an impediment to understanding. For him, it does not explain very much to say that something "fits" (p. 8). Maybe people should come up with a better metaphor. I will return to Rorty's objection in Appendix B.

the status quo, (b) collapse, or (c) undergo metamorphosis (Szabo, n.d.). The strange thing is that in social systems there can be leadership on behalf of *all three possibilities at the same time*—including leadership for competing visions of what that transformation might look like. While one part of the system might be transforming toward a new order, another part of the system might be collapsing. Complex systems rarely transform themselves all at once in a uniform, synchronized pattern, rotating together on a kind of axle. That fact right there constitutes turbulence.

An open system navigates between (a) becoming a system so closed that entropy overtakes it and (b) becoming a system so open that any sense of identity or continuity vanishes. The integrity of the system as a system can evaporate into an anarchic miasma, a diffusion of energy that actually dissipates, like the column of smoke that becomes increasingly disordered on its way upward before it fades into the night.

Open systems take in and release energy. They are permeable to their environment. They can be said to *participate* in their environment, just as you and I breathe air, eat food, and build shelters against the rain (Bohm, 1996a, p. 121; see also Laszlo, 1994, p. 45). Each of us is a bundle of turbulence— an order-seeking turbulence. So also are our organizations (Bohm, 1996a, p. 96). Open systems are at risk of becoming far-from-equilibrium because of energy being imported across system boundaries (Laszlo, 1994, p. 107). The inward flow creates the conditions for the system as a whole to change. Up to a point, the flow can simply feed the existing processes, like food for the body, such that the system continues in an uninterrupted state. Any growth would be mere extension, more of the same, expanding but not becoming essentially any different. However, at far-from-equilibrium, the influx can transform the system altogether. As Ervin Laszlo once put it: "Human societies . . . are not infinitely stressable" (2010, p. xxiii).[8] Here is an opportunity for a different kind of growth, an intensive change in the character of the system, like folding in upon itself rather than simply getting bigger (2010, p. 40).

Transformation occurs—if it occurs at all—at a bifurcation point, where it is impossible to predict how the system will change. The system enters into a "transitory phase characterized by indeterminacy and chaos" (Laszlo, 1994, p. 110). The system either breaks down or breaks through, but in either case, it threatens to break (Laszlo, 2010, p. 102).

The process of system transformation can be gradual, but then the system might leap or burst into a new order of being in discontinuous phases. It might fall into sync all of a sudden, for example, with surrounding systems (Laszlo, 1994, p. 111), as Strogatz predicted. Nevertheless, over time, as more and more

---

8. Laszlo is another of those controversial figures whose advocacy of ESP, past lives, voodoo, morphic resonance, and other occult forces may constitute pseudo-science, but will prove to be immaterial to our purposes.

open, interconnected systems reach their bifurcations, the trend is toward greater complexity. Or as Laszlo put it, "thus evolution moves from the simpler to the more complex, and from the lower to the higher level of organization" (1994, p. 110). Thus, things continue with a steady influx into and out of order, through turbulence into higher and more complex configurations (1994, p. 113). For Laszlo, this invocation of the language of chaos and turbulence is no metaphor (1994, p. 114). Consequently, leadership serves to disrupt one level of order as much as it serves to fulfill it at another level. What "fits" at one level must be shed in order to find what fits at the next level. That is to say, leadership can be seen to accompany these transitions.

An existing system reaches far-from-equilibrium by infusions of novelty, by an influx of new information or new ideas. Keep in mind that once a system enters into that turbulent phase, it often continues to transition toward a higher order, a new attractor, a new equilibrium. This means that indeed, sometimes a leader afflicts the comfortable, but then the leader also sometimes comforts the afflicted. He or she facilitates the influx to bring the system toward a higher state of being.

Consider the two ideal types for leadership proposed by Isaiah Berlin as presented in Chapter 1. One is the **idealist**, who knows where he or she wants to go next and stimulates the system to get there post-haste. The other is the **realist**, who may not know where things are going, so he or she takes slow, incremental steps, focusing less on the destination and more on the process. What Berlin fails to describe are at least three other possibilities: the **revolutionary** who has no idea where any of this is going, but he or she wants to get there quickly—someone for whom the objective is turbulence itself; the **reactionary**, who has no desire whatsoever to change—someone for whom turbulence itself is a bad thing; and finally the leader who knows where things may be going but still focuses on the process and on short-term results.

If the individual human being (psyche) undergoes a sufficient change, the ripple effect could transform the social system (polis), which in turn could transform the larger whole (history). We teach leadership studies largely in the hope that this is how it happens. Staying within the themes of this book, then, let us look at the macro for a moment.

In social theory, we can regard institutions as "transitory hardenings" and "stable states" and "coagulations" in an encompassing rhythm of intensification and diminution of some kind of energy. That's a mouthful. The structure that emerges can be highly stratified, with layers upon layers, in hierarchies, or it can be relatively unstratified, in a kind of meshwork (de Landa, 2000, pp. 260–263). Most structures are some combination of both (2000, p. 32). What Manuel de Landa urged us to do in his book is examine the flow out of which structures emerge, because these flows have dynamic properties.

In their nonlinear process, these flows (plural) alter based in part on the degree of intensification of one thing or another—for example, under conditions of urbanization or trade, or when certain events occur such as war or plague. These moments or phases of greater or lesser intensification can alter the structure, not unlike water freezing at 32 degrees Fahrenheit. The "substance" transforms into something else. Social change is what results from these moments. It may have been gradual, albeit unperceived, until a bifurcation point when it suddenly transmogrifies. These moments signify a shift, but they also contribute to further shifts in other flows (2000, p. 265). For example, the tendency to urbanize throughout Europe tended to undermine the system of feudalism, increase the likelihood of widespread epidemic such as the plague, and reduce the impact of dialect on the emergence of a vernacular. In other words, flows interact with other flows, such that their intensifications have a cascade effect on one another.

De Landa gave numerous examples in *A Thousand Years of Nonlinear History* (2000). Cities grow with an intensification of what he called matter-energy, for example, but the process by which this takes place will vary depending on human choices and other variables (2000, p. 31). As we mentioned, the intensification might result in some kind of **hierarchy** (on the one hand) or what he called a **meshwork** (on the other). These are two types of order. A hierarchy tends toward unification, centralization, and stability; a meshwork, like a market economy, for example, is horizontal, tending toward diversity, extension, and resilience. A land-locked capital city (Paris, Prague, Moscow) is likelier to build hierarchies (think in terms of a nucleus) than a port city (London, Amsterdam, New York), which is more amenable to meshworks (think in terms of a membrane) (2000, pp. 38, 50). How the intensification develops will result in quite different structures. De Landa proceeded to explain that the West (rooted in European history) came to dominate the globe in large part because of how cities developed there since the year 1000 CE. The same basic intensifications occurred in other parts of the world; yet for a variety of reasons, the West developed into aggressive, metropolitan, outward-oriented colonial powers based on meshworks. Under mounting pressures in the twentieth century, the East (which was more successful in maintaining its hierarchies) had grown in a different direction and now, on the world stage, has found that it has had to adapt its practices in order to compete (2000, p. 51).[9] The "parts" in both East and West are quite similar. That is to say, they were each working with the same basic ingredients. The question is how they came together in the way that they have, because there is more than one way to constellate. The same influx of energy into two different systems can generate more than one configuration.

De Landa took this idea of the port city where meshworks thrive and then zoomed out to explain that the West was built largely by a network of port cities that engaged each other in rivalries, wars, trade, and other cross-fertilizations (2000, p. 54; see generally Ridley, 2011). These local meshworks built large-scale meshworks and—with the Renaissance and Reformation in

9. None of which ignores the history of Asian seaports such as Shanghai and Singapore.

full flower—successfully resisted considerable centralizing pressures to unify under a single religion (such as Roman Catholicism) and a single ruler (such as Napoleon Bonaparte). These processes can be referred to as self-organization, when a given city passes through bifurcation points to new and more complex stable states. What happens along the way shapes how the process unfolds thereafter (2000, p. 55).

Hierarchies tend to conduct a process of sort-and-solidify, according to de Landa. You inventory what you have and then organize the world into logical categories, grouping things that are alike together and holding them firm (2000, p. 60). Hierarchies depend on an entitative ontology. Meshworks, on the other hand, resist this tendency. They remain more fluid, as a reflection of a more peregrinal ontology. Sorting is not nearly so important to understanding one's environment, and solidification is seen as the onset of death. That is to say, meshworks are far more adaptable, open, and uncertain. They are *in principle* dynamic.[10]

One way of thinking about this is that hierarchies gravitate toward castles (bureaucracy and uniformity), whereas meshworks gravitate toward gateways (heterogeneous groupings and diversity). Not surprisingly, hierarchies also try to solidify the belief system that justifies the hierarchy, working toward elaborate and internally consistent systems that brook no dissent. Meshworks scoff at these exertions, adopting instead more of a live-and-let live attitude. Beliefs—like languages and religions—coexist there in unsettled tensions. Meshworks are more pluralistic. As a result, meshworks are less stable but more resilient (2000, p. 107). By analogy, as populations increase and concentrate geographically into cities, epidemics become more likely (unstable), but then beyond a certain point of intensification disease becomes only endemic and the population as a whole flourishes (resilient) (2000, p. 109). Another way of saying this is that hierarchies are especially sensitive to negative feedback that is "deviation-counteracting" (2000, p. 68). This tendency promises greater stability, but at the cost of resilience.

De Landa insisted that there is not one optimal outcome toward which society migrates, like climbing a singular mountain peak. If anything, the landscape is comprised of many peaks. Things can go upward one way or another, or in several directions at once. The path forward is neither linear nor inevitable. Making matters more complicated, as we have been saying, a society will change over time, which in turn will contribute to changes in something else—in an adjacent culture or in some other domain such as politics, business, or law. These changes in turn can come back to influence everything else, in a series of mutual dependencies (2000, p. 140). He wrote that "the flow of

10. Parallels to the human brain are provocative. Whose brain is constructed as a hierarchy? And is that ideal? To what extent, on the contrary, is it better for one's brain to aspire to becoming a meshwork? A meshwork brain looks a lot like philosophy's pragmatism and accords with what we are learning about neuroscience.

cultural materials in human societies is quite open" (2000, p. 145). That fact contributes to its resilience, even if it also tends toward hierarchy—or what some theorists call hegemony. Societies do both. They close around themselves and remain open. In a system of flows going in both directions, there is bound to be plenty of turbulence, both objective and subjective turbulence. And leaders leave their fingerprints on all of it.

## Concluding Thoughts

Turbulence is an ineradicable and invigorating experience in the life span of any open system. Synchrony as an ideal for social systems in which everybody fits nicely cannot overlook turbulence as both a threat and an opportunity. This includes both subjective and objective turbulence. It includes turbulence at the individual level and at the collective level. Turbulence at the individual level casts eddies at the collective level and vice versa. At any given point in time, organizations and societies undergo multiple and sometimes contrary turbulences at different magnitudes, as the comprehending order of which they are a part makes its way in the flow of time.

Leadership sometimes sets out to quell these disturbances. It also sometimes provokes them. It keeps them within tolerable limits or rides them toward more complex configurations. In the teeth of turbulence, leadership participates in hierarchies and meshworks. Throughout the inevitable turmoil, one is guided by a sense of fitness as to where lies a harmonious way of being. Amid the noise, we might say, one can—with training and experience—detect the rudiments of a lovely tune.

# 11

## MAKING SENSE IN THE TURBULENCE

### Leadership Homeward

### Introduction to the Chapter

In the previous chapter, we looked at turbulence in transition to a new state (leaving the status quo via positive feedback loops, for example) or restoring the earlier state (countering pressures to change via negative feedback loops, for example). I said that leadership can be found in going either way. In this chapter I would like to take a closer look at one of these.

Leadership presents itself as the pursuit of novelty, a quest or mission to surpass the present and make things better. Leadership promises progress, improvement, a change in direction toward the Promised Land, over the next horizon. At its most colorful, leadership takes on metaphors of storming the heights or going on a journey, blazing a trail in a trackless wilderness, forever approximating some ideal. As the archetypal psychologist might put it, leadership participates in the energy of the puer as the Divine Child, Hero, Trickster, and Messiah—a psychopomp, as it were, not unlike Hermes, conducting the souls of others to their reward.[1] Leadership by definition has to go *somewhere*. Otherwise, it will appear to be an empty gesture, ineffectual and flat, of little or no historical interest, more of a bland inertia that requires no explanation and attracts no further attention.

---

1. In myth and archetypal psychology (see e.g. Campbell, 2008; Hillman, 2005a; Peterson, 1999, pp. 176–187; Erikson, 1958/1962; Neumann, 1954, part B), the "puer" is the image of the child, eternal youth, attuned to the promptings of transcendence directly and triumphant, ambitious without wanting the requisite drudgery and therefore refusing to grow up, forever floating above the mundane, like Peter Pan or Icarus. We would call the puer gifted yet immature. Easily lured toward adventure and supremely confident in one's divine calling, a puer character recognizes that he (or she) must leave home in order to obtain the due prize.

In his analysis of the many definitions of the term "leadership," Joseph Rost (1993) repeatedly quoted the accumulating literature to the effect that leadership implies setting direction. In 2001, Wilfred Drath included "setting direction" as one of the central leadership tasks. The same idea can be captured in a number of related terms that are not necessarily identical, yet bear a family resemblance to one another: terms such as vision, mission, objective, intent, aim, and target. Bernard Bass had referred to this understanding of leadership as "an instrument of goal achievement" (1990, p. 15f). At the very least, followers will expect the future to improve (Newark, 2018); otherwise, what was the point? In some sense, leadership as a process has to be characterized as interpersonal efforts to accomplish some intended purpose, rendered in the metaphor about movement or travel from point A to point B.

In actual practice, however, leadership also appeals to a desire to restore, to return, to recapture. It can be promoted as a reversion to a prior state, an odyssey back to familiar shores and the bosom of one's family (if not to one's ancestors). Leaders can be heard to invoke an earlier time, a golden age, making the world "great again." Pity the leader with "no ancestral tombs to protect, no relics to defend against barbarians" (Berlin, 1982, p. 316, quoting Sorel, 1889). Sometimes, in other words, the trek is not onward and upward, but instead homeward. We might wish to label these exertions as retrograde, a retreat from what calls us forward and instead more of a coming back with our tail between our legs, giving up, even hiding from our destiny. T.S. Eliot (1971) wrote that we cannot "ring the bell backward [or] follow an antique drum." Yet this debouch too is leadership, wherever it takes us, which means that the homeward journey also deserves to be the object of study.

This homeward leadership means two entirely different things. It would be advisable to describe them now, because they can easily be confused.

On the one hand, homeward leadership means a desire to undo what has happened recently and return to an earlier time. Mark Lilla (2016) referred to this temper as **reaction** and to its adherents as "reactionary," and he sees it enacted in theory and practice. In open opposition to this retrograde temper, another and a contrary temper labels itself progressive, largely to differentiate its forward-thinking and future-oriented intentions. Progressives are not for going back, they say. To them, the past was hardly worth resurrecting; the call is to improve or advance beyond where we had once been and put the past in the rearview mirror, where it belongs.

Yet that is precisely what reactionaries want to do: they argue that we have made some wrong choices. The time has come to admit our mistakes and take corrective action. They do not always agree about how far they might want to turn back the clock—to the 1950s, to colonialism, to before the Enlightenment, to the Middle Ages, even perhaps to the Garden of Eden. The reasoning is that if you once took a fork in the road earlier that seems to have been wrongheaded, the best strategy is to backtrack. That is one way to understand what is meant by homeward leadership. Moreover, sometimes, it does appeal to many people. Sometimes, it is not an unreasonable move (see e.g. Harrison, 1996, regarding the "new Coke").

Sometimes, the best move is a tactical retreat.

Even progressives, ironically, can wax nostalgic for headier days, such as the 1960s (see the lyrics of Joni Mitchell's song "Woodstock"), or like Jean Jacques Rousseau romanticize the noble savage of yore. In fact, in many instances, their agenda can resemble the reactionary agenda in that they look back on certain choices from an earlier time as regrettable or worse. Again, as with reactionaries, they do not always agree with each other about where we can be said to have made a wrong turn, but they do often lament certain projects such as industrialization, for example, or colonialism. The point is this: each "temper"—reactionary or progressive—can look to the past in order to figure out where things went wrong. But that is only one meaning of homeward leadership—and not the one I expect to elaborate.

On the other hand, therefore, is another understanding of turning homeward. Here, the appeal is not to a previous time so much as it is a search for what is timeless, to a kind of foundational and abiding truth. James Hillman, for example, would refer to "the primary forms that govern the psyche" (2013, p. 13) and "the most fundamental patterns of human existence" (2013, p. 14). Archetypes are by definition archaic and probably primal, but not in the sense of being outdated. They are enduring. They were there at the beginning, and they govern today. A homeward leadership in this second meaning of the phrase would seek that which transcends the moment, a kind of perennial wisdom, from which we occasionally fall away or even stand in open rebellion. The purpose is not so much to go back ourselves, as it is to pick up and bring something forward.

Maybe homeward leadership seeks continuity amid change. Luther wanted to go back to the scriptures. The Common Law honors enduring custom and long-standing precepts in *stare decisis*. Braudel identified a history that depicts our unaltering condition. Archer spoke of the forces that retain the familiar forms as morphostasis.

Hillman explained that we often picture history as linear: for some people, it goes up; and for some, it goes down; for some, it goes round and round (1995, pp. 226ff; Nisbet, 1969). These are templates that we overlay onto experience for our convenience. But psychologist Jordan Peterson urges a more promising imagery of a continual journey outward into the unknown and then back, gradually expanding the domain of the known without renouncing it (1999, ch. 2; also Meek, 2014). Venture too far such that you cannot go back, and you will suffer for it. Nevertheless, stay too close to home and resist venturing out altogether, and you will suffer for that, too. You take something with you into the unknown. Then you bring something back. This is a different mode of imagining the patterns of progress. It is a pattern familiar to those acquainted with the works of Joseph Campbell (1990; 2008) and Erich Neumann (1954) and the story of the hero's quest. This narrative takes seriously the idea that, notwithstanding our uneven adventures, certain things abide.

Archetypal psychology grounded in mythology is not the only way to talk about leadership that turns toward home. The same theme often arises in literature, for example, ranging from Homer's *Odyssey* to Thomas Wolfe's *You Can't Go Home Again*. The Hebrew book known as Genesis depicts the banishment of Adam and Eve from the Garden of Eden, where an angel with a flaming sword has been set at the entrance in order to prevent their return to a paradise lost. One reads along the narrative arc that rises up and must bend downward again, bringing reconciliation finally and a happily ever after. But then something of the sort appears in popular culture, where, in the end, the little girl comes to herself. She closes her eyes, clicks her heels three times, and intones, "There's no place like home. There's no place like home. There's no place like home." Indeed.

Evolutionary biology reinforces the importance for ambulatory hominids of maintaining the hearth, as a place of protection and nurture, a familiar space near where one's ancestors would have been buried. Even migratory peoples set up base camps, temporary hearths. Nevertheless, at one extreme is evidence of a cave in China known as Zhoukoudian, which appears to have served as a hearth for *homo erectus* continuously for 200,000 to 300,000 years. That duration of time could influence the psychology of descendants. Laszlo (1994) speculated that, even prior to there being a clear advantage for hominids to maintain and return to a literal hearth, the earliest humans would have been influenced deeply, even traumatically by their departure from living in the trees of Africa for far longer than 300,000 years. One might wonder whether a longing for some prehistoric Garden of Eden actually derives from our species' vestigial development of a sense of loss at having to emerge blinking into the glare of the savannah.

In physics, also, we recognize a tendency of matter to reach (and retain) an equilibrium, a steady state at rest. This is one way to describe the encompassing pattern of all material things, that ultimately the universe will reach entropy. Just as a ball bearing rolls around and around toward the exact nadir in a bowl, at a fixed point of absolute rest, we are all in one sense riding this thing toward stasis. It is only a matter of time. Even in music there is the idea of resolution, when the suspense of a more interesting dissonance ends in satisfying consonance. I have no reason to believe, in other words, that something of the sort does not impel the human mind and entire peoples. A leadership that aspires to fulfill one of the deepest longings in the human soul can possibly be not only understandable, from a scientific point of view, but also wholesome. It is the purpose of this chapter to make such a claim at least plausible.

Sometimes, to be sure, the homeward journey is a retreat, going backward. Sometimes, however, it is more of a renewal.

## The Goddess Nyx, Freud's "Death Instinct"

According to ancient Greek mythology, out of the distant, primordial chaos was born a foundational goddess depicted in black garb. Her name was Nyx or Night, the mother of a dark brood, including the twins Hypnos (sleep) and Thanatos (peaceful death). She dwells in the deepest shadow, beyond the light of consciousness, manifest primarily as a negation. Her domain at the edge of the cosmos is shrouded in mist and base metals, occluded from view, yet relentless to the end, claiming all things, embracing them at last when they finally return.

From out of her sanctuary, she will occasionally speak in oracles or dreams.

By means of slumber, she undoes what had been accomplished during the day. Likewise, she restores what the day had undone. So that through her persistent yet unseen influence, a kind of cosmic justice prevails, for with her daughter Nemesis she sets the limit to being, exacting the penalty for life itself. Writers ascribed envy to her. With good reason, humanity deplores her and calls her vile names, associating her with terror and treachery. We respond with disgust to her inheritance from the forces of disorder. To seek her is nihilism. To worship, occult. In mythology, among the immortal gods she bears an appalling visage. Even Zeus feared her power.

With regard to Nyx, my debt to the insight of Sigmund Freud is immense. He spoke of her by a different name. He called her the death instinct. In *Civilization and Its Discontents* (1930/2002), he wrote of an instinct to dissolve units and "bring them back to their primaeval, inorganic state" (p. 65f). He would develop this idea further in the "Economic Problem of Masochism" (published in 1924/1961; see also Freud, 1920/2010). I resist calling it a "death" instinct, however. The name "Nyx" seems better suited to its origins and its character. It is that in the psyche which seeks to restore the inorganic properties from out of which life emerges.

Human beings participate in the dynamics of the natural world. Moreover, we have privileged access to this reality by means of our minds. The human mind is the product of millions of years of development, going far beyond the earliest known language, back to the origin of existence itself. Out of the interplay of energies, there came into being matter. Out of the interplay of matter with energy, there came into being life. Out of the interplay of living things, there came into being *homo sapiens*. And out of the interplay of *homo sapiens*, there came us. And we in turn develop minds, all the way from the rudiments of conception through birth, education, and maturity, influenced by both nature and nurture. In this way, the mind retains many of the features from the stages or phases through which it has passed.

It was Darwin, for example, who popularized the idea that the human mind derives from animal origins. Freud simply extended the logic here by arguing that the human mind is still derived—at a far more obscure level—from *inorganic* origins. The mind is not something posited as something over against reality; no, it participates fully in it. As such, it is still a material thing, with the same crude tendencies of inorganic matter—tendencies we ascribe to water, rocks, and dust. At the risk of hyperbole, our material selves contribute to mind and in fathomless ways influence its trajectory, before reclaiming the entire operation at last in death. That is to say, the extent to which we are like water, rocks, and dust presents itself to the way that we think and feel, hope and fear. The material stuff out of which I was formed has a barely discernible voice in the way my brain works. Chances are, I live each day without being conscious of its presence—again, as with Nyx, except as a negation. Yet it is there, in the shadow, occluded by consciousness and forced to whisper at us obliquely.

The forces contributing to life—whatever we call them—struggle to overcome Nyx. To life itself, Nyx is the termination of its adventure, the opponent to be subdued, an object of horror, like the pall of doom. We resist the imagery that this death instinct is somewhere inside of us and part of us, a contribution of sorts to be reconciled. Life does not want to admit that we are material beings subject to the laws of a material world, despite our best efforts to transcend the material world by spiritual means.

Spirit is the air, the breath, the infusion of vitality required to sustain the experiment, the high-wire act that is sustainable life. But spirit has to collaborate with the body, use it, and literally animate it—ripping it first from the ground, combining elements into intricate patterns, and propelling it toward the horizon. All the while, the material body does not go uncomplaining. The body covets rest and ease and the tranquility of an existence without struggle, like a boulder that basks in the sunlight, undisturbed, for countless eons.

At his farewell address, George Washington (1796/2000) spoke wistfully of finally going "to the mansions of rest." Or General Stonewall Jackson, mortally wounded at the Battle of Chancellorsville in 1863, saying to his caretakers, "Let us cross over the river and rest under the shade of the trees." One can hear in such words the realization that at last one can lay down the burden.

According to Freud, this "death instinct" works toward reducing tensions to achieve a kind of homeostasis. To the extent this process will have become conscious, psychologists speak of **mortality salience**, a process grounded in an awareness of one's own eventual death. To paraphrase Samuel Johnson, the prospect of being hanged in the morning wonderfully concentrates the mind (Boswell, 1934, entry for September 19, 1777, vol. 3, p. 167). Ernest Becker (1973) provided the theoretical foundation for a line of inquiry known as terror management, whereby individuals cope with the grim realization that one's life ends. How do human beings wrestle with this fear? In this chapter, just to be clear, I am not talking explicitly about mortality salience; instead, at an unconscious level, the brain operates in such a way that its material substructure obeys the laws of physics. That unspoken obedience impacts how one thinks. The individual has little reason to be aware that he or she is in the grip of the death instinct. Clinicians, however, might be able to detect indirectly its influence on the functioning of the human mind. Sometimes, it manifests as a disease.

To what extent, therefore, is the medical condition known as depression the weight of Nyx on our subconscious? And to what extent is anxiety the mind's dawning awareness of her presence? Both conditions are part of a single spectrum by the psychiatric profession, and so they are probably related to each other. But is this *how* they are related? In one condition (depression), Nyx asserts herself without being detected; in the other (anxiety), the conscious mind struggles frantically to elude her. Freud referred to systems that were unprepared for the threat (depression) and systems that have been overcharged to prevent the threat (anxiety).

Popular gurus urge the patient to identify a purpose and focus on that goal. It is like a recurring theme. Finding one's purpose lies at the heart of *Man's Search for Meaning* (Frankl, 1985). In this way, you quit focusing your attention on Nyx. Look away. In conjunction, the patient is advised to confront his fears, expose himself to that which induces panic, in order to demonstrate a kind of interior courage. Recognize the extent to which your mortality is salient. Push yourself into the predicament you fear and overcome it. Prove to yourself that you can do it. In other words, find an excuse for the forces of life (which have been labeled loosely as one's libido)—find an excuse for them to resume. Activate them, discipline them, and valorize them, for they are the very forces that began this process of distancing ourselves from Nyx in the first place. Give them work to do.

So of course, the goddess presages doom and haunts our psyche; she represents the inchoate fate of all men—to die, to return to ashes and dust, to become forgotten. In a word, Nyx is the harbinger of oblivion, the derangement of a peculiar configuration and its collapse, as though it had never happened.

At the same time, however, she is a part of us. To reject her is to deny a part of ourselves, to dis-associate ourselves from an authentic aspect of who we are. Even Nyx has something to teach. As the adage puts it, the unpropitiated gods come back to haunt us. Small wonder that the ancients taught us to cultivate the art of dying and learn to die to the self. The phenomenologist celebrates the quest to encounter the goddess and touch her face, though she makes us shudder. At some point, wisdom consists in leaping down from our horse like St. Francis of Assisi and running over to the outcast leper, who is the orthogonal figure, and throwing our arms around her with affection. Nyx is like that leper: the way of all flesh.

Let me be clear: to *encounter* her is not to surrender. The advice one hears is not to accelerate the departure by dismantling the libido, throwing away the structures that constitute life, and yield to the void. This is not about suicide. Instead, the objective should be to integrate her, to give her voice, to enter the underworld like every hero and seek a boon to bring back to conscious life. We have to make peace with Nyx and not squirm to pretend she does not exist.

There is still something left for the hero to do in this world. It involves working *with* her to bestow a gift on the living.

If we find a way to do that, we recapture some of the sweetness of being alive—knowing more acutely what a strange and wonderful gift it is—while at the same time facing our eventual demise with a wan acceptance. The goal should be to befriend with her, to make our peace with the inorganic.

Dylan Thomas (1952) urged his father to rage, rage against the dying of the light . . . do not go gentle into that good night. Thus spake the forces of life. For them, the nemesis is Nyx. And that makes sense. But we have to understand at some level that this ungentle "rage" originates in a disavowal, a banishment, neglect. The puer ambition to extricate oneself from the mud and the muck, to rise, to leap out of being—anxiety in the young man as a quest for direction, to be deployed. "Release me!" Such anxiety dominates the first "Saturn Return" around the age of twenty-eight. In contrast is the senex anxiety that the game will soon be over, when you become increasingly aware again that Nyx lurks. Such anxiety dominates the second "Saturn Return" around the age of fifty-six. The laws of physics drag you back down with a long, slow, *ineluctable* descent. She was there all the time. She participated in your journey. The line representing your split consciousness (that which is alive from that which is not) runs down, straight down, through every human heart.

Let us return to Freud. Freud wrote about psychological tendencies of an earlier origin, more "preconscious" than "sub-conscious"—tendencies that are stronger and more enduring in part because they never reached consciousness in the first place. He called this the first instinct, i.e. to return to lifelessness. He then speculated that the forces of life do not exist in contradiction to Nyx. They bend toward the same outcome, ultimately, except by circuitous means. That goal, that desideratum, is to return to an earlier state or condition that was better, idyllic, golden. To that extent, they are both—life and death—fundamentally conservative drives. In either case, the goal is to reduce the experience of psychic perturbations. We might say that one of them (libido) works by addition; the other (Nyx), by subtraction.

Needless to say, followers and their leaders inspired by Nyx are unlikely to know it. They will speak in terms of restoration, reclamation, and bringing moods of havoc to a close. The turbulence of disorderly times often summons forth a strong leader to put things to right. Freud indicated why we might yearn for such a rescue. Calling it a "death instinct" obscures the role it plays in peaceful living. Leadership can be the establishment of an equilibrium, in tune with an unseen order perhaps, but also allowing for innovation and maximal freedom. Does this not capture to some extent the recurring project known as political philosophy, i.e. to unify both freedom and order as root values? This in my opinion is one way to characterize a homeward leadership.

David Farrell Krell (2019) has offered a slightly different take on this imagery of a death instinct. Relying primarily on Sándor Ferenczi, Krell hypothesizes that rather than some dry material as the base, inorganic substratum, perhaps the inorganic within us is the sea or a "thalassic regressive undertow" where once all living organisms dwelt. Upon leaving the waters, we adapted our apparatus, but we took the water with us. We are largely made of water anyway. We are conceived into an amniotic cradle. Even when we get a splinter, the body encapsulates it in watery pus to move it outward to the surface, where it can be extracted. For Krell, perhaps water is the universal element, the font of life and the ultimate destination for our mortal remains, where no records are kept. Perhaps Freud was wrong to see in our desire for serenity and ease the influence of the inorganic. "Absolute repose does not exist in inorganic nature" (2019, p. 108).

Dry, inorganic stuff or wet rhythms? Krell offers a third possibility, as well, as a substitute for the dry inorganic and the wet inorganic as the most subtle influence on our minds, drawing us toward death (2019, p. 222). He cites Herman Melville for the proposition that what resides in our brains as a kind of residue doubtless having some impact on the workings of the mind is **the dead**, our ancestors, the myriad predecessors going back to the beginning, a kind of accumulated legacy encoded in our DNA, whether it turns out to be advantageous today or not. Their constitutions—taken altogether and mixed in a unique combination—make us what we are. In any case, part of us aspires to honor—if not entirely recover—the past.

## The Omega Point and Sankofa

The Neoplatonist named Plotinus (c. 204/5–270) built an entire metaphysics around the idea that all creation (including you and me) emanated from the One, without withdrawing anything from the One (see generally Kirwan, 1995; Copleston, 1962, ch. 45; Katz, 1950). The One stands immutable forever. We might be said to have been flung, like light from the sun, into being, separable now in our experience, several stages from the blissful unity from which we began. Our destiny or fate, therefore, is to return, to become reabsorbed into the One. Until then, we remain conflicted entities, without the unity promised by the One. Plotinus called this process of reunification *henosis*, a kind of reversal or undoing, not unlike the leaping whale that splashes back into the sea.

In the twentieth century, a Roman Catholic priest named Teilhard de Chardin made a similar claim for the process by which YHWH, the divine creator celebrated in the book of Genesis, draws all things back into Himself through the Christ. Every human being and the history of all life follows the same basic trajectory from unity into differentiation, only to be reunited at the end of times at what de Chardin termed the Omega point (see Lyons, 1983).[2] This

---

2. A Russian divine named Vladimir Soloviev based his entire historical framework on the same sequence from compactness (harmony) through differentiation (sin and chaos) toward reintegration (*sophia*) (see Levine, 2019, p. 77).

teaching, known as *apokatastasis*, was by no means new, inasmuch as it appeared in one form or another in non-Christians, such as Heraclitus, and in earlier Christians, such as Origen and Gregory of Nyssa.

This image has its correlates in other cultures. Here one sees leadership as going back and not going forward. Let me mention another tradition, rooted in Africa, that turns out to be more optimistic than the mythologem of Nyx, because it is about going someplace new and bringing your treasures with you. I introduced the term earlier. What is this thing called Sankofa?

West African Ghana adhered to Sankofa depicted as a bird walking one direction while its head is turned the other way. As I stated before, Sankofa has been translated as looking backward while moving forward, but it conveys more of an adage to remember the past in order to face the future, to return to one's origins and retrieve its treasure today. Another way of saying this is as follows: do not forget where you come from. When necessary, learn your history. As a people, we are not to go back. Yet we do bring something of value with us into an unknown future.

Herman Melville once observed that the great stones used to construct the ancient Egyptian pyramids were themselves ancient long before human beings arrived on the shores of the Nile. One reason that the monument endures, he suggested, is that it was built from something far older. He wrote that "to make an eternity, we must build with eternities" (quoted in Krell, 2019, p. 224). Going forward, if we want what we do to last, then maybe we should construct it from what has lasted, namely our traditions, wherever they originated.[3]

## Populism in a Time of Complexity

In 1947, W.H. Auden published a book-length poem that won a Pulitzer Prize. It was titled *The Age of Anxiety*. The label stuck. Here we are, seventy years later, floundering still. We do not understand things. We cannot control any of it. Our global meeting place, the internet, has intensified the buzz (see e.g. Jemielniak & Przegalinska, 2020). So much that we encounter matters, even the flapping of a butterfly's wings!—putting to ruin all hope. Our condition can go dreadfully wrong overnight. A tiny virus appears and—poof!—a global economy shuts down.

The agitation necessary to sustain life has overwhelmed us. We have trouble sleeping. We have trouble paying attention. We do not know how any of it works, yet we worry it will go wrong. And, it will be our fault. When the agitation becomes too acute or chronic (or both!), we medicate ourselves and impose by means of chemicals the equanimity of a black river. Why can't life

---

3. Polanyi (1951) offered a concrete example when he wrote about liberalism, which flourished in one context that was able to capitalize on its traditions and failed in another context that had ignored its traditions (p. 122f).

just flow? Why must it surge and eddy and cascade? We do not know the answer, and we do not like it. After a while, the beleaguered brain on heightened alert shouts alarms about every little thing, bringing us to the limits of exhaustion. We want it to stop. We want it all to go away. Happily, we have been told here that if we want something, we can make it so. All we have to do is vote for it. Maybe politics will save us.

Or better yet vote against the agitation and the resulting upheaval. We stand on a bridge with Edvard Munch, prepared to open our mouths and scream. "Make it stop." Life does not have to be this way. In truth, it doesn't. When enough of us resort to politics as reflex, we get populism.[4]

Not to worry. A man on a white horse assures us that everything will be okay. The bad energy will be made to subside. What we cherish will continue. Things will even out. Defer to him, of course, and then after lunch you can go take a blanket out of the trunk of the car, lay it in the sunshine, and watch the lazy insects hover nearby until you doze. That, my friend, is the death instinct. And it is not, in and of itself, unhealthy. But it can be.

We often study leadership as a response to crisis (e.g. Hughes, Ginnett, & Curphy, 2018). And rightfully so. "We may say," wrote Terman (1904), "it happens universally that leadership is intensified in times of emergency. War, conflict and adventure are its fertile soil" (p. 426). History has less of an interest in its steady states. What draws our attention are the heroes, the outsized figures in turbulent times, commanding the waters to be still. Churchill stares down the fascist menace. Lincoln heals a divided nation. Machiavelli advises a leader to assume the mantle of chaos so that the people can go about their business unawares. The Reverend Martin Luther King Jr. speaks for a people in turmoil and rage, holding out hope that a calm and resolute march toward equality will return us to the promise of our nation's founding, when we can sing, "Free at last! Free at last! Thank God Almighty, we are free at last." The preacher's mission was fundamentally homeward. In a way, it is almost a shame that we even need leaders. Nevertheless, plainly we do.

We are a people divided. Populism is said to be on the rise circa 2020. But then so is the resistance. We are drawing up sides in some complex struggle with fuzzy boundaries and uncertain creeds. We find ourselves in a familiar, yet uncomfortable quandary between the forces of reaction and the forces of progress, each of which despises the realist politician who stands at the podium and says, "Yes, but . . ." Both sides are understandably drawn to a vision of a better age, such that they find it uninspiring and not a little pusillanimous for someone to tell them we can muddle through, drawing on our heritage while at the same time picking our way with cool deliberation through a strange land. Do we go back to Egypt or dash toward the Promised Land? Which is it? Or

4. A more sympathetic treatment of populism's role can be found at Berkowitz (2019), cf. Sanders (2019).

do we wander in the wilderness, becoming the people we were meant to be, attuned to a sovereign sense of propriety and mission? For it was Moses who had to preside over a very long and exasperating trial, going this way and that and routinely consulting the author of his misfortune.

Consumers of literature on leadership often cry out for ways to (a) tamp down the vagaries of an uncertain world and get ahold of things, imposing order, or to (b) emancipate our systems from the bloat and stagnation of inertia and instead seek a better world on the other side of chaos. Yet this is the only world we get, and it is uncertain. It just is. I hold it as a tenet of my own philosophy that we can neither stanch nor transcend the human condition. We live between the old and the new, order and freedom, legacies to uphold and opportunity to pursue. Life is conducted in an enduring *metaxy*. These two together, in a both/and configuration not unlike a dance, operate to lend us what satisfaction we can hope for. So maybe leadership lowers expectations, paying due homage to these twin and apparently contradictory aspirations without relinquishing command, calling for grim determination in the teeth of turbulence, to see its generative powers and otherwise turn the prospect of labor into an everlasting game (Carse, 1986).

What I am suggesting is that populism is the death instinct writ large, the urgings of a substructure that seeks repose, grounded in the tendencies of the material world to quit with the agitation that goes with living and instead achieve an equilibrium—an equilibrium that signals quiescence. Populist leaders promise a cessation of striving. The hunger for quiescence is neither strange nor wrong. It does have its limits, though.

## Recursive Patterns

Years ago, I drove to Ohio with my two sons in order to attend a funeral in Barberton, a city previously unfamiliar to me. After a night at a hotel on the outskirts, we dressed appropriately and set out in the morning to find the venue somewhere in the heart of town. This was before the electronic devices we now enjoy to find locations, so once I had reached the vicinity, I could not find the church itself. We circled the portion of town where it had to be, trying in the hubbub of the traffic to find different ways to go toward it. I remember at one point at a stoplight being so exasperated that I gestured and said, "Look, I know it's right over there somewhere, dadgummit. I just don't know how to get there!" Once we had passed the same landmark a third or a fourth time (I don't remember), I had become flustered. Besides, we were now too late to attend the funeral anyway. So in defeat, we retreated back to the hotel, changed our clothes, and amused ourselves for a few hours before driving back to Indiana without ever achieving what we had set out to achieve.

There is something exasperating about going around in circles. Travel around an oval often enough, the course becomes tedious. You feel as though you never get anywhere. In ordinary speech, we complain when somebody talks in circles.

Herman Hesse (2003) inserts a scene in the novel *Journey to the East* when the narrator, having gone in search, encounters his old servant Leo and rejoices because now at last they can find their way onward. He follows Leo on a circuitous path around the city, with Leo stopping intermittently at religious shrines, drawing out the suspense, to the point when the narrator—and the reader—becomes impatient. They do not seem to be going anywhere. Is this whole book one of those lame lessons that it is more about the journey than the destination?

Archetypal psychology explains the image of the uroboros, the snake consuming its own tail, signifying infinity (Neumann, 1954). It also hearkens back to the primal experience of compact reality as a swarm of undifferentiated threats, viscerally repugnant, out of which we are expected to begin the process of sorting out what's what, through a series of distinctions—the light from the dark, the wet from the dry, the waking from sleep, the living and the dead, over and over. As the neuroscientist once remarked, our brains encounter something new and immediately wonder: Can I eat it? Will it eat me? Can I have sex with it? Our brains may be designed to detect patterns within the complexity of a campfire or stream, as though our fascination with labyrinths, mazes, and other intricacies accompanies the challenge of making sense of the tangle that is paramount reality (see generally Doob, 1990). And so we rise up with gratification, having solved the Sudoku.

After a point, though, we find it oppressive to think that it goes on and on, without end, like a fractal image that looks the same at every magnitude or a Möbius strip that twists in upon itself forever. We lose any hope of progress. We start to ask ourselves why we even bother to trace the lines that lead nowhere except back to the beginning. The philosopher Friedrich Nietzsche said, in effect, yes, that is the way of things. You have two choices. You can bemoan the eternal return, as though you were condemned like Sisyphus to a purposeless toil, or you can affirm it, celebrate it, and say to yourself, this is why I am here (see Camus, 1942/1983). Let's do this thing, even if we have done this very same thing repeatedly, since time out of mind.

Images of progress intoxicate us. We exert ourselves for the sake of a better tomorrow. Dreams of utopia inspire us to study and labor, strategize, and exhort one another, excelsior! Let us amass knowledge and amass wealth, constructing tinier gadgets, faster cars, and taller skyscrapers. Those of us laboring under an achievement-oriented mindset to get someplace finally will derive a little jolt of satisfaction at the waymarks, when we get to check the box from a to-do list and say to ourselves that our exertions were worth it.

I occasionally paused while writing this book to glance at the tentative table of contents as it took shape, and I counted the number of words I had written, measuring my progress over the course of a sabbatical. So, I get it.

Anyone who has been assigned to maintenance knows how unsexy that is, to clean the toilet again, to mow the lawn again, to wash the dishes again, to keep doing the same old thing, as though it never ends. The movie *Groundhog Day* brilliantly studies the protagonist who comes to realize that he wakes up to the same exact day, no matter what he does differently to affect the outcome (see Goldberg, 2006). After a stage of bewilderment, he tries desperately to change the pattern, only to discover that his efforts are fruitless. It is the same day again. For a while, he finds the peculiar fact of his predicament to be an opportunity for mischief, but after a while that does not change anything either. He turns to despair, trying every which way to kill himself—anything to avoid waking up to the same exact radio show on the same exact day, *ad infinitum*. He keeps coming back. Once suicide proves to be futile, resignation sets in. He is stuck in a perpetual loop, with no way out. Only then does he decide, what the heck, to do the right thing in the moment, at each moment, whether it pays off later or not. He helps an old lady, he learns to play the piano, he gets to know folks personally, and in the process he does not seem to realize that even though everything around him keeps recurring, he is becoming a better man.

At one time, humanity found the cycles of this earth reassuring—the seasons, the renewal, the exchange of one thing for another, birth and death, planting and harvest, for richer for poorer, in sickness and in health. (Do we ever become bored with breathing?) We accepted the circle as a dignified rendition of our fate, a rhythm of vitality, a sense of closure that lends to life a sense of meaning that we in the twenty-first century have somehow lost in our impatience to extend, ascend, and transcend paramount reality.

Even here, we may find it within ourselves to rise up out of the daily round and look as though from the balcony down at our situation, not unlike the poor man ripped from the comforts of his chains to be brought up into the unforgiving light in Plato's Allegory of the Cave. The story does not end with him gamboling through a meadow, en route to a giddy world. He is compelled to go back down into the cave, into his chains, into the shadows, where the memory of his excursion becomes all the more painful for its transience. If he is not careful, he will think it was all a cruel dream. That would be better than the horror of realizing that he must live out his days as a slave to the lies and darkness, knowing what he knows of the sun.

Philosophers speak of the hermeneutic circle by which you move in your mind from one vantage point to another, swinging from the part to the whole and from the whole to the part, repeatedly, in order to derive meaning from a text or situation. Here is another use of the same geometric shape (a circle) to convey a repetition. Is it tedious? Perhaps. But we cannot know anything by a single glance. We must mentally circumambulate, drawing distinct impressions of the one reality, from every angle, and that includes occasionally getting outside of oneself, looking back (or down) on oneself as an object (Harter, 2017b). It also means that we must adopt the point of view of other people, empathizing, in a process that Gadamer called fusing horizons. Nevertheless, as sure as the sun rises in the east, we will return to the point of origin, back to ourselves, for we are the only thing that can occupy the where-we-are. We bring a unique perspective. We cannot wholly escape from ourselves.

Robert Avens complained in the pages of the *International Philosophical Quarterly* that both Martin Heidegger and James Hillman (of archetypal psychology fame) embrace the idea that life is lived in a circle, going nowhere in particular. The soul turns in upon itself, maybe venturing out for a bit, but then returning—perhaps with a boon. He wonders if this is not a form of nihilism. It is almost as though they had become tired of the depths of their studies and erudition and so made the effort to return to the surfaces, because at least those are real.

It is true that the human mind can cavort in realms that do not exist. Well these men in particular knew. The imagination is in principle infinite, an inexhaustible playground where a human being can get lost in the arabesque. Systematic philosophers such as Aristotle, Aquinas, and Hegel constructed impressive thought-worlds, each with its own logic. Nevertheless, something in the *psyche*—at least for most folks—must touch again the grit and the damp and the fibrous. Avens quotes Heidegger regarding "that weird and yet friendly feeling that we have always already been who we are, that we are nothing but the unveiling of things decided upon long ago" (1982, quoting Heidegger's *Schelling*, p. 185).

Perhaps the popular fascination with apocalypse reflects the same intuition. Here we are, immersed in complexity beyond comprehension, surrounded by products of human enterprise, amused more and more by fictions and corporate logos and photos of other people having a good time. We cannot master it all. Nobody ever has. It oppresses us. We certainly cannot make it dance to our liking. Perhaps here, in tales of catastrophe, is a cry for authenticity to wish it all away, consummated in one horrifying calamity, flooded once more as in the days of Noah, or incinerated by atomic bombs, or overwhelmed by zombies that do not care a whit about their wardrobe or the accuracy of their Starbucks order. Or we ourselves blow it up à la *Fight Club* or jihad. Avens sees this temptation as a retreat from our calling as intelligent creatures to make sense of things. Heidegger and Hillman might probably say in rebuttal that making sense of things requires an acquaintance with things. We have become so insulated from reality lately as to be little more than specters haunting an elaborate dreamscape, coddled as it were in what John Gray aptly called our prosthetic environment and Umberto Eco called hyper-reality. We seem to want somebody to wake us up from all that. Or make it stop. "Lay me back in my father's arms." "I want to go home."

Nevertheless, Avens has a legitimate worry. One can become so enamored of the inarticulate surface that we ignore the very real depths of science and logic and truth. Brute apprehension of the real, rubbing our nose in it, on the one hand, and fantasy, on the other hand, are not our only choices. Or, perhaps to word this another way, we can become responsible stewards of our fantasies, largely by swinging back and forth between paramount reality and our constructs—reminding ourselves again and again which is which, generating new metaphors that advance our understanding and yet cautioning ourselves (and others) about the limits of metaphor.

A mindless tour of the same old same old, like taking the same bus route every day, can become wearisome and induce ennui. "Same as it ever was." Nevertheless, we aspire to be restored to paradise and love it—snake and all. In the context of that primordial garden, therefore, we can once again venture like children into the woods and build our tree forts, so long as we care for one another, understanding that it is all a game, and that when the bell sounds across the lawn we head for home and tell Mama all about our adventures.

Is it so bad that tomorrow, we get to do it all over again?

We might quote Gadamer: "Understanding is to be thought of less as a subjective act than as participating in an event of tradition" (quoted in Simms, 2015, p. 76). I am part of what will be tomorrow's tradition. That insight alters one's perspective. By the same token, tradition persuades us that we occupy only a limited point of view. We are situated. But then so were our predecessors! And so will you be! We are all just part of an ongoing conversation, from our unique perspectives. How we acquit ourselves in the present depends upon the charity we show to both the past and the future.

## All Chapters End

The literary devices proliferate and threaten to overwhelm the understanding. Is leadership this, or is it that? Are we supposed to go one way or the other? Is leadership a fit topic for psychology, sociology, politics, history, or even (god forbid) mathematics? Here is what I recommend. Let us practice mindfulness, in the present, and ask ourselves together:

- What is the case?
- What is possible?
- Where do we need to go next?

We can be guided by lessons from the past and should take our idols with us, unafraid to cross the threshold into a strange land. If we acquit ourselves well, we can become part of that same legacy and live on in the memory of our community. Can it be said of us, as General Allenby said of Lawrence of Arabia in that iconic film, that we rode the whirlwind? Only if in the end we bestow a boon upon our people. And what greater boon than **to enlarge the future**?

Doris Kearns Goodwin, in writing about the leadership of four emblematic presidents—namely, Abraham Lincoln, Theodore Roosevelt, Franklin Roosevelt, and Lyndon Johnson —brings her study to a close with these words:

> While their personal stories came to very different ends, they were all looking beyond their own lives, hopeful that their achievements had shaped and enlarged the future. . . . For these leaders, the final measure of their achievements would be realized by their admittance to an enduring place in communal memory.
>
> *(2018, p. 345)*

# 12

## MAKING USE OF THE TURBULENCE
### Extra-Ordinary Leadership

### Introduction to the Chapter

Social synchrony occurs for a variety of reasons, sometimes because of leadership. But then so does turbulence. At any given point in time, one can find evidence of both synchrony and turbulence. Leadership entails each. You do not get synchrony without turbulence and vice versa. Sometimes, synchrony at one level entails turbulence at another. At other times, they work against one another. How does a person navigate in the tumult? In the previous chapter, I advised looking homeward, drawing from a perennial wisdom that links us across the generations. Tradition helps to guide us.

I was insistent, however, that tradition opens us to novelty. It should not altogether close us off from possibilities. We might orient ourselves by consulting the past, but we flow ever onward. If the last chapter talked about the backward glance as a kind of stabilizing force, keeping us grounded (as it were), the following chapter talks about the restless impetus to keep going forward, to venture outward. If we are like children at the beach periodically touching our mother's knee, we also wander off in increasingly wide circuits. As we get further and further away, we would be advised now and then to look back so that we keep from getting lost.

### Life as More Life and as More-Than-Life

Toward the end of his career, Georg Simmel published his views on life as transcendence, as a dynamic process, in the spirit of the peregrinal ontology that we have had reason to mention more than once. Simmel was offering a version of life as part of the flux of reality (see e.g. Goodstein, 2017, p. 74).

Simmel argued that life is a process of surpassing or transcending itself. Nature set aside life to grow past its existing form into new, more complex forms. The rest of nature tends to fall into fairly predictable patterns with mechanistic discipline, as the natural sciences keep discovering. But life . . . it constantly, even urgently, exceeds what we come to expect. Life flourishes largely because it does not stand still. It finds a way, like the weed that breaks through the concrete sidewalk. Humans exemplify this drive or urge.[1]

The source of our self-transcendence is energy that never rests. The human "will" can be said to pour this energy into existing forms. In the social world, this includes forms such as marriage and family and employment. For whatever reason, human beings have found that certain sociological forms work well. The conventional view of domination is one of those forms (1908, reprinted in 1971, ch. 7). We seem to like many of these forms. They are fairly simple. We see little reason to discard them. We replicate sociological forms readily. Even then, we are tempted to tinker with them. Maybe we find a better version. Or we try to improve what is already good. Or after some exasperating experience, we decide that maybe it was not meant for us after all, so we break off and go look elsewhere. Like water that pours into containers, our lives pour into forms, but then like water dripping onto sandstone, over time we can create our own containers. This is part of what it means for life to transcend itself. It is restlessness, adopting and adapting new forms, when not creating them whole.

In organizations, we see this vitality at work in the exertions of the entrepreneur and those who strive endlessly for innovation. We do not always swap out one existing form for another one, like switching jobs. Sometimes, we *create* alternatives that never existed before. These forms proliferate. Today, we have multiple models for education, business, politics, even marriage. New ones are always emerging. In that way, as living beings we shape the world we occupy. This, Simmel wrote, is the essence of life (1918/2010, p. 8). We flow into forms, surpass them in order to create new ones, then break them again (1918/2010, p. 13). The result is a field littered with forms—forms of scientific thought, forms of painting, forms of transportation, forms of language, and so forth. Life strews its history with forms. Moreover, these forms, as they become concrete, immediately affect what is possible next. Simmel called this an axial rotation: he wrote that "the forms or functions that life has brought forth, for its own sake and out of its own dynamic, become so autonomous and definitive that life in turn comes to serve them, subordinating its contents to them" (1918/2010, p. 25). We fabricate the boxes we live in. As Simmel put it:

> Life out of its own teleological necessities brings into existence forms of action around which, as though around an axle, life tends to be turned,

---

1. Ruth Benedict referred to this as a Faustian image of humanity (1934/2005, p. 53f). To the extent that Simmel's position resembled those of Schopenhauer (*The World as Will*) and Nietzsche (*The Will to Power*), see his study of these two philosophers in particular (1991).

so that those forms exist as an autocratic idea, and of themselves define life and its value.

*(1918/2010, p. 60)*

When confronted with these forms and their demands, we struggle once again to surpass our situation. We start all over and enter into liminal space in order to ponder the situation. We move into and back out of these forms.

Simmel argued that the push to transcend the present is characteristic of life. Life is about creating new possibilities.[2] It is my contention that an inward push embroiling a person in coordinated social action to bring about a better future appears to me to be the font of leadership.

The sequence goes something like this. Human desire motivates us to seek satisfaction. Existing forms for doing so are usually mundane. If you want an income, go get a job. But that is not the end of it. The forms we create (or reify) turn around and box us in, if we are not careful. We become alienated from that which we ourselves created (Goodstein, 2017, p. 154). "Yes, you chose this job," we say, "but over time it will interfere with your life, making demands you might come to resent." William James (1909/1996) made an equivalent observation: "most human institutions," he wrote, "end by becoming obstacles to the very purposes which their founders had in view" (p. 9).

Leadership taps into that originating energy, that pulsating vitality, trying to harness it for some discernible purpose. It guides or directs it toward an outcome. Once a leader adopts a purpose, he or she immediately sacrifices a freedom to have done other things. A leader persuades companions to limit themselves, binding themselves to some vision of the future, forsaking all others. Simmel wrote that "the antithesis of freedom . . . is purposiveness" (1918/2010, p. 29). We are free to escape our existing forms, but only on behalf of creating new ones. There is no such thing as pure potential, i.e. formless energy careening through empty space. Once this liberating energy chooses its next form, there will be a shift so that the group can focus on the necessary means for achieving that goal (1918/2010, pp. 26–30). That energy now has an outlet, and so it pours forth in a particular direction, in concert with the energies of other people.

We also learn from Simmel, however, that what we gain one day becomes the staging area for what we pursue tomorrow. The finish line recedes. Using the American football adage, we constantly move the goalposts. One never arrives. We are perpetually en route. We are strangers in a strange land condemned to wander. Witness in this regard the acquisitiveness of businesses and of empires. It would be reasonable therefore to conclude that the ultimate destination is always maximal freedom to continue the journey, giving oneself

---

2. In a similar vein, Patočka wrote, "Ours is a life in possibilities . . . in which we are involved, in which we transcend the present, are more than what is currently given" (1998, p. 145).

plenty of options. This is as much as saying not to box yourself in so deeply that you have trouble extricating yourself later. The purpose of leadership today is more leadership tomorrow. This is meant to be an infinite game.

What Simmel hoped to describe was the overarching pattern to this sequence (Goodstein, 2017, p. 155). Even during moments of introspection, we step outside of ourselves briefly to regard ourselves; we go beyond what we regard as our "selves" and occupy a space in the imagination for which we have no name (1918/2010, p. 10). We step outside to look back upon ourselves. (Ortega had a name for it: *ensimismamiento*.) In the imagination, we do the same thing with regard to our predicament, our circumstances. We swing around to behold ourselves and our present moment. We can also imagine alternatives. Even here, we exceed the ordinary limits of our thinking to think otherwise. We see a limit of some sort and then consider stepping over it. In his attempt to detect an overarching pattern, Simmel realized that the process would not be linear (Goodstein, 2017, p. 167). Nevertheless, it incorporates some form of seeing and moving beyond one's boundaries.

Life enters into forms with discernible boundaries and then almost immediately tries to transgress them.

Earlier, in the chapter on turbulence, we had reason to mention Manuel de Landa (2000). He had something to say on this topic, especially regarding social systems. That is, he tried to widen the aperture, to see this process of self-transcendence at the macro level. He hypothesized that the creation of a novel structure (or form) is usually performed by one of the most destratified elements in the preceding phase (2000, p. 266). That is to say, some marginalized group or some interest that has been neglected or ignored has the potential to trigger a shift in a new direction. At the social level, life transcends itself on behalf of those elements in society that are dissatisfied, uncomfortable, and even angry. Of course, at any given point in time there are many such marginalized groups and a multitude of neglected or ignored interests. Most of them will stay that way or disappear altogether. Only some will compete to displace the status quo, as for example during the Weimar Republic when national socialists battled in the streets with international socialists for the chance to overthrow the regime. As often as not, of course, the "destratified elements" will lose utterly. Sometimes, they will unify to win together. Sometimes, they will completely replace the status quo in open revolution. Sometimes, the powers that be will coopt the movement and fold it into its overall structure in such a way that it all survives. Sometimes, the defeat of these disaffected elements will give impetus to change, such that by losing the battle, they actually win the war.[3] The point is that the numerous flows that constitute history are

---

3. One thinks, for example, of Shays' Rebellion (1786–1787), which was forcibly put down and then petered out in the backwoods of western Massachusetts, despite giving impetus to calling the Constitutional Convention (see Harter & Clark, 2020).

complex and interlocking. A squelched uprising in one country might be part of a larger transition that succeeds elsewhere. A communist movement in Peru remains nearly inconsequential, despite the fact that communism triumphed in Cuba. While Christianity has been on the wane in Europe, it has grown exponentially in Africa. We have to see it all unfold from quite a distance in order to study *the flow itself*. Coups, rebellions, and revolutions are only manifestations of subterranean forces at work undetected, like breakouts of the plague when the conditions were right and like volcanoes that burst from out of the magma perpetually churning beneath our feet. Sometimes, you need a very long timeline to discern the patterns.

As seen from the *longue durée*, self-transcendence is an ongoing process. But now here we revisit a point I made earlier about our desire in leadership studies to isolate the so-called pin-point phenomenon. What is that narrow experience around which we pack so much cultural baggage? **I settle on self-transcendence as the pin-point**.

## Patočka on Casting Possibilities

Leadership is, in a manner of speaking, the realization of shared possibilities. I adopt the term "possibilities" as a term of art from the lectures of the Czech philosopher Jan Patočka. We can begin with a simple characterization of what it means to be human:

> [Human beings are] beings placed in the world, aware of the world and themselves, beings in the world among others and dependent on them (on others and on things) and yet living as free, not as a stone, as animals in merely external relations, but rather living an inner life.
>
> *(Patočka, 1998, p. 74f)*

What takes place as part of that "inner life" is crucial. We live as much in the sphere of our own minds as we do in paramount reality (Patočka, 1998, p. 35). "What is characteristic of us [as humans] is our variety of possibilities, a freedom from the present, from the immediately given" (Patočka, 1998, p. 33).

He wrote that, in any given situation, life can be said to "project" possibilities (1998, p. 128). Obviously, we have to be open to the horizon for this to do us any good (Patočka, 1998, p. 104). But once we are open to what might come, we cast our imagination onto the future, in anticipation (Patočka, 1998, p. 95). The array of possibilities constitutes the choice one gets to make. (Heidegger had referred to this condition as boundlessness.) Activity can be thought of as a series of these projections that we attempt to realize through our exertions, such as reaching for the spoon or landing a man on the moon. As we make the effort, the situation changes accordingly, presenting us with a new array of possibilities. Patočka wrote that "as we realize our possibilities, the constellation of our context changes, it appears ever different" (emphasis omitted) (Patočka, 1998, p. 132). The process goes on and on. Even the mind, as a person thinks, undergoes a similar process of possibility-choice-exertion-new possibilities (Patočka, 1998, p. 109).

These possibilities are not always objects that are already out there in the real world, like the sociological forms that Simmel wrote about; they belong to the future (Patočka, 1998, p. 39). They might result in something objective later, depending how we choose, but as possibilities they exist only in the imagination. When we choose a course of action, then we identify with that possibility to make it so (Patočka, 1998, p. 96).

Patočka broke the process down into discrete steps (1998, pp. 77–81), as follows:

Step one: locate yourself (where am I?)
Step two: assess the situation where you are (what is going on?)
Step three: establish your mood or disposition toward the situation (e.g. am I excited, fearful?)
Step four: identify your interests in the situation (what can I gain or lose?)
Step five: summon forth the array of possibilities (what are my choices?)
Step six: choose a possibility and take action to bring it about
Step seven: incorporate other people in the process

The last step is by no means incidental to his whole philosophy. We live among other people. We depend on them. Our possibilities must account for them. We actually discover who we are through the eyes of other people (Patočka, 1998, p. 51), which means that step one necessitates being in relationship. Leaders should not just use other people, like objects; they also learn to identify with other people. They experience a kind of shared life. As we identify with other people, we go through steps one through six together and not alone.

Doing this together is what Patočka meant by solidarity and community. This community in turn shapes the context in which we subsequently operate (1998, p. 55). Within the community, then, whenever somebody contributes to the process, we can see leadership.

In the next section of this chapter, my goal is to differentiate order and freedom. Freedom pertains to the degree that an order might be open to input. After this, we should take a closer look at the etymology of the term "influence," inasmuch as it suggests a flowing-into from elsewhere, i.e. incursions from above, downward penetrations into the mundane world. Finally, I offer an extended description about how this might work in actual practice when we look at the character of the stranger as leader. What we will see is that the metaphor of incursions works at each magnitude. As liberty is to order, leadership is to an organization, and critical thinking is to what we believe. The dynamics are similar. It is all self-transcendence.

## Concord and Liberty; Order and Freedom

The tension between civic order and freedom is part of what constitutes social life. The tension appears in the earliest records—and even perhaps in the artifacts one finds from the Paleolithic era (40,000–28,000 BCE) (see Horvath, 2013, ch. 1). Inductively, this tension appears to be a permanent part of human existence, even if the exact proportions are not constant. The tension fluctuates, quivering daily in our personal lives. The struggle to manage that tremulous tension goes by different names. Artists and philosophers and statesmen have responded in different ways. Nevertheless, it is there. And the line between order and freedom goes down, straight down, through the very heart of the phenomenon we study as leadership.

José Ortega y Gasset published a series of articles in 1940 as *Concord and Liberty* (1940/1946). There, Ortega addressed this tension explicitly. He chose the words *Concordia* and *Libertas* because they originated in the works of Cicero, who wrote in a time of historical consequence not unlike the terrible end to the European *fin de siècle* when Ortega was writing. Ortega saw parallels of liminality to his own time, as the prevailing civic order fell into violence before anything clear and wholesome could settle again over the continent.

Struggle and strife in politics are nothing new, of course; in fact, such vicissitudes contribute to learning. We adjust ourselves repeatedly to account for the shifts and missteps of experience. It is (if anything) a sign of civic vigor to undergo these struggles, not unlike an athlete competing in order to make himself stronger and more resilient. However, Cicero recognized that the civil war in Rome was something qualitatively different. Here was no surface adjustment but a full-scale transformation. That is to say that the prevailing order had for many lifetimes not only *allowed* for considerable adaptation, it required it. This capacity for adaptation had its limits. At some point, when the discord runs too deep, the order itself cannot hold. When that happens, there is a serious void. The order collapses. Concord—the "being of one heart"—evaporates. What then?

The experience is a crisis (see Ortega, 1958). Beliefs that everyone had taken for granted and relied upon are suddenly called into question. The foundation of social life trembles underfoot and then abruptly opens up into a yawning chasm. Everything a people built together teeters and then comes crashing down. Like a tree deprived of its roots, the order can be felled by a gust of wind. Everything seemingly manifests as upheaval. Later, political scientists would call it discord or anarchy. But the experience of anarchy as a political phenomenon has implications for religion, commerce, and the arts. The gods have abandoned us. All is lost. And so we lay ourselves open to any order that will have us. Part of us craves a strong man. We sigh with relief when a dictator takes from us the existential anxiety. Likewise, in their time the Romans welcomed the emperor, just as people welcomed Napoleon and

Hitler and their ilk.[4] Through the cleft in concord strides one to save us. That experience is often the origin of leadership.

I follow Ortega in his analysis largely because concord is not the same thing as order. Concord is an order we all take for granted, such that we are truly of one heart. Not every order is based on concord. Order can be based on fear, for example, or greed. Cicero had witnessed the dissolution of a cherished set of beliefs and feared what rough beast might come. Once concord no longer exists, what do we have to work with, if not fear and greed?

By the same token, then, just as concord is not identical with order but is instead a species of order, Ortega did not contend that liberty is the same thing as the absence of order. A man stranded on a raft in the middle of an empty sea can paddle in any direction he chooses, but that does not make him free. When all is liminal and we have no sense of what is up and what is down, having been cut loose into the maelstrom, this is not liberty. Concord is a wholesome order that includes liberty. It embraces another kind of both/and, predominantly to avoid the two extremes of what the political scientists would later call totalitarianism (on the one hand) and anarchy (on the other). Another way of saying this is that totalitarianism is an order contravening liberty; anarchy therefore is freedom contravening concord. Liberty occurs within a context of civic order. Liberty itself is a problem, to be sure, but a problem that any healthy concord should not only tolerate but also encourage. As liberty disappears, however, the structures tend to ossify, not unlike a corpse deprived of vital fluids. The order strangles its own quickening. It hardens.

A similar tension exists in any group or team. Without any cohesiveness, there is no group at all. Its members float away. Yet if cohesiveness is too intense, too rigid, then the group suffers from groupthink. It is not really a group any longer. It is a single thing, a monolith. It becomes a closed and unsustainable system, oblivious to its membership, oblivious to its environment, oblivious to its very nature. Ortega purchased from Cicero the idea of a supple order, a concord sustained by liberty itself.

What this implies is an adaptable social form with permeable boundaries.[5]

## What Does "Extra-Ordinary" Mean?

Sverre Spoelstra recently published a book titled *Leadership and Organization* (2018). In it, he explains what Max Weber had meant by charismatic leadership. One of the elements of charismatic leadership is a leader who is considered

---

4. The abortive caliphate known as ISIS secured territory by offering war-weary peoples at least a semblance of good governance (Revkin & McCants, 2015).
5. Jemielniak and Przegalinska recognize that a number of online collaborations dedicated to consensus, creativity, and an anti-authoritarian ethos (i.e. liberty) do go ahead to create parallel structures such as foundations, thereby formally off-loading traditional managerial functions (2020, p. 46).

**extra-ordinary**. That is the word he used: extra-ordinary. In all likelihood, one would think that extra-ordinary means distinctive by the possession of some unusual gift (such as magic) or the possession of an unusual degree of some gift (such as foresight). But Spoelstra interprets Weber to mean something else by the term, and I have to say that I agree with him.

The word "ordinary" shares the same root etymologically with the word "order." Weber devoted a lot of effort to describing social order. We all live within a social order. The charismatic leader is extra-ordinary in that *he (or she) stands partly outside of that order*. The leader is to some extent independent of that order and therefore free to call it into question on behalf of another order, a transcendent or divine order. The "extra-ordinary" leader participates in this shared order, here among the rest of us, but also in another order—a *higher* order—that informs his leadership. He occupies a portal and stands between two worlds. He is the link or *omphalos* to a greater power, an authority that comes from beyond our shared existence. This is what sets him apart and determines his authority.

I urge the image upon my readers. A leader does not belong entirely to any one level, domain, or enclosure. Leadership summons forth something from beyond this motley caravan. It brings a boon from the underworld. It requires some freedom from the prevailing ethos, some superior vantage point, permitting us to say, "Wait, it doesn't have to be this way."[6] And I mean that for all leadership, and not just for charismatic leadership. In my opinion, Weber called it charismatic leadership, when in fact he was describing leadership itself. To the extent that this happens, it is because of one's capacity to access that other order. Leadership derives from something extra-ordinary—that is, from something outside of, above, or beyond this order. In this lesson, Spoelstra has given us a different way of talking.

If one operates entirely from within a given order (the sociological form), executing functions and maintaining the system throughout its diurnal rounds, one cannot lead. At most, one manages. Leadership requires stepping outside, shedding if only for a moment the veils of convention. Leadership looks at an order as from a distance. Only then, when it all seems strange, people can see it for what it is. And possibly change it.

This liminal space of betwixt and between—part of, but not belonging to— also known as the *metaxy*: it has its terrors. Ortega had once noticed a paradox: "The man with the clear head is the man who frees himself from those fantastic 'ideas' and looks life in the face, realizes that everything in it is problematic, and feels himself lost" (Ortega, 1932, p. 170). Liminality also brings with it opportunities, if we have the gumption to try. The practice of critical thinking enables this liminality. And at the heart of this effort is the capacity (and

6. Alvesson, Blom, and Sveningsson (2017) allude to this feature of leadership only briefly (p. 214).

willingness) to swing around and really look at one's predicament, i.e. at the gruesome, knotty reality we call life. That is hard. But it can be done, even if incrementally. So, yes, I concur that leadership reflects something extra-ordinary, if we understand that term properly.

What this notion of the extra-ordinary presupposes is the existence of a separate or distinct world, a place outside or beyond what we know within our little enclosure. The leader will be the one to pass through the *aporia* and return like Joshua with good report.

## Influx as a Metaphor

The term "influence" derives from a metaphor: to flow in. For years now, I had taken the word for granted. Previously, I even found the precise meaning of the term "power" to be more interesting. Of course, scholars have been debating the definition of the term "leadership" for decades. But "influence" has such a simple and straightforward street-level value that I never recognized the importance of its etymology. Here, in this book, however, the term actually fits snugly—better than I could have guessed (see Alvesson, 2019, p. 29).

Let us begin with the claim that a single human being can operate within two different spheres. Call them what you like. They could be two different domains, such as business and law, for instance (Gardner, 2006), or they can be two different cultures. They could be two different generations. Spoelstra (2018) has written about the simple dichotomy between being inside and outside of an organization (p. 13). He avers that leadership originates from outside of the social system where it occurs. Why? Because institutions create and enforce their own way of thinking (Douglas, 1986; Hummel, 2014). In that sense, leadership is extra-ordinary, where "ordinary" means being part of an order (Spoelstra, 2018, p. 21; see also p. 131). The leader plays a role, therefore, as mediator between two spheres, a human connection from beyond the boundary. Going further, Spoelstra writes about one sphere being higher than the other, as one might imagine the mundane world situated below the spiritual or divine world (2018, p. 43), for a higher realm implies authority.[7]

Spoelstra picks up where Friedrich Nietzsche left off writing about the death of God. Religion often offers a mediating figure—a shaman, prophet, guru, sage, or savior (2018, p. 45). The leader is the one who has access to another dimension. But what does this look like if you discount religion, as Nietzsche did? Leadership still happens because mediation still happens. Martin Luther had opened the door to this way of thinking, writes Spoelstra, when he divided the idea of one's "office" (e.g. mayor, professor, carpenter) from its animating spirit (vocation or ministry). Organizational authority is different from

---

7. Mircea Eliade wrote, "The sacred always manifests itself as a reality of a wholly different order from 'natural' realities" (1957/1959, p. 10).

spiritual authority. These are not the same thing. If anything, they often clash. But without divine sanction—that is, as the significance of religion waned in Western culture—something of the sort still arises in works about leadership: see Carlyle (great man), Nietzsche (*übermensch*), and Weber (charismatic leader). The distinction is not unlike the distinction between the physical body, on the one hand, and the vital spark, on the other. Leadership quickens the collective, without which the body stagnates or coagulates or ossifies (pick your metaphor). Spoelstra writes that leadership "is a matter of bringing life to a stultifying bureaucracy" (2018, p. 52). Luther would have it that leaders embody the spirit. In his fantasy, in fact, all of us are animated by the one spirit. It does not have to be a designated person whom we call the leader.

Even those who reject both the religious dimension and the idea of there being extraordinary and necessary individuals in our midst will nevertheless invent alternatives to explain why only certain people should lead. They will appeal to something else, something other—i.e. that which sets that person apart, if only for a moment. It could be traits, for example, or expertise. Transformational leadership utterly depends on this idea of an idealized influence, inspirational motivation, and intellectual stimulation. Something special draws us toward the future. Or, by way of contrast, they so reject the threat of anything extraordinary whatsoever that they try to downplay and possibly even thwart the possibility, as they attempt to submit or subdue these unpredictable features under some version of legalism or ethics or ideology or even religion itself (2018, pp. 53–56). That is to say, to the extent there is evidence that somebody possesses such a powerful, almost mysterious mien—whether a divine calling or just awe-inspiring genius—we must hedge it in on all sides to prevent foreseeable damage. Or ostracize the great man completely, as they did in antiquity. We acknowledge its existence by rejecting it. Spoelstra identifies several trends in leadership studies that exist in part to quell the mystique of leadership—a mystique he was all too happy to reinstate (see also de Vries, 1994; Conger, 1989). As am I.

Be that as it may, leadership as a concept relies on some kind of manifestation in the social order of an authority rooted in something from outside of that order, whether sanctioned by that order and sufficiently domesticated somehow or simply sweeping through unbidden like a cleansing storm.

As with so many dichotomies in this book, I look for the both/and. We need order in our lives. We also need vitality. And if they can be made to work together, as Ortega y Gasset had illustrated from *del imperio romano*, that combination allows for the best of all possible worlds. As we saw, Ortega y Gasset regarded the Roman Empire as a particularly adroit improvisation that lasted for centuries. Order that avoids the rigidity of Max Weber's "iron cage" he referred to as concord, i.e. a being of one heart. Freedom that avoids the instability of recklessness he referred to as liberty. The trick is to secure both, because they need each other.

Another way of saying this is that we need for people to tap into this other realm, whatever it is that lies beyond the borders.

One way that Spoelstra shows he can have his cake and eat it too, combining untamed leadership and a persisting order, is in his discussion that people follow an image and not necessarily the leader himself or herself. This is something I have written about before (Harter, 2007a, ch. 4). I also bring it up in an earlier chapter, if you recall. Followers follow what they imagine the leader to be or to say or to represent. To the extent this is true (and I believe that it is), then the leader serves as either an **icon** (through whom one sees something higher) or an **idol** (through whom one sees nothing but the leader). When the leader is an icon rather than an idol, the image makes demands not only on the followers, it also makes demands on the leader, and this constrains the excesses of the charismatic leader (2018, p. 95; see e.g. Solzhenitsyn, 1984–1991, p. 339). Here, I think, Spoelstra makes an important point. The leader is—like everyone else—to be subordinated to this other sphere, this higher plane. A leader cannot do whatever he likes. He serves something, too. This way, the follower is not actually following the one we call the leader; instead, he or she is following the authority of this other sphere, as it is embodied in the leader (2018, p. 112). Although it might be an unusual way of talking, this language is very close to what James MacGregor Burns called transformational leadership (2003). Something "flows in" to the prevailing order from elsewhere, and it brings with it an implicit authority that is imperative to both leader and led.

Scientists and theologians have seen something of this imagery at several levels of analysis. The earliest Greek philosophers, for example, wrestled with the most basic notions of permanence and change. Democritus (c. 460—c. 370 BC) is regarded as one of the first to conceive of atoms, which are themselves indestructible, but which move in such a way that together they form the visible world. Why in the visible world things appear to change is because these configurations endlessly come together and come apart. What triggers these movements is the influx of something from outside of the configuration, penetrating the assemblage and thereby joining or dislodging (or altogether demolishing) what was already there. The atoms consequently adjust. Thus, we experience change.

Democritus extended his theory to the conduct of the soul. The soul too is comprised of atoms held together in configuration. Thought occurs in much the same way that the body senses the external world, i.e. by what Kirk and Raven refer to as an "impingement of congruent atoms from outside" (1966, p. 422). Jan Patočka confirms that from this perspective Democritus held that opinions fluctuate like these atoms (1998, p. 5f, n. 3, citing Cyril Bailey). "We know nothing truly about anything, but for each of us his opinion is an influx (i.e. is conveyed to him by an influx of the 'idols' [eidolon] from without)" (quoted in Schrödinger, 1954/2014, p. 89). Something from the outside of a given entity (that is, from its environment) enters or intrudes, and as a result the entity is—even if only a little bit—thereby transformed.

Many years later, William James (1907) was to make a similar claim about how we develop our belief system, and Esther Lightcap Meek (2014) put this at the very heart of knowing. Something of the same operation is thought to take place in moments of revelation, when the divine or transcendent realm "irrupts" into our own. It could be a blinding vision, a heavenly chorus, a miracle, or even a still small voice (see e.g. Steinbock, 2009). The imagery presupposes two entities or two aspects—an interior and an exterior—with an interjection that disrupts what was thought to exist as a whole.

Spoelstra contends that leadership is the result of an openness to the world beyond what we have come to know, on the other side of *aporia*. Leadership emerges from out of the *metaxy*. Perhaps it would help to give a specific example as it might pertain to leadership.

## Calling a Stranger to Lead[8]

In 1908, Georg Simmel appended a note of six pages on the social role of the stranger to a larger work on sociology. Since then, this brief "excursus" has spawned a hefty literature largely neglected in leadership studies (see Goodstein, 2017; Levine, 2015).

Part of what Simmel had been hoping to do was allude to the leadership prospects of the stranger. It begins with the idea of social distance (see Simmel, 1908/1955, p. 22).[9] Social distance is critical to understanding the stranger, because the stranger is one who is both near and far. The stranger belongs to a group as a participant with peculiar properties.[10] For one thing, he is mobile, having originated elsewhere and at all times capable of leaving, because he has few if any permanent ties to the group; he does not own land, for example, and he hasn't tried to assimilate. (Or it is just as likely that these options were closed to him by the natives.) That is to say, he is in contact with members of the group (unlike a complete alien), but he is not bound up with them. Simmel offered the example of a merchant who connects a group with the outside world. If he loses contact with the group or if he loses contact with the outside world, he can no longer trade. He needs to straddle two worlds. Simmel described the stranger as someone in or among the group but with unusual freedoms.

---

8. A previous version of this section appeared in the pages of the *Journal of Leadership Studies* (Harter, 2019a).

9. The phrase "social distance" was adopted in 2020 to refer to literal spacing in public places in order to avoid viral infections. Simmel had instead intended a metaphorical meaning.

10. For simplicity—and to accord with Simmel's usage—let us refer to the stranger as a male, even though in principle there is no reason to restrict the sociological form to men.

Of particular importance, Simmel claimed that the stranger "does not aspire to be assimilated"; instead, he occupies a determinate position in relation to the host, such as a trader, judge, or confidant (Levine, 2015, p. 73). From this proximate vantage point, close to others in one sense yet distant in another sense, the stranger has the potential to reveal to the host just how strange they are. The stranger makes it so that members of the group see themselves more objectively.[11]

Why is this important in leadership? His status *alongside* the group affords him a greater objectivity with regard to the group itself. He sees it as strange. The other members of the group recognize this about him. To some extent, this gives him privileges, as they consult him about what he perceives and confess to him things that they do not feel comfortable disclosing to one another. By the same token, he is frequently blamed for inciting dissent, because he is a foreigner with ambiguous loyalties whose presence reveals contingent elements of group life—that is to say, he reminds the group that things could be otherwise. He makes them feel uneasy.

More concretely, the stranger does at least these three things for the group: (a) he "brings qualities . . . that are not and cannot be indigenous" (Simmel, 1908/1971, p. 143); (b) he represents a point of contact with a wider world; and (c) he holds up a mirror to people in the community, witnessing in his struggles to adapt the strangeness of their own way of life. Almost like a therapist, he allows the host to know themselves differently while at the same time bringing novel ideas from the outside and expanding possibilities.

Because of these three functions, the stranger carries out special tasks for the group, either because they are unable or unwilling to do so for themselves (Karakayali, 2006, pp. 313, 326). Among these are tasks of circulation, arbitration, preserving secrecy, and dirty work. Karakayali (2006) splits this purpose into two types: linking what would otherwise be separated and hindering further division among group members, since he is from neither one side nor the other.

In this respect, the stranger contributes to group leadership, even if the stranger does not occupy the titular role of leader. Nevertheless, sometimes he does rise to a leadership position, inasmuch as Napoleon (for example) was not French, Hitler was not German, and Stalin was not Russian. Business firms sometimes recruit outsiders to assume command (e.g. Jalal & Prezas, 2012; Schein, 2004, pp. 306–308; Nelton, 1997). It is not unheard of for the stranger to lead.

Simmel wrote about group members that actually follow a stranger, as opposed to another group member (1908/1950, pp. 216–219). With some care, he compared the two options. The stranger is presumably impartial and

---

11. The experience *from the stranger's perspective* was elegantly set forth in Alfred Schütz's 1944 essay on "The Stranger."

complements the group. Also, the stranger as leader would be more closely watched, which could be a good thing. It satisfies a kind of group wariness to know that everybody will be scrutinizing this guy. The group member as leader, by way of contrast, will be more understanding, since he or she comes from the same milieu. He or she will strengthen or affirm the group, *similia similibus curantur*. A group member is less likely to be closely watched as a leader, due to an implicit trust (see Fukuyama, 1995). Simmel concluded that there are logical reasons to go either way, whether choosing a group member or a stranger to lead.

Looking to the future, then, we might speculate how these findings might inform our choices. In an era of sharp and rancorous social divisions, when neither side can tolerate the other, perhaps what we require is somebody without allegiances, somebody who brings no taint by affiliation. Maybe what we require is somebody that neither side can object to. "He may not be ours, but then he's not yours either." The prospects of an outsider taking charge can help us transcend our differences.[12]

The presence of a genuine stranger creates an opportunity for self-understanding, but it also induces anxiety and often social tension. His presence means there will be times when we see things differently from each other. Which is to say, as Simmel is translated as putting it, the strangeness keeps the relationship "from having an inner and exclusive necessity" (1908/1971, p. 148). By extrapolation, the presence of strangeness introduces a creative element that connotes freedom. Who we become to each other does not bear the burden of inevitability. As a practical implication, then, the group will tend to accept without notice that which they share with the stranger, just as two married people tend to take for granted the ways in which they are alike. Their attention is instead drawn to that which differentiates them. And it is this that stimulates novelty. A stranger brings much in the way of differences.

In sum, the stranger represents objectivity and a standard by which to critique the group. The stranger also represents the potential for creativity and freedom, which can be experienced as the threat of uncertainty and change.

Now, despite the promise of novelty and a kind of even-handedness by a stranger who leads in times of conflict, the stranger can also incite the people who were previously split to unify in opposition to him. He can be made the scapegoat. Maybe that was even the point. The natives can find common cause to oust the stranger in their midst. Such a coming together of this sort has its salutary effects for the group, as René Girard explained (see 2009). It certainly makes the stranger's position precarious.

---

12. By "outsider" I do not mean a marginalized or disaffected group member hoping to displace the existing leaders and drain the swamp, so that his people can ascend to power (see e.g. King, 2002). This kind of heretic or rebel offers a different sociological phenomenon from what Simmel was trying to describe.

One has to go back to Niccolò Machiavelli for an analysis of this kind of leadership in which an outsider comes in to transcend the differences, only to be the focal point for the two side's shared hostility (see 1532/1991). The stranger as leader gave the two groups time to turn aside from their mutual rivalry and get on with their shared lives, in a kind of respite, but then over time he instilled a deeper sense of unity in them by representing something against which they could both struggle. "He may not be yours, but he isn't ours either." Here, the burden of being an alien is seen to outweigh the benefit.

The stranger as leader provides a mechanism to interrupt the negative energy when times are tough and turn everyone away from their incessant and unproductive feuding. A stranger can be said to break the deadlock. That can be a good thing. But then very soon, the group becomes even more cohesive as it rallies against its strange leader. That can be a good thing for the cohesiveness of the group, but it will be very bad for the leader.

Here Simmel makes an intriguing (and significant) move, for he asserts that something of the sort occurs *in every relationship*—even a relationship so intimate as a marriage. Something in the other person is strange; he (or she) is not me. Therefore, technically speaking, one need not have a literal stranger in your midst to experience something similar. Simmel wrote, "A society is . . . a structure which consists of beings who stand inside and outside of it at the same time" (1908/1971, p. 15). The trick is to stand outside of the relationship you are in and confront it.

So far, we have seen in summary form what Simmel wrote about the sociological form of the stranger. Then, we noticed that he regarded the phenomenon of the stranger present in every relationship, such that you do not have to posit a foreigner in order to take advantage of what the stranger contributes to the group. A member of the group can serve the same purpose by revealing what is strange. So far as I can tell, we call this critical thinking. Further, I will suggest that Simmel was actually making a more profound observation, namely that the stranger represents something an individual person can do *in his own mind* to sharpen his reasoning: he can cultivate the stranger in himself to make himself strange to himself, in an act of reflexivity—a term that goes back to the chapter where we talked about Margaret Archer and the X factor. You do not require a literal foreigner to do this. You can (and should) do this on your own, by yourself.

Studies about ethnologists (e.g. Young & Goulet, 1994; Geertz, 1973; Nash, 1963), port cities (e.g. Cartier, 1999; Weigend, 1958), embedded journalists (e.g. Stahl, 2013; Hannah, 2007), and even philosophy (LeMoine, 2017) complement Simmel's sociological studies. Nevertheless, his treatment stands as a seminal work about the contributions to group leadership of the stranger, who occupies a unique societal niche.

We might say that consulting the stranger is a version of self-transcendence.

## One Chapter Closes, Another One Opens

We live within a world, an order of some sort, replete with various forms—forms of living, forms of thinking, forms of being in the world. This world is bounded, defined. For that's what makes it a world. We are impelled, however, to transcend or surpass this world. Life is self-transcending. Often, that impulse to transgress our boundaries would be in response to apparent *aporias* that we have termed tensions. We go looking beyond the ken for new possibilities. Concord as a state or condition of being like-minded, of one heart, requires a liberty to go in search of ways to reach beyond and return with a boon, continuously refreshing the existent order. This happens at the individual level, and we call it learning. This happens at the collective level, and we call it leadership.

This pin-point event of crossing over and coming back creates an influx into the world, a kind of *amphimixis* (Krell, 2019, p. 63). A leader therefore stands at the intersection of two worlds, mediating between them, like a stranger in our midst. Human history can be viewed from a macro perspective therefore as a nonlinear and persistent flux among these worlds, in the *metaxy*, adopting and adapting structures to perpetuate the flow onward into the indefinite future.

In the next chapter, we address two questions. First, what happens when the two worlds collide? What if the boon turns out to be more disruptive than the order can handle? Second, if we are going to make liberty the desideratum, such that we preserve the practice of transcending the present, then how do we look at suffering and death? Some adventures are lethal. You may not come back. Sometimes, even if you survive the ordeal, upon one's return, the folks back home seek to destroy you. It is almost surprising how often that happens. Sometimes, the message from beyond is to dismantle the prevailing order, kill it. And obviously, many leaders have trouble envisioning a future in which they do not get to participate. What does it mean for finite beings to choose an infinite game?

# 13

# EMBRACING *APORIAS*, SUFFERING, AND DEATH

## The Leadership of St. Francis[1]

### Introduction to the Chapter

Francis of Assisi (1181–1226) exemplifies a paradox of Christian leadership that aspires to worldly success yet also to suffering, such that it can be difficult to judge whether change can be attributable to what the leader did or to God alone, despite what the leader did. Francis himself was famously ambivalent toward leading others. Yet he did lead—not only directly in his own time, face-to-face, but also as an indirect leader in the manner described by Howard Gardner in his 1995 book *Leading Minds* (with Emma Laskin, p. 6). Francis did so despite many conventional leadership tasks being "contrary to his nature and to his spirituality" (Thompson, 2012, p. 72). He shaped European civilization, being canonized by the Roman Catholic church and becoming a popular legend.

Consulting history for the study of leadership requires an interpreter's skill (Wren, 2012). It can be tempting to pick contemporary lessons in leadership and then go back in time to show how those lessons are applied, using a retrospective glance. Historians insist, however, on the contingent and irreplaceable peculiarities of a specific time and a specific place, not to sweep that all aside in one's haste to prove abstract theories developed since the nineteenth century (Wren, 2012; Wren & Swatez, 1995). Francis lived in times that were different from today. Writers today do not share his context or his experience.

1. A version of this chapter originally appeared in Harter (2018) online at the *Theology of Leadership Journal*, http://theologyofleadership.com/index.php/tlj/article/view/6. The author would like to thank the following persons: Emily Risko, the journal's anonymous referee, and its editor, Russell L. Huizing.

One cannot simply pick up an alien épisteme and plop it down into a different context and expect it to fit.[2]

In addition, scholars in the twenty-first century are constrained by the condition of the historical record, with all of its attendant discrepancies and gaps—some of it nearly a thousand years old. Historical accounts of Francis do contradict one another (Blastic, 2012, p. 68; Thompson, 2012, pp. 154–170), and secular historians discount what they consider to be hagiography (Chesterton, 1923/2017, p. 5f; see Kehnel, 2012, p. 101). With due regard for these difficulties, the following chapter sets a broad context for the emergence of Francis, then offers a brief biographical account of his leadership, before identifying a number of implications for leadership studies today. Nevertheless, despite the predictable difficulties of doing historical research in this fashion, there is the underlying paradox of his self-abnegation, suffering, and deference to the agency of God alone—a paradox at the heart of anything to be called Christian leadership. This paradox will be addressed at the end of the chapter. It also carries over into forms of leadership that do not identify with Christianity.

The leadership of Francis does present us with a peculiar conundrum, whether we are Christian or not. Much of what follows considers Francis from within a Christian paradigm, yet by the end we will see that his leadership exemplifies an extra-ordinary character. For one thing, Francis flung himself headlong toward *aporias*, heedlessly, so long as he was responding to an inward imperative in service to a call from another dimension. In that sense, he exemplifies the leadership this book is setting forth. For another, Francis developed a relationship with suffering and death that raises the stakes, so to speak, on leadership as the crossing of boundaries, stepping athwart human limitations, in what might be the ultimate paradox: that by engaging fully in the possibilities of tomorrow, we may not live to see them fulfilled. Some visions take more than a lifetime to render. Francis accepted the risk. He even welcomed it.

## Context for Francis of Assisi

By 1181 CE Europe had been unified under the symbol of the cross for a long time. In fact, the number of years between the present (2021) and the death of Francis (1226) is 795 years. The number of years between the birth of Francis (1181) and the *Edict of Thessalonica*, which made the Nicene Creed the state religion of the Roman Empire (380), is 801 years. In this sense, Francis occupies the midpoint between the start of a Christian Europe and today.

That era of Christian dominance in Europe was not continuous and uninterrupted. Only about a hundred years before he was born, the church

---

2. This article is using the term "épistème" in the sense Michel Foucault set forth in *The Order of Things* (1966/1994).

split dramatically in the Great Schism, formally separating the Eastern Orthodox from the Roman Catholic. The upheaval led to the migration of many people from the Byzantine Empire into Umbria and other population centers in Italy. In his lifetime, adherents to the two Christian expressions made war against each other, culminating in the sack of Constantinople in 1204. At the same time, Christians were sporadically fighting the Saracen in the Crusades.[3]

To get some perspective, the crusades against the people of Islam lasted from 1095 until 1272. This series of campaigns unified Western Europe under the authority of the Pope and led to cross-cultural opportunities as traders plied the Mediterranean, helping to overcome a lingering sense of medieval insularity. The people of Assisi would have been mindful of these distant developments, despite undergoing their own clannish conflicts at home (Cusato, 2012, p. 19; McMichael, 2012, p. 129; Galli, 2002, p. 20). As a young man of means, Francis originally aspired to join his peers in the military, venturing forth to do battle abroad. Later, he would conduct his own abortive crusade to convert the infidel, inasmuch as Islam was thought to pose an existential threat to Christian Europe. From the vantage point of global politics, therefore, Francis was born into a turbulent era and participated in it.

With regard to religion (to the extent one can differentiate politics from religion in the Middle Ages), Francis was born into a different kind of turbulence. Across Europe there emerged monastic reformers and their accompanying movements—some of them resembling what Francis was to launch: a "return to a simpler and more authentic form of religious life" (Robson, 2012, p. 4).[4] Chesterton called the times "an epoch of reforms without revolutions" (1923/2017, p. 38). Galli writes that "church reform . . . was in the air that Francis breathed" (2002, p. 56). In retrospect, there was a tangible desire among Europeans for a more authentic cast to their religion (see generally Bultmann, 1956). This openness to authentic expressions of the faith would explain the sudden growth of the Franciscan order within his lifetime.

## Francis of Assisi

> Francis's admirers and modern scholars have long argued over who he "really was" and [how] his message should best be interpreted.
>
> —*Sean Field (2012, p. 208)*

---

3. The term "Saracen" was used at the time as a generic label for the adherents of Islam. In Luther's era, they were known as the Turk.

4. Michael Robson refers to St. William of Volpiano, Ranieri, and the Cistercians (2012, p. 4). William Short identifies the Humiliati, Trinitarians, and Hospitallers (2012, p. 52). Ingrid Peterson mentions the Cathars, Albigensians, and Bogomils (2012, p. 196). Mark Galli adds the Waldensians to the list (2002, p. 53).

Francis Bernardone was born into comfort. From a young age, he seems to have had an attractive personality and blithe spirit. People who knew him recognized that he was going places. But where? Chesterton called him a ringleader (1923/2017, p. 23). Together, the young men of the village were steeped in the medieval tradition of the traveling entertainers, the troubadours and acrobats who wandered from town to town in order to delight strangers. The attitude of these wayfarers towards Love as an ideal resembled extravagant poetry, a courtly romance. Bill Moyers, quoting Joseph Campbell (1988), said that "what happened in the 12th and 13th centuries 'was one of the most important mutations of human feeling and spiritual consciousness, that a new way of experiencing love came to expression.'" But the performers of the time also willingly played the clown. In this fashion, they represented both laughter and love. Something in this vagabond lifestyle appealed to the young Francis, both as the swain and the fool, for they were inextricable identities. To be in love in this way was to be a fool. You had to be okay with that.

As a boy, Francis was reported to behave in a festive and restive manner, impetuous, throwing himself into anything he did. As news from overseas told of adventure in military service, Francis decided to become a soldier. Upon leaving for battle, however, he fell ill. In his fevers, he had a dream ordering him back home—a dream which he obeyed, much to his chagrin. For two years, he struggled to figure out what else to do with his life. In the interim, his father the merchant was becoming impatient, if not ashamed. So was Francis.

It was out in the countryside that Francis encountered his worst fear. For all his gaiety and vigor, he had abhorred the figure of the leper, who represented a kind of polar opposite of what he wanted for himself. Augustine Thompson refers to his "visceral horror" of leprosy (2012, p. 9). Ailing, despised, and unlovely lepers were outcast, and only in part because of the risk of contagion. They were sad and solitary and disgusting to behold. Here on the road Francis saw a leper approaching. With characteristic impulsivity, he leapt from his horse and ran to the leper, embracing him. In that moment, he adopted a fresh perspective toward the marginalized—the sick, the hideous, and the dangerous. His heart was opened once he faced his fear. Forever after, he embraced the ideal of the universal fraternity of all creation. Care for lepers would become a central part of his life's work.

This spontaneous embrace of the alien, of the forbidding, was to signify the career of Francis. His spontaneous gestures undertaking alarming risks bespoke a singular regimen of self-mortification, or what Michel Foucault was to label self-government (2007, lecture 4). So, Francis was both on the one hand disciplined (see e.g. Bonaventure, 1867/1988, p. 46) and on the other hand impetuous. This combination is in part what qualified him for leadership.[5] He was a living exemplar of the both/and.

---

5. Compare the fact that Thompson alleges "Francis seemed to have none of the qualities usually found in a leader" (2012, p. 35).

Soon after this encounter on the byway with a leper, in prayer among the ruins of an abandoned local church, he heard a voice. This was not the dreaming of a feverish youth of the sort that he had experienced on the road to military service. The voice commanded Francis to rebuild the church. Interpreting the voice to intend literally rebuilding the ruin where he was praying, his first thought was to raise money for the project. Having so little of his own, he cheated his father on a business transaction, justifying the theft as though it were commanded by God. His father did not see it that way and—probably exasperated with his aimless and profligate child—prosecuted.[6]

Incarcerated now, awaiting trial, humiliated and constrained in the darkness, Francis underwent a change. He emerged tougher and resolute. At the hearing where he was to be tried, he confessed to the theft, reimbursed his father fully, and then in a dramatic gesture of the sort that made him interesting to know, he undressed right there in the courtroom, piling up his fine clothes for his father to reclaim. Nearly naked on a cold day, he turned and walked out of town, into the woods, and lived as a hermit at the site of that ruined church, which he started rebuilding now with his own bare hands.

A few other men in the city, inspired by his desperate example, joined him over the next two years. They also disavowed their life of privilege in order to adopt the rude way of a laboring beggar, a mendicant who would sleep outdoors in rugged conditions and eat very little. Initially, Francis believed himself to be imitating the apostles who had been commissioned by Jesus of Nazareth to go out among the people with nothing but the message of the Gospel. Gradually, he decided it was his vocation to imitate the Christ himself. Accordingly, he embraced the squalor and ridicule of a life lived with extravagant simplicity. By retaining no attachment to the things of this world, he could roam freely. He was everywhere just a visitor, a perpetual guest (Robson, 2012, p. 5). Rather than a burden, this itinerant mode of living was supposed to be experienced as liberating.

In addition to the labor of rebuilding the church, he found opportunities to preach, for Francis had decided that the voice commanding him to build the church meant something more than restoring the physical structure. If he failed to attract a congregation in the streets, he would deliver sermons to the birds. The best sermon, in his opinion, was setting an example by his deeds (Şenocak, 2012, p. 87). Bonaventure composed a biography of Francis in which he emphasized how the leadership of Francis was primarily through his example, to be imitated (e.g. 1867/1988, pp. 5ff, 30).

The little band of brothers grew to the point where it was large enough to require official sanction. This was a turning point with regard to the leadership

---

6. After all, the father had once paid a hefty ransom to recover his son from a neighboring city-state after a gruesome battle between partisans, and later he had outfitted Francis to go to war as a knight, only to have the young man give it all away to someone more in need (Galli, 2002, p. 24f). The father had apparently reached the limits of his generosity.

of Francis, because he had been living a relatively solitary life alongside a few likeminded others. But now (about the year 1209) they had to coordinate as a group. They needed management. They needed rules, to define who could join them and what everyone could expect. Francis later admitted to being uncertain how to lead. "There was no one to tell me what to do," he once said (Thompson, 2012, p. 22).

Given the example of the Christ, however, the little band was resolved to rely only on a leadership grounded in service, thereby inverting the usual pyramid of authority (see generally Thompson, 2012, p. 96f). To the extent that the community required leadership, the leader must be a minister. Not only that, but the position would be held only temporarily and was never to be sought (Robson, 2012, p. 41). According to the *Rule of 1223*, which Francis was to have a hand in composing to govern the Friars Minor, such leaders were to be elected and may be replaced as needed by their electors. Brothers were to hold their superiors accountable (Galli, 2002, p. 86). An early biographer named Thomas de Celano has been quoted as follows: "Francis saw many rushing for positions of authority. Despising their arrogance, he strove by his own example to call them back from such sickness" (quoted in Galli, 2002, p. 166).

Despite being the founder, Francis was clearly uncomfortable in administrative roles. He wanted to be out in the world, in nature, among people, and not tied up in supervision. His group should be like the troubadours, he thought, wandering merrily. By their example, as much as by their words, Franciscans would call the world to penance. By penance he did not mean the grim and reclusive practice of so many monks in his day, going about their medieval rhythms behind thick walls, but rather joyfully, free of the cloister. Nevertheless, Francis saw the occasional necessity of leading the rest of them in their vows and working with religious authorities to secure their status.[7] He accepted the title of "deacon" as a gesture to gain legitimacy (Cusato, 2012, p. 28). Many years later, however, he withdrew from any formal office, ostensibly because of malaria, although there is evidence that he had become fed up with the direction of the brotherhood (e.g. Galli, 2002, p. 137f). Or that his resignation was even an act of emotional blackmail (Dalarun, 2007, p. 100). In either case, he had held a leadership title loosely and then gave it up. This does not mean that he ever quit leading.

Plainly, Francis struggled against the idea of dominating anything or anybody. Despite the fact that he was a natural leader—or maybe because of that fact—the mature Francis resisted imposing his will on followers. Instead, on journeys, for instance, he insisted that someone else lead the expedition

---

7. It is this phase in the history of the Franciscan order that one can recognize what Max Weber (1922/1947) was to describe so famously as the routinization of charisma in *The Theory of Social and Economic Organization*. Indeed, the entire experience of the Franciscan movement reads like a case study (contra Thompson, 2012, p. 159f).

(Thompson, 2012, p. 24; Galli, 2002, pp. 18, 73; see Bonaventure, 1867/1988, p. 56f). For the purposes of his brotherhood, he sought to invert the conventional hierarchy by which authority flows downward from on high. Many texts from that era show a Francis who refused to dominate others and actually rejoiced in obedience (Dalarun, 2007, p. 23). Having said that, it is important to note that the reality was far more complicated.

It is true that Francis was no free-wheeling rogue hostile to institutional discipline; he embraced the encompassing order of the Roman Catholic Church, which is famously hierarchical (Robson, 2012, p. 42; Dalarun, 2007, pp. 32–43).[8] In fact, in many ways he was a shrewd, if not cagey operator within the power structures of the church. For example, he had bypassed local authority by subordinating the brotherhood as an organization directly to the Apostolic See, which was unusual, and then in the founding documents saw to it that the brothers were to be subordinated to himself (Dalarun, 2007, p. 74). This does not appear to be the act of somebody avoiding leadership.

For another thing, Francis occasionally behaved as a disappointed *institutor* who felt obliged to interject himself to keep the brotherhood aligned with its original purposes (e.g. Thompson, 2012, p. 25; Dalarun, 2007, p. 100; Galli, 2002, p. 128). He persisted in these efforts even after publicly renouncing any leadership. Francis had difficulty yielding to leadership. As Thompson notes somewhat drily: "The situation was truly bizarre. Francis, subject to all, was telling superiors what to command him to do" (2012, p. 81; see also p. 113; Dalarun, 2007, p. 84f). By means of his referent power, he was willing to act as though he were in charge—and act in a high-handed manner, at that (Dalarun, 2007, p. 88). Even during meetings where somebody else was presiding—somebody he had publicly named as his successor—Francis would sit at his feet and tug at his cloak to signal when he wanted to intervene (Dalarun, 2007, p. 104).

Francis also participated closely in developing the rules by which the order was to operate, the most significant being the *Rule of 1221* and the *Rule of 1223* (see generally Short, 2012, ch. 3).[9] Through (a) political maneuvering,

---

8. Francis had been duly scandalized by what he saw in Rome (Galli, 2002, p. 35), but this experience did not justify heresy or rebellion. If anything, it justified his original mission to renew the church.

9. Just before he passed away, Francis had issued a *Testament* in 1226 in which he commented on the binding force of the prevailing *Rule of 1223*—a provision that a subsequent pope cleverly rejected because Francis had insisted on being treated as an equal, despite the fact that equals cannot bind each other (Short, 2012, p. 64). This, contrary to paragraph one of chapter one of the *Rule of 1223*, in which brothers are bound to obey Brother Francis and his successors. Thus, the Holy Father ruled that the dying wishes of Francis did not pertain. This was the sort of tortured legalism that had irritated Francis. It was probably the reason he wrote the *Testament* to begin with: to preclude bureaucratic tampering with his vision. As a leader, Francis had compromised repeatedly to accommodate both institutional authority and human nature (Galli, 2002, pp. 132–137), but in his last days the *Testament* recovers something of the purity of his vision, even if church authorities treated it as a dead letter.

(b) moral suasion, and (c) authorship of the governing documents, Francis certainly exercised leadership. Yet his discomfort with day-to-day oversight tended to drive him into the field and onto the byways, where he could lead more by example than by fiat.

Having said that, however, it is important to observe that Francis cherished opportunities to obey, for in doing so he exhibited humility. And if, as Bonaventure pointed out, the leadership to which he subjected himself was faulty and brought some harm to Francis, he could rejoice in the opportunity to undergo suffering (1867/1988, p. 57). Once, being asked for a model of obedience, Francis produced a dead body: do as you like with it, he said, for the body will not resist your control. Neither will it complain. By extension, therefore, the perfect follower is a corpse. The problem was that he balked at demonstrating such compliance when it was his turn to obey.

Sometimes, he consulted his inner circle or the Cardinal Hugolino (who was to become Pope Gregory IX).[10] Other times, he ignored everybody and acted unilaterally, as though the rules did not apply to him. What to make of this uneven record?

## The Leadership of St. Francis

Gradually, the ideals that Francis and his original brothers had espoused were displaced, in part because circumstances had changed. For example, despite the commitment to equality within the brotherhood, as more learned men joined their ranks, they created a two-tiered system, with themselves in a higher rank (Şenocak, 2012, p. 89).[11] It certainly altered the egalitarian and relatively untutored mien of the earliest Friars Minor.

Looking back, Eric Voegelin lamented another outcome that was to emerge many years later. He called it a distortion by his successors of treating Francis as a spiritually imbued leader who ushers in a new age, a blessed Third Realm bringing history to its fulfillment. Voegelin blamed Joachim of Fiore (1145–1202) with promoting an apocalyptic vision in which humanity brings about in this world the paradise described in Holy Scripture. In the new age, leadership would be unnecessary, and Francis was its prophet. Francis himself would never endorse such a gnostic fantasy, yet Voegelin recognizes the impact of this vision on Dante, Machiavelli, Condorcet, Comte, Hegel, Marx, and the fascist regimes of Germany and Italy (Voegelin, 2000, pp. 178–183, 300–304). Francis himself had no such illusions, even if he had inspired them.

---

10. Jacques Dalarun claims that Hugolino had a "moderating and normalizing" effect on Francis, a man who could be free-spirited to the point of being erratic (2007, p. 95).
11. Still today, scholars disagree whether Francis accepted this shift completely (see generally Roest, 2012).

If anything, Francis cultivated the reputation of a fool, i.e. an illiterate, simple-minded man, if not an idiot (Roest, 2012). Bonaventure remarks that Francis was not stupid or lax in his study of sacred books. Reportedly, he had a terrific memory (1867/1988, p. 101). Even so, this reputation for being untutored and simple placed the merit completely on the God who had chosen him, that He should take such humble clay and breathe into it the spirit of penance. In doing so, one is less obliged to obey rules than to attune oneself with divine purpose (Peterson, 2012, p. 197). The apparent contradiction between his resistance to mindless rule-following and his teachings about the blessings of obedience is nowhere satisfactorily resolved, except that in all things the "true" leader was not to be a text but a person: the Christ (Bonaventure, 1867/1988, p. 187). Francis as a leader was less interested in ordering the lives of others as he was in attracting them to join him.

Join him, they did. The ecumenical appeal of Francis down through the centuries has been attributed to many things (see generally Dunstan, 2012). Let us look at a few examples.

First, he practiced a kind of ecumenism in his journey to the Saracen, whom he tried to convert. His followers then engaged in extensive mission and diplomatic work, which instructed them in how to conduct ecumenical dialogue. Their abstinence from wealth meant they sought no gain from their transactions. Their avowed commitment to peace and a universal brotherhood of humanity limited their tendency to denounce, deride, or otherwise derogate those of other faiths.

Second, Francis exhibited a non-conformity that Protestants claimed was a forerunner of their attempts at reform. When he expressed suspicion of institutional power, for example, and renounced participation in any hierarchy, Protestant Reformers saw someone after their own heart.[12]

Third, his quest for authenticity resonates with young people of every generation increasingly alienated by the fruits of the Industrial Revolution. Here was someone who struggled to find his place in the world—and found it by turning his back on conventional alternatives.

Fourth, his embrace of nature has found allies even today as people strive to protect and celebrate the environment. If it can be said that any crisis promises to unify people across the globe today, it is a shared dependence on the one integrated, global system in which all persons participate. For Francis, the natural world presents us with a religious community obedient to God yet without leadership (Thompson, 2012, pp. 54, 56).

Fifth, his devotion to poverty has always corresponded with a socioeconomic class that cries out for mission. Poverty appears to be a perennial

---

12. The example of the Friars Minor has inspired Protestants to form religious communities that do not smack of "papism"; in the twenty-first century, there are Anglican, Lutheran, and Reformed Franciscan brotherhoods.

condition that elicits pangs of generosity, to such a degree that many governments are now expected to devote considerable resources to its alleviation. Francis exemplified this mission.

Sixth, his respect for the vocation of women—largely because of the leadership of the lady Clare, a woman of rank and courage[13]—continues to inspire those who struggle to champion the status of women, especially within the church (see generally Godet-Calogeras, 2012).

I would hazard another reason for the ecumenical appeal of Francis, and that is his infectious joy. Just as children of every culture are drawn to jesters and enjoy the antics of the benign fool, whose smile at life evokes in them smiles of their own. That he sustained his spirits through extreme trials of suffering makes him all the more admirable in an age that demands instant cures for what ails you. He not only withstood pain and privation, but he sought them out as opportunities. Neither a whiner nor a stoic, Francis took delight even in the darkest circumstance. When the doctor prescribed cauterizing his eye, which in the thirteenth century must have been an extraordinary ordeal, it is said that Francis blessed the fire about to sear him and called it friend.

Henri Nouwen wrote that "the real and true story was told by the clowns [who] remind us with a tear and a smile that we share the same human weaknesses [and] who by their humble, saintly lives evoke a smile and awaken hope" (2013, p. 2f).

## What Is a Saint?

Francis was a kind of leader. He was also recognized as a saint in 1228. Being both illustrates the paradox of his life.[14]

In 1847, Søren Kierkegaard (1813–1855) published an essay titled "On the Difference Between a Genius and an Apostle." An apostle (or saint) might in fact be a genius, he admitted, but it is not his genius that qualifies him as an apostle. These are qualitatively different identities. Kierkegaard's essay consisted of three arguments. First, genius is inborn and then develops over time, whereas an apostle receives a call from God and does not require any special attributes or training. God will use whatever gifts or powers the apostle happens to possess. Second, genius can be judged by others. The authority of an apostle, however, comes only from God, and as Kierkegaard noted, "God cannot help men by providing them with physical certainty that an Apostle is an Apostle" (1847/1962, p. 95). In fact, if an apostle tries to use his own gifts or powers to establish his authority, without invoking the authority of the One who sent him, he thwarts the mission (1847/1962, p. 105). A genius can be tempted to displace spiritual authority

---

13. Her struggles as a leader under conditions similar to those of Francis warrant a separate monograph.
14. Alvesson and Spicer (2011) have written about the saint as a metaphor for moral leadership, whereas this section of the chapter refers to the saint as a leader—the paradox of a saint being both a saint and a leader.

with out-sized personal attributes. Third, genius serves the pleasure of the person of the genius directly and the pleasure of others indirectly. An apostle makes no promise of pleasure in this world. Often, the apostle suffers and even calls on others to suffer, as well. His message pertains to another realm altogether. According to this three-part characterization, one would be hard-pressed to see any saint as a leader, and yet Francis undoubtedly did lead. Therein lies a paradox.

William James (1842–1910) later tried to argue that saints successively withdraw from the complications of life, shedding contact with the world and withdrawing further and further—behind walls and within prayer—for the sake of inward purity (1902/1985, p. 279). To the extent that Francis tried to avoid administrative duties, that much is true, as John Mecklin pointed out (1955, p. 38). Yet Francis did not try to withdraw *from the world*. For him these dull leadership chores *were* a withdrawal from the world—and a regrettable one at that. For Mecklin, Francis comes across as so theopathic as to be grotesque, unnatural, and thus perverted (1955, p. 45). Michael Cusato, director of the Franciscan Institute, admits that Francis can seem to be "incoherent, arrogant, egotistical, and megalomaniacal . . . deeply conflicted" (2007, p. 12; see Dalarun, 2007, p. 186f). But perhaps all that this means is that Francis was a flawed human being who struggled between his gift for leadership and his disavowal of domination. He was not, as they say, a plaster saint, but a troubled and troubling individual whom God was able to use. In fact, his confusion over leadership, which kept his brotherhood in turmoil long after he had passed away, exhibits his humanity (e.g. Dalarun, 2007, p. 190). He wanted to get out from under administrative responsibility as a snare and temptation while at the same time wielding power as he saw fit, even imperiously. In short, he embodied the paradox.

Max Scheler (1933/1987) made a distinction similar to Kierkegaard's between the saint and the genius as models of exemplary persons. The saint claims access to divine revelation independent of nature, reason, or history. This experience is so profound as to shape the course of one's life thereafter—more specifically, the saint seeks to imitate God (1933/1987, p. 152f). The saint is "oriented" toward the divine and not toward this world (1933/1987, p. 155). Even among likeminded peers, the saint is unique, for he or she bears the message of the true God, and that message is embodied in the life of the saint. The holy life is in a sense a validation or illustration of the truth of the message (1933/1987, p. 154), as well as a vindication of the saint as a saint. The saint is regarded as unique, incomparable—fully saint, yet different from every other saint, even if they all imitate the one true God (1933/1987, p. 154).[15] Again, one has a hard time seeing in this the making of a leader, but then Scheler addressed the historical fact that people do in fact follow saints.

---

15. With this passage, we hear echoes of what Luther was to represent many years later about all believers imitating the same Christ without resembling one another.

Of those who can be said to follow the saint, he wrote, they follow him or her directly, becoming part of his or her life (1933/1987, p. 156). They do not follow his works (as opposed to the artist and his art, let us say, or the hero and his act of courage). There is no artifact to imitate or admire, just as there are no writings of Socrates or Jesus (1933/1987, p. 157). There is only the following itself. A "following with" rather than a "following of" (1933/1987, p. 158). Co-living, even if separated by time and space (1933/1987, p. 161). Franciscans in the twenty-first century continue to "follow with" Francis. Augustine Thompson writes that unlike other founders such as Benedict, Augustine, and Bernard, "Francis presented his followers not with a coherent rule, but with himself" (2012, p. 33; see also p. 40). So for Scheler, a saint is by definition a leader, but a peculiar type of leader. What followers imitate is his or her inestimable life—and perhaps more significantly his or her death, which it will now become necessary to address.

Not coincidentally, St. Francis had a special influence on the philosophy of Max Scheler, beyond serving as an exemplar of what it means to be a saint. Scheler had argued that the basis of moral life is grounded less in theory or tradition and more in the example of exemplary persons (White, 2005, p. 58). What somebody like Francis actually thought and expressed is secondary to what he actually did, or what might be called the form of his life (White, 2005, p. 60). This insight in itself fits the designs of Francis, who put such an emphasis on one's actions. This is also one reason so few quotations from Francis appear in this chapter.

Scheler added that one cannot really understand that exemplary person in isolation, as though ripped out of context (White, 2005, p. 62). Each life is a life in response to the larger world. Without a sense of context, one is tempted to believe that imitation means doing precisely what the exemplar did, such as stripping off one's clothing in the courtroom and walking out into the snow. That is mimicry, and not imitation. (It is called "apery" for a reason.) By way of contrast, imitation requires understanding how the action pertained to his context, so that in the present context one can do something equivalent perhaps, though not necessarily identical. Students of leadership learn to abstract from the concrete incidents to something of a pattern or archetype (see generally J. Peterson, 2017).

To qualify as an exemplary person in this sense, the role model must have made some kind of difference in the world. That is to say, the actions of an exemplary person changed the context in some fashion. The key is not so much about what the exemplary person did *in response to* contingent circumstances; instead, it is about what the exemplary person did *to change* those circumstances (White, 2005, p. 65). One of the benefits of this approach is that writers get away from treating ethics and leadership as an abstraction, a context-free exercise of the imagination, like an unmoving statue in the backyard. Trafficking in ideals and absolute truths tends to obscure the fact that the good life is always the life lived under specific conditions. Philosophers and moralists of various stripes often ignore the impact of "organic life . . . the living cosmos, and . . . bodiliness" (White, 2005, p. 68).

We turn next to bodiliness.

## Suffering and Death

Because the leadership of Francis was based to such a large extent on his life, therefore, one might take a closer look at the brutal decline of Francis—his retreat from administration, yes, but also his peculiar maladies and years of increasing peevishness that culminated in his death in 1226—for in that declining phase of life he underwent a titanic struggle between sweet accord with everything and everybody, exemplified in his famous *Canticle of the Sun*, and irascible bitterness in his suffering, as he lashed out at caretakers on a mundane level and hit a more strident tone in his admonitions against the brotherhood which he saw as betraying its founding ideals. This flamboyant temperament, coupled with inner equivocations about the usage of social power, came to the fore in his last years and showed Francis to be a perplexing and volatile mix of sentiments.[16]

In his Apostolic Letter *Salvifici Doloris* (1984), John Paul II wrote that suffering makes it possible "to release love . . . to transform the whole of human civilization into a civilization of love" (#30). Here is a language of leadership grounded in pain and anxiety. John Paul II also issued a letter to "the elderly" in 1999 which holds up decrepitude as a powerful phase in one's ministry that the present culture in the West has somehow forgotten to notice and respect—at a time that needs these lessons all the more. Just as Francis had at one time abhorred the leper before jumping from his horse to kiss one, today people might seem to abhor the elderly and the infirm.

To the extent that leadership by example serves as a legitimate form of leadership (see e.g. Hermalin, 1998; French & Raven, 1959) and to the extent saints can be regarded as leaders by example, their sufferings and death constitute a culmination, the very prototype of faithful attunement to the message of hope to which their lives are a testament. A saint is a leader largely in the way one bears the sorrows of existence.[17] In Francis, one detects an outrageous joy—not only in spite of adversity, but also because of it. Having recoiled repeatedly from leadership as administration and command, he embraced leadership as the manner by which he emptied himself in obedience to grace. In that fashion, therefore, and especially *in extremis*, Francis of Assisi was both a saint and a leader.

16. Febvre (1929) notes that with his advancing years Luther (like Francis) witnessed his followers misconstruing his message and thwarting his designs (ch. 10). This is an integral part of each man's suffering, watching the leadership that failed. But then, Febvre denies that Luther was or ever aspired to be a leader (1929, p. 272f).

17. Later, Martin Luther would assert as part of his *Ninety-Five Theses*, "The genuinely contrite love suffering and invite it" (Febvre, 1929, p. 90).

That paradox, as it were, about suffering and death was actually part and parcel of the troubadour tradition that had captured Francis as a boy. Joseph Campbell talked about "that which the troubadours celebrate, you know, the agony of the love, the sickness that the doctors cannot cure; the wounds that can be healed only by the weapon that delivered the wound" (Moyers, 1988).

It is my contention that a theology of leadership would somehow include the example of Francis, if only because for Christians it hearkens back to the example of Jesus. And yet the archetype of the saint—especially the Suffering Servant—can be found in other cultures as well (Scheler, 1933/1987).[18]

## Implications of the Leadership of Francis

Francis lived in a far different time and place, yet his example brings with it several implications for leadership in the twenty-first century. These implications are more properly understood as tensions or paradoxes.[19]

Christians who aspire to lead in this day and age will find themselves in an equivalent quandary. At one extreme, a Christian intent on leading can embrace the lessons of leadership studies about how to be effective and make his or her leadership practice nearly indistinguishable from secular leaders. At another extreme, a leader can decline to learn from these lessons and instead trust that God will accomplish His purpose no matter what they do. Francis struggled to figure out how best to lead. At times, he failed. Nevertheless, he did try. And even throughout the resulting confusion, he made a significant impact on his immediate community and ultimately the Western world. So maybe the lesson is that God can work with imperfect leaders, so long as they devote themselves persistently to His service. The question we do not have the space to ponder in this book might be framed thus: which matters more, the means of leadership or the mode?

Having said this, a leader might have to accept the possibility that he or she will not have the gratification of seeing the desired outcome. As Mother Teresa was known for saying: "God has not called me to be successful. He has called me to be faithful" (Gonzales-Balado, 2002, p. 23). In this experience, one finds a comparable suffering, to wish devoutly for something and not be rewarded with its attainment. But then this theme was already part of the canon, inasmuch as Moses was not allowed to enter into the Promised Land and Abraham, to whom was promised the land of Canaan, died owning only the narrow crypt where he and his wife's body were laid. Otherwise, he had been merely a wanderer in the land he had been promised.

---

18. One sees this, for example, in Ayoub (1978) on the *Redemptive Suffering in Islam*.
19. My book was not explicitly addressed only to Christians, even though the paradox of Christian leadership displays many of the themes this book was written to consider.

More poignantly, Francis attracted followers by means of his suffering and death. This fact strains the usual models for the bases of power (e.g. French & Raven, 1959), yet we see it exhibited again later in the lives of other Christian leaders, perhaps most recently by His Holiness John Paul II, who refused to step down from office as his condition worsened. Christian leaders who adopt this response to becoming frail or disabled should probably have a frank conversation with their closest followers about the loss of their ordinary powers, so that the community they lead can still function. And they might be more effective as leaders explaining to their followers the significance of their suffering (see e.g. Rittgers, 2012). That message would resonate most for Christians, of course. But it turns out to be an element in the hero's quest, which is universal. Leaders as human beings can be frail and decline in their powers.

Perhaps the most powerful lesson from the life of Francis of Assisi, which it seems proper to restate, is that he chose to lead more by example than by his words. Followers are quick to detect a hypocrite. And a religious person whose actions undermine his or her attempts at leadership threatens not only his or her leadership but also the cause for which they claim to lead. People will be quicker to forgive an error than a lie. Francis exemplified this lesson.

Embedded in his living example (and a recurring theme throughout his life) is the instrumentality of joy. A leader slogging through administrivia and straining openly with the chores of an office will lose some of that joy. Instead, Francis sought out excuses to celebrate and delight. He was what political historians call a Happy Warrior (see Nussbaum, 2012). He saw the blessings in all that he did and understood in his bones that some jobs were just not uplifting. The predicament remains for leaders today that, alas, somebody has to do those jobs. Not everything a leader does can be pleasant. A religious leader might examine the life of Francis and determine how best to keep a buoyant spirit while still tending to the drudgery.

Christian leaders hoping to merge their faith with their social function will be prudent to consider what that might look like. History provides a wealth of evidence, yet these instances will not be completely free from paradox. Let me be open about something, however: Christian leaders are not really my intended audience so much as I intend to reach leadership scholars and educators—the scientists, historians, philosophers, and writers, whether Christian or not—and so a word to you.

When Francis impulsively leapt from his horse to take up the leper in his arms, he did more than overcome his fears. Here is the emblematic moment to which this entire book has been building. Francis refused the conventional models of a life worth living, and he even transcended his own personal revulsion. He exposed himself fully to reality, to life lived in that reality. He literally touched a reality that horrified his peers. He risked everything for something quite simple, so simple that it would be easy to overlook. After all, the circle of his influence was much smaller than the circle of his concern (Cabrera &

Cabrera, 2015, p. 167). Nevertheless, by accepting to love in the moment within his narrow circle of influence—face-to-face, a circle of only two persons in that most intimate, unspoken dialogue—he thereby shaped the world.

Where in all the literature on leadership do we talk like this?

Love itself is a hero's quest, exposing a person to danger and despair, to suffering and death. Francis briefly stood outside of the usual framework or paradigm—the prevailing mental models of the good life—in order to encounter something more substantial. In that moment, it was a nameless beggar with a wasting disease. The fact that he struggled for the remainder of his life to craft a sufficient new model of leadership just might be the hardest lesson for the academics among us to appreciate, so let me ask: are you and I really called to bloodless theorizing, elaborating our minds, if at the same time we do not acquaint ourselves with the life we claim to want to understand? Can we in our modern world find room in our studies for the role of faith—a faith that, out of turbulence, inward and outward, and despite our many contradictions, we might witness the emergence of a beautiful order? Can we commend to prospective leaders as a daily practice the discipline of love? For there lies our hope.

We all come from different traditions. We adhere to different creeds. No matter where we travel, we encounter *aporias*. These *aporias* can instruct or annoy, but they can also liberate or destroy.

Throughout these pages, I have referred to the infinite game. I encountered the idea in a book by James Carse (1986). What exactly is this infinite game? Does it have something to do with resurrection or immortality? Not at all. In fact, it is an acceptance of the finality of death, leaving the disposition of one's soul to faith. Instead, it is an embrace of the game of this world, on this planet, into the indefinite future. It is a celebration of what is. It is a stewardship of what can be. It is an ongoing project, carried forward by our ancestors, for which we bear responsibility today, so that it persists, i.e. so that our descendants in their turn get to play. The paramount value is the game itself, life, civilization, humanity, with all of its triumphs and trials, through birth and death, round and round, in a never-ending caravan. Compatible with its enjoyment are the virtues of gratitude, openness, fallibilism, and courage. If I had to enunciate an ethic implicit in the theme of this book, it would be this. We are here, and we are together. Let us turn our gaze toward the far horizon, to go see what lies on the other side.

It will probably seem foolish to strike out for adventure. But then, Francis was quite the fool, and he infused an entire civilization with his joy.

# 14

## ARRIVING AT PORT

### Mediation and Aikido Politics

### Introduction to the Chapter

The idea of extra-ordinary leadership as the boldness to (a) step outside of the boundaries, (b) experience fully the *aporias* that present themselves, and (c) return with care to bestow a boon on the rest of us—this can seem almost like a fable. And to a great extent, it is! What (you may ask) is the concrete, practical implication of adopting such a mode in the real world? Indeed, how does the type of leadership being propounded herein promise to make a difference in the political situation where many of us in the West find ourselves today? It is one thing to generate metaphors and allude to convoluted doctrines from mathematics and science, citing poetry and myths to add a dash of color, but it is quite another to explain how it actually works. If (as I claim) my method has been genuinely pragmatic, in the philosophical sense of the term, then what I write about should also be tried in the crucible.

One way to begin that process is to show that something similar has been taking place in equivalent arenas. For this, I am indebted to Don Levine (2018), whose deathbed treatise explains a parallel between the martial arts in Japan and legal practice in the United States. According to Levine, each of these domains has evolved in a similar fashion, because they each reflect a similar mindset. It is my contention that what has happened in the martial arts and in the law can also be applied to contemporary politics. It would be the same mindset in a different domain.

The following chapter summarizes what Levine was saying before I attempt to transfer these findings to the domain of politics. Then, I take up the question illustrated in *Las Meninas* about leaders living within tensions, at the intersection, framed by paradox and perpetually threatened by contradiction. What does it mean to occupy the nexus, that exasperating *metaxy*? As a practical matter, maybe leadership begins with the realization that both/and is not a resolution of contraries, like a magical pixie disposing of every polarity; instead, maybe the conflict is constitutive of life itself. Both/and can be tragic. After posing that as a possibility, this chapter turns next to a kind of retrospective glance at what this book has accomplished, a review of sorts, where we summon once again some of the voices of several theorists who helped to frame the collage—especially we invoke Braudel, McKeon, the Cabreras, Berlin, and a smattering of good old William James.

## A Thumbnail Sketch of Aikido and Mediation

When heaven and earth become one within you, aiki and its resonance naturally make you a servant of the gods.

—*Morihei Ueshiba (2007, p. 145)*

Levine (2018) examined a range of reasons for human aggression, including biology (e.g. instinctual), culture, and self-interest (situational). As Georg Simmel observed, "the first instinct with which the individual affirms himself is the negation of the other" (1908/1955, p. 29). In contradistinction, Levine then identified a number of prominent thinkers—such as Henry David Thoreau, William James, Mahatma Gandhi, and Martin Luther King Jr.—who opposed aggression (ch. 2). One has to ask, have their teachings gained sufficient traction on a large enough scale? In order to introduce examples of a dynamic three-part model, Levine looked closely at two cultures in particular that seem to have indeed progressed from resolving conflict by means of violent struggle to increasingly peaceful means.

In Japan, in what was considered an advance over random acts of violence, blood feuds, and other forms of struggle, we see first the emergence of the feudal samurai who lived by a code known as the *bushido*. These were specialists who developed both their character by means of strict discipline as well as their skills in combat. As a result, those entrusted with violence would be inwardly constrained. They were expected to master martial arts such as swordsmanship, but also fine arts such as poetry and calligraphy, as outward expressions of having mastered themselves first. Only then would they be allowed to go out into the world protecting the people and vanquishing evildoers. In this way, violence was limited (Levine, 2018, pp. 26–29). Ritual confrontations, hedged in by gestures of honor, increasingly replaced other forms of conflict resolution. Consequently, the so-called martial arts that we know today were born. This is the transition from phase one to phase two.

Levine explained that with time these samurai no longer stepped into conflict on behalf of others but gradually assumed positions of authority, necessitating that they fight on their own behalf. The form of government they created became the shogunate, a governance by means of the warrior class, as they used their arts to obtain and enhance their power. Meanwhile, violence did not so much abate as shift toward those with a monopoly on the means of violence.

In a similar fashion, noted Levine, in the West we evolved toward our own version of the self-disciplined champion to do ritual combat, embodied best in the legal profession. After years of training and apprenticeship, the lawyer exercises restrained assertiveness against wrongdoers. Once joined by an advocate for the other side, they engage in an elaborate ritual to compete with one another as a way to resolve disputes. These professionals are expected to uphold a strict code of honor while zealously pursuing what they regard as a just outcome. Litigation is a type of contest. Simmel called it "pure conflict" because it has this purpose and only this purpose (1908/1955, p. 36).

Levine explained that with time these lawyers not only stepped into conflict on behalf of others but gradually assumed positions of authority, necessitating that they fight on their own behalf. The form of government itself became filled with lawyers, a governance by means of another warrior class, as they use their arts to obtain and enhance their power.[1] Meanwhile, violence did not so much abate as shift toward those with a monopoly on the means of violence.

What of the transition from phase two to phase three?

Levine credits Morihei Ueshiba with sublimating the samurai code toward a selfless and peaceful practice known today as Aikido, beginning in 1925.[2] In Aikido, nobody tries to vanquish another person. Instead, the objective is to convert aggression into play, in which you preserve the safety and dignity of the other person, drawing them toward exhausting their aggression and letting it become more like a dance with you. Rather than destroy or disable the foe, you are to affirm the best in them. You use the other person's energy, redirecting it, and exhibiting care for the other person. The discipline is more about mastering oneself, without having to dominate anybody else. Ueshiba wrote, "True victory is self-victory, a victory right here, right now" (2007, p. 10). If possible, an accord with the other person is reached by means of consent. Today, Levine claimed, the art is being practiced by over a million adherents around the world (2018, p. 29). This is an example of the transition from a phase two to a phase three.

Likewise, he argued, in the United States and elsewhere, disputants have discovered alternative dispute resolution (ADR) and more specifically mediation as a viable alternative to litigation (e.g. Hensler, 2017; Menkel-Meadow,

---

1. Lawyers constitute a ruling elite, whether they occupy positions of authority or not (e.g. Wollan, 1978; Green & Nader, 1975; Hain & Piereson, 1975; Derge, 1959; Rutherford, 1938).
2. A brief biographical account of his life appears in Pranin (1991, pp. 128–131, 157–163). A more extensive biography appears in Stevens (1987). Ueshiba is himself the author of several books that have been translated into English.

2015). In mediation, a professional invites disputants to come together, without representatives, and talk face-to-face about their respective positions.[3] Then with ritualized solicitation, the mediator elicits each side to practice listening to one another before engaging in mutual problem solving (Levine, 2018, p. 31f). If anything, an accord is reached by means of consent. Overall, the process turns out to be quicker, less expensive, and better able to preserve relationships when compared to traditional litigation.

The question I put to myself, as a result of reading Levine's comparisons, is whether it might be time in the practice of politics to transition in a similar way toward an equivalent type of leadership. Taking the long view, we in the West have struggled to arrive at a peaceful method for resolving political questions, centered primarily on the ritual of conducting periodic elections. The emergence of political parties guarantees that these contests are shaped by partisans, who are expected to be constrained largely by party discipline. There are consequences for candidates who flout the norm. Otherwise, they attack one another with increasing incivility, practicing what has come to be known as the politics of personal destruction. President Theodore Roosevelt even likened politics to an arena where you strive and periodically find yourself bloodied, rising once again to reengage, for only in that way do you deserve honor. The complaint has been lodged for some time that, not unlike with samurai in Japan and lawyers in the West, politicians have become careerists, using their skills to obtain and keep power for themselves and the rest of their political class. Can there be such a thing as aikido politics? Can we transition here from phase two to phase three?

## Principles of Aikido and Mediation[4]

It remains to be seen whether the domain of politics (especially electoral politics) is ready to welcome a different kind of practice—a practice more in line with Aikido or mediation. One may reasonably ask what that might look like. In order to say what that might look like in the domain of politics, first we should identify some of the core principles of Aikido and mediation.

1. Aikido. At the root of Aikido is a conceptual shift, a reorientation toward the very idea of conflict, which we ordinarily imagine as a confrontation between two warring sides, two camps, adversaries.[5] The reframing involves seeing the other person, the foe, as a partner who, by attacking you, makes a gift of their energy. They are showing themselves to be participants in the flow. You actually want them to do so, fully (Levine, 2018, p. 33). The goal is

---

3. For an overview of the practice of mediation, see e.g. Mayer (2000, chs. 9 and 10).
4. Levine also suggested ways in which Aikido and mediation could be mutually reinforcing toward this goal or objective (2018, pp. 38–41).
5. Politics is often viewed as the supreme example of either/or thinking (see e.g. Schmitt, 1927/1976).

to redirect that flow toward a shared vision. Consequently, you draw them out into the open and express gratitude for their participation. As a way of neutralizing the neurons in the brain that tell them (and you) that this will not end well, based on prior experiences with conflict, you must focus on the present and not let the past arrest the narrative (Levine, 2018, p. 34).[6] That was then, this is now.

When I began my career as a classroom instructor, my father told me not to become upset when somebody disagrees with you. They might be the only student paying attention! Elsewhere, I have seen authors of articles respond to critical reviews from anonymous referees by first thanking them for devoting so much attention to the submission and working so hard to make it better—even when the review is vicious. In the same spirit, there is evidence that many African American leaders in the Civil Rights era were grateful to William F. Buckley Jr. for having them on his television show *Firing Line* because, even though Buckley was a skilled and relentless debater who questioned them strenuously, at least he gave them a forum for their views and treated them with respect, as though their ideas had enough merit to warrant a sustained critique (Hendershot, 2016). Something of the same attitude seems to infuse Aikido. Perhaps not surprisingly, there will be parallels to the practice of dialogue.[7] Again, one looks in a new way at apparent oppositions as an opportunity.

Another feature of Aikido is to regard the attacker as a lone assailant worthy of attention, rather than as an example or representative of an unseen group. You are not fighting people who are not physically present, let alone their ideology or race.[8] With Aikido, you have to ignore everybody else and not paint your adversary as the bearer of anyone else's agenda—even if they are precisely that! This is about you and me. In fairness, of course, you do not summon your own allies to join in on your behalf either. Conflict quickly escalates when you need folks on your side to rush in, because it only makes sense that allies from the other side will sweep into the conflict as well. You have to restrict the encounter to those who saw fit to assail you directly. This is about you and me.

A worthy vision therefore is to bring about harmony in one's own life and in one's relationships, especially with rivals. Levine noted that the etymological root of the term Aikido is the Japanese term for harmony (2018, p. 41).[9] We

---

6. Patočka had urged a comparable progression, i.e. to enter into the fray, to participate, and to transcend the conflict without escaping it (Bernard, 2016, ch. 16).

7. It is no coincidence that Levine's discussion of Aikido and mediation appears in a book devoted to dialogue.

8. Simmel (1908/1955) wrote, "Each party fights, as it were, in the name of the whole group and must hate in its adversary not only its own enemy but at the same time the enemy of the higher sociological unit" (p. 50). Unfortunately, doing so has the effect of building in-group solidarity (1908/1955, p. 91f).

9. Stanley Pranin (1991) suggested it is more precisely about blending harmoniously with the attacker (p. 4).

can all work toward a better universe the more we recruit others toward that shared vision.[10]

2. Mediation. In mediation, a third party controls the process, but not the outcome of the conflict.[11] The parties do that part themselves. Obviously, they have not been able to do so yet, for whatever reason, or their conflict would not even be on the mediator's radar. In order to conduct mediation, disputants are drawn together around a table as instructed, with the mediator initiating the process, putting the focus on herself. The parties are expected to articulate their positions and deliver their version of the facts, directly to her first. But then they are instructed to hear the other party's position and version of the facts. They have to show that they heard one another. Only then can the mediator gradually work herself out of the center as she teaches the parties how to collaborate. A successful mediation leads to the parties talking directly to one another as though they have a shared commitment to problem solving. Each must say, *you* are not the problem; rather, you and I have a problem. Together, let us figure it out. Obviously, it takes a lot of work to get grievants to that point, but one of the objectives of mediation is to teach people how to manage their own disputes, so that maybe there won't have to be a next time.

Not only must attorneys who want to practice mediation unlearn models of litigation acquired in law school, anybody who aspires to mediate must see conflict as an opportunity that is less threatening and well intentioned. Some people call it peace-work. The mediator creates a welcoming climate, picking up and celebrating points of agreement as they emerge, praising the right attitudes, and reminding everybody about the shared values toward which they are moving (Levine, 2018, p. 37). To paraphrase Folberg and Taylor (1984, quoted in Levine, 2018, p. 37), mediation is a process managed by a neutral third party in which the parties (a) identify the issues to be resolved, (b) generate alternative responses, and (c) reach a consensus such that it belongs entirely to them.

Needless to say, mediators must themselves exhibit the restraint and openness they want to see in the disputants. Thus, they must discipline themselves first. Only then are they equipped to help others.

I want to make a further point. In both Aikido and mediation, the conflict comes to you. You do not seek it out. You certainly do not assault others. You respond. But you do not respond in kind. Neither is it about blocking or ignoring what is going on around you, let alone what is happening to you, as though you are a stoic. You actively absorb the energy and convert it into something else, into something productive. Therein lies the alchemy of leadership. The

---

10. For a more extensive description of Aikido for purposes of conflict resolution, see e.g. Crum, 1987.
11. Don Levine was a foremost interpreter of Georg Simmel, and Simmel published on the subject matter of conflict (1908/1955), so it makes sense that Levine peppered his remarks on conflict resolution with appropriate references to Simmel.

energy is already out there, flowing where it will—a peregrinal phenomenon. The question is how to work with it for good.

## Aikido Politics

At the risk of sounding naïve, let me try to describe what leadership informed by Aikido and mediation might look like.

First, it requires a radical re-thinking about political disputes as opportunities, exhibitions of a flow that signifies life and care. Politics does not have to be adversarial. Nevertheless, as a process it does have to bring differences to the surface. Then, in the moment of deliberation, the affected social actors must be encouraged to hear one another for the sake of a shared value of civic harmony—which is not the same thing as uniformity.[12] Instead, it means a shared participation in the spontaneous order within which we pursue our separate objectives. Each affected person gets to speak. Others are expected to listen. Then they are given an opportunity to examine the underlying rationales put forth by the respective "sides," without revisiting old grievances that no longer apply (the past) and without invoking party spirit (others). The leader keeps the focus on the shared vision of a harmonious civic order and celebrates progress, letting the affected parties hammer out the details, so that once it ends they can say that it was truly theirs and not imposed from on high.[13]

If done correctly, the encounter becomes surprisingly more like a dance to be enjoyed. This means constantly re-directing the aggression, using the energy to unbalance the clash and show how it can be used to serve others. To borrow a line from the acclaimed film *The Scent of a Woman*: when you dance the tango, if you get all tangled up, you just tango on. Implicit in all of this is the confidence that ordinary people can resolve their problems and should be expected to, a sentiment we also saw in the chapter on the Common Law. The mediating leader does control the **process**, because somebody has to, but does not control the **outcome**, so long as it results in greater opportunities for peace.

Needless to say, just as Aikido and mediation begin with the necessity of the practitioner to order himself or herself according to this same ideal, seeking internal harmony and dedicating oneself to strenuous self-discipline, so also the aikido politician must apprentice and adopt ritual practices that equip him or her for conducting these practices. Whether voters will see it or even care is another matter, but then that is why I tend to direct my own attention

---

12. One of the constraints, established earlier (Merton, 1976), is the presence of ambivalence, if not outright contradiction, in each social actor at any given point in time—a condition that uniformity frustrates, ignores, and even rejects. Ambivalence pertains to us as individuals and in collectivities. Just to be clear, this descriptive condition of ambivalence is different from pluralism as to what ought to be the case.

13. Manz and Sims (1991, p. 35) credit Lao-Tzu with the sentiment "Of a good leader, who talks little, when his work is done, his aim fulfilled, they will say: We did it ourselves."

toward local government and the development of local talent, where people can witness the effects of this kind of leadership up close. Every neighborhood is a laboratory where this type of leadership can emerge and prove itself. As we know from these pages, there are no guarantees. The prospects are daunting. The impact likely will be negligible. But aikido politics (like leadership studies generally) was not about a hero on a white horse putting the world to rights. This kind of politics has to be done collectively, even if it has to be piecemeal, in the spirit of spontaneous order. We are back to the X factor mentioned in the section on social morphogenesis: that is, each individual has to see it and buy into it and begin the practice for themselves, adapting creatively under unique circumstances where they live. After all, we do not turn the axis of culture without many hands . . . and patience.

In a business manual on applying Aikido to business leadership, David Baum and Jim Hassinger (2002) explained that leadership is intended to be deft—so swift and subtle that you almost never see it happen (§4). As a leader, you do only what is required and do it without making a display of yourself. This assumes that action of some sort is required. At times, the smart move is not to play at all, but instead to walk away (§5). In Aikido, as in other venues, sometimes discretion is the better part of valor. Over time this type of leadership diminishes the prominence of leadership itself and turns responsibility back onto the followers (§6). That is to say that Aikido leadership should not look like conventional leadership at all.

It seems incumbent upon me to mention two other themes as they pertain to what I am calling aikido politics. First, the chapter on turning homeward emphasized drawing from the past without trying to go back in time. We all come from traditions that inform our practice. Levine wrote in the very next chapter of his book after describing Aikido and mediation that pretty much every culture has some version of the value of harmony, whether by that it is understood as stoic cosmopolitanism, satyagraha, makoto, 'a^slem, berith, or the Kingdom of Ends (2018, ch. 4). He also went on to compare and contrast cosmopolitan ideals from eighteenth century France and from nineteenth century Russia (2018, ch. 5). What I am suggesting is that maybe we should draw from the past (Sankofa)—whatever that past happens to include—as we give form to the future. Second, perhaps you noticed that aikido politics means recognizing an apparent *aporia*, bringing it to the surface, searching for a way to transcend the contradictions, and then bringing back to the community what was learned in the process, in an iterative process that is literally extra-ordinary (outside the usual order of things).

Now, do we have concrete historical examples of this kind of leadership? Actually, we have many. In addition to characters in fiction, such as King Arthur, mediating is something that leaders do frequently (e.g. Papagianni, 2008; Bowles, 2005; Waldstreicher & Grossbart, 1998), whereas leading is something that mediators frequently do (e.g. Ross, Conlon, & Lind, 1990).

I would prefer to direct your attention to the many diplomats who travel the globe in order to bring warring peoples to some kind of accord. A few were themselves executives, such as Theodore Roosevelt, who won a Nobel Peace Prize for his efforts in the Russo-Japanese war in 1904–1905. Others were career ambassadors or negotiators whose impact on world history may be hard to detect, because their accomplishments are like the dog that did not bark. Sometimes, the absence of war is itself the proof of their proficiency. Besides, the best diplomats try to stay out of the limelight. I could go so far as to suggest that one of the reasons that this type of leadership has been harder to witness in the historical record is that it was often practiced by women, whose contributions have (for whatever reason) been easier for scholars to overlook (see e.g. Paffenholz, 2018; Paffenholz, Ross, Dixon, Schluchter, & True, 2016; de Langis, 2011; van Bemmelen, 1992). One leadership scholar who embodies this aikido politics is Ted Baartmans of De Presentatie Groep, located in Bloemendaal in the Netherlands. True to form, he would be ashamed when I draw attention to him.

The story is told of the closing days to the Peloponnesian war, when Sparta deputized Pausanius to go guarantee that the defeated Athenians never rose again to make mischief. Despite expectations of vengeance and destruction for the twenty-seven-year war, Pausanius brokered a peace among bitter factions within Athens, instituting widespread amnesty and the restoration of property rights to expropriated farmers. In three short years, Athens was managing peaceably under a democracy, without taking up arms against their rival ever again (Martin, 2013, p. 139). The history books rarely mention Pausanius, and when they do mention him, they rarely mention this particular episode. We overlook this species of leadership.

In *November 1916*, Solzhenitsyn (1984–1991) described Aleksandr Guchkov, president of the Third Duma, in these terms:

> [Guchkov] stood up firmly against loud and furious onslaughts from the left, from the right, and at times from the left and right simultaneously, sometimes winning support, sometimes roundly abused, but always in the belief that he was steadily steering a middle course, trying to keep the peace between Russia's rulers and Russian society, so that they could work creatively, and always in the hope that both the rulers and society would someday limit themselves and renounce their inordinate demands.
> *(p. 550)*

One may ask: if we have so many exemplars from human history, what makes me think that now is the time for aikido politics—to which I would answer that we *always* need them. It is part of a perennial condition, or what Braudel (1980) had called unaltering history. Calling for something we always need is not in and of itself a radical message.

In elective politics, a candidate who practices aikido politics will be difficult to notice. By training, such people are self-effacing and not self-promoters. They exercise discretion. They will deflect credit for their successes because the work was premised on the affected parties being the ones to have resolved their dispute. A mediator cannot boast about work that they induced others to do. In addition, as I said, the success of this kind of leadership is like the dog that does not bark. When bad things do not happen, who gets the credit? Who even notices? Nevertheless, we know who Morihei Ueshiba is. We know some famous deal brokers down through the ages. We know people in our own lives who serve in this capacity. Maybe the flaw is not in an electoral system; maybe it is more the case that we as an electorate must see with better eyes. The political structure may not require changing; maybe our minds do.

## Living Within Tensions

Because we live within a tensional world Voegelin called the metaxy, at every moment, in every direction, we can differentiate a compact reality into two or more elements. Let us call them A or B. Under the press of circumstances, we might feel obliged to choose A or B. However, that choice presupposes that we even notice the tension and conclude that something must be done about it. Many of us go through life oblivious to the tensions that constitute the social world. Alternatively, we notice, but pay no heed, perhaps because the cost of doing something exceeds the cost of letting things persist.

Leaders notice. They also experience an inward imperative to do something. They go into a particular mode because, at some point, tensions demand a response. Trusting that the system will correct itself in due time belies the fact that (a) we don't really understand our systems to begin with, (b) these systems generate unintended consequences that we may not prefer, and frankly with regard to some of the world's wicked problems (c) an evolutionary approach takes more time to complete than we probably have (Laszlo, 1994, p. 38f). Besides, the current system where all of these tensions exist is likely to perpetuate itself, actively resisting impulses to change.

A supremely satisfying outcome—and one that is rarely obvious—is when you can reconcile the two sides in a conflict. Maybe A and B are not in fact incompatible. Maybe you can have both, in full, a true win–win (non-zero-sum) solution (Fisher, Ury, & Patton, 1981). Maybe you can transcend the tension, holding them together in a generative way (Martin, 2007). If you find such an integrative outcome, the problem is really no longer a problem. That would appear to be the best outcome. The trouble goes away. It is no secret that in conflict resolution, these alternatives are characterized in a grid (Thomas, 1976; Thomas & Kilmann, 1974), and we see the same imagery in certain models of leadership (Blake & Mouton, 1964)—that is, for any two-dimensional chart, there is the either/or, the neither/nor, the both/and as a compromise, and the both/and as transcending the apparent dichotomy altogether. Each has its place. Throughout this book, we have used these options in different combinations.

St. Francis forces us to consider a possibility that lies nowhere on the grid. Maybe the best way to understand his position is by introducing a new term. Krell briefly alludes to something called **utraquism**, which is a both/and that does not dissolve the problem (2019, pp. 92–115). Kant referred to these as antinomies, and management scholars have shown how to cope with them (e.g. Martin, 2007; Fletcher & Olwyler, 1997; B. Johnson, 1996). Minogue (2013) considers ambivalence to be a condition we all experience and at some level understand quite well (p. 97). Antinomies, paradox, polarities, and ambivalence are not the exact same thing, but together they speak to a state or condition of being torn, abiding in what I am calling tensions. Utraquism is the discomfort of abiding within the tension fully without expecting it to go away. We are comprised of these tensions. We would not stand without them. We actually require the contradictions. Archer (1996) put it in these terms:

> Given their initial commitment to A, [people] are driven to engage with something both antithetical but also indispensable to it—which therefore they can neither embrace as it stands nor reject out of hand. They must struggle to extract what is necessary from B, warding off B's counter-attractions or counter-claims and avoiding the seductive labyrinth of doubt, to return to A bearing their offering.
>
> *(p. 155)*

This is a much harsher verdict than the win–win solution that makes all troubles cease. Win–win solutions sound terrific. Yet utraquism just might be the more honest position to take, even if it qualifies as a tragic philosophy. Moreover, to feel it deeply, perhaps, is the mechanism by which we feel most alive. Luther sensed it and accepted it. Francis blessed it, perhaps especially when it made no sense. In dialogue, you sharpen the differences. And so (as philosophers will warn us), the closer one gets to **utraquism** you slip quietly toward irrationalism. But, is it nonsense?

In *Las Meninas*, the tensions inherent in leadership are revealed, without resolution; they are held in a kind of suspended animation or equipoise. In dialogue, these tensions are brought to the surface and considered fully, with the anticipation that eventually they might resolve themselves the longer we talk with respect, openness, and empathy, but that possibility really never was the point. Francis embodied a tension between (a) his vocation as a saint, in which he embraced life in all of its manifestations, including leprosy, hunger, cold, blindness, and humiliation, and (b) his vocation as a leader. Trying to do both—because he was gifted at each and saw the merits of each—he suffered immensely, but one could argue that he finally made his choice. Making that choice turned out to reveal that he could be a leader precisely by being a saint.

Here, in my opinion, the example of Luther turns out to be the most interesting, inasmuch as he experienced tensions both within his own psyche and out in the world, suffering acutely, until he gained the imaginative insight that in fact everything he had feared—all the divisions and conflicts and contradictions—was in its totality fecund, intended by God to work good. The tension was not a bad thing. It was (if anything) long overdue, generative, a font of proliferation. He rejoiced to accept the tensions as they were. Moreover, he convinced many Europeans to see the world and see themselves differently, entirely with hope at the profligacy. To be fair, it must be said that many philosophers do consider Luther's position to have been irrational. But was he wrong?

Joseph Campbell (1990) confessed that he had an abiding interest in life's tensions, in the *aporias* and dichotomies that everybody faces (p. 115f). And he construed the hero's saga, told and re-told across the centuries and around the globe, as so many versions of the same basic drama in which the tension that holds us all back—the fear, the danger, the taboo, whatever it is—the hero goes directly toward, accepting to the fullest measure its penalty. As I am wont to say, the hero steps into the darkest part of the forest. After many trials, he must even visit the underworld, a place that symbolizes *aporia* as nothing else in mythology. But then, lo, the hero returns. And not only returns but also brings a boon, to bestow on his people. Here is the oldest wisdom about navigating the *aporias* in life, the apparent contradictions that hold us back from our fulfillment. The logician might find another language for this idea. The psychotherapist might require a different vocabulary for a diagnosis. Nevertheless, it is the same basic structure, the same implicate order, the imperative we all face once we adopt that mode called leadership. It goes like this. See the *aporias*, touch the *aporias*, transcend the *aporias*, bring something back to help others. One might even call this not extra-ordinary leadership, but aporetic leadership.

Eric Voegelin wrote of the equivalence of experiences and their symbols. This book of mine has tried to present a variety of equivalent experiences and their symbols:

- the experience of a civilization undergoing discord (Luther),
- the experience of disputants in a court of law,
- the experience of dialogue in which we discover just how differently we see the same world,
- the experience of metaphor as symbol that can be luminous for what it represents, but also potentially opaque when it becomes more literally understood and used,
- the experience of both synchrony and turbulence,
- the experience of the looking backward (Sankofa) while going forth,
- the experience of the tensional position of the leader (*Las Meninas*), and
- the experience of Francis celebrating the tension without being forced to resolve it.

We have looked at a variety of representations of that predicament: as conflict, *aporia*, a restless need to transcend oneself, synchrony between and among independent oscillations, spontaneous order, and flow. But the recurring image that seems to capture them all abstractly is the process of differentiation and subsequent integration, when either/or somehow becomes both/and, and the adaptive problem dissolves once you cross the boundaries you have set for yourself and see things in a new light.

This imagery of breaking out, of transgressing the boundaries, implies a homecoming. To paraphrase André Malraux, one must not return from hell with empty hands (Hindus, 1952, p. xv). The purpose is to come back and infuse the system with something new.

Another metaphor recognized by Voegelin in the works of many who struggle with this question is the imagery of depth (1990, p. 124f). Ortega (1914/1961) had rung in his career using the exact same distinction, as we saw in Chapter 6. Lightcap Meek (2014) differentiated the subsidiary and the focal. In other words, "depth" means the further level, the unanticipated space, or the ground of being or the dark heart of the forest, the point from which to assess reality. In between the macro and the micro. Voegelin wrote:

> The depth is fascinating as a threat and a charm—as the abyss into which man falls when the truth of the depth has drained from the symbols by which he orients his life, and as the source from which a new life of the truth and a new orientation can be drawn.
>
> *(1990, p. 125)*

He continued, and his words are worth quoting.

> The return from the depth with a truth newly experienced, then, is symbolized as a *renovatio* in the double sense of a renewal of truth and a renewal of man; the new man can experience the renewal of reality and truth with such intenseness that only the symbols of death and resurrection will adequately express it.
>
> *(1990, p. 125)*

## Looking Back, Yet Moving Forward (i.e. Sankofa)

Throughout the book, I have been urging an expansion of the field of inquiry for leadership studies. In doing so, I am hardly the first person to suggest these things.

1. We could expand horizontally to examine not only the leader but also the leader in **relationship** with others, so that we capture a broader array of relevant participants. William James found it useful to speak of his own "mosaic philosophy" in which a human being is aware not only of objects but also various relations among them, represented in words such "with, near, next, like,

from, towards, against, because, for, through, my" (Voegelin, 1995, p. 57). The further we go laterally, of course, the more complex things get. The context is far more extensive, intricate, confusing, turbulent, and deep than we often care to admit. It should also humble prospective leaders. Polanyi (1951) asked, "How should we consciously determine a future which is, by its very nature, beyond our comprehension" (p. 245)? A very good question.

2. We could also expand across time to look at leadership as a **process**, with a beginning, a middle, and an end—not unlike a story. In this way, we integrate many of the causal factors, seeing leadership as an event in the flow of history with its precursors in other people and features such as structures and cultures. James pointed out that not only do we experience objects and their interrelationships, but we also experience the passage of time (Voegelin, 1995, p. 58). The further we go back in time, the more we find that leadership becomes almost lost in the turbulence. Furthermore, almost as soon as we start tracking a leader's impact, the link between what a leader does and what actually occurs becomes increasingly attenuated. Nevertheless, a dynamic model more accords with the evidence.

3. We could also adopt what I was calling a **peregrinal ontology**, looking less at the figurative cars and streets as "things" and more at traffic as an ongoing flux, such that leadership is seen not as something that somebody did, whether all at once or in stages. Rather, it is something that happens in which people participate by adopting a mode of being (see Voegelin, 1995, p. 51). Mats Alvesson recently complained about the same thing, namely that leadership studies has a tendency to treat leadership as "a thing-like phenomenon [and] an 'it'" (2019, p. 34). Edgar and Peter Schein (2018) also evoke a peregrinal ontology. Leadership is what is going on all around us, at multiple levels, in multiple directions, like a massive, pulsating flow of shared influence. Part of our job is to investigate when, where, how, and why people plug in to that network.[14]

4. In addition, I have insisted that making distinctions in leadership studies is not enough. The resulting parts are reciprocal and mutually constituting (Voegelin, 1995, p. 23f). Better to regard reality as tensional, ambiguous, and exasperatingly contradictory. This condition of living in the shadow of *aporia*, as I have been calling it, appears to be not only inevitable, but even possibly necessary to the phenomenon of life. Perhaps we are constituted by our antinomies. Organizations are moving in contrary directions at the same time. Followers want incompatible things. Leaders make conflicting demands. Society and its history do not proceed as a laminar flow. Acknowledging this would undoubtedly complicate the labors of many of my peers, though it might also open up models that are more realistic.

---

14. Numbers 2 and 3 are different: 2 is a genetic understanding; 3 is a generative understanding. For more on this distinction, see Harter (2019b).

Further along these lines, therefore, encounters with paramount reality interrupt our stream of consciousness, reminding us that we belong to something bigger. We would be advised to bring an open self to these encounters, for in that way over time we enlarge ourselves (see Voegelin, 1995, p. 34ff, 61).

5. Finally, I have not recoiled from considering the possibility that leadership serves an emerging Good, whether we call this end-state synchrony or justice or harmony or an implicate order (e.g. Bohm, 1980). Mats Alvesson, whom I highly respect, denigrates this approach as Disneyland-inspired and grounded in religion (2019, pp. 31, 39). Nevertheless, something seems to be informing our efforts and guiding us toward a future that few, if any of us could have foreseen. Much as social scientists are reluctant to consider occult forces, it is not unreasonable to see something of this implicate order in the way that an acorn becomes an oak and a community forms around a market (à la Hayek). I do not presume to know what that ultimate image looks like, and I do not enjoy privileged access to its contours. I certainly do not consider it inevitable that we shall successfully realize this ideal—whatever it is. Nevertheless, something the ancient Greeks labeled *logos* works in attunement with an unseen order. What that might mean is for each generation to discern together, as we carry forward into a new world the perennial wisdom that lies within us as a resource.

William James spoke of the "next step" that always awaits us (Voegelin, 1995, p. 62). One crosses a frontier into the unknown, saying good-bye to the old self for the sake of a more capacious existence. For the pragmatist, one must remain open to the influx from paramount reality and not remain in thrall to the old constructs (or images) generated previously by a brain. Neither should we invent images that have no basis in reality. Reality is forever bigger than anything a human being can imagine.

Polanyi (1951) suggested that a polycentric order accords with the ideal of a harmony based on the relationship among the parts, not unlike the brushstrokes on a painting that derive their artistic value as a composite, or the practice of medicine in which one must coordinate among various organs and systems to achieve health (p. 216). Beauty, health, justice—these are evaluative conditions of a polycentric system. We can speak of better and worse, nearer and further from an ideal.

So where does that leave us?

Using Braudel's durations (1980), we can say that leadership studies has been conducted most profitably at the shortest duration of an event or episode (0–10 years). Going any further than that into an intermediate range of years (roughly 10–50 years) becomes difficult, for many of the reasons I have mentioned throughout this book. Singling out the implications of leadership over decades can be difficult. Trying to discern the impact of leadership over the *longue durée* (50+ years), however, becomes impossible—except to the extent that we begin trafficking in myths. What I have done here is to embrace the fourth of Braudel's dimensions, i.e. the perennial, to say that leadership is a mode that constitutes our lives together, from the roving band of hunter-gatherers to the modern, complex, global corporation, when things are dire and when they are calm, whether you command, coach, manage, or preside. For leadership betokens agency whenever a group or team, organization or society initiates and realizes a shared purpose. This is the pin-point phenomenon around which we pack other cultural baggage. And it is the pin-point that can be found in every collective that has any duration.

Using McKeon's modes of thought (2016), we can say that, to begin with, I have embraced a pluralistic approach, hoping to demonstrate and encourage others to use multiple methods in leadership studies. Nearly every mode has its uses. Nevertheless, I have come to rely most on assimilation, in which distinctions are first made, but then they are encompassed tentatively to realize an image of the whole, as we bring ourselves into attunement with an unseen order that goes by the name of the Good. It is an enactment of the sequence from compactness through differentiation toward integration, recursively taking turns on the hermeneutic circle (parts and the whole), as we approximate the Good under changing conditions.

With regard to the Cabreras' so-called rules (2015), in this book we made many distinctions, belaboring the importance of recognizing the relationship between the two sides in any dichotomy that we made—and especially the causal relationships, inasmuch as leadership betokens causation in the social world. In doing so, we adopted a perspectival approach. The student of anything occupies a point of view. So also do the participants in this practice we are calling leadership. One of the most significant distinctions made in these pages is between an entitative ontology and a peregrinal ontology, for to see leadership as a mode of participation in an ongoing flux reveals something about what it is that we claim to study and practice. One's point of view from within the flow, from within the turbulence emblematic of that flow, releases participants from a number of limitations regarding the usual schemas about leadership. Speaking of leadership as a mode of participation in realizing our shared purpose means that the shared purpose is an infinite game, a never-ending realization of order in both the *psyche* and the *polis*, where the truly interesting things happen in a spirit of openness, fallibility, and care.

If you recall, Isaiah Berlin had explained the difference between the idealist as the leader who knows where to go next but is impatient with process and the realist who does not know where any of this is going but is scrupulous about process, trusting that the process will get us where we need to go. By now, it should be obvious that this book offers an alternative. We are talking about someone who has some idea where to go yet adheres to the process. This leader—and it could be anyone, or everyone—this leader hazards the *aporias* implicit in our present circumstances, being fully exposed to their tensions, in search of a way forward that transcends the present, repeatedly, moving with boldness into the unlikelihood, and then returning with caution. Let me say that again: *move with boldness into terra incognito, then return with care.* It is a pragmatic image, like conducting an experiment, using abductive logic, but always in collaboration with others. And though we have spoken here of leadership as a process of binding ourselves to some shared purpose, this type of leadership insists on the paradox of binding ourselves to keeping the portal open, to making it possible that we do this again as needed, with a growth mindset, so that the watchword is not the Good as a fixed ideal, but instead liberty as a boundless horizon. It sounds like a paradox that openness is the destination.

Berlin was himself a pluralist. He might have embraced what Krell was calling utraquism. He would resist the idea that any one Good should predominate. A person must not appeal to justice, for example, in crushing truth or beauty. Likewise, whatever it is that leadership achieves, it must not interfere with other values that constellate our lives. Leadership is only a single mode— and arguably not the most important mode. This is one reason that maybe leadership *should be* limited, unpredictable, and so bloody complicated: we are creatures trying to do many different things that seem incompatible. In my opinion, leadership should never occlude activities such as art or science, healing or dancing, meaningful employment or play. Leadership should not stand in the way of neighborliness, worship, or family. Neither should it compete with faith or joy or love. For if we engage in leadership and find ourselves in opposition to such things, then we may be right to fail. Better for me not to have taught leadership at all.

Sometimes, leadership is not the best mode. Sometimes, it is positively destructive. Indeed, that possibility is one of the best reasons to study leadership, i.e. to inoculate the rest of us against its predations.

Still, that is no way to conclude a book about leadership. I should offer a few words of hope. Each of us may consult our respective traditions, as well as our innate sense of coherence, plus the perspectives of others to craft a way forward. *Aporias* await us. Rather than lament them, let us regard them as opportunities and cultivate in ourselves and others the discipline to change how we respond to them. Like Aikido masters, we might embrace these *aporias* and play with them, exhibiting a peculiar joy that life has brought us to this moment. We stand on the edge of a forest, listening to the fugitive pipes of shaggy Pan recede. Would it not be extra-ordinary to follow?

# APPENDICES

As an author, I struck out toward many *aporias* with boldness. I should now return with care. Leadership scholars may detect a few unresolved tensions in my own book—tensions that are more than loose ends. These appendices will try to address three of them, for the sake of thoroughness.

# APPENDIX A

## What Does It Mean That Leadership Is a Mode of Participation?

We speak as though Justice, like Truth and Beauty, is an end-state toward which we are striving, like a Promised Land in the distance, not unlike the craftsman who toils and sweats for the sake of the chair. Even here, we rely on an entitative ontology, associating leadership's purpose with the realization of a vision, i.e. some future, static ideal. We operate with an image in mind of the way things ought to be. And so we talk as though the point of the game is winning and the point of business is profit, the point of an acorn is the oak, and the point of this life that we live is our eternal reward. We construe the implicate order as an eventual (or at least hoped for) constellation that is coming to be. The hippocampus poses the question: Is this what we desire or isn't it? Well, I wonder if perhaps that is the right question.

What if the point is the becoming? The purpose of a game of chess is not the final position of the pieces. The purpose of a dialogue is not the conclusion that we reach. The point of Chopin's prelude is not the resolution; otherwise, the pianist could sit down, simply play the last chord, and walk offstage to applause. Maybe the purpose of leadership is the participating, the privilege of co-creating, being engaged in the flux.

You can walk to get somewhere. Or you can walk to get some exercise. But sometimes the purpose of a walk is the walk itself. Did you get a nice walk? Young people struggle to discern the meaning of life, as though it would be a job, a marriage, a house. But what I am asking is whether the search for meaning is the meaning. And therefore the purpose of leadership is the taking part.

Plato reports that in his old age Socrates was looking forward to the after-life. Why? Not because he would enter into a state of bliss. On the contrary, he was eager to resume the practice of engaging others in dialogue, forever. The dialogue never ends. It was for the sake of dialogue itself that he had lived and not the other way around.

We judge leadership as though it were a process of rendering some kind of outcome to be judged, as a painting would be or a book. We can even obsess over outcomes. We postpone our assessment of how well things have gone until we see the results. But maybe that's an impoverished mindset.

Maybe the purpose of peacemaking is less about peace and more about the making. Maybe science is less about the truth than it is about the study. Maybe childhood is less about the adult you become, as though all of it is preparation for something else, a prelude. Turbulence should not be defined in relation to equilibria—closer or further away from order. From a sufficient distance, turbulence has its own mesmerizing beauty, like Leonardo's deluge or the arc of chaos or, to paraphrase the poet, a primeval cradle endlessly rocking.

Theologian Hans Urs von Balthasar posited that religion could be understood profitably as a drama in which we encounter one another and tell our stories, which are part of an overarching narrative that religion seeks to tell. Religion is less about the creed (an entity) or heaven (an entity). It is the love, the walk with one another and with God, the call and response, the shared quest. Or as James Carse had it: the infinite game.

Evolution does not occur to bring anything specific into existence. It actually has no purpose. If anything, we exist to participate in evolution. Marx got it flat wrong: the dialectic does not serve the synthesis. And Freud believed that therapy was to recover a state or condition of health. Not so. I am proposing a different ontology, a step back, looking at William Cullen Bryant's innumerable caravan. What we must do, in the words of Ortega (1933), is "avoid the eventuality of a malleable and expansible horizon hardening into a world" (p. 94).

Leadership research fixates on means and ends, instrumental reason, how to accomplish something by means of other people. Consumers of our research have goals they want to achieve in the world. Given a set of antecedent circumstances, they want to know which behaviors in the present will bring about the desired consequences. And so as scholars, we try to master the principles of causation, the function of X. We see ourselves as responsible—like physicians, attorneys, and engineers—for figuring out how to work within the context to bring to fruition that which leaders have designed. Leaders first envision and draw followers toward that vision, adapting as necessary along the way. It's all about the path-goal. Leadership as transaction or transformation. How to get product out the door (in manufacturing) or to form a more perfect union (in politics).

This book has been in pursuit of a different characterization based on a peregrinal ontology, in which leadership is a performance, a mode of participation in a flow of history, the process of becoming, living as a kind of rhythm within the metaxy, on the boundary, both venturing out and coming back, helping to embody the virtues and to live not so much for the sake of Beauty (with a capital "B") but to live beautifully.

This, I think, is what Esther Lightcap Meek meant by "coming to know" when she wrote about subsidiary-focal integration as a process. It's not for the acquisition of data but for the acquaintance with reality. After all, at some point you lay the maps aside and just sit in the piazza as the sun sets, sipping your caffè while listening to the carillon. Perhaps just being a part is a superior way of knowing.

# APPENDIX B

## Countering the Risk of Radical Contingency

The most important point about a scientific system is that it should be true.
—*José Ortega y Gasset (1933, p. 11)*

Richard Rorty (1989) contemplated the meaning of a radical contingency not unlike what I have been talking about. That is to say, he took the possibility of it seriously. In doing so, he found in the writings of George Orwell a foreboding about where radical contingency might lead us. What do I mean by that?

Rorty emphasized the character known as O'Brien in Orwell's dystopian novel *1984*. O'Brien, who features in the final third of the book, is the person who tortures the protagonist, ultimately breaking his spirit because he was able to break Winston's ability to trust his own mind. By getting the poor guy to agree that 2 + 2 = 5, O'Brien moves with devastating persistence toward persuading him to denounce the woman he loves—worse, urging authorities to let the rats eat her face off rather than his own.

Rorty conducts his analysis by beginning with the prospect that if one accepts a **coherence theory** of truth rather than a **correspondence theory** of truth, you become vulnerable to an alternative coherence.[1] A correspondence theory has the merit that it has to be anchored in something we have called paramount reality. Rain is wet. The grass is green. Or as Winston kept

---

1 Gaus (2013) argued that a coherence theory is actually quite conservative, in that leaders are advised by scholars such as Hayek not to disrupt or interfere with the prevailing coherence lightly (p. 70), unless it would increase the coherence. Gaus extends this argument to show that any proposed novelty—creating, amending, or removing an existing rule—must be regarded in part by the impact of this change on the overall system of rules, the encompassing order (2013, p. 79), which of course for Hayek is quite difficult to accomplish.

insisting to himself: 2 + 2 = 4. Winston tried diligently to believe that there is a truth out there, comprised of facts and logic, so that from this external point of reference he could judge everything else and if necessary keep his distance from the propaganda and lies permeating the social system.

Rorty would support the idea that urging a fresh coherence on people can be a wholesome form of leadership, getting people to see their world in a different way (1989, p. 173). I have used words very much like that. Rorty credits Orwell with having done this about the Soviet threat, with Solzhenitsyn not far behind in exposing the delusions that liberal Westerners had of the Soviet Union and similar totalitarian regimes. But the moment of getting somebody to break free of conventional thinking is fraught with peril. How can we be certain that we aren't plunging into something far worse? As it happens, the Bolsheviks had been doing the same thing since 1917, i.e. persuading people to re-cast reality in a completely different way, ostensibly for the sake of a lofty ideal. And if Orwell and Solzhenitsyn did it in a good cause, it was because Lenin and Hitler had done it in a bad cause. Going forward, how are we to know whether following a leader across the threshold into *terra incognito* is better or worse? Aren't *aporias* there in part to warn us away for our own good? It's a fair question.

Orwell's suspicions lay with the intelligentsia, in the same way that the Common Law exists in part to resist the importunate meddling of an elite into our daily lives. Can we really trust those who are better educated and smarter than we are? They would have you think so. And progressivism often finds itself cast in those terms. Hadn't Plato urged the ideal of a philosopher-king, a benevolent despot? Hadn't we seen this again during the Enlightenment? Orwell created the character of O'Brien to show us what an intellectual can look like under the wrong circumstances (Rorty, 1989, p. 176).

First, human beings are distinct from other forms of life in that we are capable of a certain cruelty: to "tear human minds to pieces and put them together again in new shapes of your own choosing" (Rorty, 1989, p. 177, quoting Orwell). To do that, one must get the victim to flirt with incoherence. O'Brien was not saying as a matter of fact that 2 + 2 = 5. He was trying to get Winston to say it and ultimately to believe it. O'Brien was under no illusion about the truth, in his own head. His goal was to open a wedge in Winston's mind that maybe 2 + 2 really does equal 5 (Rorty, 1989, p. 178). But that's not the end goal of this exquisite torture, to get Winston to doubt the coherence of his worldview. Rather, he needed for Winston to give up on the idea that he could trust himself to think coherently. O'Brien had to destroy Winston's confidence in himself, so that forever after he would give up trying to think things through. The purpose was not to convince Winston to replace an outdated image of the world with another one, like moving from a geocentric view of the solar system to a heliocentric one; neither was it to convince him to replace an image of himself with another one. It was to give up on the idea that he could trust *any* image of the world or of himself. In effect, O'Brien destroyed

Winston's reliance on his own powers to imagine by showing just how plastic those images can be. He was showing Winston that he could be irrational and live with it. He could be cruel and live with it (Rorty, 1989, p. 179).

Strangely, Rorty contends that O'Brien's objective had nothing to do with making Winston a compliant subject who no longer posed a threat to the regime: "Torture is not for the sake of getting people to obey, nor for the sake of getting them to believe falsehoods" (1989, p. 180). Nobody doubts that rulers will go to extraordinary lengths to subdue their citizenry. We have known this since the beginning. Torture for instrumental purposes is regrettably familiar to us all, and in our weaker moments understandable if not justified. Orwell's insight is more horrifying.

Orwell was saying that O'Brien tortured Winston because he wanted Winston to suffer, to crack. O'Brien did it just for the sake doing it, to satisfy some dark, sadistic impulse, which the regime in the story happened to make possible. In a system that relies on torture, the intelligent sadist is king. O'Brien enjoyed inflicting this unique and enduring kind of pain. Earlier, I had mentioned the idea that we shouldn't valorize the criminal and insane figures from the French Revolution just because the times rewarded their worst impulses. They did in fact help to bring about a new civic order—this is true. But we stopped short of calling it leadership. It was not. But the point we return to is this: how does one judge the transition in any social change without a correspondence theory of truth? A clever torturer can always improvise a coherence that allows him to indulge his cruelty.[2] Or, to take us all the way back to the beginning of the book, when someone returns from the portion of the map that says "Here, there be monsters": how do we know that they themselves aren't the monster?[3] To his credit, Rorty (who subscribes to a coherence theory of truth) confronted this possibility head-on. So therefore should I.

Rorty believed that Orwell was not saying that his dystopia was inevitable. Only that it is possible. It is possible because it is already within us, even in our present circumstances, in our homes and in our churches and in our places of employment. And the worst of it is that any one of us can be O'Brien or Winston, sadist or victim. A belief in radical contingency has to allow for the possibility. It may not require upheavals in the global/political scene to manifest. It can be right here, across the dinner table or in a classroom. In my own opinion, Rorty was in effect pinching himself, wondering if his own philosophy was a form of Winston's confusion and self-doubt, that things could be otherwise and we could still live with it.

---

2 Rorty examined how the novelist Vladimir Nabokov showed a character doing this without much difficulty (1989, ch. 7).

3 Some would tar Christopher Columbus, whom we mentioned earlier, with this very brush (e.g. Zinn, 2015).

Strange as it might seem, Rorty even indicts dialogue as a potential technique for undermining everybody else's minds. An astute and ruthless psychotherapist can ruin the soul. A confessor, a mentor, a parent, a coach can use the excuse of engaging in a dialogue to do real damage for no real purpose. In fact, dialogue gives the exquisite torturers of the world like O'Brien a convenient venue to do their worst. The O'Briens of the world thrive on the challenge of discombobulating others (1989, pp. 185, 187). I have seen it myself. It alarms me to find students majoring in philosophy in order to equip themselves to dominate others, intellectually, because they can. Was this not the exact nature of the charges against Socrates? And to an extent, was this not one of the motives for crucifying Jesus? (Maybe even part of the reason the Catholic Church felt that it had to eradicate the Protestant Reformation, root and branch?)—that people were gathering in private conversation where unscrupulous characters could corrupt impressionable followers? How am I in these pages any different?

Rorty conceded that people who believe what he believes need dialogue to keep from going insane or turning toward the darkness (1989, p. 186). Once you adopt a coherence theory of truth and you have a capacious mind, as Rorty plainly did, you suspect that without input from others this sinister turn would be possible. How do I know that in this moment I am not being O'Brien or Winston? Something draws us into these opportunities to talk, something downright erotic, but for good purposes or ill? The damnable thing is that it could be both!

Rorty answers in the final chapter by arguing (unsurprisingly) the coherence of his entire book as it regards the importance of generating a sense of solidarity with other people by means of "imaginative identification" with others. What Christians refer to as "caritas" and Josiah Royce called "loyalty" and Wilfrid Sellars called "we-consciousness" decreases the likelihood of cruelty (1989, p. 190). The attempt to generate this sense of identification by means of some vague abstraction such as "humanity" or "rational beings" does not work; you need something more concrete. So the way to offset the risk he had just described about the prospects of torture and cruelty is to expand this we-feeling. He wrote about

> the inclusion among "us" of the family in the next cave, then of the tribe across the river, then of the tribal confederation beyond the mountains, then of the unbelievers beyond the seas (and, perhaps last of all, of the menials who, all this time, have been doing our dirty work).
>
> *(1989, p. 196)*

By expanding our familiarity, we increase the likelihood of becoming more widely solicitousness. We start from where we are, he said, then just keep growing that circle (1989, p. 198). Kenneth Minogue (2013) rejects this idea for large-scale, global societies as antiquated, impractical, and romantic. In the spirit of Hayek, the beauty of the spontaneous order we now require is that you do not have to have any acquaintance or awareness of remote people to do them good (p. 91). You can benefit them anyway by sticking to your own business. You are in no way less moral for ignoring them and their well-being.

That is one response. My response is more robust, although it relies to some extent on the coherence of my own book. So let me begin by pointing out that, first of all, my attempt here at "dialogue" is very public, not private. Second, a short review of the chapter on dialogue differentiates genuine or true dialogue from the dynamics that Rorty (and Orwell) so feared. Done correctly, you avoid many of the temptations that Rorty was worried about. If anything, dialogue should help to reduce the risk of such tactics in a group setting. But even if I were to concede that bad things can happen during dialogue, questioning the value of dialogue is like saying that pushing a little old lady into the path of an oncoming bus is no different from pushing a little old lady out of the path of an oncoming bus, since in both cases you are pushing around little old ladies. You can't blame dialogue for human nature. Third, although I agree that coherence is a criterion for establishing what is true, it is not the sole criterion. In fact, I am urging another both/and here; I have made numerous references to some version of a correspondence theory of truth. Recall that I said that the map (image) is not the territory (reality). Images must yield to reality. In SFI, one double-checks with the flashlight what seems to be the case, because if you get it wrong you could stumble over a chair in the walkway. SFI helps you avoid tripping over things. The hermeneutic circle is one way to check, to keep guarding against fantasy. The Common Law runs through multiple iterations across jurisdictions to approximate justice in the real world. Assuredly, both Luther and Francis would have contended that their faith was grounded in a Truth that transcends whatever they could imagine. Poincaré recommended that educators teach math using images, but he certainly did not disavow a reliance on mathematical proofs; he was only talking about techniques for educating children. When I disclosed that my book is more of a collage than a chain, I made a show of respect for chains of logical argumentation—my point being that this was simply not the purpose of my book. If you recall, in the chapter on turbulence, I considered the imagery of fitness, which is a version of the coherence theory of truth, and I ended up noting its limitations.

The fourth thing I would like to say is that I have also emphasized the importance of tradition—custom in the Common Law, spontaneous order, à la Hayek, the homeward leadership and Sankofa. Perennial wisdom tends to counteract strange novelties. These conservative constraints make it less likely that one would blindly or casually surrender a coherent worldview in exchange for a different one—not without considerable scrutiny. This leads to my fifth point, which is that throughout I have been making the case that the best protection against tyranny and terror is distributed leadership, getting more and more people wary and shrewd so that they can handle clever charlatans. If more social actors practiced this particular mode of participation, the chances that we would find ourselves in a regime that rewards an O'Brien goes down. This was Lincoln's plea in the Lyceum speech. This was Umberto Eco's advice regarding free speech. The more of us with critical powers, the less gullible and vulnerable we are likely to be. Rorty would seem to have anticipated this line of defense by acknowledging that the *focus imaginarius*—whatever it is that attracts our imagination—still deserves to be subjected to closer examination (1989, p. 195). True, and that takes courage and discipline. But nobody said that leadership is ever easy.[4]

4 A further possibility presents itself. In a seminar titled "In Defense of Carl Jung," James Hillman (2005b) admitted at the outset that Jung was a difficult man to be around. He was charismatic, intimidating, and a bit aggrandizing. His reactions to people were often rough, perfunctory, even rude. But is that aspect—his personality number two—perhaps intrinsic to the genius? Something in a brilliant and driven character can be cruel in service of some abstract or occult ideal that other people have trouble comprehending. To what extent, asks Hillman, is Jung exemplary of human potential? Rorty might concede that private cruelties, especially in pursuit of perfection, might be understandable. The diva makes demands, the rocker smashes his guitar, the author ignores the front doorbell while trying to finish his novel. Perhaps some inward imperative makes a person self-centered, if not insufferable. For Rorty, you should keep that stuff private and not let it bleed over into public displays, let alone into your politics. Hillman seems to be more sanguine, that perhaps cruelty (among other things) is the price one pays to suffer genius gladly. Maybe it comes with the territory. Rorty may find it all so dreadful—and Hillman doesn't discount that it is dreadful—but should we be so horrified by the possibility? I suspect that Hillman would have agreed with Rorty, that the real horror lies in the regime that cultivates and rewards the cruelty. Or should I say the genius for cruelty, such as possessed by O'Brien. *Of course* human beings can be cruel. Did you really think to stamp it out? At what cost? Rorty regarded cruelty as the worst possible thing. He said so. In his lectures, Hillman was being less monistic about it. In other words, Hillman sends us right into an *aporia*: are the best among us possibly by necessity also the worst among us? And if you occlude the worst (through prison, drugs, therapy, and so forth), are you also thereby strangling the best? It is a hard thought and beyond my powers to resolve in these pages. Nevertheless, it might re-cast one's judgment of bad leadership, ranging from the peccadillos of a Bill Clinton to the ham-handed treatment of women by notable artists so widely condemned in the Me Too movement today (see e.g. Siegel, 2019; Spencer, 2019; Ford, 2018; Gilbert, 2018; Scott, 2018; Dederer, 2017). Is it too much to ask of our leaders that they be innocuous, anodyne, paltry, domesticated, and safe?

# APPENDIX C

## A Final, Though Not Fatal Dichotomy

So, if Rorty could face the strongest indictment of his core philosophy, a move which I happen to admire, then I should probably do the same thing here. So far as I can tell, the strongest indictment against my book goes like this. How can I be a pluralist, tempted by this thing called utraquism, while at the same time believing in some ultimate, overarching harmony, an implicate order, like the picture on the jigsaw puzzle box? How can I hold the position that there is a right answer to all of our strivings, yet there is not in fact one right answer? This might seem to be the fatal contradiction. I am trying to have my cake and eat it too. It cannot be both. William James (1909/1996) called the problem "reconciling metaphysical unity with phenomenal diversity" (p. 47).[1]

I am aware of that apparent contradiction. I have devoted months—no, years—of my life to contemplating that contradiction. It is for me a philosophically interesting contradiction. I guess you could say that this has been my governing *aporia*. It is the conundrum that arose out of contemplating the words of Mary Douglas years ago. It is a problem I have felt throughout thirty years of teaching leadership studies. It also lies at the heart of my political ambivalence, where I can believe things devoutly without being drawn into crusades. It defines the paradox of my religious convictions.

And I answer it thus. As a scholar committed to a pluralistic premise, I am skeptical. As a teacher, I am hopeful. Every philosophy is comprised of these two things: its reasonings, on the one hand, and its vision, on the other (James, 1909/1996, p. 13; see also p. 251). The challenge is making them fit together.

---

1. Rorty (1989) said one has to choose: are we converging on truth or proliferating freedom endlessly (p. xvi)? Which is it? Not surprisingly, he chose the latter (1989, p. 60). We are not converging on a truth that is out there in the cosmos, he claimed (1989, p. 19). Neither are we converging on a truth in our minds or hearts. I happen to disagree.

Maybe I can explain it this way. As a mortal with bounded rationality and a narrow point of view, having been conditioned by institutional structures and the culture at large, I proceed as a scholar by acknowledging that *aporias* exist. Given my limitations, I must proceed as though pluralism is true. I do not believe as a matter of principle that either modernity or post-modernity adequately responds to this predicament. As a poor scholar, for purposes of research I am a thorough-going pragmatist. My skepticism is real. *Operationally*, I am a pluralist. "We may be in the universe as dogs and cats are in our libraries," wrote James, "seeing the books and hearing the conversation, but having no inkling of the meaning of it all" (1909/1996, p. 309). And so I proceed, like Berlin's realist, with wariness and care. That is the "mode" I must adopt as a scholar.

Yet there is a difference between what I know (or even can know) and what I believe (Ortega, 1940/2002). Accordingly, in typical both/and fashion, as a participant in a larger reality I can step out in faith, buoyed by the emergent image that is this book. To this extent, I resemble Berlin's idealist. Do not ask me as a scholar to prove somehow how it ends. But, as a teacher? In that mode? I would not walk into a classroom if I did not believe that we can each do our part to approximate the Good. Our lives together can constellate. They do constellate. Look at where human beings are, compared to where we were. Civilization is a hard-won victory that ought to be treasured. By the same token, to be fair, we are by no means done. This voyage has a direction, even if it has no destination. I have to believe that, even if I cannot prove it.

But then, think about it. Science proceeds in the exact same way as I do, holding to a vision that the universe will ultimately make sense and reward our investigations, yet getting there in baby steps, with due deliberation, double-checking our work, and only every so often lifting our gaze to take in the big picture that seems to be emerging. The hopeful large-scale vision orients us during our patient, small-scale work. We do not accuse scientists of contradicting themselves for doing this.

As an instructor, therefore, I operate as though it all makes sense. There will be profit in confronting life's *aporias*. Let others keep to the tried and true. Our souls expand as our world expands, and our world expands only as we dare. The journey toward *aporias* requires that our leaders be extra-ordinary, as I have tried to define the term: beyond the ordinary, open to the next step, willing to transgress boundaries, venturing outside the limit with boldness and coming back with care. They participate routinely in Plato's Allegory of the Cave (*Republic* 514a–520a, Plato & Bloom, 1968). I believe in my students, these extra-ordinary leaders of the future. I have to. They are soon responsible for the infinite game that you and I bequeath to them.

# REFERENCES

Ackoff, R. L. (2010). *Differences that make a difference: An annotated glossary of distinctions important in management.* Triarchy Press Limited.

Agamben, G. (2009). *The signature of all things: On method.* Zone Books.

Alisch, L.-M., Azizighanbari, S., & M. Bargfeldt. (1997). "Dynamics of children's friendships." In Eve, R., Horsfall, S., & M. Lee (eds.), *Chaos, complexity, and sociology: Myths, models, and theories* (ch. 13). Sage.

Allen, S. (2015, April 9). "Donald Levine, sociologist and former dean of the College, 1931–2015." *Uchicago news.* Retrieved 29 January 2019 from https://news.uchicago.edu/story/donald-levine-sociologist-and-former-dean-college-1931-2015.

Alpers, S. (1983, February). "Interpretation without representation, or, the Viewing of *Las Meninas.*" *Representations. 1*: 31–42.

Althaus, P. (1972). *The ethics of Martin Luther.* Fortress Press.

Alvesson, M. (2019). "Waiting for Godot: Eight major problems in the odd field of leadership studies." *Leadership. 15*(1): 27–43.

Alvesson, M., Blom, M., & S. Sveningsson. (2017). *Reflexive leadership: Organising in an imperfect world.* Sage.

Alvesson, M., & A. Spicer (eds.). (2011). *Metaphors we lead by: Understanding leadership in the real world.* Routledge.

Alvesson, M., & S. Sveningsson. (2003). "Managers doing leadership: The extraordinarization of the mundane." *Human Relations. 56*(12): 1435–1459.

Andrianova, M. (2018). "Internal dialogism of Russian postmodern literature: Polyphony or Schizophrenia?" In Freise, M. (ed.), *Inspired by Bakhtin: Dialogical methods in the humanities* [Studies in Comparative Literature and Intellectual History] (ch. 1). Academic Studies Press.

Antonakis, J., & D. V. Day (eds.). (2017). *The nature of leadership.* Sage.

Appiah, K. A. (2017). *As if: Idealization and ideals.* Harvard University Press.

Appiah, K. A. (2014). *Lines of descent: W.E.B. DuBois and the emergence of identity.* Harvard University Press.

Archer, M. (ed.). (2013). *Social morphogenesis* (chs. 1 & 8). Springer.

Archer, M. (1996). *Culture and agency: The place of culture in social theory* (revised ed.). Cambridge University Press.

Arendt, H. (1970). *On violence.* Houghton Mifflin Harcourt.

Arendt, H. (1968). "Introduction." In Benjamin, W. (ed.), *Illuminations: Essays and reflections.* Mariner Books.

Arendt, H. (1958). *The human condition.* University of Chicago Press.

Arendt, H. (1953). "Ideology and terror: A novel form of government." *The Review of Politics. 15*(3): 303–327.

Aron, R. (1967). *Main currents in sociological thought* (vol. II) (R. Howard & H. Weaver, trans.). Anchor Books.

Auden, W. H. (1947). *The age of anxiety.* Random House.

Avens, R. (1982). "Heidegger and archetypal psychology." *International Philosophical Quarterly. 22*(2): 183–202.

Ayoub, M. (1978). *Redemptive suffering in Islam.* De Gruyter Mouton.

Back, K. (1997). "Chaos and complexity: Necessary myths." In Eve, R., Horsfall, S., & M. Lee (eds.), *Chaos, complexity, and sociology: Myths, models, and theories* (ch. 4). Sage.

Bair, D. (2003). *Jung: A biography.* Little, Brown and Company.

Baker, S. D. (2007). "Followership: The theoretical foundation of a contemporary construct." *Journal of Leadership & Organizational Studies. 14*(1): 50–60.

Bakhtin, M. (1992). *The dialogic imagination: Four essays.* University of Texas Press.

Bakhtin, M. (1986). *Speech genres and other late essays* (V. McGee, trans.). University of Texas Press.

Ball, P. (2014, July 3). "The scientific problem that must be experienced: To understand turbulence we need the intuitive perspective of art." *Nautilus* ISSUE 015. Retrieved 28 February 2016 at http://nautil.us/issue/15/turbulence/the-scientific-problem-that-must-be-experienced.

Barabási, A-L. (2003). *Linked: How everything is connected to everything else and what it means for business, science, and everyday life.* Plume.

Bass, B. (1990). *Bass & Stogdill's handbook of leadership* (3rd ed.). New York: Free Press.

Bastiat, F. (1850/2007). *The law.* Ludwig von Mises Institute.

Baum, D., & J. Hassinger. (2002). *The Randori principles: The path of effortless leadership.* Dearborn Trade Publishing.

Becker, E. (1973). *The denial of death.* Free Press.

Bell, R., Roloff, M., van Camp, K., & S. Karol. (1990, Winter). "Is it lonely at the top? Career success and personal relationships." *Journal of Communication. 40*(1): 9ff.

Benedict, R. (1934/2005). *Patterns of culture.* Mariner Book.

Benjamin, W. (1968). *Illuminations: Essays and reflections.* Mariner Books.

Berejikian, J. (1992, September). "Revolutionary collective action and the agent-structure problem." *American Political Science Review. 86*(3): 647–657.

Berkowitz, P. (2019, Winter). "Conservatism and the people." *City Journal.* Retrieved 25 March 2019 from www.city-journal.org/conservatism-populism-peter-berkowitz.

Berlin, I. (2001). *The power of ideas* (H. Hardy, ed.). Princeton University Press.

Berlin, I. (1996). *The sense of reality.* Farrar, Strauss, & Giroux.

Berlin, I. (1982). "Georges Sorel." In Berlin, I. (ed.), *Against the current: Essays in the history of ideas* (pp. 296–332). Penguin.

Bernard, M. (2016). "Patočka's figures of political community." In Tava, F. & D. Meacham (eds.), *Thinking after Europe: Jan Patočka and politics* (ch. 16). Rowman & Littlefield.

Bernstein, R. (1997). "Pragmatism, pluralism, and the healing of wounds." In Menand, L. (ed.), *Pragmatism: A reader* (pp. 382–401). Vintage Books.

Bertalanffy, L. von. (1968). *General system theory* (revised ed.). George Braziller.

Bevan, W., Albert, R. S., Loiseaux, P. R., & P. N. Mayfield. (1958). "Jury behavior as a function of the prestige of the foreman and the nature of his leadership." *Journal of Public Law.* 7: 419.

Beveridge, W. (1950). *The art of scientific investigation*. Blackburn Press.

Beversluis, J. (2000). *Cross-examining Socrates: A defense of the interlocutors in Plato's early dialogues*. Cambridge University Press.

Bion, W. R. (1976/1994). "Emotional turbulence." In *Clinical seminars & other works*. Karnac Books.

Bird, R. J. (1997). "Chaos and social reality: An emergent perspective." In Eve, R., Horsfall, S., & M. Lee (eds.), *Chaos, complexity, and sociology: Myths, models, and theories* (ch. 11). Sage.

Black, H. C., Nolan, J. R., & M. J. Connolly. (1979). *Black's law dictionary*. West.

Blackstone, W. (1765–1769). *Commentaries on the laws of England*. Clarendon Press. Retrieved 4 May 2018 from http://files.libertyfund.org/files/2140/Blackstone_1387-01_EBk_v6.0.pdf

Blake, R., & J. Mouton. (1964). *The managerial grid: Key orientations for achieving production through people*. Gulf Publishing Co.

Blastic, M. (2012). "Francis and his hagiographical tradition." In Robson, M. (ed.). *The Cambridge companion to Francis of Assisi* (ch. 4). Cambridge University Press.

Bobbio, N. (1944/1948). *The philosophy of decadentism: A study of existentialism* (D. Moore, trans.). Basil Blackwell.

Bobrick, B. (2001). *Wide as the waters: The story of the English Bible and the revolution it inspired*. Penguin.

Boháček, K. (2018). "Between Socrates and the Stranger: How dialogic are Plato's dialogues?" In Freise, M. (ed.), *Inspired by Bakhtin: Dialogical methods in the humanities* [Studies in Comparative Literature and Intellectual History] (ch. 2). Academic Studies Press.

Bohm, D. (1996a). *On creativity*. Routledge.

Bohm, D. (1996b). *On dialogue*. Routledge.

Bohm, D. (1980). *Wholeness and the implicate order*. Routledge.

Bonaventure, with Manning, H. E. (1867/1988). *The life of St. Francis of Assisi: From the "Legenda Sancti Francisci."* TAN Classics.

Boorstin, D. (1992). *The creators* (pp. 398–407). Vintage Books.

Borges, J. L. (1937/1993). "The analytical language of John Wilkins." In Vázquez, L. (trans.), *Other inquisitions 1937–1952* (pp. 101–105). University of Texas Press.

Boswell, J. (1934). *Boswell's life of Johnson* (G. Birkbeck Hill, ed.; rev. L. F. Powell). Clarendon Press.

Boulding, K. (1989). "A bibliographical autobiography." *PSL Quarterly Review.* *42*(171): 365–393.

Boulding, K. (1956). *The image: Knowledge in life and society*. University of Michigan Press.

Bowles, H. R. (2005). "What could a leader learn from a mediator? Dispute resolution strategies for organizational leadership." Working Papers: MIT Center for Public Leadership. Retrieved 7 May 2019 from https://core.ac.uk/download/pdf/4420401.pdf.

Box, G. E. (1957). "Evolutionary operation: A method for increasing industrial productivity." *Journal of the Royal Statistical Society: Series C (Applied Statistics).* *6*(2): 81–101.

Boyd, R., & J. A. Morrison. (2007). "F.A. Hayek, Michael Oakeshott, and the concept of spontaneous order." In Hunt, L. & P. McNamara (eds.), *Liberalism, conservatism, and Hayek's idea of spontaneous order* (ch. 5). Palgrave Macmillan.

Braudel, F. (1980). *On history* (S. Matthews, trans.). University of Chicago Press.

Brettell, C. (2002, Fall). "The individual/agent and culture/social in the history of the social sciences." *Social Science History. 26*(3): 429–445.

Brooke, X. (2003). "A masterpiece in waiting: The response to *Las Meninas* in nineteenth-century Britain." In Stratton-Pruitt, S. (ed.), *Velazquez's Las Meninas* (ch. 3). Cambridge University Press.

Brouwer, C., & M. Schaefer. (2011). "This art has chemistry: New exhibit kicks off the U.S. celebration of IYC 2011." *Chemistry International*. Retrieved 30 April 2019 from www.degruyter.com/downloadpdf/j/ci.2011.33.issue-3/ci.2011.33.3.4/ci.2011.33.3.4.pdf.

Bryman, A., Stephens, M., & a Campo, C. (1996). "The importance of context: Qualitative research and the study of leadership." *The Leadership Quarterly. 7*(3): 353–370.

Buber, M. (1965). "Dialogue." In Buber, M. (ed.), *Between man and man*. Macmillan.

Bultmann, R. (1956). *Primitive Christianity*. Collins.

Burns, J. M. (2003). *Transforming leadership: A new pursuit of happiness*. Grove Press.

Cabrera, D., & L. Cabrera. (2015). *Systems thinking made simple: New hope for solving wicked problems*. Odyssean Press.

Caldwell, B. (2014). "Introduction." In Hayek, F. (ed.), *The market and other orders* (B. Caldwell, ed.). University of Chicago Press.

Camic, C., & H. Joas (eds.). (2004). *The dialogical turn: New roles for sociology in the post-disciplinary age*. Rowman & Littlefield.

Campbell, J. (2008). *The hero with a thousand faces* (3rd ed.). New World Library.

Campbell, J. (1990). *The hero's journey: Joseph Campbell on his life and work* (P. Cousineau, ed.). San Francisco: New World Library.

Camus, A. (1942/1983). *The myth of Sisyphus*. Vintage International.

Capra, F. (2007). *The science of Leonardo: Inside the mind of the great genius of the Renaissance*. Anchor Books.

Caputo, J. D. (1986). *The mystical element in Heidegger's thought*. Fordham University Press.

Cardozo, B. (1921). *The nature of the judicial process*. Yale University Press.

Carlsnaes, W. (1992). "The agency-structure problem in foreign policy analysis." *International Studies Quarterly. 36*: 245–270.

Carlyle, T. (1841/2011). *On heroes, hero-worship, and the heroic in history*. CreateSpace Independent Publishing Platform.

Carnap, R. (1934/1995). *The unity of science* (M. Black, trans.). Thoemmes Press.

Carnegie, D. (1936). *How to win friends and influence people*. Simon & Schuster.

Carse, J. (1986). *Finite and infinite games: A vision of life as play and possibility*. Free Press.

Cartier, C. (1999). "Cosmopolitics and the maritime world city." *Geographical Review. 89*(2): 278–289.

Chesterton, G. K. (1923/2017). *St. Francis of Assisi*. CreateSpace Independent Publishing Platform.

Ciulla, J. (2019). "Leadership and ethics." In Riggio, R. (ed.), *What's wrong with leadership? Improving leadership research and practice* (ch. 5). Routledge.

Ciulla, J. (ed.). (1998). *Ethics: The heart of leadership*. Quorum Books.

Clark. K. (1939). *Leonardo da Vinci*. Penguin.

Cohen, M. (1962, April–June). "The aporias in Plato's early dialogues." *Journal of the History of Ideas. 23*(2): 163–174.

Coke, E. (2003). *The selected writings and speeches of Sir Edward Coke* (S. Sheppard, ed.). Liberty Fund.

Collinson, D. (2019). "Critical leadership studies." In Riggio, R. (ed.), *What's wrong with leadership? Improving leadership research and practice* (ch. 14). Routledge.

Collinson, D. (2014). "Dichotomies, dialectics and dilemmas: New directions for critical leadership studies?" *Leadership. 10*(1): 36–55.

Collinson, D. (2005). "Dialectics of leadership." *Human Relations. 58*(11): 1419–1442.

Collinson, D., Grint, K., & B. Jackson. (2011). "Introduction." In Collinson, D., Grint, K., & B. Jackson (eds.), *Major works in leadership studies* (vol. 1). Sage.

Conan Doyle, A. (1892). "The Memoirs of Sherlock Holmes: Silver Blaze." *The Strand Magazine.*

Conger, J. A. (1989). *The charismatic leader: Behind the mystique of exceptional leadership.* Jossey-Bass.

Copleston, F. (1962). *A history of philosophy* (vol. I, part II). Image.

Coyne, C. J. (2008). "The politics of bureaucracy and the failure of post-war reconstruction." *Public Choice. 135*(1): 11–22.

Cronin, T., & M. Genovese. (2012). *Leadership matters: Unleashing the power of paradox.* Paradigm.

Crossley, N. (2011). *Towards relational sociology.* Routledge.

Crum, T. (1987). *The magic of conflict: Turning a life of work into a work of art.* Touchstone.

Csikszentmihalyi, M. (1990). *Flow: The psychology of optimal experience.* Harper and Row.

Csikszentmihalyi, M., & K. Sawyer. (2014). "Creative insight: The social dimension of a solitary moment." In *The systems model of creativity* (pp. 73–98). Springer, Dordrecht.

Cupit, G. (1999). *Justice as fittingness.* Oxford University Press.

Curtin, J. L. (2004). "Emergent leadership: Case study of a jury foreperson." *Leadership Review. 4*: 75–88.

Cusato, M. (2012). "Francis and the Franciscan movement." In Robson, M. (ed.), *The Cambridge companion to Francis of Assisi* (ch. 1). Cambridge University Press.

Cusato, M. (2007). "Foreword." In Dalarun, J. (ed.), *Francis of Assisi and power* (A. Bartol, trans.). Franciscan Institute Publications.

Cusher, B. E. (2015). "Leaders in conversation: The dialectic model of leadership education in Plutarch's Lives." *Journal of Leadership Education. 14*(2): 198–2008.

Cusher, B. E. (2014). "How does law rule? Plato on habit, political education, and legislation." *The Journal of Politics. 76*(4): 1032–1044.

Cusher, B. E. (2013). "From natural catastrophe to the human catastrophe: Plato on the origins of written law." *Law, Culture and the Humanities. 9*(2): 275–294.

Cusher, B. E. (2010). "Rousseau and Plato on the legislator and the limits of law (Doctoral dissertation)." University of Toronto. Retrieved 23 June 2018 from https://tspace.library.utoronto.ca/handle/1807/24341.

Dafermos, M. (2018). "Relating dialogue and dialectics: A philosophical perspective." *Dialogic Pedagogy* (vol. 6). Retrieved 29 January 2019 from https://dpj.pitt.edu/ojs/index.php/dpj1/article/view/189.

Dalarun, J. (1999/2007). *Francis of Assisi and power* (A. Bartol, trans.). Franciscan Institute Publications.

Damasio, A. R. (2006). *Descartes' error.* Random House.

Dawkins, R. (1976/2006). *The selfish gene.* Oxford University Press.

de Bracton, H. (1569). *De legibus & consuetudinibus Angliæ (The Laws and Customs of England).* Retrieved 23 June 2018 from http://bracton.law.harvard.edu/index.html.

Dederer, C. (2017, November 20). "What do we do with the art of monstrous men?" *The Paris Review*. Retrieved 1 June 2019 from www.theparisreview.org/blog/2017/11/20/art-monstrous-men/.

de Diego, E. (2003). "Representing representation: Reading *Las Meninas*, again." In Stratton-Pruitt, S. (ed.), *Velazquez's Las Meninas* (ch. 5). Cambridge University Press.

de Landa, M. (2000). *A thousand years of nonlinear history*. Swerve Editions.

de Langis, T. (2011). "Across conflict lines: Women mediating for peace." In *12th annual colloquium findings*. The Institute for Inclusive Security.

Denning, S. (2007). *The secret language of leadership: How leaders inspire action through narrative*. Jossey-Bass.

Deresiewicz, W. (2010, March). "Solitude and leadership." *The American Scholar*. Retrieved 6 May 2017 from https://theamericanscholar.org/solitude-and-leadership/#.

Derge, D. R. (1959). "The lawyer as decision-maker in the American state legislature." *The Journal of Politics*. *21*(3): 408–433.

Derrida, J. (1993). *Aporias* (D. Dutoit, trans.). Stanford University Press.

de Saussure, F. (1959). *Course in general linguistics* (W. Baskin, trans.). McGraw-Hill.

Dessler, D. (1989, Summer). "What's at stake in the agent-structure debate?" *International Organization*. *43*(3): 441–473.

de Vries, M. F. K. (2005). *Lessons on leadership by terror: Finding Shaka Zulu in the attic*. Edward Elgar Publishing.

de Vries, M. F. K. (1994). "The leadership mystique." *Academy of Management Perspectives*. *8*(3): 73–89.

de Vries, M. F. K., & D. Miller. (1985). "Narcissism and leadership: An object relations perspective." *Human Relations*. *38*(6): 583–601.

Diamond, J. (2011). "Why do some societies make disastrous decisions?" In Brockman, J. (ed.), *Culture*. Harper Perennial.

Distin, K. (2005). *The selfish meme*. Cambridge University Press.

"disturb." *Oxford English Dictionary*. Retrieved 28 February 2016 from www.oxforddictionaries.com/definition/english/disturb.

Donaldson, C. D. (1950, November 29). "Investigation of a simple device for preventing separation due to shock and boundary-layer interaction (NACA EM L5OBO2a)." National Advisory Committee for Aeronautics.

Donaldson, W. (2017). *Simple_complexity: A management book for the rest of us*. Morgan James Publishing.

Donati, P. (2013). "Morphogenesis and social networks: Relational steering not mechanical feedback." In Archer, M. (ed.), *Social morphogenesis* (ch. 11). Springer.

Doob, P. R. (1990). *The idea of the labyrinth from classical antiquity through the Middle Ages*. Cornell University Press.

Dopfer, K., Foster, J., & J. Potts. (2004). "Micro-meso-macro." *Journal of Evolutionary Economics*. *14*: 263–279.

Douglas, M. (1986). *How institutions think*. Syracuse University Press.

Drath, W. (2001). *The deep blue sea: Rethinking the source of leadership*. Jossey-Bass.

Drucker, P. (2006). *Managing in turbulent times* (reprint ed.). HarperBusiness.

Duncan, T., & C. Coyne. (2015, January 10). "The political economy of foreign intervention." In Boettke, P. & C. Coyne (eds.), *Oxford handbook of Austrian economics*. Oxford University Press.

Dunstan, P. (2012). "The ecumenical appeal of Francis." In Robson, M. (ed.), *The Cambridge companion Francis of Assisi* (ch. 17). Cambridge University Press.

Durkheim, E. (1895/1938). *The rules of sociological method* (S. Solovay & J. Mueller, trans.). Free Press.

Dweck, C. (2016). "What having a 'growth mindset' actually means." *Harvard Business Review. 13*: 213–226.

Editors. (2015, April–June). "Debating the Longue Durée." *Annales HSS. 70*(2): 215–217.

Edwards, W. (1954). "The theory of decision making." *Psychological Bulletin. 51*(4): 380–417.

Eire, C. (2016). *Reformations: The early modern world, 1450–1650.* Yale University Press.

Eliade, M. (1991). *Images and symbols: Studies in religious symbolism.* Princeton University Press.

Eliade, M. (1957/1959). *The sacred and the profane: The nature of religion* (W. Trask, trans.). Harcourt, Brace & World, Inc.

Elias, N. (1970/1978). *What is sociology* (S. Mennell & G. Morrissey, trans.)? Columbia University Press.

Eliot, T. S. (1971). "Four Quartets." In Eliot, T. S. (ed.), *The complete poems and plays (1909–1950)* (pp. 117–145). Harcourt, Brace & World, Inc.

Elliott, E., & L. D. Kiel. (1997). "Nonlinear dynamics, complexity, and public policy: Use, misuse, and applicability." In Eve, R., Horsfall, S., & M. Lee (eds.), *Chaos, complexity, and sociology: Myths, models, and theories* (ch. 6). Sage.

Eno, B. (2011). "A big theory of culture." In Brockman, J. (ed.), *Culture* (ch. 4). Harper Perennial.

Erikson, E. (1958/1962). *Young man Luther: A study in psychoanalysis and history.* W.W. Norton & Company.

Erlmann, V. (2010). *Reason and resonance: A history of modern aurality.* Zone Books.

Fairhurst, G. T. (2001). "Dualisms in leadership research." In Jablin, F. & L. Putnam (eds.), *The new handbook of organizational communication: Advances in theory, research, and methods* (ch. 11). Sage.

Farfel-Stark, L. (2018). *The telling image: Shapes of changing times.* Greenleaf Book Group.

Febvre, L. (1929). *Luther: A destiny.* E.P. Dutton & Co.

Feld, S. (1998). "They repeatedly lick their own things." *Critical Inquiry. 24*(2): 445–472.

Fiedler, F. E. (1972). "How do you make leaders more effective? New answers to an old puzzle." *Organizational Dynamics. 1*(2): 3–18.

Field, S. (2012). "Franciscan ideals and the royal family of France (1226–1328)." In Robson, M. (ed.), *The Cambridge companion to Francis of Assisi* (ch. 13). Cambridge University Press.

Firebaugh, G. (2001). "Ecological fallacy." In *International encyclopedia for the social and behavioral sciences* (Vol. 6) (pp. 4023–4026). Pergamon Press.

Fisher, R., Ury, W. L., & B. Patton. (1981). *Getting to yes: Negotiating agreement without giving in.* Penguin.

Fletcher, J., & K. Olwyler. (1997). *Paradoxical thinking: How to profit from your contradictions.* Berrett-Koehler Publishers.

Forbes-Pitt, K. (2013). "Self-organization: What is it, what isn't it and what's it got to do with morphogenesis?" In Archer, M. (ed.), *Social morphogenesis* (ch. 6). Springer.

Ford, C. (2018, November 5). "We let 'male genius' excuse bad behaviour—but what about the loss of female genius?" *The Guardian.* Retrieved 1 June 2019 from www.theguardian.com/commentisfree/2018/nov/06/we-let-male-genius-excuse-bad-behaviour-but-what-about-the-loss-of-female-genius.

Foucault, M. (2007). *Security, territory, population: Lectures at the Collège de France, 1977–78* (G. Burchell, trans.). Springer.

Foucault, M. (1966/1994). *The order of things: An archeology of the human sciences* (Anon., trans.). Vintage Books.

Frankl, V. E. (1985). *Man's search for meaning.* Simon and Schuster.

Freedman, D. H. (1992). "Is management still a science?" *Harvard Business Review. 70*(6): 26.

Freise, M. (2018). "Introduction." In Freise, M. (ed.), *Inspired by Bakhtin: Dialogical methods in the humanities* [Studies in Comparative Literature and Intellectual History]. Academic Studies Press.

French, D. (2019, June 24). "Politics is not war." *National Review. LXXI*(11): 13f.

French, J. J., & B. H. Raven. (1959). "The bases of social power." In Cartwright, D. (ed.), *Studies of social power* (pp. 150–167). Institute for Social Research.

Freud, S. (1930/2002). *Civilization and its discontents* (D. McLintock, trans.). Penguin.

Freud, S. (1920/2010). *Beyond the pleasure principle* (C. J. M. Hubback, trans.). International Psycho-Analytical Press. Retrieved 3 September 2017 from www.bartleby.com/276/.

Freud, S. (1924/1961). "The economic problem of masochism." In *The standard edition of the complete psychological works of Sigmund Freud, Volume XIX (1923–1925): The ego and the id and other works* (pp. 155–170). Hogarth Press.

Fukuyama, F. (1995). *Trust: The social virtues and the creation of prosperity.* Free Press.

Gadamer, H. G. (1976). *Philosophical hermeneutics* (D. Linge, trans.). University of California Press.

Galli, M. (2002). *Francis of Assisi and his world.* Intervarsity Press.

Gammaitoni, L., Hänggi, P., Jung, P., & F. Marchesoni. (1998). "Stochastic resonance." *Reviews of Modern Physics. 70*(1): 223–287.

Gardner, H. (2006). *Changing minds: The art and science of changing our own and other people's minds* [Leadership for the Common Good]. Harvard Business Review Press.

Gardner, H., with E. Laskin. (1995). *Leading minds: An anatomy of leadership.* Basic Books.

Gastil, J. (1994). "A definition and illustration of democratic leadership." *Human Relations. 47*(8): 953–975.

Gaus, G. (2013). "The evolution, evaluation, and reform of social morality: A Hayekian analysis." In Peart, S. & D. Levy (eds.), *F.A. Hayek and the modern economy: Economic organization and activity* (ch. 3). Palgrave Macmillan.

Gaus, G. (2007). "Social complexity and evolved moral principles." In Hunt, L. & P. McNamara (eds.), *Liberalism, conservatism, and Hayek's idea of spontaneous order* (ch. 8). Palgrave Macmillan.

Geertz, C. (1973). *The interpretation of cultures: Selected essays.* Basic Books.

Geniusas, S., & D. Nikulin (eds.). (2018). *Productive imagination.* Rowman & Littlefield.

Gibb, C. (1947). "The principles and traits of leadership." *Journal of Abnormal and Social Psychology. 42*: 267–284.

Gibbon, E. (1830). *The history of the decline and fall of the Roman Empire.* J.O. Robinson.

Giddens, A. (1993). *New rules of sociological method* (2nd ed.). Stanford University Press.

Gilbert, S. (2018, October 12). "The men of #MeToo go back to work." *The Atlantic.* Retrieved 1 June 2019 from www.theatlantic.com/entertainment/archive/2018/10/has-metoo-actually-changed-hollywood/572815/.

Gilligan, C. (1982). *In a different voice.* Harvard University Press.

Girard, R. (2009). *I see Satan fall like lightning* (J. Williams, trans.). Orbis Books.

Gleick, J. (2003). *Isaac Newton.* Vintage Books.

Godet-Calogeras, J. F. (2012). "Francis and Clare and the emergence of the Second Order." In Robson, M. (ed.), *The Cambridge companion to Francis of Assisi* (ch. 7). Cambridge University Press.

Goethals, G. R., & G. J. Sorenson (eds.). (2007). *The quest for a general theory of leadership.* Edward Elgar Publishing.

Goethe, Johann Wolfgang von. (1817/1994). "Giuseppe Bossi: On Leonardo da Vinci's *Last Supper* at Milan." In Goethe, J. (ed.), *Essays on art and literature* (E. von Nardoff & E. von Nardoff, trans.) (pp. 37–59). Princeton University Press.

Goldberg, J. (2006, February 2). "A movie for all time." *National Review.* Retrieved 21 May 2019 from www.nationalreview.com/2006/02/movie-all-time-jonah-goldberg-2/.

Gonzales-Balado, J. (ed.). (2002). "In my own words: The words of Mother Teresa." *Coptics.info*. Retrieved 17 January 2018 from www.coptics.info/Books/Jose_Luis_The_Words_of_Mother_Teresa.pdf.

Goodstein, E. (2017). *Georg Simmel and the disciplinary imaginary.* Stanford University Press.

Goodwin, D. K. (2018). *Leadership in turbulent times.* Simon & Schuster.

Green, M. J., & R. Nader. (1975). *The other government: The unseen power of Washington lawyers.* Grossman Publishers.

Grint, K. (2010). *Leadership: A very short introduction.* Oxford University Press.

Grint, K. (2005). "Problems, problems, problems: The social construction of 'leadership'." *Human Relations. 58*(11): 1467–1494.

Gronn, P. (2002). "Distributed leadership as a unit of analysis." *The Leadership Quarterly. 13*(4): 423–451.

Gustavson, C. (1955). *A preface to history.* McGraw-Hill.

Guthrie, S. (1993). *Faces in the clouds: A new theory of religion.* Oxford University Press.

Gutmann, B. (1935). "The African standpoint." *Africa, Journal of the International African Institute. 8*(1): 1–19.

Habermas, J. (2001). *The liberating power of symbols: Philosophical essays.* MIT Press.

Hain, P. L., & J. E. Piereson. (1975). "Lawyers and politics revisited: Structural advantages of lawyer-politicians." *American Journal of Political Science.* 41–51.

Hall, J. (1949). *Living law of democratic society.* Bobbs-Merrill.

Hannah, J. R. (2007). *A portrait of war: Case studies of the Operation Iraqi Freedom media embed program* (Doctoral dissertation). BEARdocs. Retrieved 21 May 2019 from https://baylor-ir.tdl.org/handle/2104/5057.

Harrison, E. F. (1996). "A process perspective on strategic decision making." *Management Decision. 34*(1): 46–53.

Harsanyi, D. (2019, June 24). "More Harding, please, less Wilson." *National Review. LXXI*(11): 52.

Harter, N. (2019a). "Calling a stranger to lead." *Journal of Leadership Studies. 13*(1): 1–3.

Harter, N. (2019b). "Eric Voegelin's 1944 'Political theory and the pattern of general history': An account from the biography of a philosophizing consciousness." In Robinson, S., Trepanier, L., & D. Whitney (eds.), *Eric Voegelin today: Voegelin's political thought in the 21st century* (ch. 9). Lexington Books.

Harter, N. (2018). "Saint and leader? The example of St. Francis of Assisi." *Theology of Leadership Journal. 1*(1). http://theologyofleadership.com/index.php/tlj/article/view/6.

Harter, N. (2017a, October 18). "Martin Luther and the translation of the Bible into German." *VoegelinView.* Retrieved 29 April 2019 from https://voegelinview.com/martin-luther-translation-bible-german/.

Harter, N. (2017b). "No one, everyone, anyone." *Leadership and the Humanities. 5*(1): 41–50.

Harter, N. (2016). *Foucault on leadership: The leader as subject* [Routledge Studies in Leadership, Work and Organizational Psychology]. Routledge.

Harter, N. (2015). *Leadership and coherence: A cognitive approach.* Routledge.

Harter, N. (2007a). *Clearings in the forest: On the study of leadership.* Purdue University Press.

Harter, N. (2007b). "Leadership as the promise of simplification." In Hazy, J., Goldstein, J., & B. Lichtenstein (eds.), *Complex systems leadership theory: New perspectives from complexity science on social and organizational effectiveness* (pp. 333–348). ISCE Publishing.

Harter, N., & C. Clark. (2020). "Eric Voegelin on the seemliness of symbols: Shays' Rebellion." In Bezio, K. & G. Goethals (eds.), *Leadership, populism and resistance.* Edward Elgar.

Harter, N., & S. M. Heuvel. (2018). "Is there still a place for the study of great leaders? *International Leadership Journal. 10*(2): 75–84.

Harvey, M. (2004). "Literature." In Goethals, G., Sorenson, G., & J. M. Burns (eds.), *Encyclopedia of leadership* (Vol. II) (pp. 915–918). Sage.

Harvey, M., & R. Riggio (eds.). (2012). *Leadership studies: The dialogue of disciplines* (ch. 6). Edward Elgar.

Havre, S., Hetzler, B., & L. Nowell. (2002). "ThemeRiverTM: In search of trends, patterns, and relationships." *IEEE Transactions on Visualization and Computer Graphics. 8*(1): 9–20.

Hawthorne, N. (1879). *The scarlet letter.* Riverside Press.

Hayek, F. (2014). *The market and other orders* (B. Caldwell, ed.). University of Chicago Press.

Hayek, F. A. (1976). *Law, legislation and liberty* (vol. 2). University of Chicago Press.

Hayek, F. (1974, December 11). "Nobel Prize lecture." *nobelprize.org.* Retrieved 29 April 2019 from www.nobelprize.org/prizes/economic-sciences/1974/hayek/lecture/.

Hayek, F. (1973/2012). *Law, legislation and liberty* (vol. I). Routledge.

Hayek, F. (1952). *Individualism and economic order.* Routledge & Kegan Paul.

Hays, S. (1994, March). "Structure and agency and the sticky problem of culture." *Sociological Theory. 12*(1): 57–72.

Heidegger, M. (1981/1995). *Aristotle's Metaphysics Θ 1–3: On the essence and actuality of force* (W. Brogan & P. Warnek, trans.). Indiana University Press.

Heifetz, R. (1994). *Leadership without easy answers.* Harvard University Press.

Heifetz, R. A., & D. L. Laurie. (1997). "The work of leadership." *Harvard Business Review. 75:* 124–134.

Hendershot, H. (2016). *Open to debate: How William F. Buckley put liberal America on THE FIRING LINE.* Broadside Books.

Hensler, D. R. (2017). "Our courts, ourselves: How the Alternative Dispute Resolution movement is re-shaping our legal system." *Dickinson Law Review. 122:* 349.

Herdener, M., Esposito, F., di Salle, F., Boller, C., Hilti, C. C., Habermeyer, B., . . . & Cattapan-Ludewig, K. (2010). "Musical training induces functional plasticity in human hippocampus." *Journal of Neuroscience. 30*(4): 1377–1384.

Hermalin, B. E. (1998). "Toward an economic theory of leadership: Leading by example." *American Economic Review. 88*(5): 1188–1206.

Hermans, H. J., Kempen, H., & van Loon, R. (1992, January). "The dialogical self: Beyond individualism and rationalism." *American Psychologist. 47*(1): 1, 23–33.

Hesse, H. (2003). *The journey to the east: A novel.* Macmillan.

Hillman, J. (2013). *Uniform edition of the writings of James Hillman* (vol. 1). Spring Publications.

Hillman, J. (2005a). *Uniform edition of the writings of James Hillman* (vol. 3). Spring Publications.

Hillman, J. (2005b). "In defense of Carl Jung." *Intellectual Deep Web*, posted 10 September 2017 to *YouTube*. Retrieved 1 June 2019 from www.youtube.com/watch?v=NVLYIVg6_50.

Hillman, J. (1995). *Kinds of power*. Spring Publications.

Hillman, J. (1975). *Re-visioning psychology*. Harper & Row.

Hindus, M. (1952). "Introduction." In Chambers, W. (ed.), *Witness*. Regnery Gateway.

Hofkirchner, W. (2013). "Self-organisation as the mechanism of development and evolution in social systems." In Archer, M. (ed.), *Social morphogenesis* (ch. 7). Springer.

Hogan, R., & R. B. Kaiser. (2005). "What we know about leadership." *Review of General Psychology*. *9*(2): 169.

Hogue, A. (1966). *Origins of the common law*. Liberty Fund.

Hollander, E. P. (1992). "Leadership, followership, self, and others." *Leadership Quarterly*. *3*(1): 43–54.

Hollander, E. P. (1978). *Leadership dynamics: A practical guide to effective relationships*. Free Press.

Holquist, M. (2002). *Dialogism: Bakhtin and his world* (2nd ed.). Routledge.

Horsfall, S., & E. Maret. (1997). "Short-term changes in the domestic division of labor." In Eve, R., Horsfall, S., & M. Lee (eds.), *Chaos, complexity, and sociology: Myths, models, and theories* (ch. 14). Sage.

Horvath, A. (2013). *Modernism and charisma*. Palgrave Macmillan.

Hosking, D. M. (1995). "Constructing power: Entitative and relational approaches." In Hosking, D., Dachler, P., & K. Gergen (eds.), *Management and organization: Relational alternatives to individualism* (pp. 51–70). Avebury.

Hosking, D. M. (2011). "Organising, leadership and skilful process." In Collinson, D., Grint, K., & B. Jackson (eds.), *Leadership: Classical, contemporary and critical approaches*. Sage.

Hughes, R., Ginnett, R., & G. Curphy. (2018). *Leadership: Enhancing the lessons of experience* (9th ed.). McGraw-Hill.

Hummel, R. P. (2014). *The bureaucratic experience: The post-modern challenge*. Routledge.

Hunt, L. (2007). "The origin and scope of Hayek's idea of spontaneous order." In Hunt, L. & P. McNamara (eds.), *Liberalism, conservatism, and Hayek's idea of spontaneous order* (ch. 3). Palgrave Macmillan.

Ignatieff, M. (1998). *Isaiah Berlin: A life*. New York: Metropolitan Books.

Isaacs, W. (1999). *Dialogue and the art of thinking together*. Currency.

Isaacson, W. (ed.). (2010). *Profiles in leadership: Historians on the elusive quality of greatness*. W.W. Norton & Company.

Jacobson, M. (1993). *Art for work: The new Renaissance in corporate collecting*. Harvard Business School Press.

Jahanbegloo, R. (1991). *Conversations with Isaiah Berlin*. Phoenix Press.

Jalal, A. M., & A. P. Prezas. (2012). "Outsider CEO succession and firm performance." *Journal of Economics and Business*. *64*(6): 399–426.

James, W. (1909/1996). *A pluralistic universe*. University of Nebraska Press.

James, W. (1907). *Pragmatism: A new name for some old ways of thinking*. Longmans, Green, and Co.

James, W. (1902/1985). *Varieties of religious experience*. Harvard University Press.

Jarvis, C., & P. Gouthro. (2015). "The role of the arts in professional education: Surveying the field." *Studies in the Education of Adults*. *47*(1): 64–80.

Jaspal, R., Carriere, K., & F. Moghaddam. (2016). "Bridging micro, meso, and macro processes in social psychology." In Valsiner, J. et al. (eds.), *Psychology as the science of human being: The Yokohama manifesto* [Annals of Theoretical Psychology] (ch. 15). Springer.

Jaspers, K. (1986). *Basic philosophical writings: Selections* (Edith Ehrlich, Leonard H. Ehrlich, & George B. Pepper, ed., trans., with introductions). Ohio University Press.

Jaspers, K. (1953/1964). "Leonardo as philosopher." In Jaspers, K. (ed.), *Three essays* (essay #1) (R. Manheim, trans.). Harcourt, Brace & World, Inc.

Jaspers, K. (1941). "On my philosophy." In Kaufmann, W. (ed.), *Existentialism from Dostoyevsky to Sartre*. Meridian Books. Retrieved 12 January 2018 from https://mercaba.org/SANLUIS/Filosofia/autores/Contempor%C3%A1nea/Jaspers/On%20my%20Philosophy.pdf.

Jelliffe, D. (1967, March). "Parallel food classifications in developing and industrialized countries." *The American Journal of Clinical Nutrition. 20*(3): 279–281.

Jemielniak, D., & A. Przegalinska. (2020). *Collaborative society*. MIT Press.

Jepperson, R., & J. Meyer. (2011). "Multiple levels of analysis and the limitations of methodological individualisms." *Sociological Theory. 29*(1): 54–73.

John, King of England. (1215/1995). *Magna Carta* [English trans. of the *Charter of Runnymede*]. The British Library Board. Retrieved 22 December 2015 from www.bl.uk/magna-carta/articles/magna-carta-english-translation.

John Paul II. (1984). *Salvifici doloris*. Retrieved 28 August 2017 from http://catholicsociety.com/documents/john_paul_ii_letters/Salvifici_doloris.pdf.

John Paul II. (1999). "To the elderly." Retrieved 28 August 2017 from http://w2.vatican.va/content/john-paul-ii/en/letters/1999/documents/hf_jp-ii_let_01101999_elderly.html.

Johnson, B. (1996). *Polarity management: Identifying and managing unsolvable problems*. HRD Press.

Johnson, S. (2001). *Emergence: The connected lives of ants, brains, cities, and software*. Scribner.

Jokisaari, M. (2017). "A social network approach to examining leadership." In Schyns, B., Hall, R., & P. Neves (eds.), *Handbook of methods in leadership research*. Edward Elgar.

JuriGlobe, a research group of the Faculty of Law, University of Ottawa. "Common Law systems and mixed systems with a Common Law tradition." Retrieved 22 December 2015 from www.juriglobe.ca/eng/sys-juri/class-poli/common-law.php.

Kaczmarczyk, M. (2018). "Toward a dialogical sociology." In Freise, M. (ed.), *Inspired by Bakhtin: Dialogical methods in the humanities* [Studies in Comparative Literature and Intellectual History] (ch. 4). Academic Studies Press.

Kahn, C. (1979). *The art and thought of Heraclitus*. Cambridge University Press.

Kamen, R. (2018). "Arts-based research in the natural sciences." In Leavy, P. (ed.), *Handbook of arts-based research* (ch. 29). Guilford Press.

Kamen, R. (2012, August). "Art as a catalyst for connections in chemistry." In *Abstracts of papers of the American Chemical Society* (Vol. 244). AMER CHEMICAL SOC.

Kantonen, T. A. (1941). *The message of the church to the world of today*. Augsburg Publishing House.

Kaplan, R. E., & R. B. Kaiser. (2003). "Developing versatile leadership." *MIT Sloan Management Review. 44*(4): 19–26.

Karakayali, N. (2006, December). "The uses of the stranger: Circulation, arbitration, secrecy, and dirt." *Sociological Theory. 24*(4): 312–330.

Katz, J. (1950). *The philosophy of Plotinus*. Appleton-Century-Croft.

Kegan, R. (1982). *The evolving self*. Harvard University Press.

Kehnel, A. (2012). "Francis and the historiographical tradition in the order." In Robson, M. (ed.), *The Cambridge companion to Francis of Assisi* (ch. 6). Cambridge University Press.

Kellerman, B. (2016). "Leadership—It's a system, not a person!" *Daedalus. 145*(3): 83–94.

Kellerman, B. (2014). *Hard times: Leadership in America*. Stanford Business Books.

Kellerman, B. (2004). *Bad leadership: What it is, how it happens, why it matters*. Harvard Business Press.

Kelly, A. (2001). "A revolutionary without fanaticism." In Lilla, M., Dworkin, R., & R. Silvers (eds.), *The legacy of Isaiah Berlin* (pp. 3–30). New York Review Books.

Kemp, M. (2004). *Leonardo*. Oxford University Press.

Kerr, S., & J. M. Jermier. (1978). "Substitutes for leadership: Their meaning and measurement." *Organizational Behavior and Human Performance. 22*(3): 375–403.

Kierkegaard, S. (1847/1962). "'On the difference between a genius and an apostle." In Kierkegaard, S. (ed.), *The present age* (A. Dru, trans.) (pp. 89–108). Harper Torchbooks.

Kim, D. H. (1993). *Systems archetypes I: Diagnosing systemic issues and designing high-leverage interventions*. Pegasus Communications.

King, A. (2002). "The outsider as political leader: The case of Margaret Thatcher." *British Journal of Political Science. 32*(3): 435–454.

Kirk, G. S., & J. E. Raven. (1966). *The PreSocratic philosophers.: A critical history with a selection of texts*. Cambridge University Press.

Kirwan, C. (1995). "Plotinus." In Honderich, T. (ed.), *The Oxford companion to philosophy* (p. 689). Oxford University Press.

Klenke, K. (2008). *Qualitative research in the study of leadership*. Emerald.

Kline, R. (2017). "Mediation analysis in leadership studies." In Schyns, B., Hall, R., & P. Neves (eds.), *Handbook of methods in leadership research* (ch. 8). Edward Elgar.

Koczela, S. (2019, January 9). "Why Elizabeth Warren's likability won't matter." *CNN*. Retrieved 15 January 2019 from www.cnn.com/2019/01/08/opinions/elizabeth-warren-koczela/index.html.

Koerner, E. F. (1992). "The Sapir-Whorf hypothesis: A preliminary history and a bibliographical essay." *Journal of Linguistic Anthropology. 2*(2): 173–198.

Koestler, A. (1970). "Beyond atomism and holism—the concept of the holon." *Perspectives in Biology and Medicine. 13*(2): 131–154.

Krell, D. F. (2019). *The sea: A philosophical encounter*. Bloomsbury Academic.

Krippendorf, K. (2018). "Discourses in the design of cultural artifacts." In Freise, M. (ed.), *Inspired by Bakhtin: Dialogical methods in the humanities* [Studies in Comparative Literature and Intellectual History] (ch. 5). Academic Studies Press.

Kroeber, A. L., & C. Kluckhohn. (1963). *Culture: A critical review of concepts and definitions*. Vintage Books.

Kuhn, T. S. (2012). *The structure of scientific revolutions* (50th anniversary ed.). University of Chicago Press.

Kumaran, D., & E. Duzel. (2008). "The hippocampus and dopaminergic midbrain: Old couple, new insights." *Neuron. 60*(2): 197–200.

Kumaran, D., & E. A. Maguire. (2006). "An unexpected sequence of events: Mismatch detection in the human hippocampus." *PLoS Biology 4*(12): e424. Retrieved 16 May 2019 from https://doi.org/10.1371/journal.pbio.0040424.

Ladkin, D. (2015). *Mastering the ethical dimension of organizations: A self-reflective guide to developing ethical astuteness*. Edward Elgar.

Lakoff, G., & M. Jackson. (1980). *Metaphors we live by*. University of Chicago Press.

Laszlo, E. (2010). *Chaos point: 2012 and beyond*. Hampton Roads Publishing.

Laszlo, E. (1996). *The whispering pond: A personal guide to the emerging vision of science*. Element.

Laszlo, E. (1994). *Vision 2020: Reordering chaos for global survival*. Gordon & Breach.

Lawson, H. (1985). *Reflexivity: The post-modern predicament*. Open Court.

Lawson, T. (2013). "Emergence and morphogenesis: Causal reduction and downward causation?" In Archer, M. (ed.), *Social morphogenesis* (ch. 4). Springer.

Lazego, E. (2013). "Network analysis and morphogenesis: A neo-structural exploration and illustration." In Archer, M. (ed.), *Social morphogenesis* (ch. 9). Springer.

Lee, M. (1997). "From Enlightenment to chaos: Toward nonmodern social theory." In Eve, R., Horsfall, S., & M. Lee (eds.), *Chaos, complexity, and sociology: Myths, models, and theories*. Sage.

LeMoine, R. (2017). "Foreigners as liberators: Education and cultural diversity in Plato's *Menexenus*." *American Political Science Review*. *111*(3): 471–483.

Lévi Strauss, C. (1978). *Myth and meaning: Cracking the code of culture*. Schocken Books.

Lévi-Strauss, C. (1963). *Structural anthropology* (C. Jacobson & B. G. Schoepf, trans.). Basic Books.

Levine, D. (2018). *Dialogical social theory* (H. Schneiderman, ed.). Routledge.

Levine, D. (2015). *Social theory as a vocation: Genres of theory work in sociology*. Transaction Publishers.

Levine, D. (2006). *Powers of the mind: The reinvention of liberal learning in America*. University of Chicago Press.

Levine, D. (1995). *Visions of the sociological tradition*. University of Chicago Press.

Levine, H. (2014). *On Freud's screen memories*. Routledge.

Lewis, M. (2019, January 4). "I'll say it: Elizabeth Warren isn't likable." *Daily Beast*. Retrieved 15 January 2019 from www.thedailybeast.com/ill-say-it-elizabeth-warren-isnt-likeable.

Lilla, M. (2016). *The shipwrecked mind: On political reaction*. New York Review Books.

Lincoln, A. (1953–55). *The collected works* (R. Basler, ed.). Rutgers University Press.

Little, D. (2010). *New contributions to the philosophy of history*. Springer.

Liu, J., Li, J., Feng, L., Li, L., Tian, J., & K. Lee. (2014). "Seeing Jesus in toast: Neural and behavioral correlates of face pareidolia." *Cortex*. *53*: 60–77.

Lloyd, G. E. R. (1992). *Polarity and analogy* (part I). Hackett.

Lord, R. (2019). "Leadership and the medium of time." In Riggio, R. (ed.), *What's wrong with leadership? Improving leadership research and practice* (ch. 8). Routledge.

Losada, M. (1999). "The complex dynamics of high performance teams." *Mathematical and Computer Modeling*. *30*(9–10): 179–192.

Luhmann, N. (2008/2010). *Love: A sketch* (K. Cross, trans.). polity.

Luther, M. (1908/1954). *Commentary on Romans* (J. T. Mueller, trans.). Kregel Publications.

Luxenberg, A. (2003). "The aura of a masterpiece: Responses to *Las Meninas* in nineteenth-century Spain and France." In Stratton-Pruitt, S. (ed.), *Velazquez's Las Meninas* (ch. 2). Cambridge University Press.

Lyons, J. A. (1983). "The Cosmic Christ in Origen and Teilhard de Chardin." *Religious Studies*. *19*(1): 108–109.

Mabry, M. (1971) "The relationship between fluctuations in hemlines and stock market averages from 1921 to 1971." Master's Thesis, University of Tennessee, 1971. Retrieved 12 January 2019 from https://trace.tennessee.edu/utk_gradthes/1121.

Maccarini, A. (2013). "The morphogenetic approach and the idea of a morphogenetic society: The role of regularities." In Archer, M. (ed.), *Social morphogenesis* (ch. 3). Springer.

Machiavelli, N. (1532/1991). *The prince* (Skinner & Price, eds.). Cambridge University Press.

MacIntyre, A. (1997). *The unconscious: A conceptual analysis*. Thoemmes Press.

Mantegna, R., & E. Stanley. (1996, October 17). "Turbulence and financial markets." *Nature*. *383*: 587–588.

Mantzavinos, C. (2016, Winter). "Hermeneutics." In *The Stanford encyclopedia of philosophy* (E. Zalta, ed.). Retrieved 15 January 2019 from https://plato.stanford.edu/archives/win2016/entries/hermeneutics/.

Manz, C. C., & H. P. Sims Jr. (1991). "Superleadership: Beyond the myth of heroic leadership." *Organizational Dynamics. 19*(4): 18–35.

Manz, C. C., & H. P. Sims Jr. (1989). *Super-leadership: Leading others to lead themselves.* Berkley Books.

Martin, C. (2013). "Hayek and the Nomothetes." In Peart, S. & D. Levy (eds.), *F.A. Hayek and the modern economy: Economic organization and activity* (ch. 6). Palgrave Macmillan.

Martin, R. (2007). *The opposable mind: How successful leaders win through integrative thinking.* Harvard Business Review Press.

Marty, M. (2004). *Martin Luther.* Viking Penguin.

Marx, K. (1978). *The Marx-Engels reader* (2nd ed.) (R. Tucker, ed.). W.W. Norton & Co.

Maslow, A. H. (1939). "Dominance, personality, and social behavior in women." *The Journal of Social Psychology. 10*(1): 3–39.

Matusov, E., & K. Miyazaki. (2014). "Dialogue on dialogic pedagogy." *Dialogic Pedagogy: An International Online Journal, 2.*

Mayer, B. (2000). *The dynamics of conflict resolution: A practitioner's guide.* Jossey-Bass.

McCusker, M., Foti, R., & E. Abraham. (2019). "Leadership research methods." In Riggio, R. (ed.), *What's wrong with leadership? Improving leadership research and practice* (ch. 1). Routledge.

McFadden, N., Rathert, G., & R. Bray. (1952). "The effectiveness of wing vortex generators in improving the maneuvering characteristics of a swept-wing airplane at transonic speeds (NACA RM A51J18)." National Advisory Committee for Aeronautics.

McGrath, A. (2001). *In the beginning: The story of the King James Bible and how it changed a nation, a language, and a culture.* Anchor Books.

McGregor, D. (1966). *Leadership and motivation.* The MIT Press.

McKeon, R. (2016). *On knowing: The social sciences* (D. Owen & J. Olson, eds.). University of Chicago Press.

McMichael, S. (2012). "Francis and the encounter with the sultan (1219)." In Robson, M. (ed.), *The Cambridge companion to Francis of Assisi* (ch. 8). Cambridge University Press.

Meadows, D. H. (2008). *Thinking in systems: A primer.* Chelsea Green Publishing.

Mecklin, J. M. (1955). "The passing of the saint." *American Journal of Sociology. 60*(S6): 34–53.

Medina, J. (2009). *BrainRules.* Pear Press.

Meek, E. L. (2014). *A little manual for knowing.* Cascade Books.

Meindl, J. (1995). "The romance of leadership as a follower-centric theory: A social constructionist approach." *Leadership Quarterly. 6:* 329–341.

Mencken, H. L. (1923, June 11). "Next year's struggle." Reprinted in Moos, M. (ed.). (1956). *H.L. Mencken on politics: A carnival of buncombe* (pp. 59–63). Johns Hopkins University Press.

Menkel-Meadow, C. (2015). "Mediation, arbitration, and alternative dispute resolution (ADR)." In *International encyclopedia of the social and behavioral sciences.* Elsevier.

Merton, R. (1976). *Sociological ambivalence and other essays.* Free Press.

Merton, R. (1949/1968). *Social theory and social structure.* Free Press.

Mihata, K. (1997). "The persistence of 'emergence'." In Eve, R., Horsfall, S., & M. Lee (eds.), *Chaos, complexity, and sociology: Myths, models, and theories* (ch. 3). Sage.

Mill, J. S. (1872/1988). *The logic of the moral sciences.* Open Court.

Mill, J. S. (1859/1992). *On liberty and other writings.* Cambridge University Press.

Minogue, K. (2013). "Hayek and the conditions of freedom." In Peart, S. & D. Levy (eds.), *F.A. Hayek and the modern economy: Economic organization and activity* (ch. 4). Palgrave Macmillan.

Mitchell, J. "Woodstock." Retrieved 20 February 2018 from http://jonimitchell.com/music/song.cfm?id=75.

Monbiot, G. (2016, April 15). "Neoliberalism—the ideology at the root of all our problems." *The Guardian.* Retrieved 6 January 2018 from www.theguardian.com/books/2016/apr/15/neoliberalism-ideology-problem-george-monbiot.

Montouri, A., & R. Purser. (1997). "Social creativity: The challenge of complexity." *Pluriverso. 1*(2): 78–88. Retrieved with different pagination on 6 March 2019 from https://s3.amazonaws.com/academia.edu.documents/31567997/Social_Creativity-_The_Challenge_of_Complexity.pdf?AWSAccessKeyId=AKIAIWOWYYGZ2Y53UL3A&Expires=1551909665&Signature=tNwx7UG02ln0Ee41XF%2BhUFKGiJQ%3D&response-content-disposition=inline%3B%20filename%3DSocial_Creativity_The_Challenge_of_Compl.pdf.

Montouri, A., & R. Purser. (1995). "Deconstructing the lone genius myth: Toward a contextual view of creativity." *Journal of Humanistic Psychology. 35*(3): 69–112.

Morgan, G. (1997/2006). *Images of organization* (2nd ed.). Sage.

Moul, W. (1973, September). "The level of analysis problem revisited." *Canadian Journal of Political Science. 6*(3): 494–513.

Moyers, B. (1988). "Ep. 5: Joseph Campbell and the Power of Myth—'Love and the Goddess'." *Joseph Campbell and the Power of Myth.* Moyers & Co. Retrieved 25 March 2019 from https://billmoyers.com/content/ep-5-joseph-campbell-and-the-power-of-myth-love-and-the-goddess-audio/.

Muller, J. (2007). "The limits of spontaneous order: Skeptical reflections on a Hayekian theme." In Hunt, L. & P. McNamara (eds.), *Liberalism, conservatism, and Hayek's idea of spontaneous order* (ch. 10). Palgrave Macmillan.

Munger, M. (2007). "Culture, order, and virtue." In Hunt, L. & P. McNamara (eds.), *Liberalism, conservatism, and Hayek's idea of spontaneous order* (ch. 9). Palgrave Macmillan.

NASA Earth Observatory image by Dr. Alice Alonso, using Landsat satellite data from the U.S. Geological Survey. (2015). Story adapted from Laura Rocchio, NASA Landsat Science Outreach. Retrieved 12 January 2019 from https://climate.nasa.gov/climate_resources/178/suwannee-blackwater-river-meets-the-sea/.

Nash, D. (1963, Summer). "The ethnologist as stranger: An essay in the sociology of knowledge." *Southwestern Journal of Anthropology. 19*(2): 149–167.

Nelson, D. L., Quick, J. C., Hitt, M. A., & D. Moesel. (1990). "Politics, lack of career progress, and work/home conflict: Stress and strain for working women." *Sex Roles. 23*(3–4): 169–185.

Nelton, S. (1997). "Hiring an outsider as a top executive." *Nation's Business. 85*(2): 53–56.

Nestingen, J. (1982). *Martin Luther: His life and teachings.* Fortress Press.

Neumann, E. (1954). *The origins and history of consciousness* (R. F. C. Hull, trans.). Princeton University Press.

Newark, D. (2018). "Leadership and the logic of absurdity." *Academy of Management Review. 43*(2): 198–216.

Niebuhr, H. R. (1951). *Christ and culture.* Harper Torchlight.

Nisbet, R. (1969). *Social change and history: Aspects of the Western theory of development.* Oxford University Press.

Nissley, N. (2002). "Arts-based learning in management education." In Wankel, C. (ed.), *Rethinking management education for the 21st century* (ch. 2). Information Age Publishing.

Norton, R. (2018, February 5). "Unintended consequences." *The Library of Economics and Liberty*. Retrieved 12 January 2019 from www.econlib.org/library/Enc/Unintended Consequences.html.

Nouwen, H. (2013). *Clowning in Rome: Reflections on solitude, celibacy, prayer, and contemplation*. Image.

Nussbaum, M. (2012). "Who is the happy warrior? Philosophy, happiness research, and public policy." *International Review of Economics*. 59: 335–361.

Olshansky, D. (2002–2018). "Mikhail Bakhtin." *Gallery of Russian Thinkers, International Society for Philosophers*. Retrieved 28 January 2019 from https://isfp.co.uk/russian_thinkers/mikhail_bakhtin.html.

Ortega y Gasset, J. (1940/2002). "Ideas and beliefs." In Ortega y Gasset, J. (ed.), *What is knowledge?* (appendix). State University of New York Press.

Ortega y Gasset, J. (1975). *Phenomenology and art* (P. Silver, trans.). W.W. Norton & Co.

Ortega y Gasset, J. (1972). *Velázquez, Goya, the dehumanization of art, and other essays* (A. Brown, trans.). W.W. Norton & Co.

Ortega y Gasset, J. (1961). *History as a system and other essays toward a philosophy of history* (J. Miller, trans.). W.W. Norton & Co.

Ortega y Gasset, J. (1914/1961). *Meditations on Quixote* (E. Rugg & D. Marin, trans.). University of Illinois Press.

Ortega y Gasset, J. (1958). *Man and crisis* (M. Adams, trans.). W.W. Norton & Co.

Ortega y Gasset, J. (1957). *Man and people* (W. Trask, trans.). W.W. Norton & Co.

Ortega y Gasset, J. (1940/1946). *Concord and liberty* (H. Weyl, trans.). W.W. Norton & Co.

Ortega y Gasset, J. (1933). *The modern theme* (J. Cleugh, trans.). W.W.Norton & Co.

Ortega y Gasset, J. (1932). *The revolt of the masses*. W.W. Norton & Co.

Orwell, G. (1940). "Inside the whale." In Orwell, G. (ed.), *Inside the whale and other essays*. Victor Gollancz Ltd.

Osborn, R., Hunt, J., & L. Jauch. (2002, December). "Toward a contextual theory of leadership." *Leadership Quarterly*. 13(6): 797–837.

Otteson, J. (2007). "Unintended order explanations in Adam Smith and the Scottish Enlightenment." In Hunt, L. & P. McNamara (eds.), *Liberalism, conservatism, and Hayek's idea of spontaneous order* (ch. 2). Palgrave Macmillan.

Paffenholz, T. (2018). "Women in peace negotiations." In Aggestam, K. & A. Towns (eds.), *Gendering diplomacy and international negotiation* (pp. 169–191). Palgrave Macmillan.

Paffenholz, T., Ross, N., Dixon, S., Schluchter, A. L., & J. True. (2016). *Making women count-not just counting women: Assessing women's inclusion and influence on peace negotiations*. UN Women.

Papagianni, K., & Centre for Humanitarian Dialogue. (2008). *Power sharing, transitional governments and the role of mediation*. HD Centre for Humanitarian Dialogue.

Parten, M. B. (1933). "Leadership among preschool children." *The Journal of Abnormal and Social Psychology*. 27(4): 430–440.

Patočka, J. (2018). *An introduction to Husserl's phenomenology* (E. Kohák, trans.). Open Court.

Patočka, J. (2002). *Plato and Europe* (P. Lom, trans.). Stanford University Press.

Patočka, J. (1998). *Body, community, language, world* (E. Kohák, trans.). Open Court.

Peart, S., & D. Levy (eds.). (2013). *F.A. Hayek and the modern economy: Economic organization and activity*. Palgrave Macmillan.

Peirce, C. S. (1884/1992). "Design and chance." In Peirce, C. S. (ed.), *The essential Peirce: Selected philosophical writings* (N. Houser & C. Kloesel, eds.) (vol. 1). Indiana University Press.

Peirce, C. S. (1877/1955). "The fixation of belief." In *Philosophical writings of Peirce* (ch. 2). Dover Publications.

Pelikan, J. (1987). *The excellent empire: The fall of Rome and the triumph of the Church.* Harper & Row.

Pelikan, J. (1964). *Obedient rebels: Catholic substance and Protestant principle in Luther's Reformation.* Harper & Row.

Pelikan, J. (1950). *From Luther to Kierkegaard: A study in the history of theology.* Concordia Publishing House.

Peterson, I. (2012). "The third order of Francis." In Robson, M. (ed.), *The Cambridge companion to Francis of Assisi* (ch. 12). Cambridge University Press.

Peterson, J. (2018). *12 rules for life: An antidote to chaos.* Random House.

Peterson, J. (2017). *The psychological significance of the Biblical stories* (episode 21). Retrieved 19 August 2017 from https://jordanbpeterson.com/2017/06/episode-21/.

Peterson, J. (1999). *Maps of meaning: The architecture of belief.* Routledge.

Petsoulas, C. (2001). *Hayek's liberalism and its origins: His idea of spontaneous order and the Scottish Enlightenment.* Routledge.

Pettegree, A. (2015). *Brand Luther: 1517, printing, and the making of the Reformation.* Penguin.

Pfeffer, J. (1977). "The ambiguity of leadership." *Academy of Management Review.* 2(1): 104–112.

Phillips, J. (2006). "Reconstruction in Mississippi, 1865–1876." *Mississippi History Now.* Retrieved 14 May 2019 from www.mshistorynow.mdah.ms.gov/articles/204/reconstruction-in-mississippi-1865-1876.

Piaget, J. (1950/2005). *The psychology of intelligence* (M. Piercy & D. E. Berlyne, trans.). Routledge.

Pinker, S. (2019). *Enlightenment now: The case for reason, science, humanism, and progress.* Penguin Books.

Pinnow, D. (2011). *Leadership: What really matters.* Springer.

Pittinsky, T. L., & S. Simon. (2007). "Intergroup leadership." *The Leadership Quarterly.* 18(6): 586–605.

Plato & A. Bloom. (1968). *The republic: Translated with notes and an interpretive essay by Allan Bloom.* Basic Books.

Plucknett, T. (1956/2010). *A concise history of the common law.* Liberty Fund.

Poincaré, H. (1914/1996). *Science and method.* St. Augustine's Press.

Polanyi, M. (1951). *The logic of liberty: Reflections and rejoinders.* Liberty Fund.

Politis, V. (2009). "Aporia and searching in the early Plato." In Judson, L. & V. Karasmanis (eds.), *Remembering Socrates: Philosophical essays* (ch. 6). Oxford University Press.

Polley, D. (1997, September–October). "Turbulence in organizations: New metaphors for organizational research." *Organization Science.* 8(5): 445–457.

Pollock, F. (1890). *Oxford lectures and other discourses.* Macmillan and Co.

Popper, K. (1966). *The open society and its enemies* (vol. 2). Routledge and Kegan Paul.

Porpora, D. (2013). "Morphogenesis and social change." In Archer, M. (ed.), *Social morphogenesis* (ch. 2). Springer.

Pranin, S. (1991). *The Aiki News encyclopedia of Aikido.* Aiki News.

Pratt, J. (2001, February). "It's lonely at the top: But must it be?" *Home Health Care Management and Practice.* 13(2): 155–158.

Přibáň, J. (2016). "Resisting fear." In Tava, F. & D. Meacham (eds.), *Thinking after Europe: Jan Patočka and politics* (ch. 5). Rowman & Littlefield.

Price, B. (1997). "The myth of postmodern science." In Eve, R., Horsfall, S., & M. Lee (eds.), *Chaos, complexity, and sociology: Myths, models, and theories* (ch. 1). Sage.

Price, T. (2005). *Understanding ethical failures in leadership.* Cambridge University Press.

Prince, L. (2005). "Eating the menu rather than the dinner: Tao and leadership." *Leadership. 1*(1): 105–126.

Proust, M. (2003). *In search of lost time* (C. K. Scott Moncrieff, T. Kilmartin, & D. J. Enright, trans.). Modern Library.

Raelin, J. A. (2003). *Creating leaderful organizations: How to bring out leadership in everyone.* Berrett-Koehler Publishers.

Reilly, K. (2017, January 22). "Read Hillary Clinton's 'Basket of Deplorables' remarks on Trump supporters." *TIME.com.* Retrieved 23 June 2018 from http://time.com/4486502/hillary-clinton-basket-of-deplorables-transcript/.

Rescher, N. (1998). "Fallibilism." In *The Routledge encyclopedia of philosophy.* Taylor and Francis. Retrieved 9 February 2019 from www.rep.routledge.com/articles/thematic/fallibilism/v-1. doi:10.4324/9780415249126-P019–1.

Rescher, N. (1995). "Aporia." In Honderich, T. (ed.), *The Oxford companion to philosophy* (p. 41). Oxford University Press.

Revkin, M., & W. McCants. (2015, November 20). "Experts weigh in: Is ISIS good at governing." *Brookings.* Retrieved 25 July 2018 from www.brookings.edu/blog/markaz/2015/11/20/experts-weigh-in-is-isis-good-at-governing/.

Rhodes, J. (2013, June 1). "What is the metaxy? Diotima and Voegelin." *Voegelin-View.* Retrieved 13 May 2019 from https://voegelinview.com/what-is-the-metaxy-diotima-and-voegelin/.

Ricke-Kiely, T., & D. Matthias. (2013). "The power of observation: Teaching leadership." *Journal of Nonprofit Education and Leadership. 3*(2): 82–96. Retrieved 8 May 2017 from http://js.sagamorepub.com/jnel/article/view/4969.

Ridley, M. (2011). *The rational optimist: How prosperity evolves.* Harper Perennial.

Riggio, R. (ed.) (2019). *What's wrong with leadership? Improving leadership research and practice.* Routledge.

Riggio, R., Ciulla, J., & G. Sorenson. (2003). "Leadership education at the undergraduate level: A liberal arts approach to leadership development." In S. Murphy & R. Riggio (eds.), *The future of leadership development* (ch. 12). Lawrence Erlbaum.

Rittgers, R. K. (2012). *The reformation of suffering: Pastoral theology and lay piety in Late Medieval and Early Modern Germany.* Oxford University Press.

Robson, M. (2012). "Introduction." In Robson, M. (ed.), *The Cambridge companion to Francis of Assisi.* Cambridge University Press.

Roest, B. (2012). "Francis and the pursuit of learning." In Robson, M. (ed.), *The Cambridge companion to Francis of Assisi* (ch. 20). Cambridge University Press.

Roosevelt, T. (1910). "Citizenship in a republic." Delivered at the Sorbonne, Paris. *Wikisource.* Retrieved 30 April 2019 from https://en.wikisource.org/wiki/Citizenship_in_a_Republic.

Rorty, R. (1989). *Contingency, irony, and solidarity.* Cambridge University Press.

Rosenau, J. (1990). *Turbulence in world politics: A theory of change and continuity.* Princeton University Press.

Ross, W. H., Conlon, D. E., & E. A. Lind. (1990). "The mediator as leader: Effects of behavioral style and deadline certainty on negotiator behavior." *Group & Organization Studies. 15*(1): 105–124.

Rost, J. (1993). *Leadership for the twenty-first century.* Praeger.

Rothbard, M. (1990). "Concepts of the role of intellectuals in social change toward laissez faire." *Journal of Libertarian Studies. 9*(2): 43–67.

Rousseau, D. (1985). "Issues of level in organizational research: Multi-level and cross-level perspectives." *Research in Organizational Behavior.* 7: 1–37.

Rustow, D. (ed.). (1970). *Philosophers and kings: Studies in leadership.* (pp. 208–247). George Braziller.

Rutherford, M. L. (1938). "Lawyers as legislators." *The Annals of the American Academy of Political and Social Science. 195*(1): 53–61.

Ryle, G. (2009). *The concept of mind.* Routledge.

Sabine, G. (1947). *A history of political theory.* Henry Holt and Company.

Sala, F. (2001). "It's lonely at the top: Executives' emotional intelligence self [mis] perceptions." *Consortium for Research on Emotional Intelligence in Organizations.* Retrieved 8 May 2017 from www.eiconsortium.org/reports/its_lonely_at_the_top_executives_ei_misperceptions.html.

Sanchez-Hucles, J. V., & D. D. Davis. (2010). "Women and women of color in leadership: Complexity, identity, and intersectionality." *American Psychologist. 65*(3): 171.

Sanders, P. (2019). "Leadership and populism: A parallel reading of Hannah Arendt and Franz Neumann." *Leadership.* Retrieved 25 March 2019 from https://journals.sagepub.com/doi/abs/10.1177/1742715019837807#articleCitationDownloadContainer.

Sartori, G. (1997). "Understanding pluralism." *Journal of Democracy. 8*(4): 58–69.

Schein, E., & P. Schein. (2018). *Humble leadership: The power of relationships, openness, and trust.* Berrett-Koehler.

Schein, E. (2004). *Organizational culture and leadership* (3rd ed.). Jossey-Bass.

Scheler, M. (1933/1987). "Exemplars of person and leaders." In Scheler, M. (ed.), *Person and self-value: Three essays* (M. Frings, trans.) (pp. 127–198). Martinus Nijhoff.

Schmitt, C. (1927/1976). *The concept of the political* (G. Shwab, trans.). Rutgers University Press.

Schrödinger, E. (1954/2014). *Nature and the Greeks.* Cambridge University Press.

Schutz, A. (1944, May). "The stranger: An essay in social psychology." *American Journal of Sociology. 49*(6): 499–507.

Schyns, B., Hall, R., & P. Neves (eds.). (2017). *Handbook of methods in leadership research.* Edward Elgar.

Scott, A. O. (2018, January 31). "My Woody Allen problem." *New York Times.* Retrieved 1 June 2019 from www.nytimes.com/2018/01/31/movies/woody-allen.html.

Searle, J. (1984). *Minds, brains and science.* Harvard University Press.

Searle, J. (1980). "*Las Meninas* and the paradoxes of pictorial representation." *Critical Inquiry. 6*(3): 477–488.

Sells, B. (ed.). (2000). *Working with images: The theoretical base of archetypal psychology.* Spring Publications.

Senge, P. (1990). *The fifth discipline.* Currency Doubleday.

Şenocak, N. (2012). "Voluntary simplicity: The attitude of Francis towards learning in the early biographies." In Robson, M. (ed.), *The Cambridge companion to Francis of Assisi* (ch. 5). Cambridge University Press.

Short, W. (2012). "The *Rule* and life of the Friars Minor." In Robson, M. (ed.), *The Cambridge companion to Francis of Assisi* (ch. 3). Cambridge University Press.

Siegel, E. (2019, March 13). "Censure the artist, but never censor the art." *The Artery, 90.9 WBUR.* Retrieved 1 June 2019 from www.wbur.org/artery/2019/03/13/censure-the-artist-but-never-censor-the-art.

Simmel, G. (1918/2010). *The view of life: Four metaphysical essays with journal aphorisms* (J. Andrews & D. Levine, trans.). University of Chicago Press.

Simmel, G. (1916/2005). *Rembrandt: An essay in the philosophy of art* (A. Scott & H. Staubman, trans.). Routledge.

Simmel, G. (1991). *Schopenhauer and Nietzsche*. University of Illinois Press.

Simmel, G. (1908/1971). *Georg Simmel: On individuality and social forms*. University of Chicago Press.

Simmel, G. (1908/1955). *Conflict & the web of group-affiliations* (K. Wolff, trans.). Free Press.

Simmel, G. (1908/1950). *The sociology of Georg Simmel* (K. Wolff, trans.). Free Press.

Simms, K. (2015). *Hans-Georg Gadamer* [Routledge Critical Thinkers]. Routledge.

Simon, H. (2000). "Bounded rationality in social science: Today and tomorrow." *Mind & Society*. 1(1): 25–39.

Simon, H. (1990). *Reason in human affairs*. Stanford University Press.

Simon, H. (1982). *Models of bounded rationality* (vol. 2). MIT Press.

Sinek, S. (2017). *Leaders eat last: Why some teams pull together and others don't*. Penguin.

Skiena, S., & C. Ward. (2013). "Who's biggest? The 100 most significant figures in history." *Time*. Retrieved 13 November 2016 from http://ideas.time.com/2013/12/10/whos-biggest-the-100-most-significant-figures-in-history/.

Sky, E. (2015). *The unraveling: High hopes and missed opportunities in Iraq*. Perseus Books.

Smith, A. (1776/1950). *An inquiry into the nature and causes of the wealth of nations*. Methuen.

Smith, J. E. (1969). "Time, times, and the 'right time': 'Chronos' and 'kairos'." *The Monist*. 53(1): 1–13.

Smith, P. (1964). *The historian and history*. Alfred A. Knopf.

Smith, T. (1997). "Nonlinear dynamics and the micro-macro bridge." In Eve, R., Horsfall, S., & M. Lee (eds.), *Chaos, complexity, and sociology: Myths, models, and theories* (ch. 5). Sage.

Solzhenitsyn, A. (1984–1991). *The red wheel*. Farrar, Straus and Giroux and University of Notre Dame Press.

*Southern Pacific Co. v. Jensen*, 244 U.S. 205 (1917) MR. JUSTICE HOLMES, dissenting.

Spencer, M. (2019, February 23). "This is not an apology for Woody Allen, but we can still watch his films." *National Review*. Retrieved 1 June 2019 from www.nationalreview.com/2019/02/woody-allen-movies-judge-artistic-merit/.

Spoelstra, S. (2018). *Leadership and organization: A philosophical introduction*. Routledge.

Stacey, R. (2003). *Sir William Blackstone and the Common Law: Blackstone's legacy to America*. ACW Press.

Stahl, R. (2013, July 14). "Innerview: David Campbell on embedding." *The Vision Machine*. Retrieved 26 October 2017 from http://thevisionmachine.com/2013/07/innerview-david-campbell-on-embedding-2/.

Steinbock, A. (2009). *Phenomenology and mysticism: The verticality of religious experience* [Indiana Series in the Philosophy of Religion]. Indiana University Press.

Stevens, J. (1987). *Abundant peace: The biography of Morihei Ueshiba, founder of aikido*. Shambhala.

Stone, P. (2008). *Opting out? Why women really quit careers and head home*. University of California Press.

Stone, P., & S. Edwards. (1970). *1776: A musical play*. Viking Press.

Storey, J., & G. Salaman. (2009). *Managerial dilemmas: Exploiting paradox for strategic leadership*. Wiley.

Storing, H. (1987). "William Blackstone, 1723–1780." In Strauss, L. & J. Cropsey (eds.), *History of political philosophy* (3rd ed.) (pp. 622–634). University of Chicago Press.

Stratton-Pruitt, S. (2003). *Velázquez's "Las Meninas"* [Masterpieces of Western Painting]. Cambridge University Press.

Strogatz, S. (2003). *Sync: How order emerges from chaos in the universe, nature, and daily life*. Hachette Books.

Stroup, W. (1997). "Webs of chaos: Implications for research designs." In Eve, R., Horsfall, S., & M. Lee (eds.), *Chaos, complexity, and sociology: Myths, models, and theories* (ch. 10). Sage.

Sugden, R. (1989, Fall). "Spontaneous order." *Journal of Economic Perspectives. 3*(4): 85–97.

Swart, T., Chisholm, K., & P. Brown. (2015). *Neuroscience for leadership: Harnessing the brain gain advantage* [The Neuroscience of Business]. Palgrave Macmillan.

Szabo, G. (n.d.). "Edgar Morin on evolution of complex systems." *Academia.edu.* Retrieved 10 March 2019 from www.academia.edu/9721654/Edgar_Morin_on_Evolution_of_Complex_Systems.

Tainter, J. (1990). *The collapse of complex societies.* Cambridge University Press.

Taleb, N. (2010). *The bed of Procrustes: Philosophical and practical aphorisms.* Random House.

Tava, F., & D. Meacham (eds.). (2016). *Thinking after Europe: Jan Patočka and politics.* Rowman & Littlefield.

Taylor, A. E. (2001). *Plato: The man and his work.* Dover.

Taylor, C. (2002). "Gadamer on the human sciences." In Dostal, R. (ed.), *The Cambridge companion to Gadamer* (ch. 6). Cambridge University Press.

Temple, C. (2010, September). "The emergence of Sankofa's practice in the United States: A modern history." *Journal of Black Studies. 41*(1): 127–150.

Terman, L. (1904). "A preliminary study in the psychology and pedagogy of leadership." *The Pedagogical Seminary. 11*(4): 413–451.

Thietart, R. A., & B. Forgues. (1995). "Chaos theory and organization." *Organization Science. 6*(1): 19–31.

Thomas, D. (1952). *In Country Sleep, and other poems.* New Directions.

Thomas, K. (1976). "Conflict and conflict management." In Dunnette, M. D. (ed.), *Handbook of industrial and organizational psychology* (pp. 889–935). Rand McNally.

Thomas, K., & R. Kilmann. (1974). *Thomas-Kilmann conflict mode instrument.* XICOM.

Thomas, N. (2018). "Mental imagery." In *The Stanford encyclopedia of philosophy* (E. Zalta, ed.). Retrieved 30 April 2019 from https://plato.stanford.edu/archives/spr2018/entries/mental-imagery/.

Thompson, A. (2012). *Francis of Assisi: A new biography.* Cornell University Press.

Tillich, P. (1966). *The future of religions.* Harper & Row.

Tolstoy, L. (1959). "The difficulty of defining the forces that move notions (L. Maude & A. Maude, trans.)." In Gardiner, P. (ed.), *Theories of history.* Free Press.

Townsend, P. (1999). "Won't get fooled again." Spirit Music Group.

Toynbee, A. (1957). *A study of history.* Oxford University Press.

"turbulent." *Oxford English Dictionary.* Retrieved 28 February 2016 from www.oxforddictionaries.com/definition/english/turbulent.

Turner, F. (1997). "Foreword." In Eve, R., Horsfall, S., & M. Lee (eds.), *Chaos, complexity, and sociology: Myths, models, and theories.* Sage.

Ueshiba, M. (2018). *The art of peace* (J. Stevens, trans.). Shambala.

Ueshiba, M. (2007). *The secret teachings of Aikido* (J. Stevens, trans.). Kodansha International.

Uhl-Bien, M., & R. Marion (eds.). (2008). *Complexity leadership: Conceptual foundations.* Information Age Publishing.

Uhl-Bien, M., Marion, R., & B. McKelvey. (2007). "Complexity leadership theory: Shifting leadership from the industrial age to the knowledge era." *The Leadership Quarterly. 18*(4): 298–318.

Utley, G. (2003). "*Las Meninas* in twentieth-century art." In Stratton-Pruitt, S. (ed.). *Velazquez's Las Meninas* (ch. 6). Cambridge University Press.

Vaihinger, H. (2014). *The philosophy of as if.* Routledge.

Vaill, P. (1989). *Managing as a performing art: New ideas for a world of chaotic change.* Jossey-Bass.

van Bemmelen, S. (1992). *Women and mediation in Indonesia* (Vol. 152). Koninklyk Instituut Voor Taal Land.

van Vugt, M., & A. Ahuja. (2011). *Naturally selected: The evolutionary science of leadership.* HarperCollins.

Vernon, R. (1978). *Commitment and change: Georges Sorel and the idea of revolution.* University of Toronto Press.

Vico, G. (1744/2001). *New science: Principles of the new science concerning the common nature of nations* (3rd ed.) (D. Marsh, trans.). Penguin.

Villaseñor, J. (1949). *Ortega y Gasset, existentialist: A critical study of his thought and its sources* (J. Small, trans.). Henry Regnery.

Vlastos, G. (1982). "The socratic elenchus." *The Journal of Philosophy. 79*(11): 711–714.

Voegelin, E. (2002). *Collected works* (vol. 6) (D. Walsh, ed.; M. J. Hanak, trans.). University of Missouri Press.

Voegelin, E. (2000). *Collected works* (vol. 5) (M. Henningsen, ed.). University of Missouri Press.

Voegelin, E. (1998). *Collected works* (vol. 22; part V; § 1). University of Missouri Press.

Voegelin, E. (1995). *Collected works* (vol. 1) (J. Gebhardt & B. Cooper, eds.). Louisiana State University Press.

Voegelin, E. (1991). *Collected works* (vol. 27) (R. Pascal, J. Bain, & J. Corrington, eds.). Louisiana State University Press.

Voegelin, E. (1990). *Collected works* (vol. 12) (E. Sandoz, ed.). Louisiana State University Press.

Voegelin, E. (1987). *Order and history* (vol. V). Louisiana State University Press.

Voegelin, E. (1957). *Order and history* (vol. III). Louisiana State University.

Voegelin, E. (1956). *Order & history* (vol. I). Louisiana State University Press.

Volz, H. (1963). "German." In Greenslade, S. L. (ed.), *The Cambridge history of the Bible* (pp. 94–110). Cambridge University Press.

Vroom, V., & A. Jago. (2007, January). "The role of the situation in leadership." *American Psychologist. 62*(1): 17–24.

Waldstreicher, D., & S. R. Grossbart. (1998). "Abraham Bishop's vocation; or, the mediation of Jeffersonian politics." *Journal of the Early Republic. 18*(4): 617–657.

Wang, X. (2018). "Voices in images." In Freise, M. (ed.), *Inspired by Bakhtin: Dialogical methods in the humanities* [Studies in Comparative Literature and Intellectual History] (ch. 7). Academic Studies Press.

Warner, N. (2011). "Leadership in literary perspective." In Harvey, M. & R. Riggio (eds.), *Leadership studies: The dialogue of the disciplines* (ch. 14). Edward Elgar.

Washington, G. (1796/2000). "Farewell address to the people of the United States." *Senate Document no. 106–21.* Retrieved 11 February 2018 from www.gpo.gov/fdsys/pkg/GPO-CDOC-106sdoc21/pdf/GPO-CDOC-106sdoc21.pdf.

Weber, M. (1922/1947). *The theory of social and economic organization* (A. A. Henderson & T. Parsons, trans.). Free Press.

Weick, K. (1995). *Sensemaking in organizations.* Sage.

Weigend, G. (1958, April). "Some elements in the study of port geography." *Geographical Review. 48*(2): 185–200.

Wendt, A. (1987, Summer). "The agent-structure problem in international relations theory." *International Organization. 41*(3): 335–370.

Wheatley, M. (1992). *Leadership and the new science.* Barrett-Koehler.

White, J. (2005). "Exemplary persons and ethics: The significance of St. Francis for the philosophy of Max Scheler." *American Catholic Philosophical Quarterly*. 79(1): 57–90.

Whitehead, A. N. (1978). *Process and reality: An essay in cosmology*. Free Press.

Wilber, K. (1998). *The marriage of sense and soul*. Broadway Books.

Wiley, N. (1988, Fall). "The micro-macro problem in social theory." *Sociological Theory*. 6: 254–261.

Will, G. (1984). *Statecraft as soulcraft*. Simon and Schuster.

Williston, S. (1920). *The law of contracts*. Baker, Voorhis & Co.

Wills, G. (1994). *Certain trumpets: The call of leaders*. Simon & Schuster.

Wilson, S. (2016). *Thinking differently about leadership: A critical history of leadership studies*. Edward Elgar.

Wilson, W. (1952). *Leaders of men* (T. H. Vail Motter, ed.). Princeton University Press.

Wollan, L. A. (1978). "Lawyers in government: 'The most serviceable instruments of authority'." *Public Administration Review*. 38(2): 105–112.

Wren, T. (2012). "The discipline of history and the understanding of leadership." In Harvey, M. & R. Riggio (eds.), *Leadership studies: The dialogue of disciplines* (ch. 6). Edward Elgar.

Wren, J. T., & M. J. Swatez. (1995). "The historical and contemporary contexts of leadership: A conceptual model." In Wren, T. (ed.), *The leader's companion: Insights on leadership through the ages* (pp. 245–252). The Free Press.

Wright, S. (2012). "Is it lonely at the top? An empirical study of managers' and non-managers' loneliness in organizations." *The Journal of Psychology*. 146(1–2): 47–60.

Yammarino, F., & S. Dionne. (2019). "Leadership and levels of analysis." In Riggio, R. (ed.), *What's wrong with leadership? Improving leadership research and practice* (ch. 2). Routledge.

Yammarino, F., & J. Gooty. (2017). "Multi-level issues and dyads in leadership research." In Schyns, B., Hall, R., & P. Neves (eds.), *Handbook of methods in leadership research*. Edward Elgar.

Yenor, S. (2007). "Spontaneous order and the problem of religious revolution." In Hunt, L. & P. McNamara (eds.), *Liberalism, conservatism, and Hayek's idea of spontaneous order* (ch. 6). Palgrave Macmillan.

Young, D., & J-G. Goulet (eds.). (1994). *Being changed: The anthropology of extraordinary experience*. Broadview Press.

Zamora, D., & M. Behrent (eds.). (2016). *Foucault and neoliberalism*. Polity Press.

Zinn, H. (2015). *A people's history of the United States: 1492-present*. Routledge.

Zuckert, C. (2002). "Hermeneutics in practice: Gadamer on ancient philosophy." In Dostal, R. (ed.), *The Cambridge companion to Gadamer* (ch. 9). Cambridge University Press.

Zwijnenberg, R. (1999). *The writings and drawings of Leonardo da Vinci: Order and chaos in early modern thought* (C. van Eck, trans.). Cambridge University Press.

# INDEX OF NAMES

# INDEX

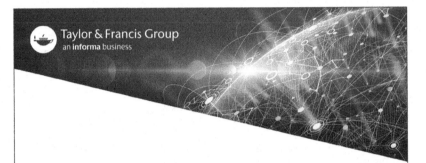